The Writer's Circle

Reading, Thinking, Writing

The Writer's Circle

Reading, Thinking, Writing

Sarah Morgan

Rockhurst College

Michael Vivion

*University of Missouri,
Kansas City*

St. Martin's Press
New York

ACKNOWLEDGMENTS

"The Cerebral Snapshot" from *Sunrise with Seamonsters* by Paul Theroux. Copyright © 1985 by Cape Cod Scriveners Company. Reprinted by permission of Houghton Mifflin Co.

"Say It Only if It's Tried and True" by George Gurley. Reprinted by permission of *The Kansas City Times* © 1984, all rights reserved.

"Lessons in Bringing Up Baby" by John Leo. Copyright 1984 Time Inc. All rights reserved. Reprinted by permission from *Time*.

"Apartheid Protester Finds KU Kept Clipping on Her" by Jared Byer. Appeared in *The Kansas City Times*, December 12, 1985. Reprinted by permission of Jared Byer.

Excerpts from *How to Make Money on Wall Street* by Louis Rukeyser. Copyright © 1974 by Louis Rukeyser. Reprinted by permission of Doubleday & Co., Inc.

Excerpts from *Gorillas in the Mist* by Diane Fossey. Copyright © 1983 by Diane Fossey. Reprinted by permission of Houghton Mifflin & Co.

Excerpts from "The Language of the Catcher in the Rye" by Donald P. Costello in *American Speech*. Copyright © October 1959 by D. Costello and reprinted by permission of author.

Excerpts from *From Reverence to Rape: The Treatment of Women in the Movies* by Molly Haskell. Reprinted by permission of Holt Rinehart, 1973.

Excerpts from *The World Atlas of Wine* by Hugh Johnson. Reprinted by permission of Simon & Schuster, 1971.

"The Ragged Edge" by Jim Atkinson. Reprinted with permission from the December issue of *Texas Monthly*. Copyright 1982 by *Texas Monthly*.

Excerpts from "U.S.–Soviet Relations" by Walter Laqueur. Reprinted by permission of *Foreign Affairs: America and the World 1983*. Copyright 1984 by the Council on Foreign Relations, Inc.

"Some Attitudes of Returning or Older Students of Composition," by Patricia Connors in *College Composition and Communication*. Copyright © 1982 by the National Council of Teachers of English. Reprinted by permission of publisher.

Excerpts from "Uncle Dad" by C. W. Smith. *Esquire*. March, 1985. Reprinted by permission of C. W. Smith. Copyright © 1985.

"Missile Center–U.S.A.," by David Chamberlain. Copyright © 1985 by *Harper's Magazine*. All rights reserved. Reprinted from the March 1985 issue by special permission.

Excerpts from "Little Taipei" by Andrew Tanzer. Reprinted by permission of *Forbes Magazine*, May 6, 1985. Copyright © 1985 by Forbes Inc.

Excerpts from "Obligation to Endure" in *Silent Spring* by Rachel Carson. Copyright © 1962 by Rachel L. Carson. Reprinted by permission of Houghton Mifflin Co.

"An Educational System That Has No Losers: Academic Preparation for All" by George Hanford. From *Vital Speeches of the Day*. Reprinted by permission of City News Publishing Co., Kansas City, June, 1985.

Acknowledgments and copyrights continue at the back of the book on page 354, which constitutes an extension of the copyright page.

To the Teacher

We planned this text to respond to students' anxieties about writing, and we present a variety of approaches to alleviating that anxiety. The text recognizes that there is no one "writing process"; that students already have developed a complete set of writing behaviors, which have been used to produce complete pieces of discourse; and that the way to improve student writing is to improve thinking, reading, and writing behaviors. To accomplish this goal, students must first examine the way they write now. They then should be introduced to a variety of alternatives with which to approach invention, organization, paragraphing, style, revision, and editing. Our text provides such an introduction. We explore a range of prewriting techniques, we offer approaches to revision, we show how revision and invention recur throughout the various steps of writing, we separate revising and editing, and we present activities to help students make realizations about writing for themselves. At the same time, there are a few holdovers in our text from the traditional "product" approach. We recognize the need for an occasional five-paragraph essay. We haven't thrown away the topic sentence, the thesis statement, the modes of development, or the inverted pyramid completely—although we have qualified the extent of their usefulness and modified the ways in which they are used.

What then is this text? It is a rhetoric. Throughout the various drafts of the text, we have kept in mind our belief that the students we teach write in a world of complicated social relationships. To this end we have tried to keep audience and purpose as central focuses. We also realize that these social relationships are complicated. To that end we have tried to consider the powerful effects of the nature of particular writing occasions. We have also tried to provide students using this text with a series of thoughtful ways to examine and execute their writing tasks. We emphasize throughout that learning to read, to think, and to write are integral parts of the same intellectual process—hence the name *The Writer's Circle*. This is not, however, a text that treats these parts with equal rigor. This is a writing text for freshmen, and as such is merely one small step in a neverending process.

A question that has engaged us during our careers is, "What exactly do we mean when we say that we teach writing?" Can writing be taught? Yes, but perhaps only "writing" as the relationship of theoretical descriptions to a physiointellectual act. Can teachers teach students *how* to write? Probably not. Students can be taught to develop concepts of good writing and to recognize excellence when they see it. They can be taught patterns which some writing in the past has assumed. They can be taught traditional strategies for approaching various writing occasions. They can be taught vocabulary and syntax and how to use them to pass the SATs. They can be taught patterns of thinking. Even if all these things have been taught, however, "writing" has not been taught, but rather disparate pieces of the process have been conveyed.

Fortunately, students can learn how to write; they can learn to put all these disparate pieces together. Even more fortunately, we can help by providing them with good exercises, intelligent assignments, and sensitive and critical responses to their writing and by our willingness to read their work while it is still in the developing stages.

Students already know a lot about writing when they come to us; it is *not* our responsibility to teach them how to write—even if we could. In one semester or one quarter we can expect to do no more than to provide approximately 1/28 of their formal exposure to school writing. Therefore, we have tried to write with a voice and tone that addresses students directly and to provide techniques and strategies that reflect an overview of the best current research and applications in the field. Rather than presenting students with *the* approach to writing, the text explores several intelligent approaches to the problems inherent in writing.

Acknowledgments

We wish to express our appreciation to the writers and teachers who shared their expertise with us by responding to the various drafts of this text: Lou Agosta of Kansas State University; Bob Cullen of the University of California at Los Angeles; Eric Gould of the University of Denver; George Hatch of Georgia State University; Larry Kent of William Rainey Harper College; George Miller of the University of Delaware; Jo Tarvers of Rutgers University; Tomas Vallejos of the University of Houston/Downtown; Barbara Weaver of Ball State University; and Jim Williams of Johnson County Community College.

We further wish to thank our editors at St. Martin's Press: Michael Weber, Julie Nord, and especially Susan Anker, whose flexibility and firmness guided the writing of this book from incubation through completion. We thank also those teachers, professors, and colleagues who helped us develop a love of literature, writing, and teaching and encouraged us to make those pursuits our own. Although a list of those for whom we feel appreciation would in itself be of book length, we must thank here James Merriman of Wichita State University; Susan Miller of the University of Utah; Jake Kobler and Lee Miller of North Texas State University; Joseph Comprone of the University of Louisville; and the composition staff of the University of Missouri at Kansas City. We thank also our students for teaching us what we know about how they learn to write.

And, finally, we thank our parents and our children, to whom we dedicate this book.

Sarah Morgan
Michael Vivion

Contents

CHAPTER   THREE

Patterned Strategies for Generating Ideas   50

C H A P T E R   F O U R

The Shaping Process   85

C H A P T E R   F I V E

Revision: Early Stages   121

CHAPTER SIX

Revision: Later Stages, Editing   145

CHAPTER SEVEN

Convincing Others: Argument and Persuasion 200

CHAPTER EIGHT

Writing About Literature   242

CHAPTER NINE

Writing from Formal Research 304

EPILOGUE

The Writer's Circle 343

To the Student

Writing is not a nice, tidy sequential activity that follows a predetermined series of rules and procedures. Writing is inherently and inescapably messy. Different writers use widely differing techniques and approaches. Ernest Hemingway's writing practices were not those of F. Scott Fitzgerald. The same writer frequently tackles different writing occasions (or assignments) with different techniques and approaches. The steps followed by the writer of an annual financial report differ markedly from those of a feature writer doing a story on skiing at Vail.

This disparity makes teaching writing difficult; it makes writing a composition text almost impossible. We can give you neither the ten essential steps to becoming a writer nor the ten essential steps to writing a successful paper. Even if we could identify the steps, we could not establish the one correct sequence in which to arrange them. Writing is a series of starts and restarts, a series of discoveries and reviews; the writer moves forward, stops to look back, checks direction, and moves on—sometimes on the same path, sometimes not. For some people the journey ends here. Others have to repeat the process. (This constant circular process led to the title *The Writer's Circle.*) For all, there is the danger that when all the steps have been taken, and often repeated, the result at the end may not match in quality the great effort expended in creation.

This is the potentially grim side of writing. There is another side, a side which results in your writing going public, being read and appreciated by others. This aspect of writing can be as exhilarating as the performing arts. And some things can be taught. We can't give you the exact steps or the exact sequence, but we can help.

We can help you teach yourself how to write better. We can identify the various steps in the writing process. We can help you see how you can make the most of each step. If we're successful, we can help you modify the writing process you have now and develop one that works better for you.

Although we cannot separate the writing process into neat, sequential steps, we can categorize the types of activities that take place when writers write. In this text we attempt to assist you in improving in each of the following:

1. Generating ideas and collecting data.
2. Moving from general ideas toward a specific idea.
3. Writing drafts of your ideas.
4. Rethinking ideas.
5. Reseeing what you've written.
6. Revising your ideas and your words.
7. Developing a more pleasing style.

So give the study of writing your attention and most sincere effort. The improvement you make in your writing can help you academically, socially, and professionally.

The Writer's Circle

Reading, Thinking, Writing

CHAPTER ONE

The World of Writing

All writers look for a way out of writing. But writing is like serving a jail sentence—you're not free until you've done your time on the rock heap.—Paul Theroux

Attitudes about Writing

Almost everyone reading this text has experienced moments of deep frustration with writing, especially with writing for English classes. Even professional writers like Paul Theroux have experienced difficulties with writing. The blank white page staring back at the face of a frustrated writer; the one sentence that just isn't working or that just doesn't look "right"; the completed theme with red marks and marginal comments obscuring the original sentences and paragraphs; the grade, somehow not as good as expected or hoped for and certainly not equal to the time and effort spent writing the paper; the completed manuscript rejected for the tenth time by an unappreciative publisher: These memories combine with others to make writing a task many of us would gladly avoid or trade for something simple like digging irrigation ditches through Death Valley.

No writing teacher can promise to eliminate all these unpleasant moments, but fortunately much can be done to make the writing process easier and more rewarding. This text is an effort to accomplish that goal through a collaboration of writing teachers and student writers, a collaboration that minimizes the teacher's role as teacher/evaluator and emphasizes the teacher's role as reader/responder.

Most of us develop our aversion to writing gradually. There was a time, perhaps now hidden deep in your memory, when you enjoyed writing. Somewhere in your elementary school experience writing was fun. You told stories to your teachers, wrote them down, illustrated them with brightly colored stick

1

drawings, and read them aloud to your classmates, teachers, and often to your parents. For these efforts you received universal approval and encouragement. You were praised for your originality, your creativity, your imagination. Somewhere along the line, however, someone changed the rules. Suddenly red marks started appearing on your papers: Spelling errors were circled, incorrect verb forms were underlined, hieroglyphics such as AWK and FRAG began appearing in the margins, and the smiling faces or stars at the bottoms of your papers turned into letter grades.

EXERCISE 1–1

Before you go any further, we'd like you to stop for a moment to reflect on what you remember learning about writing in previous English classes. Make a list of all the rules of composition that you remember being taught. What do you remember being told about sentences, about how to begin and end them? About paragraphs? About the proper length of sentences and paragraphs? What do you remember being told about the kinds of words your writing should contain? Were you ever told that certain rules govern the structure of paragraphs? Make a list of these rules, then work with the rest of the class to prepare a master list on the board, in groups, or in class discussion.

The "Rules" of Writing

If your list of rules from the previous exercise is typical, you were given throughout your education a list of some "truths" about writing to live by. Sometime in the process of learning these rules (probably around seventh grade), the emphasis in your school writing shifted from writing stories to writing themes. You learned that a theme has an exact number of paragraphs—usually five—that a theme consists of an introduction, a body, and a conclusion. You learned that the thesis statement appears at the very end of the introduction, that each paragraph in the theme's body begins with a topic sentence, that a conclusion is a summary—a retelling—of the body. You also learned a list of rules. Never begin a sentence with a conjunction. Never use fragments. Never use the passive. Never use contractions. Never use "I" or "you." (Some of us were even taught that sentences and paragraphs had appropriate and specific lengths. One English teacher we know tells her students that no sentence should be longer than 23 words, no paragraph longer than seven sentences.) Points were taken off for each of your transgressions because you had sinned against the "absolute" laws of composition.

When an occasional rebellious student would ask why many of the authors whose work was being read in class violated these absolute rules, the reply was predictable: "These are professional writers. They know the rules, so they can decide when to violate them for effect." As a consequence of this rule-oriented instruction, many of you probably learned that the way to success—a good grade—was to pay more attention to following the rules than to what you had to say. You knew that you could get at least a "C" if your mechanics were right, a "B" if you could provide some specific examples. Others of you became so worried about the rules that writing became excruciatingly difficult; some never got enough of the rules right and failed in their efforts so frequently that they simply gave up trying to write better.

We hope this description doesn't match your experience. Perhaps sometime in your schooling you met a teacher who asked you to think, who wasn't satisfied with superficial thought packaged in a standard container, who urged you to experiment with your ideas, to play with language. We hope so, because the world of writing you are entering in college and that you will encounter after you graduate presents you with writing occasions which demand that you go beyond the superficial and test your thinking abilities. Don't worry. You will still have opportunities to use those forms you learned in the past; now, however, they should no longer dominate your writing experience. Instead, they will become what they should have been all along—options, alternatives that you may consciously choose or ignore. This book examines your options as a writer and helps you practice them so that you can draw on a wide variety of approaches when you undertake various writing tasks.

Thinking, Speaking, Writing

The Personal World of Thinking

Let's consider for a moment the relationships among thinking, speaking, and writing. Thinking by itself is obviously a personal experience. Through our inner contemplation we organize and establish a sense of our relationship with the world, with our environment, with our society, with the other people in our lives. We can silently reach decisions about morality, ethics, the nature of love, the meaning of life itself—or even about which movie to see. The thinking we do is as varied as the designs of snowflakes; often our thoughts meander about aimlessly, sometimes through pieces of reality, sometimes through creations of fantasy; often our thoughts follow a direct line of pursuit (chasing the answer to a problem, for example); frequently our minds retreat into memory or speculate about the future. Sometimes we think in patterns, at other times in associations; often our thoughts reflect a certain amount of chaos.

None of this thought, however, places us in action in the world. Except in the most philosophical sense, thinking must be translated into action before it is useful. Thought may, of course, be translated into physical action, but our most common vehicle of translation is speech. We try out our ideas on others, engage in debate, express our emotions, present reports, give speeches. Sometimes we even talk things over with ourselves.

The Social World of Talking

Our speech patterns reflect some of the same variety found in our thinking. When speaking formally, we usually follow a logical progression. Speaking informally, however, we are likely to jump from subject to subject, to utter statements apparently unrelated to any current conversation. When we speak, grammatical correctness is usually less important than the idea we are trying to communicate. Even English professors often speak in incomplete sentences and make errors in pronoun agreement. Another characteristic of speech is that it usually occurs instantaneously; no quicker is something thought than it is out of our mouths, a speech characteristic most of us regret from time to time. Fortunately, unless someone has a tape recorder on, those words immediately become unrecorded history. We could deny them or modify them— either because of imperfect memory or by design, perhaps because we don't always want to be held responsible for what we've said.

Another important feature of speech is the role of the listener. When we talk, a good listener provides an immediate and valuable response. Our listeners can question us, tell us how they interpret what we're saying, tell us what they think. Also we can often judge our listener's responses to our words by their physical reactions. Listeners nod and smile and we recognize agreement; they frown and we suspect dissent. These immediate responses allow us to elaborate, to pursue a new tack, or to modify our views completely. Translating thinking into writing, however, is a different proposition.

The Historical World of Writing

Writing is rarely instantaneous. The hand moving across the paper or across the keyboard is much slower than either thought or speech. The pauses while composing last longer than most of those during thought or speech. Once written, an idea is both history (for the writer) and present (for the current reader), as well as future (for all readers to come). The written word provides a permanent record which may be left unmodified or changed at a future date. The conventions of writing are, therefore, frequently more formal than those of speech. Sentences, because they are readily available for scrutiny, can more easily be shaped into patterns of elegance or complexity. We can change words to create more vivid or precise images or meanings. We can organize our ideas into paragraphs for the convenience of our readers. We can even add virtually unlimited illustrations, charts, or photographs as counterpoints to our words. We can produce books, indeed volumes, focusing on one subject simply because readers can turn to our words at their convenience and because they can generally read much more effectively than they can listen. Writing, then, offers many advantages.

On the other hand, writing has some definite disadvantages. One obvious disadvantage is that for writers the audience is rarely present to provide immediate response. Writers must imagine and make decisions about how their words, sentences, examples, and ideas will affect the audience. Then they must wait long periods before they discover their audience's reaction. A student in a writing class might have to wait a week or more to see the teacher's response. A professor might wait six months to see a journal editor's response to his manuscript and then another 18 months until publication. Beginning novelists might wait years before someone other than an editor even reads their novels.

The following exercises ask you to think about how you write, about what kinds of writing are most comfortable for you; they ask you to examine your own writing process. Once you become more aware of the way you write, you'll be better able to incorporate the suggestions for improvement made in this text. You'll be better able to judge which of the strategies we suggest will alleviate your own difficulties in writing.

EXERCISE 1–2

Think about your own intellectual experiences. Using them as the source, write a quick page discussing the differences you have noticed in your own thinking, speaking, and writing. You may not at first even realize that there are differences. That's fine, though, because once you've written about how you think, how you speak, and how you write, you can compare each experience with the others and come to some conclusion about how the three activities differ. If you need an example of such a comparison to help you get started, read the following response:

Sample Response to Exercise 1–2:

```
                Thinking--Speaking--Writing

     I usually think in bed at night. I can't stop
myself. Ideas just keep coming. I find it hard to stay
on the subject. Ideas just seem to jump in without
order or logic. Sometimes I come up with good ideas
and plans when I'm doing this kind of thinking.
Unfortunately I usually forget most of them by
morning. To keep the ideas, I have to talk them over
with someone or I have to write them down. If I don't,
they're gone.
     Talking is much the same way. I sometimes give
talks before groups. I don't like to give canned
talks, so I usually just use a few notes. I like the
spontaneity associated with talking through a subject.
I like the feeling of energy and creativity. Sometimes
this happens when I talk in class. The trouble is that
I'm so busy talking that I can't remember exactly what
I've said. Even 15 minutes later I can only remember
the generalities. I need a tape recorder--which takes
too much time--or a secretary to keep minutes.
```

```
     As much as I hate to write, I need writing for a
permanent record of what I've done. I can go back to
it. Change it. Add things. But mostly I need it for
remembering. It doesn't come as freely as the other
two but it's more valuable. In fact, sometimes
writing's a real pain. Can't write fast enough to keep
up with my ideas. I have to make notes to myself just
to keep up--at least I don't lose anything.
     Let's see--what else. Writing needs tools. Each
tool makes me function differently. Composing on the
computer is different from my yellow legal pad.
Harder. I like writing on the pad so I can see what
I've written, spread it out around me. I guess I like
chaos.
```

EXERCISE 1–3

Write a description, including as much detail as possible, of the way you go about completing a writing assignment. Focus on one particular assignment you've done recently. Explain the assignment, then describe, as thoroughly as you can, your steps from beginning to end. Where did you write? your room? the library? in a classroom? What did you write on? computer? a legal pad? How did you begin the assignment? Did you do some research? discuss your ideas with a friend? take preliminary notes? How long did it take to finish the writing task? What problems did you have? Were you able to solve them? How successful and in control did you feel as you worked on the assignment? How successful were your results?

The purpose of this assignment is to describe, as accurately as possible, a process that you use. Pay attention to detail—do not worry at this stage about creating perfect sentences or a polished essay.

EXERCISE 1–4

Write a comparison of two writing assignments you've recently completed, one that was positive and rewarding and one that was frustrating, even maddening. As you write, try to discover what made one writing task so positive and the other so negative. Some possibilities: the assignment itself, your state of mind when you wrote, your understanding of what you had to do, your confidence in handling the assignment.

Once again, we are more concerned with your content than with perfection.

EXERCISE 1–5

Quickly make a list of the types of writing you do. Include every type of writing you can think of, from assembling a Christmas list to writing a documented paper for a psychology class. Once you've made the list, look it over and select one or two types with which you are generally comfortable—types that cause you little pain and even some delight. Then write a page about that type of writing, trying as you write to discover why you are more comfortable with that type than the others. Again, you may not know the reasons for your ease with a particular type when you begin this exercise, but as you describe and explain your feelings, some reasons will emerge.

✗ Skills and strong
writing is important.

The Importance of Writing

Despite its difficulties, writing clearly offers a greater depth and breadth of possibility than speech. Through writing of all kinds we have the opportunity to explore the full extent of our mind's capacity to think and create. Our fantasies are recreated in the science fiction of Ray Bradbury and the tales of J. R. R. Tolkein. Our emotions find life in the novels of Charlotte Brontë and Leo Tolstoy. James Joyce recreates the mind's ability to give meaning to a world of minutiae. Our sense of man's spirituality is exemplified in the Bible, the Koran, the Talmud. Ideas on social order are argued by James Madison, Karl Marx, and Jean Jacques Rousseau. Humanity's foibles and shared frailties are illuminated by Thornton Wilder, Jonathan Swift, and Emily Dickinson. Less noble, but no less a part of our lives, is the writing that allows modern life to function. Reports, pamphlets, manuals, laws, and contracts all work together to allow society to function.

No less important to college or university students is the role that writing plays in education. The writing you do in college comprises a significant part of the learning process. You take notes during lectures; you write essay exams which both organize material and lead you to your own conclusions; you summarize and review articles and books; you paraphrase your reading; you take notes for research; you write papers which require you to handle large chunks of information and to reach tenable conclusions. In sum, much of your learning—and your teachers' measurement of that learning—takes place through your writing.

The importance of writing in your life does not suddenly stop with graduation. Biologists and chemists write up research results. Police officers write extensive reports, as do social workers and physicians. Government workers produce a sea of documents. Those in business write letters, memos, evaluations, reports. Even in this age of high expectations about the future of the computer, someone has to compose the documents which are processed.

Research by Professors James Paradis and David Dobrin of MIT shows, for example, that professionals in technical fields spend over one-third of their professional time on projects that demand writing skills. They further discovered that an engineer's writing skills often directly affect his or her chances for promotion. A study done by the College of Engineering at the University of Wisconsin—Madison showed that the amount of writing engineers do usually increases as they advance in their careers (both studies are cited in Anne

Eisenberg, "The Rise of the Writing Class," *IEEE Potentials,* February 1984, p. 26).

The amount of writing you do after graduation depends on the field you enter and the position you hold. But most professions require some writing— writing undertaken for various purposes and addressed to various audiences. What follows are brief descriptions of the writing tasks performed by professionals in physical therapy, business, and accounting. Each description was written by the professional named. As you read their remarks, consider how closely the types of writing they undertake resemble those required in your chosen major.

Catherine Rush Thompson is a physical therapist who works independently with the Kansas City, Missouri, school system. She says:

Writing is critical to the health professional. The physical therapist relies on written information for three major reasons: (1) to monitor a patient's condition; (2) to communicate professional information; and (3) to record data pertinent to administrative duties.

Documentation of a patient's status includes subjective information (information provided by the patient and his/her family), objective information (measurement of performance and health information), an assessment or evaluation of the patient's condition, and planning for an appropriate therapeutic program. This charting of data is used to analyze treatment programs and their effectiveness.

Finally, the medical professional relies on permanent records for accountability. Should there be any question about the procedure used or a decision made, the physical therapist can refer to written information which supports his/her professional judgment. In addition, reimbursement for services performed and protection from liability make documentation mandatory.

Here's an example of a physical therapist's documentation:

```
        12-5-85 Mary Brown complained of pain in her
    left elbow this morning. Dr. Harris ordered hot packs,
    which were applied for 20 minutes. The patient
    appeared to tolerate the treatment well. She will
    return to clinic tomorrow a.m. for follow-up
    examination and treatment.

                        Catherine Rush Thompson, R.P.T.
```

Timothy J. Ryan, assistant general manager of an international industrial company, estimates that he spends 20 hours a week writing. His estimates of the kinds and amounts of writing required by his position follow:

Hours Weekly

Sales Proposals 5
Contract Administration 5
Periodic Business Reports 5

Hours Weekly

Interoffice Memos 2.5
Sales Letters 2.5

As assistant general manager of a company that sells large industrial process equipment for the separation of liquids and solids, I operate first as a sales manager and have a number of administrative duties. Some of the department managers report to me in lieu of the general manager since he travels a great deal.

As noted in the above list, the first three types of writing are the most important for my job. We are primarily a sales and service company, so most of us take some type of active sales role.

The sales proposal forms the basis of our business with a prospective customer and therefore has the highest priority. Since we import our equipment from Austria, our price is relatively high in the marketplace. To put this price in a better light we always include in the quotation a total cost evaluation that considers operating costs as well as capital costs as they compare to alternate systems. If considered favorably, the proposal becomes an integral part of the customer's request for approval and is then widely circulated.

I get involved with contract administration when a customer has a problem that affects either payment or further progress of the project. After I investigate the problem, my letter represents the company's position and (usually) suggests a method for resolution.

The periodic business reports provide a scorecard of our actual performance as it compares to budget objectives. More important, they outline marketing trends and company strategy for the next 12-to-18-month period. These reports are approved by our president and then forwarded to management in Austria for review and approval.

Accountant Robert L. Deskins says that although writing is not the major part of his work, it is an important one. Many of the reports and statements he prepares for clients are accompanied by written explanations and recommendations that must be as clear, precise, and accurate as the reports and statements themselves. Here is Deskins' description of his responsibilities as a writer:

At first glance writing would appear to be of minor importance for a Certified Public Accountant. What does a C.P.A. do? He prepares tax returns, financial statements and analyses—all using numbers, not words. If writing is ignored, however, and only the numeric presentations are made, several things could go wrong.

If the C.P.A. does not prepare a clear written statement of the service to be performed, a statement to be signed by the client, there can be legal liability. Courts are more likely to rule against C.P.A.s in disagreements if there is no clear understanding of the extent of work to be performed. This written statement, called an engagement letter, is a contract between the parties and must clearly specify the responsibilities of all parties.

Preparing financial statements also requires a written report which describes the extent to which a reader can rely on the information presented. Other statements may be required to outline what the C.P.A. found, to provide a detailed explanation of certain sections, and to modify the standard report if emphasis is needed or an opinion has changed.

If proposals to prospective clients are not well written, they will not be well received. Marketing one's services requires that tax and financial information be sent to clients, newspapers, and others in written form. This information—explanations of complex tax laws or formulas—must be understandable to readers or they will look elsewhere for the information they need.

It is frequently helpful to attach to a tax return a statement describing an unusual situation because I.R.S. computers will mark a tax return for audit if an unusual dollar amount is noted. After the return is marked, it will be reviewed by an individual, and it is at this point that an explanation of the unusual situation may prevent the return from being audited. If an audit notice is sent, however, the C.P.A. will need to write up the steps to be followed in the audit presentation in order to have all necessary documents and evidence ready. Once an audit is completed, it may be necessary to appeal an unfavorable ruling by going to the Appeals Office of the I.R.S. It is extremely important at this point to use clear and precise language in the written explanation defining the client's position.

The ramifications of ineffective writing could thus be somewhere between embarrassment and loss of business to forfeiture of one's license to practice. Clients who have been misinformed because of the C.P.A.'s inability to clarify a situation in writing may simply take their business elsewhere or, in more serious cases of increased liability, may take legal action. Writing is a part of the C.P.A.'s job and, like the other parts of the job, it should be done as effectively as possible.

As each of these accounts shows, writing plays an important part in the business and professional worlds. Professionals, business persons, and workers must communicate with others. They must issue and acknowledge instructions, analyze conditions, offer and accept services, propose and plan. Much of this communication is done in writing, for writing often allows for greater reflection and clarity than speech. In addition, as these accounts show, writing seems to clarify responsibility, to state what will be or has been done and why.

So novelists, poets, columnists, and investigative reporters are not the only people who write. Some people write to express themselves. Some people write to create beauty. Others write to reveal an inequity or to explore a situation they find interesting. And some people write for the very practical reason that the smooth operation of their jobs depends on an exchange of information with others.

EXERCISE 1–6

Interview someone in a profession you might be interested in to find out how much and what types of writing are required. Then write a report of your findings and compare them to what you expected. (For some tips on conducting a good interview, see Chapter 9.)

Read the following essay by Paul Theroux, author of *The London Embassy*. It offers a unique description of the power of writing.

The Cerebral Snapshot

Paul Theroux

It is my good fortune that I've never owned a camera. Once, when I was in Italy, I saw about three dozen doves spill out of the eaves of an old cathedral. It was lovely, the sort of thing that makes people say *if only I had a camera!* I didn't have a camera with me and have spent the past two-and-a-half years trying to find the words to express that sudden deluge of white doves. This is a good exercise—especially good because I still can't express it. When I'm able to express it I'll know I've made the grade as a writer.

And recently I was driving through Kenya with a friend of mine. It was dusk, an explosion of red shot with gold, and the setting sun and the red air seemed to be pressing the acacias flat. Then we saw a giraffe! Then two, three, four—about ten of the lanky things standing still, the silhouettes of their knobby heads protruding into the red air.

I brought the car to a halt and my friend unsheathed his camera and cocked it. He snapped and snapped while I backed up. I was so busy looking at the giraffes that I zig-zagged the car all over the road and finally into a shallow ditch.

The giraffes moved slowly among the trees like tired dancers. I wanted them to gallop. Once you've seen a giraffe galloping—they gallop as if they're about to come apart any second, yet somehow all their flapping limbs stay miraculously attached—you know that survival has something to do with speed, no matter how grotesque, double-bellied and gawky the beast may be.

My friend continued to fire his camera into the sunset, and pretty soon all the giraffes had either loped away or had camouflaged themselves in the trees. Both of us, rendered speechless by beauty, nodded and we continued along the road.

After a while my friend told me that we should have stayed longer with the giraffes. Why? Because he didn't get a good look at them.

"See," he explained calmly, "if you take a picture of things—especially moving things like giraffes—you don't really see them." He said he would have had trouble explaining what the giraffes looked like except that he had seen some in the Chicago Zoo. I could only agree and I told him about my Italian dove episode.

The next day, when we saw another herd of giraffes, he pushed his camera aside and we both sat there—it was a blazing Kenyan noon—and watched the giraffes placidly munching leaves and glancing at us, pursing their lips in our direction.

No camera is like no hands, a feat of skill. And if you know that sooner or later you will have to explain it all, without benefit of slides or album, to your large family, then as soon as you see something you start searching the view for clues and rummaging through your lexical baggage for the right phrases. Otherwise, what's the use? And when you see something like a galloping giraffe which you can't capture on film you are thrown back on the English language like a cowboy's grizzled sidekick against a cactus. You hope for the sake of posterity and spectators that you can rise unscratched with a blossom.

[October 5, 1965]

EXERCISE 1–7

Answer the following questions. Try to fill at least one side of a page. Use direct references to Theroux's essay to support your ideas.

1. What does Theroux say about writing that corresponds to your own feelings?

2. How are his feelings different?

EXERCISE 1–8

Theroux's essay focuses on the power of language to recreate experience. Discuss what you think makes this essay an example of powerful writing. Use specific examples to support your ideas. Again, try to fill at least one page.

EXERCISE 1–9

Make a list of things you have seen which no photograph could do justice to (e.g., your grandmother's face, Mt. Rainier covered with snow, a race horse going down the stretch). Bring your list to class and be prepared to discuss with your classmates the specific characteristics of the items on your list which make them defy the power of photography. After you've discussed the items on your list, pick three and write a brief paragraph on each explaining how to capture their essence in words.

The next chapter suggests ways of generating ideas for your writing. Then it covers ways of refining your ideas, of deciding whether they are usable, of working those ideas into a thesis that clarifies your purpose—to yourself and to your reader.

The following article shows how an event as apparently insignificant as a chance encounter with a junkyard dog led George Gurley to write a piece that grew into a meaningful engagement with an idea: the slippery nature of our language.

Say It Only if It's Tried and True

Meaner than a junkyard dog . . ."

You've heard that expression. But just what degree of *meanness* does it convey? Junkyard dog. Visions of lean, lunging dobermans with chiseled teeth gnashing at human flesh. But if you've never confronted a junkyard dog . . . ? "A junkyard dog is almost as mean as Leroy Brown," you say. Singer Jim Croce put it this way: "Bad, bad Leroy Brown . . . meaner than a junkyard dog."

Very good. But again: If we're not personally acquainted with Leroy, how do we know how mean *he* is? For all we know Leroy Brown and the junkyard dog may both be docile. They may be jellyfish. Or at least only semi-mean.

Expressions such as "meaner than a junkyard dog" should always be tested in the field before used. In other words, we must seek out a junkyard and throw ourselves upon the mercy of the junkyard dog, exposing our persons to all his unmuzzled ferocity. We must face his wrath. We must know the savagery of tooth and claw.

First, we have to find a junkyard. We want a place that spells junk j-u-n-k. Not a place that spells junk j-u-n-q-u-e. A place that displays piles of treadless tires, refrigerator compressors, mountains of mattress springs, oil-blackened Johnson rods, the guts of extinct autos. Not the kind of place that displays hand-painted milk cans suitable for exhibiting pussy willows.

Easier said than done. There aren't many establishments in the Yellow Pages that come right out and call themselves junkyards. We call our first "salvage yard."

"Hello, we're doing a survey on junkyard dogs . . ."

"This is NOT a junkyard!" Click.

Dogged pursuit of the subject reveals that few junkyards employ the services of dogs any more. If thieves want something, they're going to get it. ("We just let them take what they want," says one cynic.) They'll poison your dogs. They'll hit them with a baseball bat. Dogs are expensive. Dogs dig under your fence and run away.

One man had a dog. This dog was so mean that only that one man could feed him. And the dog bit *him*. He bit the hand that fed him. (If only we could find *that* dog. . . .)

Dogs scare your customers off. If your dogs bite someone, you get sued. One junkyard proprietor relies on phantom dogs. He has signs that say

"Beware of Dogs." But he has no palpable dogs. When someone asks where his dogs are, he says, "I've put them up."

The search for the junkyard dog takes us to the nether reaches of the city's digestive tract. Cars and appliances that are consumed in Mission Hills wind up here, "pre-owned" materiel.

At last we find what we're after: five mean-looking dogs roaming menacingly behind an 8-foot-high chain link fence topped with barbed wire. The proprietor invites us to meet them. We prepare ourselves for swift dismemberment in the interests of participatory journalism. He opens the gate and calls the brutes.

"Princess, Precious, Sissy." . . . Hmmmmm. "They won't bite," he says. Not even if you tried to climb over the fence at night? "No, they're good dogs. Someone broke in last month, and they just trotted over to my house. Here, Precious. That's a good girl." Precious lies down in the shade and falls asleep.

You'd expect these mean junkyard dogs to eat a power lunch—raw horsemeat or alligator tartare. But no, they do lunch on Church's fried chicken. Extra crispy, no doubt.

OK. So you're back from the junkyard. You've had your 250 stitches. The doctors were able to save one of your arms, three of your fingers. You cower in the corner whenever you hear an "arf," a "woof" or a "bow-wow." Psychiatrists diagnose your case as mild catatonic canine-phobia. Otherwise, you're fit as a fiddle feeling great.

And now you know how mean a junkyard dog is.

Let's all learn something from this. Let's stop saying, "I'll be back in two shakes of a lamb's tail," until we've been out among the lambs with our stopwatches and found out whether that's quicker or slower than a wink. "Ugly as sin," "Loose as a goose," "Drunker than a boiled owl." Let's get out there in the field and put these propositions to the test.

—George Gurley

EXERCISE 2–1

Write a summary of Gurley's article in which you illustrate your understanding of the three points he makes about our language.

EXERCISE 2–2

1. Pack up some paper, lots of it, and two or three of your favorite writing tools. If you have an unobtrusive tape recorder, pack it as well. Go somewhere you don't usually go, find a comfortable spot with no traffic and take a few minutes to acclimate yourself to the spot. Then turn on your tape recorder, take out your paper and writing tool, and saturate yourself in your environment. For thirty minutes record everything you observe around you. Be as specific as you can.

2. At the end of the thirty minutes, pack up and head for wherever it is that you write best. Listen to your tape recorder, reread your notes. Try to find one sensory impression which leads you from your senses to an idea. Make a list of as many ideas as you can. Don't discard any because you feel they're too wild. (You might even record an observation as curious as the one President Reagan once made: that trees are pollutants. Even unusual ideas might lead to new ideas.)

3. Write an informal essay (a legible first draft without grammatical or mechanical corrections) of about two pages on one of the ideas that tickles your fancy.

The previous assignment may have given you some trouble at first. But perhaps eventually you had a rush of ideas and finally found one you could play with for a couple of pages. Maybe somewhere in the process you even found yourself having fun.

In the following section, we present methods, collectively called *prewriting*, which you can use to approach a wide variety of writing situations. These methods—like the previous exercise—are designed to help you tap all the levels of your experience *to find a topic or to develop a topic* for a paper in any kind of class. No doubt some of the methods will work better for you than others in different situations. But before you can decide what works best, you need to understand and practice the prewriting methods. Care enough about your writing to practice them, to experiment with them, and then to integrate the most useful into your own writing process.

Responding to Your World

The Journal

If you know you are going to be choosing your own topic for essays this semester, you should start looking now for those topics that allow you to engage your reader. One way to begin your search is a journal. A journal allows you to examine your experience—both primary and secondary—and to find workable topics. If you already know that you have some papers to write and you know the general or specific topics, you can use the journal to focus on those topics and to begin examining them more thoroughly.

There are many types of journals, from those of Henry David Thoreau and Joan Didion, which were designed for a reader, to those of Thornton Wilder, which were used as a personal source for other writings and were published after his death. (Journals for personal use, like Wilder's, are usually published only after the author's death.) The most productive journal for your purposes is one that allows you to explore your ideas freely without the intention of presenting them to a critical reader. You should feel free in your journal to play with both language and ideas. Don't worry about grammar, punctuation, spelling, or sentence structure. And don't worry that your ideas are not yet fully developed. You might discover along the way that you have ideas you didn't know you had.

We must add one important qualification. The journal is not a diary, not merely a record of what happens to you during the day. Read the following sample diary.

Diary Entry:

> Dear Diary,
>   Today I had a history quiz. Think I did great.
> Think I'll treat myself to a sundae at Winstead's.
> Maybe I'll see Jack and Frank. Hope so! I need a date
> for Saturday night.
>   Also ate lunch with Sue. No more cafeteria. We
> went to Fedora's. Going to the spa at 7:00.

This type of entry will do you little good in the pursuit of a topic. It might satisfy the requirements of completing so many pages of journal entries, but it probably will not help you find a topic nor will it help you become a better writer. By contrast, the following entry, which has the same subject matter as the previous diary entry, goes on to examine the student's responses to what happened during a day. As you can see, she has discovered ideas which might be worth pursuing.

Journal Entry:

> History quiz today. I don't understand why I
> have to memorize all those names and dates. I used to
> think I'd like to major in history but now I don't
> know. Isn't there another way to teach this course?
> Can't—shouldn't—history be alive? Didn't anyone
> historically famous ever have an interesting life? I
> wish the professor would put American history in
> context with what was happening in other parts of the
> world. Hans, my new German friend, claims that
> Americans are provincial. Are we? Oh well.
>   I feel fat but keep on eating—sundaes—at
> Winstead's. Why do I feel so guilty? Why are Americans
> so concerned with being thin and beautiful? Bo Derek?
> Tab commercials? The lust for perpetual youth? Is that
> why Mom bought us spa memberships? I don't want to
> compare myself to models and actresses but I do it all
> the time—fool! I buy all the right clothes too. Calvin
> Klein loves me.

The journal entry takes the ideas expressed in the sample diary a step further; it reflects on them. The author of the journal entry explores her feelings about the study of history and about the origins of her self-image. She also finds that she has contradictory thoughts about each topic. She feels fat but keeps eating; she finds her constant comparison of herself to screen and magazine images silly but admits that she can't help making those comparisons.

This journal entry suggests ideas that can be expanded into topics for essays. The writer could further explore her dissatisfaction with the way history is taught, perhaps suggesting ways to bring the subject to life or arguing the merits of teaching history regardless of how dryly it is taught. She could explore the compulsion to eat that makes so many people unhappy with themselves. She could explore the images of perfection to which so many people compare themselves, perhaps tying the comparisons they make to the motives behind advertising or the effects of lowered self-esteem.

In the journal entry, possibilities exist that never come to the fore in the diary entry. Using the journal to reflect on ideas and events helps you to discover what ideas you have, allows you to speculate upon those subjects that interest you and have some effect on your life. The ideas you play with in the journal may become the ideas you organize and explain in a full-blown essay.

EXERCISE 2–3

Write several journal entries and select one to bring to the next class for discussion.

Reading

Another way to find a topic or develop ideas for an assigned topic is by keeping a different kind of journal—the reading log. But before we discuss exactly how to use the reading log in your writing, we need to digress briefly to discuss the role that reading plays in developing your writing skills. Much of the writing that you do in college is directly or indirectly related to what you've read. Essay tests, research reports, and reviews all connect writing directly with reading. Lab reports, certain kinds of philosophical essays, and reports of primary research all rely on initial reading to develop necessary concepts. Unfortunately, many students are not prepared for the kinds of reading they have to do in college. They report that they read well for facts and information but they have difficulty isolating underlying assertions and concepts and making inferences.

This text helps you become a better reader in two ways. Throughout we emphasize the role reading plays in the writing process. We also focus on the ways readers and writers think when they approach a communication task. The first step you can take is to commit yourself to becoming a more active reader. This commitment involves consciously integrating reading and writing.

First you must realize that you will have to write or talk about every piece of writing which is or might be important to you. For you to grasp the content of a piece of writing, you must somehow engage it intellectually. If you don't engage it, you read words—not ideas—and your retention of the material is brief.

The Engaged Reader

The active reader begins to engage the material immediately. The first step is context: When and where does the piece appear? Who wrote it? What's the title? An article on entreprenurial trends for women might well have a different focus if it appears in *Inc.: The Magazine For Growing Companies* or *The Wall Street Journal* or *Redbook*. A 1986 article carries different significance from one written in 1956. An article on foreign policy written by Jesse Helms is sure to be different from one by Ted Kennedy. What level of sophistication can you expect from an article titled "In and Out of Work: 'How Can We Manage on an Unsteady Paycheck?'" published in *Family Circle*? Would you expect more from the title "In and Out of Work: Managing the Entrepreneur's Uneven Cash Flow"?

The active reader is also aware of purpose. We read for different reasons: to gain important information, to search for potentially valuable information, to substantiate our own feelings and opinions, to see what our opponents have to say, to help us make up our minds, to find out how to behave, to gain advice, to laugh, to feel sad, to be reminded of our pasts, to help us better understand ourselves and the world around us.

Although there are many reasons for reading, active readers usually know why they are reading a particular piece. This awareness causes them to read each piece differently. If they know the piece contains valuable information, they read slowly and carefully, perhaps taking notes. If they are searching for information, they skim until they find the pertinent sections. If they're reading an opponent's work, they consciously examine the argument and the proof as they read. If they're reading casually, they might discover their purpose while reading. We decided to include the George Gurley article in this text, for example, when one of us was reading his column for enjoyment. When it became evident that the column was about the nature of language rather than junkyard dogs, the purpose for reading shifted.

Active readers often write while reading. When they are confused or enlightened or informed, they take notes or underline or write in the margins or talk with a friend. They feel the need to have some sort of conversation with the author of the words they're reading. Since real conversation is impossible, they create their own internal dialogues. Writing about what they've read, either while reading or after, helps the reader gain control of the material and retain it longer. For these reasons, we're going to ask you to keep a reading log.

The Reading Log

Instead of a response to the world of your primary experience, the reading log is a response to the world of your secondary experience. Many times as you read newspapers, magazines, novels, even your textbooks, you find yourself responding to the ideas. Sometimes what you read simply reminds you of something in your life. In your sociology text, for example, you're reading about the effects of winter in northern climates. You think about the year you spent in the Upper Peninsula in Michigan and the "cabin fever" that you and your family suffered. If you don't stop to write this response down, the idea might be gone forever. If you were keeping a reading log, the idea would be yours to use if you needed it.

Your response to reading is often emotional; the ideas you encounter may substantiate or conflict with one of your beliefs. You read in the newspaper that the legislature is thinking of cutting state support of education by 3%. Last year your school suffered from lack of supplies and the best teacher quit because of low pay. In a reading log you could record your response to this new legislative initiative. Or you might read in a magazine that unionism in the 1980s has lowered productivity in American industry. You and your family have a long affiliation with unions, and you are familiar with the case of a union which has increased productivity significantly. A reading log might help you turn this observation into an essay for your English class, your political science class, or your business class.

Finally you might read something that you simply find interesting and might like to store away for future use. In this case, the most likely response to your reading would probably be a concise summary of what you've read. When you write a summary, keep the following points in mind:

1. Make sure you include all the specific details you might need. Having to find the article again and reread it would take valuable time.
2. If the author has said something in language you particularly like, include it as a direct quotation.
3. Remember that a summary is designed to capture the meat and the spirit of what you've read.
4. Record all the publication data. You'll need it if you ever use the source in a paper. (See the section on documentation in Chapter 9.)

Your reading log might be in the following format:

NAME   _____

DATE   _____

PUBLICATION DATA   _____

_____

_____

_____

RESPONSE TO WHERE PIECE APPEARED (FORUM), AUTHOR, AND TITLE

INITIAL PURPOSE FOR READING PIECE

FINAL PURPOSE

RESPONSE TO CONTENT

As you read the following sample reading-log entry, notice that many of the ideas could serve as topics for essays. The article on which the sample is based is presented first; the reader's response follows.

Lessons in Bringing Up Baby

Jerome Kagan's conversion came during a 1971 trip to Guatemala. Until then, Kagan, now 55 and a developmental psychologist at Harvard, had assumed that "the differences you see in five-year-olds, ten-year-olds and adults were all determined primarily by environmental experience, in the family, the peer group, the school." In Guatemala he made a startling discovery: children who received no intellectual stimulus at all during early childhood, who were often kept isolated in dark huts for years, blossomed into happy, lively and intelligent youngsters. Even children who had suffered illness and neglect as toddlers turned into vital and alert ten-year-olds.

The Guatemala trip ended what Kagan now calls "the Don Quixote phase" of his career, which was dedicated to showing that children are shaped primarily by their environment. Kagan subsequently developed his "minimal continuity" theory. It is the subject of his provocative new book, *The Nature of the Child* (Basic Books; $22.50). Environment is important, according to Kagan, but biology, particularly brain development, strongly guides the child in the first few years of life and accounts for much of the child's moral and emotional life.

Children begin to know right from wrong at about the time that important emotions develop, says Kagan, or around the end of the second year. A child who has been hitting playmates generally stops doing so at that age, when empathy for others is first felt.

Unlike most observers of children, Kagan does not think that conscience is learned, or built into a child by parents. "Our culture," he says, "is doing something very dangerous by saying that morality is learned, that if a 15-year-old kid mugs an old lady, he probably never learned a conscience. I think that *all* children, provided they have an intact nervous system, know before they are three that hurting another is wrong. We can expect a conscience of every child. We don't have to build it in. All we have to do is arrange the environment so they don't lose it."

Similarly, Kagan believes that the turmoil of puberty is a byproduct of brain development. "When you become adolescent," he says, "you become cognitively able for the first time to evaluate the consistency of the beliefs you hold. You automatically detect inconsistency, and that creates uncertainty." A child who considers his father wonderful and wise may suddenly realize that the father screams a lot or drinks too much. "Now the child has a problem: Is the father good or bad? That creates a tension until it's worked out. I think the tension of adolescence is due in large measure to this cognitive conflict, not because the hormones are running in the bloodstream."

Kagan has focused on inborn temperamental differences in children and finds that although some are influenced by the environment, some are more stable than others. About 10% of children, he says, are born with a tendency to be "shy, timid, frightened, vigilant, fearful." On the other end of the scale, another 10% "tend to become sociable, extraverted, bubbly, spontaneous, the kind of children every parent wants." In a group of Boston-area children Kagan has been studying from the second to the sixth year of life, not one child in the fearless group has become fearful, while about a third of the fearful children are becoming more extraverted, largely because of parental pressures.

Among Kagan's fearful children, a sudden shout or a mild challenge in classroom work produces unusual changes in heart rate, dilation of the eyes and tension in the vocal cords. Parents of the fearful children report that as infants, their youngsters suffered colic, sleeplessness and allergies, while the fearless children "just had nothing wrong with them." This evidence strongly suggests a genetic base to temperament.

The current trend among many child psychologists to emphasize bonding and early attachment in children is way out of line, Kagan believes. An infant girl with a close attachment to a mother who promotes passivity, fear of boys and a noncompetitive attitude toward schoolwork, for example, is likely to be ridden with conflict and anxiety during adolescence. "Thus," Kagan says, "it is not obvious that a secure attachment at one year will be beneficial for an indefinite period of time."

Kagan's central idea is that human development is marked by discontinuity: "A lot of habits and characteristics are lost, repeat lost, in early childhood." From his finding he concludes that preschool for toddlers is unnecessary. Most children, as long as they have contact with other people and objects to explore, will flourish with or without early schooling. Kagan's 1978 book, *Infancy,* found no significant difference between children reared at home and those farmed out to a good day care center. Says he: "Our notions about how parents affect children are too simple." In his view, parenting is important but not the all-powerful influence that many child experts believe.

Not everyone in the field shares Kagan's sunny views of child development. "It's a bit Pollyannaish, based more on his easygoing view of the world than on any solid research," says New York City Child Psychologist Louise Kaplan, author of *Adolescence* and *Oneness & Separateness,* a book on infancy. "Not everything that happens to a child determines its future. He's right about that and it needs to be said. But he underrates the importance of attachments, and he minimizes the effects of what happens to some children." Nevertheless, Kagan's work has stirred the world of child psychology and pushed many specialists to rethink their opinions. His message may reassure some parents and dismay others: since much of a child's development takes place independent of parents, the hand that rocks the cradle does not rule the world.

—By John Leo; reported by Ruth Mehrtens Galvin/Boston

Sample Reading Log Entry

NAME   K. M. Jackson

DATE   November 1, 1984

PUBLICATION DATA   TIME, October 22, 1984

''Lessons in Bringing Up Baby''

By John Leo

Reported by Ruth Mehrtens Galvin

page 97

RESPONSE TO WHERE PIECE APPEARED (FORUM), AUTHOR, AND TITLE

I always read *TIME*. I usually trust it to present well-informed articles. I don't know anything about the authors, but they interview some people whose names I've seen in my child psych texts. Wonder how the authors knew they were experts? I like the title—going to talk about how to raise children. Isn't that an old movie title? Sounds like it will challenge the role of the environment.

INITIAL PURPOSE FOR READING PIECE

I paid close attention because I'm taking a child psych class, and I wanted to see how this article compared to my class.

FINAL PURPOSE

I took some notes because I realized that I might be able to use the article in class discussion, on an essay, or in my final paper.

RESPONSE TO CONTENT

An article about a psychologist who has written two books on children. He says that there is probably a ''genetic base for temperament''—that kids are not shaped just by environment but by biology, so that biology shapes much of the child's moral and emotional life. It must help form personality and disposition then. This interests me because I can see in my own behavior tendencies to behave in certain ways that I've always had. When I was a baby, my mother says, I didn't like to be held much. But I liked to see what was going on. So they'd prop me up with pillows in a cardboard box (before infant seats) and there I would sit, watching the world. At nine months I was crawling out of my crib, hanging to the railing until rescued. In stores I climbed racks and counter tops. It seems I had a quiet but independent sort of temperament at an age so young that it couldn't be learned. But environment must have had a part? I'm not sure if this is a rehash of the old ''nature—nurture'' argument, but I can see how it affects lots of things: how I understand myself, how kids should be reared by their parents, how schools can best teach kids, how we understand the ways kids relate to each other, how early tendencies matter and could be (not?) changed later in life.

EXERCISE 2–4

The above log entry accomplishes several purposes. It helps the reader clarify his beliefs about the article's content. It helps him relate what he's read to his own life. It provides him with potential material for another class. It begins with summary, moves toward personal experience, and ends with a question of belief. Individually, in small groups, or as a class, make a list of possible topics that can be gleaned from the above log entry. Then discuss ways those topics might be used or writing occasions for which they might be suitable.

EXERCISE 2–5

Read the following article and write a reading log entry on it. For the Response to Content section of the entry, combine personal response, statements of belief, and summary. Bring your responses to class; be prepared to compare your entry with those of your classmates. This log entry will be used for a later assignment, so either keep it in a collection of log entries (Exercise 2–8) or in your writing notebook (Exercise 2–10).

Apartheid Protester Finds KU Kept Clipping on Her

LAWRENCE, Kan.—When Shawn Holstrum went to the financial aid office of the University of Kansas last August to determine why she was not being allowed to enroll for fall classes, she was shocked to see a newpaper article about an apartheid protest in her loan file.

The article, which Miss Holstrum said was taken from the *Lawrence Journal-World,* identified her as one of the people arrested during a demonstration staged at the Kansas University Endowment Association building last spring. The endowment association has been the target of several protests by groups that want the association to eliminate its investments in companies that do business in South Africa.

The article "was the second piece of paper in the file, and my name was circled in red," Miss Holstrum said. "I started wondering if my arrest was the reason a hold had been put on my enrollment."

Miss Holstrum said she was an active member of the KU Commitee on South Africa during the spring semester and was arrested for criminal trespass at two apartheid protests conducted at Youngberg Hall, the endowment association's building on the western edge of campus.

When she called the endowment association's loan office to find out why the article was in her file, Miss Holstrum said she was told that it should not be there but that it would have no bearing on her enrollment status.

"The man I talked to kind of laughed if off and said some secretary must have put it in there as a joke," she said. "He said that the hold had been put on my enrollment because I hadn't repaid my short-term loan."

Miss Holstrum said she was told she would not be allowed to enroll until she repaid a $350 short-term endowment association loan that had been due in June. The 19-year-old freshman did not attend school during the fall semester but said she plans to pay off the loan and enroll for the spring semester.

Endowment association loan officer Bill Shunk said he decided last spring to insert the newspaper articles in the files of "five or 10" students who had loans through the endowment association and had been arrested during demonstrations against the organization.

"When the article came out we decided to check to see who had student loans with us," he said. "We didn't use the information in any way with regard to loans. It was just for our own information. There was nothing wrong with it. We can put what information we want in the files."

Mr. Shunk said the practice has been discontinued and the newspaper clippings have been removed from the students' files.

"It was just a one-time thing," he said. "And the articles did not affect whether or not someone would receive a loan."

—Jared Byer, Kansas City Times, Dec. 12, 1985

EXERCISE 2–6

Write one reading log entry on an article of your choice to bring to the next class for discussion.

The Electronic Media Response Log

An electronic media response log is a variation of the reading log. Every day of your life you are subjected to a barrage of messages from radio and television. On the radio you hear song lyrics, commercials, and talk shows. On television you see specials, sitcoms, music videos, soap operas, commercials. You are constantly surrounded by ideas, many of which prompt emotional and intellectual responses. By becoming an active listener and viewer through the use of a media log, you can discover many ideas suitable for an essay for one of your college classes. Take a look at this sample:

Sample Electronic Media Log

October 26, 1984
9:00, NBC

Last night's *Hill Street Blues* was good; the show is usually good, in fact. As I was watching I began wondering how writers and producers name the characters they use on the show. That subject came up because there was a character, a cop, named Randy Buckman on the show. I used to know somebody named that. What I wonder is, how far do producers or writers have to go to assure that they are not using somebody's name? They must use names that actually belong to somebody, I know, but I wonder if before they name a cop a certain name they check to make sure no cop actually has that name. How would they check? I'm thinking of the disclaimer that often comes in books and movies—any resemblance of the characters or story to any person living or dead is purely coincidental. Another thing about names—how they select the name to match the character's character. Something I read in the last week or so talked about how the writers of *Cagney and Lacey* came up with their names. They wanted to use something out of *Butch Cassidy and the Sundance Kid* but they weren't allowed to. Finding out would probably involve psychological studies of some sort—how some names conjure certain images in our minds. Priscilla sounds feminine, Elizabeth sounds dignified, Margaret sounds very self-sufficient. In my mind, anyway. I know studies have been done about how teachers react to certain names—I read about it in psychology classes and in some magazines.

Come to think of it, I never knew a Randy Buckman. The person I was thinking of has a different first name. What tricks memory can play. The PBS show on the brain might talk about that.

This sample begins with a reflection about a television show, a reflection born of the writer's association of a fictitious name with a real one. The entire sample is based on one question the writer had, a question about how characters on television are given names. That reflection leads to others; by the end of the entry, the writer has several ideas that could be developed into full-length essays. Here's a list of some of those ideas:

1. The rules or procedures that govern the naming of fictional characters.

2. The effect of the fictional character's name on the audience.

3. The connection between a name and how others treat somebody because of that name.

4. The way our prejudices about names are formed.

5. The way a memory is recalled through association.

You may have noticed other topics as you read the sample from the electronic media log. The entry took only about five minutes to write; the result is at least five ideas for essays, five ideas that may never have occurred to the writer if she had not been keeping the log. These five ideas could be used in a number of ways. Numbers three and four could be the basis for a personal essay in an English class or for a research paper in a psychology class. The first idea could be used in a communication or media class for an essay or research paper about ethics, slander, or libel laws. The second and fifth ideas could be used in a number of classes—composition, communication, literature, creative writing, education, psychology. Actually, all the ideas could be used in composition were the writer to discuss the idea in relation to her own life or perceptions.

The sample electronic media log entry is not an essay; it's an exploration of ideas prompted by the writer's viewing of a television show. Had the writer not recorded her initial reflection—the use of a name that sounded familiar—she would have no record of that reflection or the others that followed it. Without a record of these ideas, it's unlikely that she would ever have thought of them when it came time to write a paper for a class. But the entry now serves as a repository for those ideas, ideas she can take up at a later time.

The electronic media response log, like the reading log and the journal, are tools for the writer—tools whose purpose is to allow ideas to surface and play among themselves. Writers need those ideas.

EXERCISE 2–7

Write one electronic media log entry to bring to the next class for discussion. Use the following form:

Sample Electronic Media Log Format

NAME _____

DATE _____

BROADCAST DATA **(date, time)** _____

(network, station) _____

(authors, reporters, etc.) _____

PURPOSE FOR WATCHING/LISTENING

RESPONSE

RESPONSE

EXERCISE 2–8

For the next twenty-one days experiment with these forms of generating ideas. For the first seven days keep a journal of your responses to the world around you. Then for the next seven keep a reading log. For the last seven keep an electronic media log. At the end of these three periods, review what you have written and bring to class a list of five possible topics for future papers for this class or others you are taking this semester. Be prepared to discuss in class why you think each of these would make a good subject for a paper.

The following short essay presents David Ray's response to the news story of the disaster at the Union Carbide plant in Bhopal, India. Notice that the writer uses the incident to make his own point.

Fewer Mosquitoes in Bhopal

It wasn't a sick joke. It wasn't Black Humor. It wasn't the New Metafiction. It was simply a news announcement over the radio, and the announcement was this—that in Bhopal, India, where in late 1984 a disaster at a Union Carbide pesticide plant killed at least 2500 people and left over 150,000 blinded, insane and otherwise damaged, there has been a drop in the malaria rate.

The announcement gave me pause. I don't have a computer, but I could easily take the population of Bhopal, subtract 2500, and comman sense dictated to me that the malaria rate would be down, because there would be fewer people. Also, because the explosion sent pesticide across the landscape in the middle of the night, I could presume that there were far fewer mosquitoes, as well as people, in the Bhopal area. Also, the survivors would have residues of pesticides throughout their bodies, no doubt giving them some immunity from mosquitoes, if not from other problems.

But I wondered too if we weren't looking a little too hard for more evidence that even in the worst excesses of industry there is still some gain. Chemistry is, after all, *better things for better living.* And our belief in *progress,* particularly when it comes to the gifts the West gives the developing countries, runs far too deep to be upset by a mere disaster. Furthermore, there would be much to learn from a disaster. The malaria rate drops, and, as in Bhopal, experts on germ warfare fly in from several countries to autopsy the victims and study the lingering effects of deadly gases, not too dissimilar to those projected for our future wars. And no doubt that same habit of thinking will find benefits to announce regarding the goals of those future wars. Don't we, after all, live in the best of all possible worlds? Even the Bhopal disaster gave us the benefit of a lower malaria rate, and some guinea pigs for germ warfare studies. What would Gandhi think of it all—the people he loved donating their tissues for slides, to be studied to make war somehow more acceptable, cosmetic, perhaps sweetly scented? I suppose that next we'll hear that India should be grateful that Union Carbide is helping the nation with its population problems.

Since the Bhopal disaster we've read about malfunction at the West Virginia plant of the same company. These mishaps, like accidents in nuclear plants, are duly listed and claimed to be of little significance, and not worth the trouble and expense of preventing. Incidentally, most of the people exposed to the gas leaks in West Virginia happen to be black people—it just happens to work out that way. If a larger disaster like that at Bhopal happens in West Virginia it will be interesting to hear what Union Carbide has to say about the malaria rate, and whether the victims there will also turn into fodder for germ warfare studies. Of course, at the moment, company officials are claiming that major bungling at their plants can't happen in America, as in troubled Third World countries.

One thing's for sure: Those blinded by pesticide are not the only ones who are blind. Of course the malaria rate is down in Bhopal, and so is the sensitivity and common sense of industrial propagandists and news announcers here in the U.S.

Searching Your Mind and Memory

Freewriting

Another method of exploring your ideas is freewriting, a technique borrowed from psychology and free association, which is useful both in finding a topic and exploring a topic to generate ideas. When you practice freewriting, you sit down with a pen—or a typewriter or computer—and a blank page (or screen), and proceed to fill it up with whatever thoughts come to mind. You include anything and everything that crosses your mind. When you get stuck, don't stop to think. Instead write "I can't think of anything to say" over and over until a thought—any thought—breaks through. You'll discover that this technique works on a very simple principle. If we told you right now to stop reading this text, close your eyes, and think of nothing for the next 60 seconds, you would discover that the first thing that happens is that thoughts immediately force their way into your mind. Try it. The same thing happens during freewriting. As soon as you start to write "I can't think . . . ," thoughts race through your mind. Record them, no matter how nonsensical they may seem. Write as fast as you can. Don't worry about sentence structure, grammar, eloquence, or mechanics. What you're after right now are ideas that might lead to a topic or a good idea to narrow the topic you have. Later, when you're deep into the process of writing the essay, you can worry about revising and editing. Read the following samples for an idea of the shapes freewriting can assume.

Sample Freewriting on American Dream

The American Dream. I first heard the term years ago when the local PBS station ran a program of that name. ''American Dream Machine,'' I think. I don't remember much about the program except that it was comprised of a series of short sketches or vignettes, some of which were animated. But I do remember that it characterized American life, our dreams and aspirations and the incongruities that made those dreams and aspirations seem silly or trivial.

But I'm not sure that the dreams are silly or trivial. The ''American Dream'' conjures for me a series of images: houses with flowers and lace curtains and fresh cookies, cars shining as their owners wax and rub, cars, buses and trains filled with people in suits and dark blue uniforms (with their names printed on the pocket), all going to work so that they can pick up paychecks and shop for more cars and lace curtains. I see images of people playing softball in parks, playing frisbee on the Nelson Gallery lawn. Images of children crying and pouting, pointing to planes in the sky as they squeal in delight and wonder. I see at once a comparison of my life to my parents' and to my grandparents', lives shaped in different places at different times. But the hopes and aspirations are the same: to stay healthy and well, to find meaningful work, to maintain ties with those we love, to improve our lives materially. There is a sense that all things are possible in the comparison, for each generation has come closer to the Dream than the previous one, closer in terms of education and material goods. But that's not true in all families. If there is no progression, I wonder, does the Dream die?

If each generation's hopes of living the Dream never come true, how long does the Dream keep living for that generation? I think that must make people angry, jealous even. I see it in my own life when I see people who seem to be living my fantasy of the American Dream more fully than I do.

Sample Freewriting on American Dream

```
American Dream. Impossible topic. It goes clear back
to the beginning. Columbus, old Leif Erickson, Ponce
de Leon: the search for new lands and cities of gold.
Then the Puritans. Different kind of gold—freedom.
Religious freedom, political freedom, class freedom.
Then everyone could own land and that became part of
the dream. Then the pioneer spirit. Lots of sons and
tales of new land. OK. We can go on and have things
better, better than the ancestors. And that became
part of the dream. Is that how we came to want a
bigger and better mousetrap, toaster, microwave, VCR,
stereo, car. Oh, I could write the whole thing on how
much the car's become part of the dream. Henry Ford.
Do it better. Instant mobility. No more wagon trains.
Sex. Now it's part of the dream. From back seats to
bachelor apartments. Been writing so long my fingers
hurt. What a price to pay—education. Used to be part
of the dream just to get a degree. Now degree is a
means to one very particular end—$, $, $. Buy a ski
condo in Denver, buy Rollex watches. My dream. To
never have to write any more papers for English!
Married? New car (there it is again)? Good job? House?
Why is this American? Sounds just like what my cousin
in Germany wants. Is the American Dream contagious?
```

Notice that these two pieces of freewriting are very different. The first is very tightly written. It stays on topic, has good transition, good mechanics and grammar. In fact, it's almost a first draft. The second one, however, is loose. It jumps from topic to topic. It doesn't develop any of the ideas very deeply. It most definitely is an exploration. Which one is better? In this case, "better" depends on the writing processes of the author. We all go about writing differently. Freewriting is designed to help you explore and develop a topic. Do it however you must to accomplish these two goals.

EXERCISE 2–9

Individually, in groups, or as a class, make a list of topics suggested by one of the above freewriting samples.

Brainstorming

A technique similar to freewriting is brainstorming. Brainstorming demands the same spontaneity that freewriting does, but it doesn't require sentences or phrases, and it doesn't require that you move across the page from left to right. *The purpose of brainstorming is simply to get as many ideas as possible on paper and as quickly as possible.* You can write single words or short phrases;

you can use the whole page almost in the same way that you make a collage. One idea suggests another. Brainstorming may not be completely new to you. At least once in the past you have probably played the free association game. Soneone says a word; you respond immediately with the first word that comes to mind. He or she says another word or repeats the word you gave in response. You could continue this process to the limits of your endurance. Brainstorming ideas for an essay works in much the same way. If you don't try to censor or judge the quality of your ideas, then your subconscious mind can play freely with ideas. One idea suggests another until you have a page or more filled with suggestions. Some teachers advise turning your paper sideways before you brainstorm. Somehow this shift from the normal boundaries stimulates ideas to flow even more easily.

Both freewriting and brainstorming demand that you turn off that censor in your head. What follows is a brainstorming example on The American Dream. Not a pretty sight, is it? It's messy, disorganized, and may be difficult to make sense of. The writer has listed anything that came to his mind on the subject of "The American Dream." He's written words, phrases, questions. He's set some of his thoughts off by using boxes, arrows, and dashes. Some of the material appears as a list, other material almost in outline form. He repeats himself.

Such disorder may be distasteful, and in a final paper it would surely be condemned, but at this point in the prewriting process, disorder is almost a necessity. Brainstorming allows your memory to play, allows your powers of association to brew, so that you can discover what ideas you have about a topic. Look over the sample in Figure 2–1 to see how brainstorming worked for one writer.

Preliminary writing such as brainstorming helps you to discover ideas, to separate and consider the ideas, feelings, and objects that shape your attitudes, beliefs, and positions. This preliminary writing uncovers possibilities. Then the first trauma is behind you. These techniques can be repeated as often as you need them to generate new ideas, support for your original idea, or subtopics of your original idea. In other words, these techniques can be repeated throughout the writing process—but more about that later.

The prewriting methods we've introduced thus far are designed to tap the wealth of your personal experiences and ideas. For the writer without a topic, these methods provide options. Even if you have a topic, prewriting opens up the possibility of discovering new directions, new ideas, and material which might support them. Thus far, however, we've demonstrated only initial kinds of prewriting. What comes next?

Beyond Initial Prewriting

What do you do next with prewriting? Before we continue we must repeat a warning: *Now is not the time for a final judgment of the quality of your ideas.* You've explored some ideas in your logs or in your freewriting, but you're

FIGURE 2-1

The good life, the easy life
   house, car, clothes

job education social life

fun, travel, ballgames, movies
   barbeque in the backyard

shopping centers, sales, good deals on
   cars & clothes

looking good, making an "appearance"

school → college → work → marriage = the progression

repeat the parents' life: show gratitude by doing well

a nice, ordered life no big arguments
   Dorris Day & Rock Hudson in Pillow Talk
   Eight is Enough
   Partridge Family
   Leave it to Beaver
      ward in a suit
      June in pearls and heels

_____
      ↓

the real life
   Nikes and sweats (Even this is
                       middle class!)

   dishes to wash
   two careers
   what about kids

Work — advancement
      vacations — at least two weeks
              trendy — ski Colorado
                    sun in St. Martin

Dream also to movie up in class
   Be able to say "film"
   Attend the opera, symphony
   wear a mink and drive a Mercedes

Americans want to identify with larger successful
   groups: companies, Universities, smokers of
   particular cigarettes: The Bandwagon
   Is this why spectator sports are so popular?

Dream available to all

   bootstraps
   entrepreneurs
   education
   military

what does a parent
   want for a newborn
      child: health
         popularity
         a better life - job, etc
         to have more
         For our children
            to relive our lives

where does the
Dream come from?
TV, Movies, books,
from what what we see,
people we look
up to

contrasts with the
wedding — start.
of dream - ceremony -
dress - up - gifts
So clean, so
antiseptic

can everyone, does everyone
participate? What are the
American Dreams of the
very rich and very poor?

still looking for a direction or a focus; you won't know what works best until you've probed more deeply into the ideas from your prewriting. At this stage you've already made considerable progress toward defining a direction for your writing.

Proceeding from initial prewriting toward a rough draft requires rereading your prewriting with the goal of finding an idea or ideas worth pursuing. After rereading, return to some form of prewriting for a short time. Rereading usually stimulates new ideas or additions and modifications to old ones; use prewriting again to explore the new directions suggested by your rereading. Then you should have several possible ideas to pursue.

Narrowing the Topic

At this stage in writing a paper an author has generated a great deal of information and has identified several possible choices. Some decisions have to be made in order to establish the direction the paper will take.

Look at the brainstorming example in Figure 2-1. Do you see any ideas which could serve as the direction or focus for a paper? One good way to discover the possibilities inherent in any piece of prewriting is to group into categories the ideas and details you've written down. As the student who did the brainstorming in Figure 2-1 reread, he discovered various ideas about the American Dream and modified his original brainstorm.

He also noticed that there were certain ideas which could be grouped together, so he began sorting his brainstorming into categories. He labeled the first item and each of the others which might fit in the same category "A." Then he labeled the next item which didn't fit with the first category "B." He repeated this procedure until all the items were sorted. Those which either didn't appeal to him or which seemed unique were marked "O." (He chose to use letters, but he could just as easily have used numbers or any other method for sorting. The prewriting of some writers looks like abstract painting; some items are circled, others underlined, still others boxed and triangled, some connected by arrows. Precisely how you proceed is not as important as beginning to see the relationships among your ideas.) What he came up with appears in Figure 2–2. Next he physically separated the categories so he could get a clearer picture of what he had to work with (see Figure 2–3).

When he finished, he had ten possible directions for his paper. He labeled the general topics as follows:

A. The Good Life

B. The Role of Career in the Dream

C. The Material Side of the Dream

D. Marriage and the Dream: The Ideal and the Real

E. The Bandwagon and the Dream

F. Flaws in the Dream?

G. The Parents' Role in the Dream

H. Sources of the Dream

FIGURE 2-2

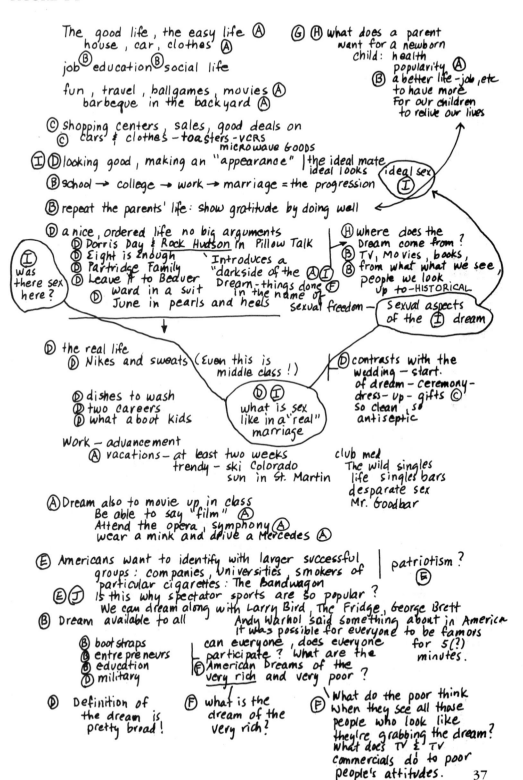

FIGURE 2-3

A	B
good life, easy life house, car, clothes fun, travel, barbecue ballgames, movies the dark side of sexual freedom trendy vacations, Colorado, St. Martin images from TV, movies opera, symphony, popularity wear mink, drive a Mercedes	job, education, college school, work, marriage, repeat parents' life, grateful to work, formed from TV, movies, books, people we look up to like teachers, available to all—bootstraps, opportunity, education
C	**D**
house, car, clothes, sales, shopping centers, good deals on cars, wedding gifts, toasters, micros VCRs	marriage, Doris Day, Rock Hudson Eight is Enough, Partridge Family, Leave It to Beaver, June with pearls & heels, Ward in a suit real life with Nikes and sweat suits—dishes to wash—kids mother, weddings, ceremony, gifts, clean & antiseptic— parents' goals & models—to do better, two careers, sex? nice ordered life no fights
E	**F**
Americans want to identify: successful groups, cigarettes companies, universities, teams: The Bandwagon	How do the very rich and poor fit? Can everyone participate? What do the poor think when they see others grabbing the brass ring? What do TV and commercials do to poor people's attitude? What is the Dream of the very rich? the dark side of the Dream ideal vs. real
G	**H**
when child is born, parents want: popularity, good life health, child to do better, to live on in child	dream formed by parents, TV, movies, books, what we see, people we look up to— teachers, etc.
I	**J**
sex on family TV sitcoms? sex life in marriage sexual aspects of the Dream ideal sex Fridge, George Brett? the dark side of the Dream Club Med, singles bars, Mr. Goodbar, desperate sex	Sports, why are they so much a part of the Dream? Is it so we can dream along with Larry Bird

I. The Sexual Aspects of the Dream

J. Sports and the Dream

Once the writer arranges the items into categories, he should read them again in their new groupings, thinking about each group and the interest and reason he might have for writing about it. Some categories may seem too boring or too obvious. Others may seem too flimsy, too unsubstantial. Still others may be too complex or unwieldy. So from the outset he may want to dismiss some categories as unworkable. Or he may want to do additional free-writing or brainstorming on one or more of the categories, looking for a way to make its ideas less boring or more substantial, less complex or more manageable.

In the example we've been considering, the student becomes most interested in the disparity he perceives between the Dream's ideal of marriage and the actuality he observes. He chose to work with topic "D." From his initial prewriting he thus developed the following more restricted topic, phrased as questions: Can the American Dream be a potential cause of problems in a marriage or even lead to divorce? Does the Dream create unrealistic expectations which can create unhappiness and despair, and end in divorce?

In the begining of the text we mentioned that sometimes writers begin without a topic, whereas others have a topic from the start. No matter where you started, by the time you complete this initial prewriting, you will all be at approximately the same stage. The only difference is that those who began with a topic have taken fewer steps; the rest, however, should be limbered up and ready to go.

Notice that the title of this section is "Narrowing Your Topic." That's what you've been doing since you started—moving from broad, general ideas toward more well-defined, manageable ideas. In the process, you've also generated specific details which will be useful when you begin the first draft. One way to imagine this process is to think of language as a ladder of abstraction.[1]

"The Abstraction Ladder"

When we speak of "topic," we are speaking on a general, abstract level. If, for example, we say that the topic of this text is *writing,* we are abstracting at a high level of generalization. An even higher abstraction would be to say that the topic of the text is *education.* These abstractions would help a librarian decide where to categorize the text in a collection (see Documentation, Chapter 9), but they wouldn't help teachers decide whether this might be appropriate for their classes. To be useful to a potential reader, more concrete labels are necessary. Figure 2–4 illustrates the move down the ladder of abstraction from the more general toward the more specific.

[1]For a complete discussion of the role of abstraction in communication, see S. I. Hayakawa, *Language in Thought and Action,* (New York: Harcourt Brace Jovanovich, 1978).

FIGURE 2-4

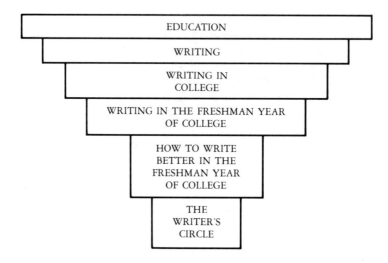

We can talk about our subject more specifically as we move toward more concrete statements. Inexperienced writers sometimes begin writing on a topic which is too high on the ladder of abstraction. The topic is so large that it's impossible to find a point of view or focus for a piece of writing shorter than a small book. These kinds of papers usually end up sounding like encyclopedia entries.

At what stage in Figure 2–5 do you think you'd find your topic for a political science class?

An attempt to write on American governmental policy would produce an encyclopedia or a series of books. American foreign policy in Nicaragua is good for a book or two. The decision to support the contras is worth at least a term paper. Only when you get down to the last two do you approach a topic narrow enough to provide a good focus for a college essay.

Here is a common writing situation you will face: You are given a general topic—a paper on suicide for your sociology class, for example—and are required to narrow it any way you choose. Once again, the way you narrow your topic depends on your knowledge and your interests, but it also depends on your audience and your purpose. (The importance of audience and purpose is discussed in Chapter 3.)

Using Initial Prewriting: Journals and Logs

In any case, one of your tasks is to examine your primary and secondary experience to find a way to engage your readers meaningfully. The first three methods suggested previously—the journal, the reading log, and the media log—are still effective for gathering your ideas, but there is a difference. Now you have a focus for your exploration. Let's say, for example, that you're taking

FIGURE 2-5

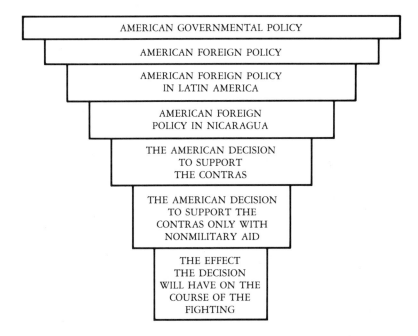

a class which is examining the American Dream. Your journal entries are now focused on developing your own ideas. You might remember some of your own earlier dreams: wanting to own a 10-speed bike, to make the cheerleading squad, to climb Mt. McKinley, to score the winning points. You might then speculate as to how these earlier dreams relate to the larger concept of the Dream. Or you might know a neighbor who poured his family's life savings into a new business in his pursuit of the Dream. These memories might lead to an excellent topic for an essay.

Your reading might also give you direction, so keep a reading log focused on your topic. You might be fortunate, and *Newsweek* might do a cover story on your topic—The American Dream. Even if you aren't so lucky, newspapers, magazines, books, and even ads can offer a variety of ideas. If formal library research is allowed, you could also check the library's card catalog or the *Reader's Guide to Periodical Literature* for reading material on your topic. Remember, though, that if you use any ideas or information from secondary sources, you are obligated to document their use in your paper. So while you are recording responses to your reading, be sure to record the necessary publishing data. (Documentation is discussed in Chapter 9.)

Use your media log in the same way. Check the detailed guide to the radio and television programming for your area. You'll be surprised at the number of programs on both radio and television that deal with ideas and issues related to those you encounter in your college classes.

EXERCISE 2–10

For the rest of the semester we recommend that you keep a writing notebook which combines the journal, the electronic media log, the reading log, and any other exploratory writing—like freewriting—you do. Use the form or technique which seems appropriate for the subject you're working on. This notebook should provide you with material for future essays in this class and others.

Using Initial Prewriting: Freewriting and Brainstorming

Freewriting and brainstorming are also useful techniques once you've found your topic and are looking for a thesis or a way to support it. You can use these techniques as ways to expand upon ideas you've discovered through your journal, your logs, or your lists. After you've found your topic, focus your freewriting and/or your brainstorming on the specific topic you have chosen. The procedures for using these techniques, however, remain the same as described in the previous section.

In effect, then, you may use the same techniques to find a topic, to expand a topic, and even to narrow a topic. Using brainstorming, freewriting, logs, and journals, you may explore a topic and then narrow it to something manageable, supportable, and interesting. Suppose for your first essay in this English class you are asked to write about an instance when your expectations of a person proved wrong once you met that person. Your audience is the class, and your purpose is to communicate what you expected, what you found, and what effect the discovery had on you.

Where should you begin? You have a general topic but nothing specific. So you must work toward an idea by brainstorming, freewriting, or addressing the subject in your logs or journal. Suppose that first you brainstorm, listing every person you can think of who differed from what you expected:

Surprises

S's boyfriend	Mr. Stanley
Dad's boss	Who else ???
First grade teacher	Amy
Dr. L., professor	Wes
Dr. Smith	Georgia
Willa, J's friend	

When you can't think of anymore, stop. (But you may have to force yourself.) Look at the list. It doesn't tell the writer much yet, but it's a good beginning. The writer is closer to finding a topic than she would be if she'd just *thought* about what she could select. The final paper may use none of the subjects on the brainstorming list, for using other prewriting techniques may bring a better subject to mind. To continue the narrowing and selection of a topic, the writer freewrites next, focusing on each of the possibilities already listed.

Surprises-Freewriting

1. S's boyfriend—I first met him a couple years ago. I had heard a lot about him—that he was athletic and smart, from the East. I expected someone brash and conceited, someone I wouldn't like. But I found someone nice, modest, polite, kind. Not too different from what I'd look for or admire in a friend. The effect? I liked him. But what else? Nothing startling.

2. Dad's boss—I'd heard that he was forceful, dynamic, efficient. But nothing like that showed—just seemed ordinary. Don't know very well, anyway. I was puzzled, that I know.

3. First grade teacher—Expected an ogre. Someone who wouldn't let me talk or go to the bathroom or do anything I wanted to. Someone who had the power to punish me, get me in trouble. I wanted her to like me from the start. She was kind and funny, though, and did like me. I *did* get into trouble, though, once or twice unfairly. Maybe her kindness, and the way her opinion mattered to me, has affected the way my other school years went.

4. Dr. L., professor—Maybe I thought of him because of first grade—same sort of thing. I'd heard that he was difficult, made students squirm, liked to catch them wrong. Screwed up my first exam. But then my next assignment I did well on—his opinion of me changed, too. He was demanding, I found, and did sort of enjoy seeing students squirm when they were not prepared, but he liked students better when they knew the answers or could at least make good tries.

5. Willa, J's friend—I expected glamour, sophistication, efficiency. I expected not to like her. Well, I don't like her. But not for any of those reasons. She's not glamourous. I don't know about sophistication. Efficient, yes. But I don't like her because of other stuff—too friendly but I don't think she is or could be my friend. Maybe my premonition was right—no reason to like her, even if she wasn't what I expected.

6. Mr. Stanley—Forget it. He's a neighbor and nice, but I don't want to write about him.

7. Amy—We got to know each other through notes at
work. Didn't see her for a long time. Physically she's
not what I expected, and her background is different,
too. But that doesn't seem to mattter.

8. Wes and Georgia—Forget it.

9. Dr. Smith—No.

The freewriting has helped the writer to isolate some support for each topic.
She's briefly stated the reasons for choosing one topic over another. Notice,
though, that she's addressed the three components—what she expected, what
she found, and the effect of the discovery—to varying degrees. At times she
dwells on expectations, as with the first grade teacher, and at other times she
dwells on the effects, as with Willa, J's friend. At this point the writer might be
tempted just to select any one of the people named, but she's not quite ready
to do so. Some of those people would be better for the assignment than others, so to figure that out, she writes in her journal about the possibilities.

Surprises—Topics for Essay

Need to figure out what to do this paper on. I
brainstormed and did some freewriting on what I came
up with. But I don't know.
I don't think I can write about Wes or
Georgia. Just not enough to say. And Amy I like, but
there's just not enough there either. Mr. Stanley,
too. He's nice but *too* boring to write about. Dad's
boss I could do—he interests me because he's so
different, but I don't really know him well and would
have to base my opinion on only the two or three times
I met him.
That leaves first grade, S's boyfriend, and
Dr. L. and W.—Willa. I don't know.
Not S.'s boyfriend. Nothing startling enough.
I mean, I was wrong and so what. I still like her and
him and they like me and he wasn't obnoxious—So what?
No good.
Maybe Willa. She wasn't what I expected at
all—quite opposite. Maybe I don't like her because I
can't—don't want to—believe she's like she is. I mean,
I couldn't stand her before we met, probably because
of J. So the feelings caused by the expectation won't
be changed by the reality.
Dr. L. I don't know. I *sort* of expected all
along that I'd like him. And what I had expected was

basically right except that he wasn't mean. Just
demanding. I don't know that I can recreate the terror
I felt when I signed up for his class.
      OK. So I've decided against most everything
except Mrs. B. in first grade and Willa. I'm leaning
toward Willa. I can recall *so well* what I thought
she'd be and I can certainly tell what she is. The
interesting part is that I still don't like her. That
might make my paper different—everyone else I've
considered I didn't like before we met and then I
liked them. I don't quite know about the effect,
though. I'll have to think hard about that as I'm
doing the first draft. What I might be able to do is
something like saying I dislike her because I want to
for reasons that have nothing to do with what I
expected or what I found. I don't know.

The journal entry led the writer to a decision; it helped the writer to select, to narrow her topic. By considering each possibility for her paper *as* a topic, by discussing in her journal how she felt about writing on each possibility, she was able to narrow her topic—a person who differed from what she expected—to a specific topic, a subject: how Willa differed from the writer's expectations and what effect this difference had on the writer.

The writer chose Willa because of the interest she had in her own feelings toward her. She also found an approach, an angle to be used: Meeting Willa and discovering her to be nothing like the writer imagined, the writer still disliked her. The writer has stumbled upon a question, an inconsistency that could be the focus of the paper. This inconsistency will probably center on the way the feelings created by the expectations remain or grow even stronger once they are proved false.

It has probably become obvious to you by this time that very few writers use all the techniques for getting started that we give you in this text. If they did, they would probably never start writing. We are showing you a variety of methods because accomplished writers ultimately develop personal methods of approaching each piece of writing. Since writing is a craft, however, apprentices need to experiment with different techniques in order to find out which works best for them. Just as apprentice artists experiment with various brush techniques before settling on one, so apprentice writers need to experiment with the techniques of their craft to develop a method most suitable to them.

The prewriting techniques presented here are not necessarily exclusive, however. One writer might combine the journal with freewriting; another might use freewriting and brainstorming together. We would like you to discover both what works best for you to make you feel more comfortable about writing and also what works best for you to produce more successful writing. Before you can accomplish these goals, you *must* experiment with the techniques.

EXERCISE 2–11

Return to the paper in which you examined the way that you go about writing (Exercise 1–3). What parts of your process are working; what parts need to be modified? Write a brief, informal paper (to be discussed in class) in which you explain how you could alter your writing process to make it work better. Discuss the usefulness of the prewriting techniques presented so far. Which ones have been most helpful? If a technique does not become part of your writing behavior through extensive practice, then it will be useless to you. We present more ideas about prewriting later in the text, but for now experiment and become comfortable with those offered up to this point.

The Nature of the Thesis

You might now be developing questions about a term which student writers have been hearing since the beginning of their instruction in writing essays: the thesis. What exactly is a thesis? What's the difference between a topic and a thesis? How do you recognize one? How do you come up with one? How do you move from a reading log on the American Dream to a thesis?

Before we can go any further we need to discuss more completely what we mean when we say "thesis." First, there is no universal definition, nor does a thesis always take the same shape. A thesis in an essay about your childhood home differs from one in a paper arguing that the American two-party political system is antiquated. Indeed, to confuse matters even further, you've probably noticed that many of the essays you've read contain no direct statement of thesis at all. Therefore, there are two terms which must be defined: *thesis* and *thesis statement*. Briefly, a thesis is your own idea, vision, view, opinion, belief, focus, stance—all these words and others are often introduced in discussions of the thesis—on a particular topic. A working definition of *thesis* might then be the following: *A thesis is the idea behind your paper which limits and controls its shape and content.* In other words, a thesis is the idea you have in your mind about what you want to say and what you hope to accomplish by transferring this thought to paper. (The precise nature of the thesis changes as considerations of audience and purpose change. Ideally you should read this section on thesis simultaneously with those on audience and purpose. But since you can't, read the next chapter as soon as possible.)

Many students have been taught that writers always start with a thesis when they begin an essay, that coming up with a thesis is the first step in prewriting. This is sometimes the case. When our colleague began the letter to the San Francisco rental car agency (p. 13), for example, he already had his thesis in mind. He felt that the agent had made a mistake in representing the company's insurance policy; therefore he felt that he deserved a refund. His task in writing was to document his point as carefully and persuasively as possible. This kind of writing resembles deductive thinking or reasoning. He began with a point, then collected and arranged his material to prove or support it. When you begin with a definite thesis in mind, you use the journal, the logs, the lists, and the free association techniques to generate ideas and information to help you develop or prove your point.

Generally, however, you don't have a clear thesis in mind when you begin. You know that you want to (or have been told that you have to) write a paper about the American Dream, suicide, or education, but you're not sure what the thesis should be. For these writing occasions, you can use brainstorming and freewriting to generate information and ideas from which you eventually derive a thesis. This is Sherlock Holmes' method. He examines all the clues and evidence, then he arrives at a conclusion. This way of thinking and reasoning is called inductive (although Holmes calls it "deduction").

Often writers choose not to make a direct statement of thesis within a paper. Instead they present their topic and support in a way that leads readers to arrive at the idea behind their writing. This is called an *implied thesis*. A paper written in this way demands careful attention from both writer and reader. The writer must select and arrange ideas and details carefully so the reader does arrive at the author's thesis. The reader must follow the logic carefully, noting the details of development and the arrangement so each sign from the author is considered in the proper context. Writing such a paper takes considerable skill.

Sometimes, however, writers make direct statements of the thesis; we call such a direct statement a *thesis statement*. In this case, the writer translates the controlling idea into a clearly written statement which appears directly in the paper. Some teachers routinely require a thesis statement, and some kinds of writing—essay exams or papers designed to persuade or argue, for example—almost demand a thesis statement. You should be comfortable enough with both ways of presenting a thesis so that you can use whichever is most appropriate to the piece you are writing. But we strongly recommend that you always keep a written thesis statement available. You can refer to it throughout your writing as a check to make sure you're staying on the topic and as a prompt for new ideas.

Some Sample Thesis Ideas:

1. For a lab report: Following the steps described in this report will lead to the discovery that the compound being analyzed is simple table salt (NaCl)

2. For an article on the charms of your neighborhood: Although Hyde Park has problems similar to other urban areas, the charm of its restored Victorian houses, its wide tree-lined boulevards, and its variety of life styles make this neighborhood one of the most liveable in the city.

3. For a paper on the American Dream in a class on women in society: For the American housewife, the dream of labor-saving appliances has turned into a nightmare of increased work and shattered expectations.

4. For a paper on suicide in a media class: Television programs on teenage suicide may contribute to an increased suicide rate.

5. For a business class on corporate structure: The separation of a textbook publishing house into school, junior college, and university divisions is inefficient and directly results in a loss of profit.

In all the examples above, the thesis statement is simply a way of controlling your thinking, and ultimately your writing, about a particular topic. You generally arrive at this thesis through a great deal of prewriting, thinking, reading, and through observing the world around you. Remember that at the beginning stages in your writing the thesis is not etched in stone. As you continue to generate ideas, to read, to reflect, and finally to write, you should remain open to the possibility that your original idea can change considerably as you go.

EXERCISE 2–12

Reread the entries in your journal, your reading log, and your media log. Find five ideas which you think might be worth expanding. Write five controlling ideas which could serve as focuses for papers. Bring these sentences to class and be prepared to discuss (1) why they make good ideas for essays, and (2) what you would have to do to explore them further.

EXERCISE 2–13

During the group discussion of your five controlling ideas, take notes on the responses your classmates give to your suggested topics. You'll need to reread these notes later while you're writing. Are your classmates interested in your ideas? Listen to their suggestions for refining them and listen to their response to your proposed plans for development. Choose two of your controlling ideas; do a brainstorm on one and a freewrite on the other. You'll need to turn everything in, so don't throw anything away. (Save all five. You'll need them for several exercises in the next chapter.)

EXERCISE 2–14

Review the theses you developed in Exercise 2–12. Discuss which of them would make good ideas for papers. Write a paragraph for each thesis focusing on what you would have to do with each in order to write a good essay.

This section on generating ideas has covered a lot of ground. We've presented several methods through which you can explore your interests and respond to what you read, see, think, and hear. Having something to say is essential in writing, and these methods help you discover what you have to say.

They can help in several ways as you write in this class and others. First, you may use one or more of these invention techniques when you are given an open assignment, an assignment in which you must come up with the topic for your paper yourself. You may look back through the journal or the logs you have kept for an idea to work with. Or you may begin a new, fresh bout of brainstorming or freewriting to help you discover a topic.

But these techniques can also help when you've been assigned a topic. The results of freewriting and brainstorming sessions may help you to construct a thesis. Keeping a journal or log on the topic also helps, especially if the assignment is one made far in advance. If, for instance, your psychology professor tells you in January that a long paper on some stage of early childhood development is due the end of April, you can select one or two stages that may be of interest and begin to keep a log on them. You can brainstorm or freewrite on those stages. You can draw on what you recall about your own childhood, what you observe in your own children, your nieces and nephews, or the child behind you in the bank line who wipes his chocolate-covered hands on you or wants to show you how far he can spit. You can record these observations, as well as reflections on TV programs, films, and feature articles, in a log or journal that can supplement any required research.

So these methods can help initially by providing ways in which you can decide upon a topic. But they can also help after you've selected a topic and are in the process of drafting your paper. If you get stuck, if you don't know where to go next, brainstorming or freewriting on the problem section of the paper may help you to get moving again. Continuing your journal or log entries as you work on the draft keeps the topic fresh in your mind and may supply you with good examples to illustrate your points. Glancing back through the journal serves the same purposes and may also remind you of a point or idea that you had forgotten.

Use these methods anywhere in your writing process. Use them to come up with an idea, to sustain it, or to test a new one. Later in the book, we'll discuss some additional methods of generating ideas, methods that build upon these early ones. So for now, become comfortable with these; discover what works for you in various situations. Continue to use these methods as you add to your writing process the strategies discussed in the next section, a section that presents ways to continue the shaping process.

CHAPTER THREE

Patterned Strategies for Generating Ideas

Art is the imposing of a pattern on experience, and our esthetic enjoyment in recognition of the pattern.—Alfred North Whitehead

So far, most of the prewriting techniques we have presented have encouraged you to work with the spontaneous part of your mind that calls up knowledge, memories, and ideas from your unconscious to your conscious, where you can then begin to process them. These kinds of prewriting rely on the power of the creative chaos in your brain to supply you with material for your writing. The kinds of prewriting you encounter in this chapter, while still using the spontaneous nature of thinking, allow you to draw on that part of your mind which yearns for a more systematic and organized approach to an intellectual challenge. These techniques allow you to generate ideas while helping you to see patterns of organization at the same time.

The Journalist's Questions

If you've ever taken a journalism class, you're probably familiar with the following set of questions, which reporters use as a checklist for gathering data: WHO? WHAT? WHERE? WHEN? WHY? (HOW? is sometimes used as well.) Reporters use these questions to ensure that they've gathered the essential facts for a news story. They then use the same questions to organize their lead paragraphs.

Read the following paragraph from *The New York Times* (June 6, 1986):

> WASHINGTON, June 5—The United States announced today that it was banning the sale to Syria of eight chemicals that might be used to help Iran develop mustard gas and nerve gases for use in its war against Iraq.

Notice how the paragraph answers the questions:

Who?	The United States
	Syria
	Iran
	Iraq
What?	ban on sale of chemicals
Where?	Syria
	in Washington (where decision was announced)
When?	today
Why?	chemicals might be used to develop mustard gas and nerve gases for Iran's war against Iraq

These questions are powerful because they elicit the same basic information we need to fill in the grammatical structures which make up our language. In the following example, the questions are used to generate a sentence:

Who?	Fred
What?	Roped (We already have enough information for a grammatical sentence; the rest of the information is for our audience's enlightenment and interest.)
Where?	At the rodeo
When?	Friday
Why?	For fun
How?	Not very well

Here's a possible sentence from this information: "Fred had fun roping at the rodeo on Friday, but he didn't do very well." Of course, you could add more information by asking further questions. WHO went with him? WHO won the rodeo? WHAT horse did he ride? WHAT other events did he enter? WHERE was the rodeo? WHEN was it on Friday? WHY didn't he do well? If you included all this information, you could end up with an overly complicated sentence. However, through the process of deciding what you want to say to your audience, you select only the information that suits your purposes. You might end up with the following sentence: "Fred rode Augie, his new pinto, at the rodeo in Payson last Friday night, but he lost to Jack Fletcher on the last ride of the night when Augie lost her balance and fell."

The questions give you new perspectives which change the shape of the sentence. We've *added* words to convey new information; we've *deleted* some words; we've *substituted* some specific words for some vague ones; we've *rearranged* the information in the sentence; and we've *combined* some of our information. In other words, by generating new ideas, we change not only the content but also the final form. The same is true for both sentences and essays. *Revising begins in prewriting because each new idea, each modified idea, changes the possibilities for the shape and direction of the final product.*

Asking this set of questions helps you generate information in the very first stages of prewriting and helps you refine your thinking, thus influencing both development and eventual structure at later stages in the process.

The following list of questions compiled by a student preparing an essay on the American Dream shows how simple questions can lead a writer to consider a variety of perspectives. Notice that the student was not a slave to the questions; rather, she used them as springboards for generating ideas her own way.

1. What is the American Dream?
2. Who does the American Dream apply to?
3. How does the American Dream affect poor Americans?
4. Where does the American Dream take our minds?
5. Does the American Dream make us more determined?
6. Why doesn't everyone share the Dream?
7. Where does the Dream lead us?
8. When do we stop dreaming?
9. When did the American Dream begin to develop?
10. When have major changes taken place in the nature of the Dream?
11. How do parents affect young people's Dreams?
12. How do we make our Dreams come true when all odds are against us?
13. What is the purpose of the Dream?
14. How will the Dream affect me if not attained?
15. Where do most of us hear about the Dream for the first time?
16. When do most of us hear about the Dream for the first time?
17. Why do people give up?
18. Why is the Dream so hard to achieve?
19. When does the Dream become a nightmare?
20. Why do we need an American Dream?

The student hasn't begun to answer the questions yet; indeed she won't necessarily answer all of the questions. First she reexamines her list to see which directions she wants to explore. Then she answers only those questions she considers pertinent. One of her first steps might be to sort her list into related questions, as we ask you to do in the next exercise.

EXERCISE 3–1

Divide the student's twenty questions into groups which might form the basis for a cohesive essay. (For example, the answers to questions 1, 9, 10, 11, 13, 15, 16, and 20 could lead the student to discuss how she, or someone else, developed a version of the American Dream.) At the top of each of your group-ings, write the principle you used to establish your category.

You can also use these questions to discover the right audience for a partic-ular piece. (For some students, this works even better than the audience checklist on p. 90.) The following illustrates how the questions can be used to focus an essay on the general topic, "Something in my neighborhood which irritates me: trash."

Who needs to read the essay? My neighbors. The people who walk by on the way home from Burger King and Texas Tom's. The com-muters who use our street. The city inspectors.

Where can I find a forum to reach them all? Newspaper. Neighborhood newspaper. Neighborhood newsletter. Letter to inspectors. An-nouncement on walls of restaurants. Can't reach everyone with one forum!

Who's my most important audience? My neighbors. Somebody in city gov-ernment?

Where is the best forum? Neighborhood newsletter—it goes to every house; might get some walkers as well. City newspaper—start a campaign.

What do I need to include? A description of the types of trash: paper, kitchen garbage, old cars, household items, trashy houses. A com-parison with other cleaner neighborhoods. Mention the causes?

What should I exclude? Old cars, trashy houses, anything which might make my neighbors mad and ruin any possible communication.

Why? My neighbors can't afford to fix their houses and they love their cars.

When? Next issue comes out in a month.

How can I convince them to listen to me? What will impress them? Aes-thetics. Property values, community/neighborhood spirit. Law. Health. Friendliness.

What might keep us from communicating? Different values. Different ed-ucational levels—different vocabulary. Use of esthetic and legal ar-guments.

We could take this further, but from what we have done already you should see that our relationship with our audience is becoming clearer. At the same time the specific purpose and the precise shape of the paper is beginning to emerge.

EXERCISE 3–2

Use the journalist's questions to examine the potential audience for a paper you're currently writing. If you aren't working on one, choose one of the top-ics from Exercise 3–11 on page 79.

Clustering

In her book *Writing the Natural Way,* Gabriele Rico describes clustering as "a nonlinear brainstorming process akin to free association but which creates a visual design or map to help the writer conceptualize, abstract, and organize." Clustering uses the mind's ability to group pieces of information and ideas into distinct categories. The author of the cluster in Figure 3–1 tries to reconcile a paradox: How can discipline and freedom be related?

FIGURE 3-1

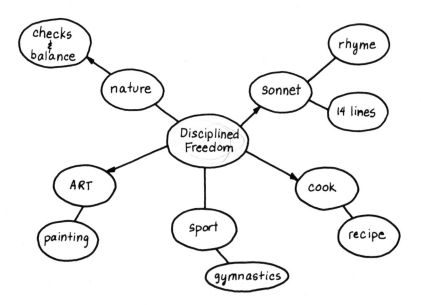

The cluster led to the following first draft.

I struggle with "disciplined freedom" because I know that it is the only real way to be free because form gives meaning to content; but I have an egotistical, anarchic streak in me that wants to have no order placed on me. Yet, when I read a sonnet, or hear a symphony, or visit a garden, I know that it is the discipline or form which reveals the beauty that anarchy can only obliquely hint at. Also, I know that the only time I'm productive is when I have some order imposed on my day. When my day is "free," I never seem to find time to make the bed, and, somehow, then, at the end of the day, I feel as if the day were lost. However, I love the idea of "free" days even if I waste them—so I struggle with the concept of "disciplined freedom."

—GABRIELE RICO

A cluster, as we're using the term, begins with a central idea represented by a key word or phrase. Then it combines brainstorming and the ladder of abstraction to generate ideas. Clustering is similar to brainstorming in that to do it you must tap your mind's ability to produce ideas in association with one another. It relies on your ability to perceive levels of abstraction and to arrange items in these levels into groups or categories. Like the writing that follows it, the cluster in Figure 3–1 illustrates that the primary role of clustering is to explore a subject. There are many stages between the two pieces of prewriting presented above and a final draft.

Let's take several subjects from their beginning stages to show different ways that clustering works.

Lately there has been a good deal of controversy on the status of athletics on college campuses. Let's say that you've been assigned this general topic by the professor in one of your classes on coaching. You begin to cluster by writing your general topic in the middle of a blank sheet of paper, as in Figure 3–2.

FIGURE 3-2

One way to continue is to begin to divide your larger topic into smaller units—in other words, move down the ladder of abstraction (Figure 3–3).

FIGURE 3-3

The writer doing this clustering is starting to see that the issue of collegiate athletics can take several possible directions. At this stage, however, he has a choice to make. He can continue to separate categories from the main idea—adding "improves public's image and support of higher education," for example—or he could proceed by taking his first branches—pods?—further down the ladder of abstraction toward more concrete specifics. He can always come back and add ideas to the main pod. If he were to choose the latter option, his next step might resemble Figure 3–4.

FIGURE 3-4

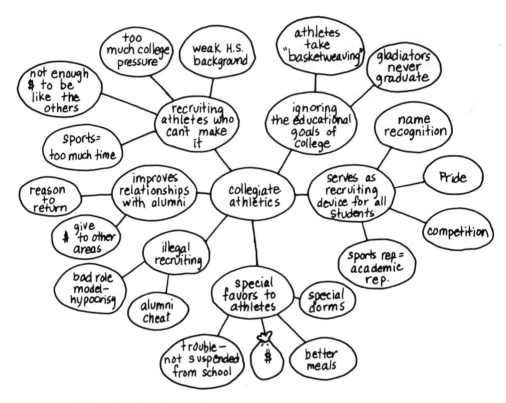

The writer should now begin to see that there is a complex topic beginning to take shape. Now's the time to begin to ask some of those questions we discussed earlier (pp. 50–53): What's the writing situation? Who's the audience? What's the purpose? Since this is a class paper, this writer needs some answers. What kind of paper does the professor expect? A paper loaded with secondary sources? One in which the writer did significant personal research with interviews and surveys? An examination of his personal philosophy? The creation of a philosophy for a hypothetical junior college? Perhaps even something like a White Paper (a paper stating an institutional position on an issue) which examines the status of intercollegiate athletics at your campus? The answers to these questions help determine both the shape the paper takes and how long it has to be. Some editors and teachers believe a paper has to be long enough to get the job done—just like a dog's legs. But, how big the job is depends on the writing situation, the audience, and the writer's purposes. If you are writing for a teacher, you should determine class expectations and choose your subject and its focus carefully.

In the collegiate-athletics example, for instance, our hypothetical writer has carved out a subject broad enough to warrant term-paper status. If he kept the topic as broad as it now is and wrote a one-week, five-page paper, he would probably end up with a paper full of generalities and would be disappointed in the results.

In any case, the writer has more work to do. He's still operating at a relatively abstract level; he needs to pinpoint specifics to give his paper substance and a more controlled direction. If he's writing that term paper on the status of collegiate athletics, he must find out what details he already knows about his topic. He could cluster more, as in Figure 3–5 (see page 58).

During this process the writer might even discover a category not considered during the initial steps: athletes, for example, who have pulled themselves up from poverty because of their athletic skills and who have either earned degrees and found a profession, or those few who have gone on to make their fortunes in pro ball. After going this far with clustering, the writer should have a good idea what direction he wants the paper to follow. Notice also that the paper's future organization is taking tentative shape. His next step is to develop a tentative thesis statement and to begin the first draft.

The approach we just illustrated is not the only one the writer could have taken. Let's go back to the initial cluster (Figure 3–3). Perhaps after reviewing this initial cluster—or the next one in the process (Figure 3–4)—the writer immediately sees a more focused subject that interests him more than the others. Perhaps articles on illegal recruiting have been abundant lately, and he wants to take advantage of this timeliness. In that case, he would begin to cluster only the one category, as in Figure 3–6 (see page 60).

Notice that this is the most detailed cluster so far. The writer produced only two subgroups under this topic in the original cluster; he found more this time, at least in part because he had limited his scope and focused his attention on one small segment. Notice also that he hasn't yet begun to look for concrete examples to support the theme. You can also see that a fairly specific tone and point of view is beginning to emerge. You should note that the author still has several possible directions to explore:

1. A analysis of the problem.
2. A paper on punishment for violations.
3. The detailed story of one violation.
4. The causes of the problem.
5. Solutions to the problem.
6. A comparison of ideals with reality.
7. A paper saying it's not the problem it's made out to be.
8. A suggestion to reorganize the NCAA.
9. An argument for greater control of collegiate athletics.
10. A paper on the effect of TV on the problem.

FIGURE 3-5

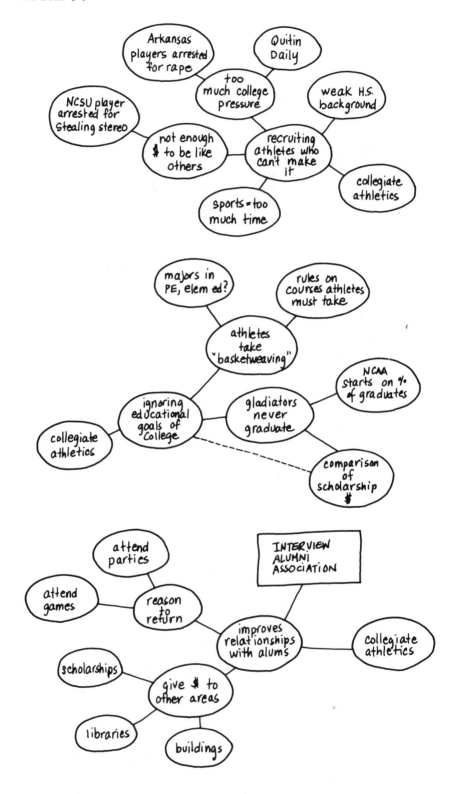

FIGURE 3-5 (continued)

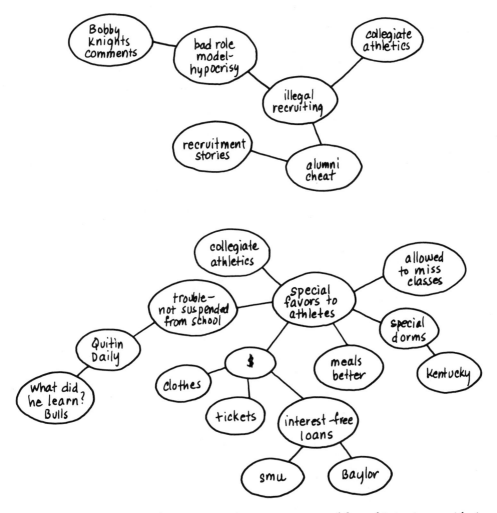

Of course, the author must continue to narrow and focus his topic, considering the role his audience, purpose, and forum play in developing a thesis and support.

Many students prefer clustering to other forms of prewriting; others make different choices. You'll never know which you prefer unless you experiment and practice. For that reason, here is a series of exercises to help you try clustering on for size.

EXERCISE 3-3

Copy the cluster design in Figure 3-7 (page 61) with the center circle filled in. You fill in the rest. There is no single way to complete this exercise as long as you keep your mind focused on the relationship between the phrase in the middle and what you're writing in the subcategories. If your ideas extend be-

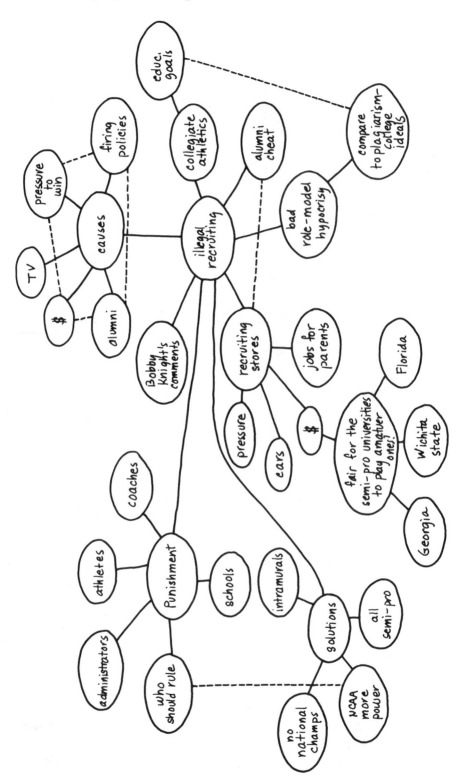

FIGURE 3-6

FIGURE 3-7

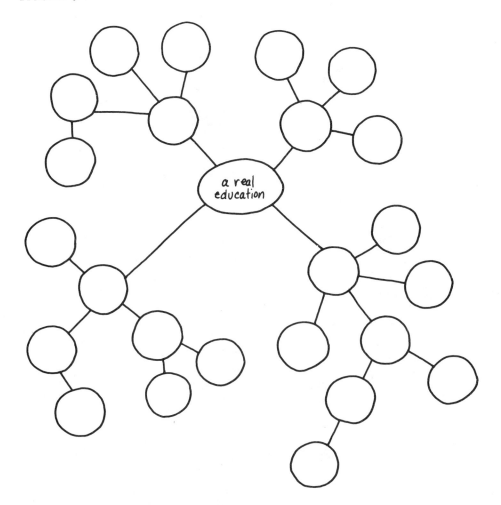

yond the structures we've supplied, add new circles. Bring your cluster to class. Discuss with your classmates the thought process which occurred as you filled in the blanks. The clusters you create for yourself will probably *never* be as symmetrical as the models we've provided. Use ours for practice, as a way of getting used to the feel of clustering.

EXERCISE 3–4

Now create your own mental shapes using the following words as your centers. Once again, be prepared to explain to your classmates how your thinking proceeded for each.

1. femininity
2. maturity
3. a day that mattered
4. best friends
5. parenthood

FIGURE 3-8

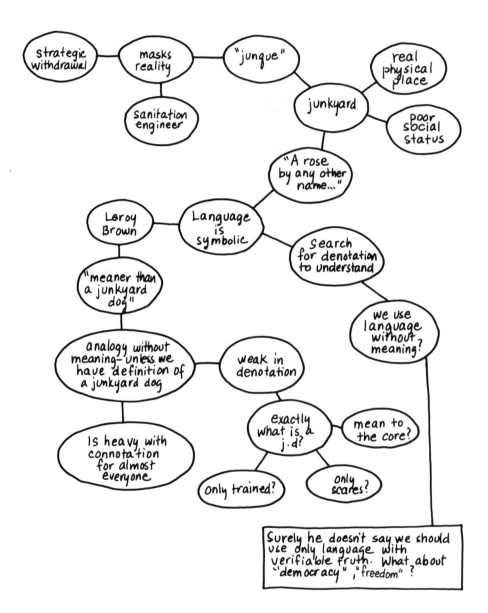

EXERCISE 3–5

> Review your clusters. Pick the two you find most interesting and write brief paragraphs explaining what kind of essay could be written based on each one. Include the writing situation, your audience, your purpose, and your tentative thesis.
>
> For some students, clustering also serves as an effective device for understanding reading assignments in classes across the disciplines. Clustering as prewriting works from a topic or central idea out toward *creating* supporting ideas; clustering as a study technique works from a central idea or topic out toward *identifying* and *organizing* supporting ideas. Clustering as prewriting is designed to find or clarify focus; clustering as reviewing is designed to reinforce a reader's perception of a written text.
>
> The clusters, shown in Figures 3–8 and 3–9 on George Gurley's article about the junkyard dog (pp. 15–16) illustrate two different readings of the article—both leading to similar conclusions.
>
> In both cases the readers now have a review of the article. Each writer has an idea of the author's main point and a visual schema of the supporting points. The clusterings serve much the same purpose as an outline, a map of a piece of writing. A series of clusters done over the course of a semester also serves as a convenient study guide.

EXERCISE 3–6

> Cluster the article "Lessons on Bringing Up Baby" on page 00. In your central circle, place either the general topic or what you think the thesis is. Group the main and subpoints around the center. If you begin with the general topic, place your interpretation of the article's thesis in the lower right-hand corner of your paper in a separate circle. Bring your clusters to class for comparison with those of your classmates.

The Power of Perspective

Shifting for Focus

As you already know, writing is much more complicated than just getting an idea, writing about it, and then polishing your prose. Each of the steps we've discussed involves many kinds of thinking and acting. The steps also overlap considerably. Many times, the way you think about a topic has much to do with how you finally decide to arrange your thoughts in the paper. Often, an inexperienced writer turns first thoughts into final draft without the necessary steps between. Even writers centuries ago were aware of this problem. Cicero, an ancient Roman writer, said that a writer needs to learn to see a subject from all possible sides before the actual writing begins. Let's consider preparing to

FIGURE 3-9

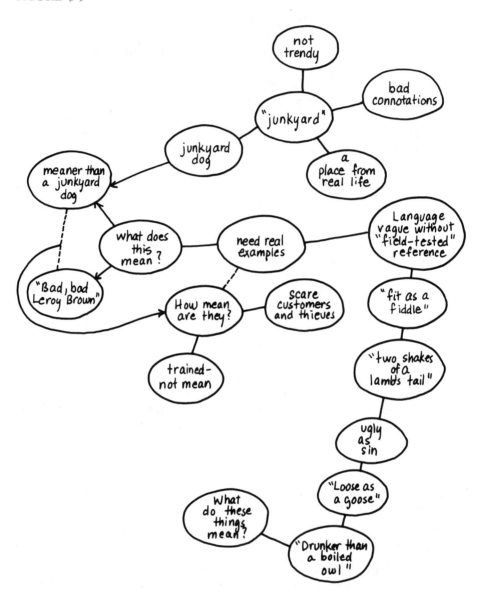

write an essay about a piece of sculpture as an example. As you walk around the sculpture, your perception of it changes. As you change your point of view, the focus of what you see changes as well.

EXERCISE 3–6

Bring to class a small piece of sculpture or three-dimensional art. Choose one to place in the center of the room. If possible, arrange your desks in a circle so that each class member gets a different view of the object. Do a freewrite description of and response to what you see. Describe in specific physical detail what you see, tell how you feel about it, what it reminds you of, how it's different from similar things you've seen. After you finish, read the responses aloud. Discuss how the responses from the various parts of the room differ. Discuss their similarities.

Physically shifting your point of view is only one kind of changing focus. You can also change your intellectual focus. Let's return to the example of the piece of sculpture. If you were to write a formal essay about the sculpture, you could write about much more than its physical appearance. You could write about how well it corresponds or fails to correspond to the physical reality that you know. If it fails to correspond, you could write about why the artist created this different view of reality. Was the artist's sense of beauty or view of the nature of art different from yours? Was the artist making a point about the nature of reality by using distortion? You could write about the sculpture's physical composition and how this composition is realized through a particular texture or shape. You could write about how the materials the artist chose produce a specific aesthetic effect. You could write about how the sculpture is similar to or different from other sculptures created during the same period. You could write about how this particular sculpture fits into the artist's lifelong artistic development or about how it fits into a particular period of creative work.

What you know about your subject and the way that you think about it shape the content of your essay. In the same way, the nature and direction of your thinking also shape the organization and arrangement of the details in your paper. For example, if you are interested in why the artist chose to present what you think is a distorted view of reality, then you become involved in searching for the reasons behind the differences you observe. You also have to define for your audience precisely what your view of reality is and how this view contrasts with the one represented by the sculpture. If you are interested in the sculpture's place in the history of art, then your paper must in some way consider the movements and trends in art that preceded, coincided with, and followed the sculpture's creation.

These are only some of the possibilities inherent in this example, but by now you see that your developing subject, thesis, purpose, and audience are actually shaping the way you think and the kind of material that will appear in your paper. How easily these different possibilities come to you is determined largely by how well you know your subject. If you don't know very much about art, you might now be thinking that you never could have come up with so many ideas about a piece of sculpture. On the other hand, if you know quite a bit about art, you might have seen many more possibilities than the ones that we have given you. The approaches to generating ideas and information that we have presented thus far will not help you create ideas on a subject about which you know nothing; they will, however, help you find out and shape what you do know. They are designed to make the most of the knowledge that you already have—to open up your mind to new ways of seeing things.

Patterned Thinking

The approaches we are presenting in this part of the text are connected more directly with patterned thinking than were those presented previously. Earlier we showed you how to tap the spontaneous part of your thinking. This section focuses on how to use patterns of thought which are inherent to all thinking Western minds. In general, when we think, certain patterns recur constantly: *narration, description, exemplification, cause and effect, comparison and contrast, classification and division, and definition.* From the discussion on how we could write about the sculpture, you can see that these patterns of thought rarely occur in isolation, separate from one another. More frequently, they occur mixed together—and not always in a neat, tidy way. Examine, for example, these two lines:

For example, if you are interested in why the artist chose to present what you think is a distorted view of reality, then you become involved in searching for the reasons behind the differences you observe. You also have to define for your audience precisely what your view of reality is and how this view contrasts with the one represented by the sculpture.

Your theme, if you were to follow the thinking in these two lines, would involve cause and effect, definition, comparison and contrast, and—since you would be writing about a physical object not in your audience's sight—description. In turn, the paper you write would have paragraphs comprised of these same kinds of thinking.

This correspondence between thinking and writing allows writing teachers to talk about narrative paragraphs, cause and effect paragraphs, descriptive paragraphs, etc. Paragraphs can be broken down this way because writing is codified thinking. *One warning,* however: Very often you find more than one kind of thinking in any one paragraph, in much the same way that you find more than one kind of thinking in any given essay.

In the following pages we present a brief review of each of the patterns of thought, patterns you've been developing since childhood. Then we show you how you can use these patterns in your prewriting and right after your rough draft.

Narration

The kind of thinking that you are probably most familiar with is sequential thinking associated with narration. Narration, of course, forms the basis of plot in fiction, but you also use it in telling someone a story about something that happened to you. In both these cases, narration tells what happened, when it happened, who did it, where it was done, and sometimes why it happened.

Telling a friend about what happened at the ballgame last Saturday night is a simple form of narration.

There are, however, other kinds of writing which use the same kind of sequential thinking that underlies the telling of a story. Written history also tells who, what, when, where, and why. Events are recorded sequentially. When you write instructions for putting something together or when you describe a process such as photosynthesis, you are also concerned with events—except now you call them steps and generally you are no longer concerned with who.

Events form the structure of all the different kinds of writing described above, but our main focus is not always on events. Perhaps in the story you want to tell, the location of the events plays a central role. For example, you're telling a story about a scary Halloween night; part of the reason the events were so scary is that you were alone in a crumbling Victorian mansion. You would want to include the details of the setting to add to your story's effect (description). Even your narration of last Saturday night's ballgame might call for another kind of thinking. Perhaps you might want to use the events at the game to show that this year's team is superior to the one you played on last year (comparison). A historian is not only concerned about getting the events of history in the correct order; she might also be concerned about why certain events happened and their ramifications (cause and effect). In other words, no matter why we are writing, we use different kinds of thinking to make the strongest possible case for what we say.

In the following paragraph, the author uses narrative thinking to show that the stock market remains a consistently sound investment.

But however noble the contribution of the securities industry may be to the national economy, what you are probably wondering is what contribution it is likely to make to your personal economy. And here the evidence is more reassuring than one might suspect from a casual inspection of the financial bloodshed occasioned by the market's brutal zigzagging of the last decade. For one thing, the market is now a better-regulated and safer place for the small investor. For another, it has still been a place where, in any reasonable long-range perspective, the average investor could count on seeing the money he had saved make money for him. There have been various statistical studies that tried to put a number on this; perhaps the most famous was conducted by the Graduate School of Business at the University of Chicago under the sponsorship of the nation's largest brokerage firm, Merrill, Lynch, Pierce, Fenner & Smith. The school's Center for Research in Security Prices began with January 1926—before the Great Crash of 1929—and concluded that an investor over the next forty years, picking stocks at random without guidance or research, would have averaged a return on his investment euqal to 9.3 percent a year compounded annually. A later extension of the study over the next five years, which included the 1969–70 slump, reduced that figure only a fraction, to 9 percent, and found that, taking the decade of the 1960s as a separate entity, an investor who was around from start to finish would have averaged an 11 percent return, including dividends and growth of capital. Even when the university updated its figures through the end of 1974, when the market was wallowing in the worst bear market of the generation, it found the average return from 1926 to that low point was still 8.5 percent—and projected a sharply higher average return for the rest of this century. In short, by whatever long-term test we apply, the stock market has been a place where even average results have been impressive. Professional investors, such as mutual funds, naturally aim to beat those averages, and so— with patience, intelligence and the information in this book—should you.

[Louis Rukeyser, *How to Make Money in Wall Street* (Garden City, N.Y.: Doubleday, 1976), pp. 5–6.]

Description

Generally, when we think of description we think of sensory images—how something looks, tastes, feels, smells, and sounds. We have read description all our lives—in the fairy tales our parents read to us, in the novels and short stories we read, in travel magazines, in advertisements. But description, like the other kinds of thinking, rarely appears in isolation. Description is usually used for a purpose related to some other kind of thinking. Want to persuade your roommate or your parents to spend this Spring Break on a beach in Texas? Then describe the slowly breaking surf, white sand dunes, and tanned sunbathers to win them over. Depending on exactly how you used this description, you could be using classification and division, exemplification, or even definition.

Certain kinds of description, however, are not so clearly focused on the physical. A professor might ask you to describe the characteristics of the American cowboy film in the 1970s. In your answer, you might cite the types of characterizations used, attitudes toward violence, settings, attitudes about Indians, levels of realism, movie stars most frequently cast—the list is almost endless. As you are describing the American cowboy film of the 1970s, you are coming very close to defining this particular period in film history.

The author of the following passage uses vivid description to establish the powerful first impression gorillas in the wild make.

I shall never forget my first encounter with gorillas. Sound preceded sight. Odor preceded sound in the form of an overwhelming musky-barnyard, humanlike scent. The air was suddenly rent by a high-pitched series of screams followed by the rhythmic rondo of sharp *pok-pok* chestbeats from a great silverback male obscured behind what seems an impenetrable wall of vegetation. Joan and Alan Root, some ten yards ahead on the forest trail, motioned me to remain still. The three of us froze until the echoes of the screams and chestbeats faded. Only then did we slowly creep forward under the cover of dense shrubbery to about fifty feet from the group. Peeking through the vegetation, we could distinguish an equally curious phalanx of black, leather-countenanced, furry-headed primates peering back at us. Their bright eyes darted nervously from under heavy brows as though trying to identify us as familiar friends or possible foes. Immediately I was struck by the physical magnificence of the huge jet-black bodies blended against the green palette wash of the thick forest foliage.

[Diane Fossey, *Gorillas in the Mist* (Boston: Houghton Mifflin, 1983), p. 3.]

Exemplification

Exemplification—using examples to make your point—is the most commonly used of all patterns of thinking. Some researchers have suggested that over half of all professional writing relies on exemplification as its central method of proving points. Once again, we need to emphasize that these different ways of thinking and organizing are almost always found in combination. In fact, can you imagine any kind of thinking that does not draw on examples? Even a long story told to prove a point, like a parable or a fable, is nothing more than a form of extended example. The question is not, then, whether or not to use examples, but rather how to use the most effective examples in the most effective way. In the following excerpt the author offers a collection of examples to support his assertion that a fictional character knowingly violates grammatical rules.

Holden is a typical enough teenager to violate the grammar rules even though he knows of their social importance. His most common rule violation is the misuse of *lie* and *lay,* but he also is careless about relative pronouns ("about a traffic cop that falls in love"), the double negative ("I hardly didn't even know I was doing it"), the perfect tenses ("I'd woke him up"), extra words ("like as if all you ever did at Pency was play polo all the time"), pronoun number ("It's pretty disgusting to watch somebody picking their nose"), and pronoun position ("I and this friend of mine, Mal Brossard"). More remarkable, however, than the instances of grammar rule violations is Holden's relative "correctness." Holden is always intelligible, and is even "correct" in many usually difficult constructions. Grammatically speaking, Holden's language seems to point up the fact that English was the only subject in which he was not failing. It is interesting to note how much more "correct" Holden's speech is than that of Huck Finn. But then Holden is educated, and since the time of Huck there had been sixty-seven years of authoritarian schoolmarms working on the likes of Holden. . . .

[Donald P. Costello, *"The Language of The Catcher in the Rye," American Speech,* XXXIV (Oct. 1959), p. 179.]

Cause and Effect

Cause and effect thinking can begin with either the cause or the effect, but its purpose is either to ascertain why something happened or to try to figure out what would happen following a particular action. Although this kind of thinking is more sophisticated than the previous ones, it is another with which you are already familiar. Consider the following situations: You are unusually quiet when you are around your boyfriend's friends; the flowers by the fence haven't bloomed this year; you always make good grades in biology. If you were looking for the reasons for these situations, you would be engaging in cause and effect thinking. You have the effects; you're looking for the causes, the reasons the conditions or situations exist. In these examples, you might discover the following causes: Perhaps, you reason, you are quiet around your boyfriend's friends because they talk so much that you never get a chance to speak, or because they are so brilliant they intimidate you, or simply because they bore you. The flowers might not be blooming because the winter was so cold that the ground froze more deeply than usual, or because the new puppies you bought trample them. You get good grades in biology because the course was fairly easy, or because your mother, a biology major, tutors you, or because you have an aptitude for science. Determining the precise causes is important because you have to choose a course of action based on your reasoning. It would be unfortunate to change your major to biology, for example, if it's your mother who has the real aptitude for science. *One caution:* An effect may have more than one cause. Just because your boyfriend's friends are brilliant doesn't necessarily mean that they aren't also boring!

You can also think in the other direction. You are trying to decide whether to take a trip to Vermont; you have to decide whether to transfer to another university; you've been offered the lead in next semester's musical. Each of these decisions, when translated into action, causes other events in your life. If you take the trip to Vermont, you will have to work overtime for the next month. If you transfer, you will lose thirty credits. If you take the role, you will have to spend twenty hours a week in rehearsal.

Notice also that causes can produce more than one effect. Working overtime will put a strain on your studies. Losing thirty credits will delay your graduation for a year. Spending twenty extra hours a week in the theater will force you to quit your job.

In the following discussion of sexual repression in film, the author examines the broader history of the source of sexual repression in the United States.

Our heritage of sexual repression—one that the Hollywood film does not so much create as imitate—is double-edged indeed, giving rise to the need to elevate (spiritualize) on the one hand, and to standardize (explain, debase) on the other. Our sexual emancipators and evangelists sometimes miss half of the truth: that if puritanism is the source of our greatest hypocrisies and most crippling illusions, it is, as the primal anxiety whose therapy is civilization itself, the source of much, perhaps most, of our achievement. In movies, as in individuals, the sublimation of the sexual drive can be for some a poisoning influence while for others, it is the source, in compensating energy and action, of creative achievement. That the early suffragettes should not have been perfect homebodies, or that there is a strong puritanical streak in the women's movement, should come as no surprise.

[Molly Haskell, *From Reverence to Rape: The Treatment of Women in the Movies* (New York: Holt, Rinehart, Winston, 1973), p. 125.]

Comparison and Contrast

Comparison and contrast ranks with exemplification as one of the most frequently used patterns of thought. In our spoken language, we realized the power of comparison long ago. If we want to convince our friends that a new space adventure movie we have just seen is excellent, we might say that it compared favorably with *Star Wars,* a movie we know our friends admired. Or if we want to convince someone that this year's Royals aren't very good, we might want to contrast this year's team to a better Royals' team from the past. (*Note:* People often use the word *compare* to mean both to tell how things are alike and how they are different. This is particularly good to know if you're taking an essay exam and your professor asks you to compare two things. She might be looking for both similarities and differences. Usually, however, when you compare you work only with similarities. When you contrast, you work with differences.)

Although we are constantly comparing and contrasting things from our daily lives, this kind of thinking often causes problems in writing because of the complexities involved in organizing a well-structured comparison. In the following paragraph the author explores the difficulty of establishing a criterion for wine regions. He uses comparison/contrast to illustrate his point.

> There was no question of finding one style or one set of criteria to apply to every map. For the very fact which is most enthralling about wine is that no two regions have the same standards, or place emphasis on the same things. In Burgundy there is the most complex grading of fields ever attempted: Each field, and even parts of fields, being classified in a hierarchy which is cut-and-dried. In parts of Bordeaux there is a formal grading of properties; not directly related to the land but to the estates on it. In Germany there is no land classification at all, but an ingenious hierarchy of ripeness. In Champagne whole villages are classed, in Jerez soils of certain kinds, in Italy some traditional wine zones, but not others.

[Hugh Johnson, *The World Atlas of Wine* (New York: Simon and Schuster, 1971), p. 8.]

Classification and Division

No doubt, you recognize these two related types of thinking as ones you use frequently. Remember back in elementary school when your teacher gave you a picture like the one in Figure 3–10?

FIGURE 3-10

Then you were asked which picture didn't belong in the group. To make this decision you use the pattern of thinking called classification and division. An-

FIGURE 3-11

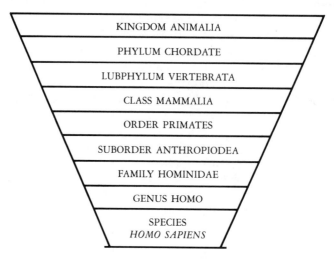

KINGDOM ANIMALIA

PHYLUM CHORDATE

LUBPHYLUM VERTEBRATA

CLASS MAMMALIA

ORDER PRIMATES

SUBORDER ANTHROPIODEA

FAMILY HOMINIDAE

GENUS HOMO

SPECIES
HOMO SAPIENS

other example is from high school biology. Remember the classification system Carolus Linnaeus developed for plants and animals (Figure 3–11)?

As you see, this method of thinking is also familiar.

Other words that can be associated with this kind of thinking are analysis and synthesis. When we analyze, we take whole things apart; we move from the general, the abstract, toward the specific, the concrete. When we synthesize, we look at all the parts and try to fit them into a coherent whole.

The following paragraph presents a discussion of the German language by classifying it among language families; note that the paragraph also makes use of comparison.

On an even broader scale, those students who have studied Latin are struck by the fact that the grammar of German seems often more akin to Latin than to English. And such comparisons could be expanded to point up similarities to such languages as Greek, Sanskrit, and Russian. In other words, it would soon become clear that German is related not only to that group of languages we have called *Germanic,* but also—even if usually less obviously—to other and more distant tongues. In fact, the Germanic languages are related to the following linguistic groups: Albanian, Armenian, Baltic, Celtic, Greek, Hittite, Indic, Iranian, Italic, Slavic, and Tocharian (in addition to certain other less available languages of antiquity). These languages—or language groups—are subsumed under the term "Indo-European." The German language, therefore, in point of its broadest generic classification, is an Indo-European language belonging to the Germanic group.

[John T. Waterman, *A History of the German Language* (Seattle: University of Washington Press, 1966), p. 3.]

In the following paragraph the author analyzes the zones of the marine environment.

The marine environment can be divided into zones on the basis of the illumination of the water. The shallowest zone—which reaches to a depth varying from 65 to 390 feet (20 to 120 meters), according to certain conditions, mainly the latitude and the transparency of the water—is called the euphotic zone (euphotic means good light). In this, all the red rays and some of the blue are absorbed. The vegetation endowed with chlorophyll receives sufficient solar energy here for photosynthesis to occur. The lower limit of the euphotic zone coincides with the "compensaton depth," the greatest depth at which plants are able to manufacture a quantity of food substances equivalent to—and thus compensatory for—the quantity that they consume in order to live. Below the euphotic zone lies the oligophotic zone (oligophotic means little light), which receives only the most penetrating rays of the solar spectrum. This zone extends to a depth of one to two thousand feet (300 to 600 meters), with an average of about 1600 feet (500 meters). In this zone the classic chlorophyll-carrying organisms are lacking, since the light intensity is too low to allow them to manufacture a quantity of food substances equal to the amount which they require to live. Below the oligophotic zone extends the aphotic zone (no light), which is totally deprived of light, and is therefore not capable of sustaining any plant life.

[Menico Torchio, *The World Beneath the Sea* (London: Orbis Publishing, 1972) p. 12.]

Definition

When we define something, we are trying to find its shape, its parameters. If we are writing to an audience that knows considerably less than we do, then definition becomes particularly important. If, for example, a zoologist were to write an article imploring people to contribute to a fund to save the reticulated giraffe, an endangered species, he might be wise to tell his audience what "reticulated" means; otherwise he might not receive the kind of widespread support he is seeking. In fact, for some audiences he might also want to define exactly how a species is put on the endangered list. (Notice that if he did this, he would be defining the limits of "endangered" and presenting an account of a process—once again combining modes of thinking.)

The following paragraph uses definition—notice that the paragraph also contains narration and comparison—to make a comment about the age in which we live.

Baroque is a mysterious term. Some scholars (Benedetto Croce among them) believe that it derived from an artificial word (b-a-r-o-c-o) invented by medieval scholars to teach dull pupils a particularly intricate form of logical reasoning, the fourth mode of the second figure of the syllogism, to be exact. Others think it is the old trade name for the oddly-shaped monstrous pearls still known as *pearle barocche* in Italy. The two hypotheses are not in contradiction. Somehow the term came to be used metaphorically to describe anything pointlessly complicated, otiose, capricious and eccentric, similar to rarely used syllogisms or irregularly bulging pearls: twisted theories, elliptical and over-ornate poetry, elaborate and gaudy architecture. Later it came to define a whole period in history, the Baroque era, in which Baroque men thought Baroque thoughts, led Baroque lives, surrounded by Baroque art. The age had a more than casual resemblence to our own.

[Luigi Barzini, *The Italians* (New York: Bantam Books, 1965), p. 311.]

EXERCISE 3–7

Read David Ray's essay on page 30 again. Write an outline of each paragraph, but instead of listing the topics, list the modes of thinking he uses in each.

Modes of Thinking as Prewriting

Some students find it helpful to use these modes of thinking during their prewriting. They use something we call the *thinking grid* both to generate ideas and to help focus them. This grid takes a while to get used to because it asks you to think about writing using all the modes of thinking we've just discussed. After you've done this, you consider which pieces of information best serve your audience and your purpose.

Before we introduce the grid, let's consider an example. Assume you own a cabin in Green Mountain Falls right outside of Colorado Springs. A friend of yours in Mississippi has written you about possibly purchasing it. Since you are eager to sell it, you want to send him a letter increasing his interest and ultimately leading to the sale of the cabin. The modes of thinking can help you generate a variety of ideas to make your letter persuasive.

Narration. You could recount the events of one particularly memorable vacation your family had at the cabin. You could *narrate* the events of one typical day of Rocky Mountain vacation.

Description. You might want to *describe* the beautiful scenery surrounding the cabin and, of course, you need to include a thorough description of the cabin itself.

Exemplification. Instead of presenting a sequential narration of events of one vacation or one particular day, you might instead choose to *provide examples* of vacation activities available to the owner of such a cabin. Or you might want to *provide examples* illustrating several advantages of owning the cabin.

Cause and Effect. You might want to include in the letter some possible *effects* of owning the cabin. You could even include the *effects* of not acting on such a good deal in the immediate future.

Comparison and Contrast. You could *compare* owning a cabin to renting one each season. If your friend was also thinking about cabins in another part of Colorado, you could *contrast* the area around Colorado Springs with other parts of the state.

Classification and Division. You might choose to structure your letter around the general theme of advantages of buying this cabin. Then you could *divide* the letter into distinct parts which explore each of the different kinds of advantages.

Definition. One of your strategies might be to *define* just what makes for a good vacation home, or you might be able to use the definition of a "good deal."

Using the modes of thinking generates a variety of possible approaches to your task. You probably also noted that in all likelihood you would not use any one of the modes by itself when you finally composed the letter. In fact, an effective letter would have to combine two or more of them. For example, can you imagine a good narrative about one of your vacations not including a description of watching the sun glittering off the mountain peaks while you were in the lift line at one of the neighboring ski resorts? Or, what use would there be in dividing the advantages of owning the cabin without supplying specific, concrete examples? You might choose one of the modes as your basic organizing principle, but you would be forced to use many of the others to make your letter effective.

The Thinking Grid

Here's a sample of what the grid looks like before it's used as a prewriting (or revising) tool. Think about your topic in each of the ways indicated on the grid, writing your results in each category. When it's complete, you can reconsider your focus in view of the additional information provided by the grid.

THINKING GRID	
TOPIC	FOCUS
NARRATION	DESCRIPTION

EXEMPLIFICATION	CAUSE AND EFFECT
COMPARISON	CONTRAST
CLASSIFICATION AND DIVISION	DEFINITION
REVISED FOCUS	

EXERCISE 3–8

Pick out something you own that might be worth selling. Fill out a complete Thinking Grid on the item you've chosen.

EXERCISE 3–9

Select one of the patterns of thinking as your main approach and write at least one page of sales persuasion about the item from Exercise 3–8. (Don't use description as your main approach.)

EXERCISE 3–10

Try to sell the item again (writing at least one page). This time, combine at least three of the patterns in your paper.

The grid is much simpler to use than it might appear. You can use it as controlled freewriting or brainstorming, or as a way to ask yourself key questions before you begin writing. It also can help you sort and organize your thoughts, and ultimately your paper. Below is a Grid done on a local neighborhood.

THINKING GRID

TOPIC: Hyde Park
neighborhood

FOCUS: To show
that it's *al-
most* good

NARRATION

Tell the neighborhood's history—the steps it's gone
through to become what it is
today: fancy ⟶ integration
⟶ segregation ⟶ race
riots ⟶ gentrification
tell the story of a ''typical'' neighbor or narrate the
history of a typical house
(large, one-family dwellings,
some with servants' quarters,
divided and partitioned).
Tell the history of Leper
West.

DESCRIPTION

Describe the different
houses, the people who
live there—give the
reader a real sense of
physical place. Describe the weirdos who
wander through . . .
the junkyards—some of
the old cars

EXEMPLIFICATION

Good neighborhood
restoration, new people, mixture of people, beauty, convenient to downtown restaurants, neighborhood
activities, good values for
young people, group activities
Bad neighborhood
Shabby houses, noise, crime,
neighborhood conflicts,
fires, too many strangers, on
edge of prostitution and drug
territory

CAUSE AND EFFECT

Why did the neighborhood become what it
was? Is?
war, depression, segregation, ''White
Flight,'' racism.
Help from realtors,
bankers, politicians,
new money from yuppies
Why crime? Its effects?
Stop it: crime watch,
crime patrol, block
meetings, pressure on
police

Schools better $\longrightarrow$ more
$ and more parent
help = better neigh-
borhood
Action line telephone
number $\longrightarrow$ better re-
pairs, cleaner yards

COMPARISON   **CONTRAST**

Tell what it was like when Leper West was in action:
fires, alcoholics sleeping in the gutter, naked, fat
women. Show how tame it's become—only an isolated mur-
der in the front yard.
Compare present state with early 20th century—not too
bad, boulevards and trees still there, most houses
still there.
Compare Hyde Park to one of the other old neighborhoods in this town or another town (Cincinnati, Cleveland, or Pittsburgh would be good because the towns
are similar).
Compare/weigh(?) good with bad, point by point.

CLASSIFICATION AND DIVISION   **DEFINITION**

Tell different historical ar-   define gentrification-
chitectural styles   use Washington, D.C.
Categorize family types: sin-   shirtwaist, prairie,
gles, families, homosexual,   bungalow, Victorian,
apartment dwellers   etc ''urban''
Life styles
Analyze the kinds of problems: crime (what kinds?),
trash, crowded, neighbors
with different values.
Possible categories of
''good'' living
1) Education 2) Security
3) Beauty 4) Entertainment
5) Pride 6) Community feeling

REVISED FOCUS: Despite the crime and urban problems, Hyde
Park is a place where people enjoy life in the neighborhood

Filling out the grid generates a great deal of possible material for an essay. Also, it usually leads to questions which need to be considered before actual writing begins. In the exercise above, working through the grid prompted the author to change his mind about how he felt about his topic. He began by thinking that his neighborhood was "almost" a good place to live; by the time he had worked through the grid, he had decided that living there was good.

We can also see that the original subject is still, at this stage, too broadly defined. The grid, however, opens up a writer's mind to new directions, while suggesting methods of organization. Below are three other possible modified topics suggested by the material generated in the grid.

Modified Topics Suggested by the Grid

1. There's enough material in the grid for a paper showing how a deteriorated neighborhood can be revitalized—Hyde Park becomes an extended example. The possible audience could be neighborhood associations now facing problems Hyde Park faced five years ago.

2. There's enough material for a piece area real estate brokers could include in their brochures touting the neighborhood's positive values.

3. There's enough material to write an analysis of the neighborhood for a company considering purchasing three houses in the neighborhood for young executives and their families who will live in the city during one-year training periods.

Follow us through a review of the first of the modified focuses to see how the original subject might be refined.

1. In this paper the author would draw on a variety of types of thinking. Basically, the topic calls for an examination of cause and effect. What steps were taken to produce the desired results? This question suggests another possible method of organization. The author could present the specific steps residents took to revitalize the neighborhood, in effect creating a blueprint. If the steps do not have to be followed precisely in sequence for the effort to be successful, the author may choose to group the steps into categories and arrange them in an appropriate order—least to most important, for example. The classifications might look something like the following: *preconditions* (housing must be inexpensive, must be an attractive location, must be suitable for restoration), *realtor involvement, neighborhood association, low-interest development money (bank involvement), involved city government, means to fight crime, school improvement, planning, eyesore elimination, publicity.* The author might choose to define/describe the features of Hyde Park, analyze its problems, and show how solutions were found. In other words, the same topic, the same basic thesis, can produce a variety of different papers depending on what methods of thinking you apply to a particular writing problem.

EXERCISE 3–11

List three other possible focuses deriving from the grid. Tell which sections you would use to support each focus.

EXERCISE 3–12

>Imagine that *you* have a vacation home to sell. Place it in your favorite part of the United States. Complete a blank grid for it. You may brainstorm, freewrite, or simply list possibilities in the same way that we did earlier. (We should caution you that if you list possibilities you still need to generate specific details for your writing in a following step.)

EXERCISE 3–13

>Peruse your writing notebook or turn back to some of your earlier prewriting. Choose a topic you think might be appropriate for an essay. (If you need to, review pp. 14–15 for the definition of an appropriate topic.) Write it at the top left of your paper; if you have a tentative direction in mind, write it at the upper right of the grid. Go through each section of the grid filling in as much information under each as possible. Brainstorm, freewrite, ask questions, make lists—use any technique you want, just get as much out as you can. If you come to a part of the grid where you draw a blank, don't worry about it now. Not all topics lend themselves easily to all the different ways of thinking. You may also find some ways of thinking more productive than others, depending on your topic. If you can't think of a topic, use one of the topics below.
>
>1. Something about your neighborhood which makes you angry/happy/sad.
>2. Something you would change about the university.
>3. Something you've read lately which made you angry/happy/sad.
>4. The shape of the family in 20 years.
>5. What you would change about human nature.
>
>(These are ideas to get you started—general topics, not thesis statements.)

EXERCISE 3–14

>Reread the material you wrote on your grid for Exercise 3–13. Make a list of possible thesis statements which could be developed from the material you have generated. Come up with at least five. Be prepared to show how you derived each of them. What material would you keep for each thesis? What material could you use if it were modified?
>
>[*Note:* Some students become frustrated unless all the topics on the grid are completely filled in. They think that unless each of the ways of thinking is productive that the grid isn't working. That's not necessarily true. Different topics naturally lend themselves to different kinds of thinking. Try to fill it in as completely as you can. As with the other kinds of prewriting/prethinking techniques we have suggested, the grid becomes more helpful to you with practice. You have to use it several times before you begin to see it as an effective technique for your own writing. If after trying it several times, you discover that it is not a productive way for you to go about writing a paper,

then don't use it. We offer these different approaches to writing so you can find the ones which make you a better and more efficient writer. Adopt the ones that work for you.]

The Thinking Grid as Organizational Strategy

For some students, the grid is also an effective step between the first stages of prewriting and writing the first draft. These students use other prewriting approaches to narrow their topic to a tentative thesis; then they use the grid to help them organize their thinking and to fill in the gaps. For example, let's say you've brainstormed or freewritten on the ways that your university has affected the quality of life in the adjoining neighborhoods. You've come to the tentative conclusion that the nonstudents who live in the area have been negatively affected by the university's seemingly haphazard policy of property acquisition and development. You are ready to rough out a first draft from your preliminary thinking, but you are overwhelmed by the randomness of your prewriting. The grid offers you a way to begin sorting your material.

Place a blank grid in front of you and sort your information, placing each of your thoughts into an appropriate square. If you feel that some items belong in more than one square, then put them in more than one. If you have new ideas—and you probably will—write them down on the grid. When you are finished, you have a preliminary organizational map of your paper. You can get a visual picture of the information you have and how it fits together. From this point it is easier to decide on a strategy for tackling your first draft.

In our search for examples to use in this section, we found that few paragraphs offer pure examples of one mode of thinking and organization. If these *pure* modes are so hard to find, what good will they do you? If you learn to explore the various patterns, you might derive the following benefits:

1. Using a variety of patterns opens up thinking.

2. Opening up thinking brings to the foré a variety of evidence.

3. A paper with a variety of evidence is harder to refute than one which draws predominantly on one mode of thinking.

4. Variety in thinking leads to variety in writing, which is pleasing to read.

EXERCISE 3–15

Return to one of your logs. Find a piece of prewriting that you did as an exercise but haven't yet turned into a paper. Use the grid as your next step in exploring the topic. Start the same way that you did in Exercise 3–13, including both the topic and your tentative focus. After you finish the grid, write at the bottom of the page the focus which now seems most appropriate for a paper you would like to write.

Assignments from Other Disciplines with Exercises

Assignment #1. The following assignment is from Introduction to Art History, a freshman-level class that gives students the opportunity to gain "a basic understanding of the visual arts: the factors that enter into the production of a work of art and how they reflect the different characteristics of the cultures and individuals that produced the work."

Write three short (500–600 words each) papers on selected works of art that are assigned in class. In preparing your papers, you should begin by looking at the object and taking careful notes on the material used, size, technique, style, etc. Examine it more than once. The second and third times you will see things that you overlooked the first time. Begin to *analyze* as you take notes. *How* has the artist achieved the visual effect? How are the formal elements organized, using what principles of composition? How does this enhance (or detract from) the impact of the work?

In writing the paper, it is good practice to begin with a brief description before proceeding to your analysis. You might, for example, mention the size of the work and the materials that are used. If figures are involved, how many are there? How are they placed? What is the compositional arrangement? Symmetrical? Asymmetrical? How do the color, technique, and other aspects of style help the artist make his statement? Remember that a good description is the best basis for a good analysis, and a good paper presents the reader with concrete images based on your *observations,* rather than simply stating your generalized opinions about the work. Finally, write and *rewrite* until you have said what you want to say in the most succinct way.

—ASSIGNED BY PROFESSOR GERALDINE E. FOWLES.

EXERCISE 3–16

Notice that this assignment calls for prewriting, several different modes of thinking, and rewriting. We should also add that Professor Fowles makes it clear that she expects students to edit their papers carefully.

1. Write a description of how each of the following prewriting techniques might be used to your advantage if you were undertaking Professor Fowles' assignment: brainstorming, freewriting, clustering.

2. Write a brief discussion of the modes of thinking that the assignment calls for. Tell what role each of them *might* play in your essay.

Assignment #2. The following sample assignment is an essay exam from an upper-division class in environmental psychology:

1. Please define in two or three complete paragraphs (a) environmental psychology, (b) characteristics of environmental psychology and/or historical antecedents, (c) how the field might be similar to and different from the other areas of psychology, e.g., social psychology. Use information from notes and from the text where applicable.

2. Please select two models/theories relevant to environmental psychology. Describe these models and the implications for study of environment-behavior relations (e.g., environmental stress, arousal, environmental load, adaptation level, behavioral constraint, ecological factors).

3. Levy-Leboyer described current research in environmental psychology as a function of data type and "methods." Please describe the data types, the methods, and their interactions. Data types: Action on Environment, Perceived Effect of Environment on Behavior, Non-Perceived Effects of Environment on Behavior, Environmental Cognition, Environmental Evaluation, Attitudes toward Environment. "Methods": Discrete Observation, Systematic Observation, Performance, Factual Questioning, Games/Simulation, Attitude and Personality Questionnaire, and indirect methods.

4. Please describe internal, construct, and external validity, and important threats to each type of validity for research in environmental psychology.

5. Define the following terms:

variable:
measurement:
reliability:
validity:

6. Describe the relationships (tradeoffs) between the three types of validity we discussed in class and strategies for research.

—PROFESSOR LARRY SIMPKINS.

EXERCISE 3–17

Unless you're a psychology major, you probably wouldn't have much luck answering the questions above. On the other hand, if you had the information and you had done the exercises having to do with the modes of thinking, you would understand how each of the questions could be answered to the professor's satisfaction. Review the essay exam, and for each of the questions tell what mode of thinking is demanded by the question. Some questions might call for more than one. Don't forget the first cardinal rule for taking an essay exam: *Read the questions or instructions carefully*.

Assignment #3. The following assignment is an essay exam for Western Civilization to 1600: Your essay should consist of five solid, well-argued paragraphs, including an introduction and a conclusion. Be sure to document your statements with references to the readings.

Based on your reading of Sarah Pomeroy's article, how does Aristophanes's description of women in Athenian society in *Lysistrata* represent either an exaggeration or distortion of the way women actually lived in fifth-century B.C. Athens? Pay special attention to women's legal and political status, economic privileges and responsibilities and the importance of the family in society.

—ASSIGNED BY PROFESSOR JIM FALLS.

Although you may never have read either Pomeroy or Aristophanes, if you understand the section on modes of thinking you realize that this essay demands comparison and contrast within the context of the classification and division the professor has provided.

EXERCISE 3–18

Write a tentative outline for the previous essay.

Assignment #4.

Any mutually agreeable computer science topic is acceptable. Preferably the topic should deal with operating systems in some way. The list of future trends listed on pages 16–17 of the text might give you some ideas. Explain how you are going to handle the topic (i.e., "trace the history of . . . ," "analyze and explain the components of . . .," "discuss the advantages and disadvantages of . . .," "compare and contrast . . .," etc.). Topic choice should be neither too narrow nor too wide. It is possible to change topics or the handling of a topic later, but all steps already completed will have to be redone.

—ASSIGNED BY PROFESSOR RON MCCLEARY.

This assignment is for a beginning computer operating systems class. Notice the amount of freedom and responsibility given to the student.

EXERCISE 3–19

Write a paragraph explaining how what you have learned in this writing class would help you undertake the computer science assignment (Assignment #4).

The next chapter examines the processes inherent in moving from prewriting—both spontaneous and patterned—to the first drafts of your writing. In this chapter, you can see how the thinking activities you've been working with in Chapters 2 and 3 are useful in the later stages of writing.

CHAPTER FOUR

The Shaping Process

Elegance in prose composition is mainly thus: a just admission of topics and words; neither too many nor too few of either; enough of sweetness of sound to induce us to enter and sit still; enough of illustration and reflection to change the posture of our minds when they would tire; and enough of sound matter in the complex to pay us for our attendance.—Walter Savage Landor

We hope you have found some of the ways to approach writing presented in the previous chapter useful in helping you get started. All of them, however, make demands on you as both a reader and a writer. As a reader you must be able to *reread* the material you have generated and make decisions about it. This rereading begins with a consideration of purpose and audience.

Purpose

One way you can check your direction before you get too far into writing a paper is to decide early on what your purpose and audience are. No matter what kind of thesis or main point you have developed—even if you're writing a piece, such as a factual report, which has no real thesis—there is always the issue of the writer's motivation or underlying purpose. Why are you writing? What do you hope to accomplish?

The answers to these two questions vary, of course, depending on the writing occasion. In general, the answers to the questions can be divided into three broad categories: In college you generally write to express yourself, to inform, or to persuade. These generalizations, however, are of limited use while you're writing on a specific topic. Your answers need to be personalized and directed toward your writing. Let's say, for example, that you are writing up the results of an experiment in chemistry. Why are you writing? Perhaps you are writing to describe the steps you went through to analyze an unknown substance and to present your results. What do you hope to accomplish? If you are writing for an exam, you want to demonstrate to your instructor that you understand the procedures necessary to do the analysis, that you followed the procedures correctly, and that you achieved the desired results. If you are writing up the results of an original experiment, you are trying to describe the procedure so that another researcher could replicate it and reach the same conclusions. In the first case, you know what your professor (your audience) wants, and that knowledge determines the depth and breadth of your answer. In the second case, you know that your audience needs to be able to repeat your experiment exactly. Every small detail needs to be recorded. In all likelihood, your report in the second case would be much more detailed than the report for your professor. In addition, you probably want to delve into the implications of your procedure for your field. In both examples, your final piece of writing is shaped by your purpose and your audience.

Our colleague's letter to the rental car agency (p. 13) offers a different perspective on purpose and audience. What he hoped to accomplish was to get a refund—not just to get a complaint off his chest. He was, therefore, motivated more by his purpose than by his audience. He chose his examples to illustrate the details of the transaction so the agency could see the nature of the error. If he had wanted merely to air the complaint and vent his anger, he would have been less detailed and would have focused more on the clerk's incompetence and rudeness. His purpose for writing in that case would have been simply to make himself feel better.

EXERCISE 4–1

Write an explanation of what you would need to accomplish in each of the writing situations that follow.

a. You must write a note to your work-study supervisor, who has demanded to know why you were rude to a faculty member who came to you for assistance.

b. You must write a proposal for the Student Senate to present to the Faculty General Assembly, asking that elective courses be graded on a Pass-Fail basis if a student so desires.

c. You must write a letter to your best friend after a particularly nasty quarrel.

d. You must write the minutes of a community service organization's meeting.

e. You must write a research paper on light and dark symbolism in *The Scarlet Letter* for an English course.

In short, before you start to write, you might want to write a short note to yourself describing why you are writing and what you hope to accomplish.

Audience

Deborah C. Andrews, an assistant professor of technical writing at the University of Delaware—Newark, has discovered that employees trying to improve their writing skills most frequently ask her to teach them to do audience anal-

 # consider audience

ysis and list defining audience as one of their main difficulties. (Anne Eisenberg, "The Rise of the Writing Class," *IEEE Potentials,* February 1984, p. 28). In other words, the challenge of defining your audience and learning to write for it is one that stays with you long after leaving college.

Analyzing or defining your audience is a skill that may become somewhat formalized when you write. But it is a skill which you practice daily in talking to others. Consider, for example, your last date. Suppose you had dinner, then went to a concert—Bruce Springsteen, Rickie Lee Jones, the Chicago Symphony. You had a marvelous time—the music was great, your date lively and charming. What do you say the next day when one of your parents asks you whether you enjoyed yourself? Probably: "Yes. The music was really good. The hall was crowded, though, and we had trouble finding a parking place." Later, on the phone with your best friend, you are more expansive: "It was wonderful! Bruce Springsteen was *too good*! He did two encores. We went wild; the whole crowd did! And Jim is so much fun. I've never laughed so much in my life. I think I'm in love!!" The next day at the library you run into an acquaintance from one of your classes, someone you have always felt in competition with and whom you just don't like very much. Here, you are more likely to be a bit standoffish: "I went to the Springsteen concert with Jim the other night. Did you get a chance to go? Too bad. You missed a great concert. The reviewer in the paper said that it was The Boss's best performance of this tour. Jim got great seats, too—we were practically on stage."

What's the difference? Same story, different audience. What you tell people and how you tell it, whether in speech or writing, depends on who these people are, on what your relationship with them is, on how much they know and on how much you think they need to know. In both speech and writing you shape content and presentation to meet the audience's requirements, requirements you become aware of when you consider the audience.

When you communicate, you give the audience an impression of yourself. At times you may want the reader to believe that you are sassy and bold; at other times you may want to appear timid, polite, enthusiastic, restrained, sorrowful, or happy. What you tell people and how you tell it are also shaped by the impression you want to leave.

The content and presentation of a piece of writing, then, are determined not only by your audience's requirements, but also by your purpose in writing. In the concert example, what you tell your parents is tempered by your belief that they really don't want to hear you rave about Bruce Springsteen because they don't like him much. Yet you do want your parents to know you had a good time; they are interested in you. Your best friend is interested in you, the date, and Bruce Springsteen. So you try to give her a clearer, more detailed account of the evening. When you talk to the acquaintance from school, though, you are hoping to make her just a little jealous; at least you want to drive home that she missed something that you enjoyed tremendously.

Your conversation with each has been guided by your awareness of audience and purpose. Different audiences demand not only a different emphasis or focus but different details, different tones, different approaches. So, too, does your purpose in writing demand that you carefully select the emphasis, tone, approach, and supporting details that will help you achieve what you intend.

How, then, do you determine the audience's requirements? Early in the writing process—at least by the first draft if not during prewriting—you should begin to form an idea of your audience and its requirements. Then keep that audience in mind during the entire process—through all drafts and revisions, even as you edit. Here's a checklist, a series of questions to guide your thinking about your audience. Write the answers down; form a concrete image of the audience so that you can shape your writing to meet its requirements. If your writing is directed by the qualities and characteristics of your audience, you are bound to increase your effectiveness as a writer.

Audience Analysis Guide

1. What is your relationship with your audience?

If you are relatively friendly with the members of your audience, you can rely to some extent on their good will. Generally you can use a more relaxed tone and diction. If you do not know your audience, a friendly tone might seem patronizing or condescending, and they would probably resent it. Have you ever received a letter from someone you didn't know who was trying to sell you something by addressing you as though you were a long-lost friend? Remember how irritated you felt? You have to earn your audience's trust and respect.

2. What kind of acceptance or resistance can you expect from your audience?

If you know your audience is generally hostile toward you or what you have to say, you must work to establish some common ground, to create some basis for potential agreement or compromise. You must establish your credibility. The audience needs to know that you have considered various possibilities before deciding that your thesis represents the most reasonable position. State the objections your audience might have to your thesis, cite opposing viewpoints that some members of the audience might hold. As you plan your paper, plan to answer the objections readers might have. In this way you show your readers that you have explored your subject thoroughly. You may not persuade them to accept your position, but you will have enabled them to see how you arrived at your thesis.

3. What do they already know about your subject?

You must try to predict how familiar your audience is with your subject. If they have no more than a general knowledge, you may need to begin your paper with significant background material. You would also want to avoid using highly technical and specialized terms or explanations. You might even need to supply some crucial definitions. On the other hand, if they already know a great deal about your subject, you don't want to bore them by repeating details or explanations they already know. As an example, consider explaining to people who don't understand or care for baseball why the Kansas City Royals offered George Brett a lifetime contract. How important would George's batting average be to them?

4. *How interested is the audience in your subject?*

If you know that the members of your audience are already interested in or concerned about your subject, then you can be more straightforward in your approach. You don't have to stir your employer's interest, for example, in a report on corporate earnings. Conversely, if your readers have only limited original interest in what you're writing about, you'll have to work harder to catch their attention. For instance, you are presenting a proposal for a client to rezone some land from residential to commercial. You aren't sure the city council will be interested in the plan, so you begin with something designed to get their attention and arouse their interest—100 percent of the area's nearby residents have signed a petition supporting the rezoning proposal. Once you have their attention, your case has a better chance of receiving full and careful consideration. As a general rule, people don't like to be bored—not even while they're doing business, so do your best to present your material in the most lively way possible.

5. *What will they need to know to understnad or accept your thesis?*

This question is related to how much your audience knows about your subject, but the focus has shifted to the nature of your thesis. If you are presenting a complex thesis, then explaining things clearly and organizing logically become critically important. Are there terms or processes that need to be explained? Do your readers need graphs or charts to understand your point? Perhaps you need to divide your paper into clearly marked sections so readers can follow your reasoning more easily.

6. *What are the special language requirements for this particular audience?*

What language does your audience speak? What language do they respect? What kind of language do they expect from someone presenting a thesis like yours? The answers to these questions help to shape the nature of the language you use; they tell you what level of formality, familiarity, and technicality you should use. Complicating the matter somewhat is your own ability to manipulate the language. You must use language that you are comfortable with as well. Have you ever heard an adult try to speak to a younger person using the current "in" expressions?

7. *How do you want them to feel about you and your subject when they finish reading your piece?*

This question takes us back to a consideration of purpose. If you know what you are trying to accomplish in a piece of writing and you've done a good job addressing your audience, the likelihood of success is much greater. You can now reread your piece from your audience's point of view and judge your writing's effectiveness.

8. Have you designed your paper to appeal to your audience's sense of emotion, reason, and ethics?

Most effective writing contains these three appeals. You should attempt to determine what kinds of examples and evidence will reach your audience and make them respond favorably to your thesis. You should organize your proofs and presentation so your audience can see the logic of your mind at work. You should be honest with your evidence. You should make clear any ethical or moral judgments inherent in accepting your thesis. (For a fuller treatment of audience consideration, see Chapter 8 on argument and persuasion.)

Audience Analysis Checklist

1. What is your relationship with your audience?
2. What kind of acceptance or resistance can you expect from your audience?
3. What does the audience already know about your subject?
4. How interested is the audience in your subject?
5. What will they need to know to understand or accept your thesis?
6. What are the special language requirements for this particular audience?
7. How do you want them to feel about you and your subject?
8. Have you designed your paper to appeal to your audience's emotion, reason, and ethics?

EXERCISE 4–2

Take from your writing notebook the five thesis statement ideas you wrote for Exercise 2–13. Choose two of the them. Decide on a possible audience for each and do a detailed audience analysis for each. Bring your analysis to class for discussion. Now select a dramatically different audience for each of the two theses and do a detailed analysis of the new audience. During class discussion, compare the two audiences and explore how your thesis and paper would differ for each one.

EXERCISE 4–3

For each of the theses from Exercise 4–2, write a statement of purpose that would give you direction if you were to turn these ideas into papers. Be as specific as you can. Bring both to class for discussion.

Reviewing Your Prewriting

At this stage in your writing process, you have already decided on a topic, done substantial prewriting, sorted and pruned the prewriting, arrived at a tentative thesis, decided on a purpose, and analyzed your audience. After rereading your material carefully, you must now decide whether you have an acceptable thesis or if you need to modify or rethink it. If you are satisfied for now with your main point, you must then make a series of decisions concerning the material you have generated. You must decide if you need *to add support* to make your point stronger. You must decide if you need *to delete material* which is not appropriate to or which does not support your point. You should also check to see if you might be able *to substitute* more powerful or pertinent material for the weaker parts of your prewriting.

You probably have already begun to come up with some tentative ideas about the way you want *to arrange* the ideas in your essay. In any case, you must decide if you need *to combine* any of your subpoints or evidence to organize your material more effectively. In other words, even though you're still at the planning stage of writing, you are checking whether you need to revise what you have already done. In most cases, even the most experienced writer discovers that some changes, some revisions, need to be made.

At this stage, you become an active reader of your own writing. In order to make those decisions discussed above, you have to go back to your material with new eyes. Now you have a controlling idea to guide your rereading, so the first step is to return to your brainstorming, freewriting, journal, or logs, but this time with your tentative thesis written out in front of you. Here is the first question you ask yourself: What supports my idea? Use a highlighter or a colored pen. Mark everything you think might be useful in your paper. If you have any thoughts about how to use the material or if you have any new thoughts, write them in the margins. (Don't throw anything away or cross anything out yet; you still might refocus your thinking and might need what you've lost.)

Now spread things out in front of you. Label your first idea. You can simply label it #1 or letter A. Or, if you see immediately that it belongs to a particular subtopic, you can give it a category name. Let's take the American Dream thesis as an example. Your first idea might be related to time-saving appliances. Label it. Then go through the rest of your ideas and put the same label on everything that might fit into the same category. Then move onto the next idea—dreams of leisure time, for example. Repeat the labeling process. Follow the same sequence until all your ideas are labeled. Write on only one side of the paper; flipping pages wastes time and muddles the total picture.

You are probably making several interesting discoveries. First, you notice that you have some ideas with no companions. That raises a question: Do these ideas really fit into your paper? If they don't, you can relegate them to the probably-won't-use file. If you still think they fit, you must ask if you need to generate new ideas to develop them further. Or you need to recheck to see if perhaps they fit into one of the other categories.

You might also discover that some of your items fit under more than one label. Go ahead and put all the appropriate labels on them. Later on while you're writing, you might see that these overlaps signal ideas which should be connected in your paper. In fact, one of your major discoveries should be that you are beginning to see one or more possible organizations for your paper. What are now separately labeled categories or subpoints later become the different parts and even paragraphs of your paper. (For more on organization, see pp. 94–101.)

Before you undertake the actual planning of your paper, however, some other thinking steps must be taken. At this point it's sufficient that you have all your ideas grouped. It's good practice, though, to transfer ideas from their original locations to a separate place. This allows you to see the ideas you're planning to use without the surrounding clutter of unused ideas. Some writers simply transfer the ideas onto separate sheets of paper. Others like the cut-and-paste approach: They take some scissors, cut out the ideas they plan to use, and tape them in groups on blank paper. Others prefer simply to paper-clip the different ideas together for easier rearrangement later.

The rest of this chapter is designed to help you make those planning decisions listed earlier and to help shape your first draft.

Reconsidering Your Thesis

Your next step takes you back to your thesis. You should be concerned with the effectiveness of your thesis through all the stages leading up to the final draft. We've already discussed the care you need to take in developing the first version of your thesis. Remember: *Don't hold on to that first effort too tightly.* After you reread the material you have generated, you might find new insights that modify your thesis. You might even discover that you've changed your mind about the way you believe or that an entirely new approach comes to mind. Don't worry. This happens to us all. Frequently the new idea is more thoughtful and more exciting than the original idea. Trust yourself. Run with it; you have a variety of techniques to use to explore the new idea. If it doesn't work out, you can always return to the original. You may even discover when you finish the first draft that you've altered your thesis. In that case, feel free to modify the original idea. Remember that you're not completely committed until the piece of writing has reached its final audience.

EXERCISE 4–4

Choose one of the topics from your writing notebook or one you are ready to begin developing into a final essay. Take it through the prewriting and reviewing steps. Check your thesis and write at least two possible new versions (revisions). Decide which one fits most closely with what you want to do.

Everything you do from this point on is controlled by the idea that remains after you've completed the prewriting and reviewing steps described in the first part of Chapter 3. *Remember, however, that your thesis and your approach can be changed at any stage until the paper reaches its final readers.*

The First Draft

Many inexperienced writers encounter difficulty the moment they begin to write the first draft—even if they've followed steps similar to the ones described in the preceding pages. This difficulty results from what we might call the obsession with perfection. Some writers feel that they have to get everything right on the first attempt. They feel that every word, every sentence, every paragraph must come out of the pen in perfect form. When they come to the first place where they fall short of perfection, they stop and reach for that perfection. Very often the results are the opposite of what they intend. Instead of finding the perfect solutions to their writing problems, they become blocked. Nothing comes. The creative flow dries up. This approach to writing is hard to change because writing behaviors have been developed gradually though the years. It might be some consolation to know that if you've gone through a careful planning stage these problems are less likely to occur. But if they do occur, there are ways to modify your behavior.

A piece of writing is something like a piece of clay. You can keep working on it until it gets too dry or until you fire it in a kiln. One sure way for it to dry out is to worry too long over things that can be fixed later. *The most important key to success in this early stage is to get the shape of your ideas on paper.* If you come to a word you aren't sure how to spell or aren't sure is the one that conveys the exact shade of meaning you want, make yourself a note in the margin: For example, use "sp?" or "word?" to remind yourself to come back later. If you have two possible words or even sentences in mind, write down both of them and leave yourself a note to come back later. Leave your dictionary or thesaurus closed on your desk. You're on a roll; let your ideas flow. What you most want to avoid is getting hung up—especially in the first few paragraphs.

Handling Blocks

Sometimes, however, the ideas just stop. Have faith. There are ways to get them going again. You might simply want *consciously to relax,* stare out the window, and let your subconscious mind do some work. Anne Tyler makes this comment on inspiration: "While I was painting the downstairs hall I thought of a novel to write." (Sometimes if you get too distracted by what's going on elsewhere, you have to refocus your attention on your paper. But, surprisingly, these pauses often lead to new ideas.) One professor we know meditates to get his ideas flowing again. Another begins a household chore.

If relaxing doesn't work, then attack the problem. You are already familiar with a variety of techniques. Brainstorming and freewriting can be used during this part of the writing process as well as during prewriting. Or try asking yourself some questions—and writing the answers down:

- What do I *know* that I want to include in the rest of the paper?

- Why am I stuck now? (It might be because the music's too loud, because you're hungry or tired, because you only have 15 minutes left before your favorite soap is on.)

- What ideas can I get from what I've written already?

Annotating

The last question suggests another way out of your block. Reread your original thesis and your statement of purpose and audience. Then read what you've written so far. As soon as you've done this, make some notes in the margin or on another sheet of paper. Write down quickly what comes to mind. Let the creative part of your mind play freely. *One warning:* Don't read what you've written so far with a critical eye. You are not looking for mistakes. At this point, you're more like an explorer looking for signs to predict what adventures lie ahead.

With a little luck the notes you take should suggest some new directions. If they don't, then it is time for a break, time to let your ideas incubate. Take a walk, a nap, a shower. Some writers consider this kind of pause a natural part of the writing process. While you're taking this break, your unconscious should help you work on your problem. Come back to the paper when you're fresh and when you have an extended period of time to devote to writing.

If your pause, conversely, is not due to a lack of ideas but rather to *new* ideas interfering in your writing, then you have an easier solution. Take a minute to write your new ideas in the margin so you don't forget them. Don't count on your memory; too many good ideas slip away between conception and application. Don't hesitate to include these new ideas; some of the best ideas appear while you're writing rather than during the planning stages. Writing is discovery. In other words, be prepared to invent (look for new ideas) at any time during the writing process.

Arranging Ideas for the First Draft

As you've learned from the discussion of the shaping process, every piece of writing starts to assume a shape from the moment you begin thinking about a topic or doing some prewriting on it. Often, through extensive prewriting, you discover what shape you want your writing to take. As you gather your ideas, and determine which fit together, which belong in the same categories, you begin to discover that presenting them in a certain order might make sense to your readers. The purposes of a first draft, then, are to get your ideas down on paper to help you clarify the focus of the essay for yourself and to discover an order you think will help readers understand your message and purpose. The focus and order may be changed in subsequent drafts, of course, but you must have a first draft before your writing can benefit from revision.

You can also consider the first draft a process of finding the relationships among the ideas you have generated in prewriting and of arranging these ideas in a coherent way. What you have to say, why you are saying it, and to whom you are saying it usually determine the form of your writing; these same considerations should also help determine the arrangement of the ideas you present.

No matter which path you take to arrive at this point in writing the first draft, your working thesis, your statement of purpose, and your sense of audience serve as guides. Keep them in front of you and refer to them frequently while writing. Should you have a question about the appropriateness of the direction your writing is taking, check your progress against these guides. Sometimes you will change directions; sometimes you will modify your guides.

Drafting from the Working Thesis

Instead of plunging through the first draft with no specific arrangement in mind, you may decide to plan or organize this first draft by asking yourself questions about the thesis from which you are working. As an illustration, reconsider this thesis developed earlier in the text (p. 77–79):

> Although Hyde Park has problems similar to those of other urban areas, the charm of its restored Victorian houses, its tree-lined boulevards, and its variety of life styles make this neighborhood one of the most livable in the city.

What questions can you ask about this thesis that will lead you to a tentative arrangement of ideas? (Remember that *everything* until the final, edited draft is tentative.) Try this question: *What points must I establish to convince my reader that my thesis is true?*

To answer it, examine the thesis to see what claims it makes. They are:

- that Hyde Park has urban problems;
- that it has charming, restored, Victorian houses;
- that it has tree-lined boulevards;
- that it has a variety of life styles; and,

- that the problems don't seem so severe when the amenities are considered.

If you review the claims, you have a list of the points that need to be established for the reader to understand how you reached your conclusion. Your next task could be determining either how to establish those points or how best to arrange them to reach the reader most effectively. Notice that the wording of the thesis suggests one possible arrangement. This arrangement could be effective because you move from background material and from a belief which you do not hold (that the neighborhood is plagued by problems) toward the real subject of your paper (Hyde Park) and the belief that you do hold (it's a good place to live).

There are alternatives. You could begin with a delightful description of the neighborhood, introduce the urban problems to show that you're aware that not everyone might see it that way, then proceed by showing how the good points outweigh the bad. If you chose this approach, you might feel the need to minimize the extent of the problems. Both approaches arrive at the same conclusion.

Both these approaches assume an author who probably lives in Hyde Park and who wants to show the neighborhood off at its best (or a realtor with extensive holdings in the neighborhood). With a different audience—an urban developer, for example—and a different author—an urban analyst hired by the developer—the writing resulting from the analyst's research would be quite different from either of the other two approaches. More details about the nature of the problems, housing costs, tax structure, etc., would be included. The arrangement, however, could follow either of the two approaches suggested above.

As you develop your working thesis into a thesis statement, list your points in the order you plan to address them in the paper; that is the order the reader expects. If the order in your working thesis doesn't seem logical, change it.

Your first question, then, when you draft from a working thesis is: *What points must I establish to make the audience understand my point of view and the reasoning behind my conclusion?* The second question is: *How can I arrange these points to best accomplish my purposes?*

Drafting from an Outline

Closely allied to drafting from a working thesis is drafting from an outline. Here, too, you need to determine which points must be established for the reader to understand your position. To determine those points you have to answer the two questions listed above. But outlining *may* go further toward helping you arrange your ideas, for, in order to make an outline, you need to glean from the information generated through prewriting those details that can help you support each point.

A point is supported by examples and illustrations, by explaining and elaborating. These supporting details may be gathered from the prewriting material or may be generated and inserted as the writer completes the outline. The visual representation of your points in an outline often suggests patterns of arrangement as well.

Because an outline contains much detailed information, because it is a precise plan of the order in which points and supporting material are to be presented, it may reveal early on any places where your argument is weak. This outline, too, is tentative, possibly requiring additions, deletions, substitutions, new combinations, and rearrangements.

Here's a sample outline of the Hyde Park thesis:

```
              LOVE THY NEIGHBOR(HOOD)

          Although Hyde Park has problems similar to
     those of other urban areas, the charm of its restored
     Victorian houses, its tree-lined boulevards, and its
     variety of life styles make this neighborhood one of
     the most livable in the city.

       I. Urban problems
          A. Crime
          B. Traffic
          C. Density
          D. Trash
      II. Restored Victorian homes
          A. Architecturally interesting
          B. Historically significant
          C. Economically affordable
     III. Boulevards
          A. Old parkways lined with trees
          B. Shade
          C. Sidewalks
      IV. Life Styles
          A. Occupations
          B. Family status
          C. Entertainment interests
```

After completing an outline, writing the first draft is a matter of establishing the importance and validity of each point, then establishing the relationships between the parts of your paper and their collective relationship to the thesis. The outline is a guide designed to be used with the thesis statement, the statement of purpose, and the audience analysis. [*Note:* Sometimes an outline can be made after the first draft as a step in revision. If you make an outline of your first draft, you can see the parts of your paper more clearly and decide more easily how effective your arrangement is.]

Drafting from Cut-and-Paste

Both drafting from the thesis and from an outline rely on the author's ability to see potential patterns after the points or claims in a thesis are isolated. For many writers, isolating points suggests one or more approaches to effective organization. Other writers, however, rely on a form of cut-and-paste to find their patterns of arrangement. From their prewriting they know their topic can be divided into parts. They approach each part as a separate writing task and write as completely as possible on each part. Then they cut-and-paste.

On a table or another sheet of paper, they arrange and rearrange the patterns until they find the one that makes the most sense. Some writers connect the parts with scotch tape; others like to use paper clips. Others use the mark-and-move feature of word processing programs to experiment with different arrangements.

Prewriting processes and the grouping and separating that follow provide most writers with several possible effective arrangements. If, however, you reach this stage and cannot perceive an acceptable order in your material, here is some generic advice:

1. Begin your paper with anything your readers must know to read the rest of your paper—definitions, history, background material, etc.

2. Establish your relationship with the readers. Are you writing as expert to nonexpert or peer to peer? Is your tone concerned, angry, or friendly; serious or humorous; formal or informal? Are you striving to be informative or persuasive?

3. Use an obvious arrangement like chronological, spatial (i.e., left to right, top to bottom) for a paper relying heavily on description, from simplest to most complex, from least important to most important, from problem to solution, from question to answer.

4. Use anything you can to get the first draft on paper. You can always rearrange later.

Drafting from Methods of Organization

We've presented several ways of writing the rough draft: working with a cut-and-paste approach, working from a preliminary thesis, working from an outline. One of these techniques may work better for you consistently than the others; one may work best for you only for certain kinds of writing tasks. As with prewriting techniques, it's best to experiment with each type so you become familiar with each one and gain enough experience to use whichever seems most effective for a particular writing assignment. In general, the more controlled approaches are more effective the longer and more complicated your piece is. You may also find that some combination of drafting techniques leads you to your best arrangement or organization of ideas.

Another drafting technique you may want to try is one in which you work from the more or less established methods of organization. This technique, as well as those mentioned above, is shaped by the material you have to present and your approach to that material. We call the following methods of organization "established" because much writing fits into these categories. In fact, any piece of writing most likely exhibits the characteristics of several of the categories at the same time.

These categories of arrangement or methods of organization appear so frequently in writing because they reflect methods by which we think, methods by which we shape our thoughts. These methods work by replicating a writer's thought processes so the audience sees not only *what* the writer believes, but also *how* she has reached that particular conclusion.

Although these methods are treated more extensively in Chapter 3, pp. 66–75, we are repeating them here because they can help you arrange ideas in your first draft. The categories are:

1. *Narration/Process*—examining events in chronological or sequential order;

2. *Description*—exploring a focal point, generally visually oriented, to direct the reader's attention;

3. *Exemplification*—detailing main points divided into subpoints, each supported by qualifications of and examples illustrating the subpoints;

4. *Cause/Effect*—presenting a point, then showing the forces that created it, or presenting a point, then showing what results from it;

5. *Comparison/Contrast*—showing, *item by item,* the similarities or differences between two or more ideas, concepts, or things;

6. *Classification*—arranging subpoints according to an abstracted general principle;

7. *Division (analysis)*—separating a larger idea into its constituent parts, based on a stated philosophy;

8. *Definition*—establishing the parameters of a point.

If, for example, you are writing a paper for other fundraisers on the successful fund-raising activities of the local repertory theater company, you could do any combination of the following:

1. Tell the story of the fund-raising activities, including the efforts of the key characters. Or give a step-by-step account of the procedures followed by the organizers, noting successes and failures.

2. Describe the activities, their purpose, their results.

3. Give examples of successful fund-raising activities.

4. Show the reasons for (causes of) your success—hard work, good planning, sheer luck—and/or the effects—better productions, higher morale, increased revenue.

5. Compare and contrast this year's efforts with last year's. Show why this year's were more successful.

6. Classify the fund-raising efforts—volunteer efforts/professional efforts, early/middle/late efforts, indirect contact efforts/direct contact efforts.

7. Analyze the efforts and their success. Divide the efforts into components—direct mailings, solicitation of businesses, grants from the local arts council, free-ticket contests, media advertising.

8. Define "successful fund-raising activities" and show how the local company's projects fit that definition, or define "traditional fund-raising activities" and show how the local efforts broadened the definition.

Some professional or experienced writers do not concentrate consciously on the arrangement of ideas. They find that the form their writing takes just appears. For these writers, a great deal of prewriting and organization takes place unconsciously; the way they think about a problem shapes the arrangement. You also may have found that for some pieces of writing, arranging and organizing presented no problem, but other pieces demanded painstaking work before you developed a satisfactory organizational scheme. That's to be expected; different writing occasions make different demands on writers.

As you begin a rough draft, look first at the material you have accumulated. Look for a method of organization, an ordering of ideas inherent in the ways you think about your material. If none appears, practice the techniques for drafting suggested in this section. By working through these techniques, you should arrive at a satisfactory form for your first draft. Although almost any piece of writing could assume any one of a number of forms, the best form links your message, your purpose, and your audience.

A Summary of Advice for Writing the First Draft

1. Start the writing process far enough before the due date so you can follow all the prewriting and writing steps.

2. Don't linger too long on small details. Like a hockey team on a power play, you should go straight to the goal, which, for you, is to get your ideas arranged on paper.

3. Use marks to indicate places where you might have a problem with words, punctuation, sentence structure, or paragraphing. You can always come back, but going forward may not be as easy.

4. Develop techniques to combat your blocks.

   • Allow moments for incubation. Let your body and mind relax so thoughts can surface. For some writers, formal meditation serves this purpose. Some even take relatively long breaks from writing.
   • Don't forget the power of brainstorming and freewriting. Often, a two-minute burst of brainstorming or freewriting can get you back on track.

5. Occasionally, during a pause, reread your original thesis and purpose.

You can change these at any time, but they act as guides to thinking through your paper while writing, and they help you keep your focus.

6. At times it's good to reread what you've written. You might get new ideas or reaffirm and strengthen your current course.

7. Take notes on all new ideas, either in the margin or on a separate sheet of paper. Don't lose good ideas.

8. Keep an open mind about revision.

You've probably noticed that the process of drafting is a very active stage in the writing process. For one thing, new ideas are constantly being generated even while you're writing your first draft. You write these down and make notes, already planning your second draft. The perceptive writer takes advantage of all this creative energy and uses it to sustain the next stage in the process.

While you're writing and generating new ideas, you're also taking some initial steps in revising—not in editing, but in revising. When we speak of revision, we're not referring to changes in grammar, spelling, punctuation, and word choice. These items are considerations for editing and—except for noting problems as you go—are dealt with *after* you have a full, complete draft. By making notes while you are writing, you are establishing a plan for your future editing. Revision, at this stage, is making those changes, however large or small, that help you keep the focus of your essay on your original idea— later you can reread and rework your draft(s) to improve the effectiveness of your presentation.

EXERCISE 4–5

For this assignment you need the rough draft for a writing assignment. Follow the method of marginal annotation suggested above. Bring this rough draft with notes, and a xeroxed copy, to class. Pair up with someone in your writing group or one of your classmates. Read your rough draft aloud as your partner follows along on the copy. Discuss your marginal notes; include your editing plans, your suggestions for the next draft, and your new ideas. Be sure to relate your discussion to your proposed thesis and your statement of audience and purpose. (It might be convenient to bring to class extra copies of these as well.)

This exercise is designed to get advice from a potential reader and to question your own thinking and planning. Take notes on what your partner says. Also, be prepared to discuss problems that you had while writing the first draft. You can learn from listening to how others have solved their problems. [*Note:* If you're one of those writers who absolutely has to write the introduction in near-final form before going on, read the next section before you begin this assignment.]

The Special Case of the Introductory Paragraph

When and What

The introductory paragraph often causes writers more problems than any other part of the writing process. It's the first paragraph which, after all, introduces the topic to be addressed, establishes the tone of the paper, and identifies the nature of the writing occasion. We suggest that if the introduction causes you problems, go on with the rest of the paper and come back to the introduction after you've finished the paper. Yes, the introduction can be written last, especially if writing it first is creating a writer's block. Instead of worrying about the introduction, just use your tentative thesis statement and your description of your purpose as guidelines. You might find it useful to copy the thesis, statement of purpose, and audience as though they were your introductory paragraph. Copying them establishes them even more firmly as your guides. (Don't forget, however, to go back and revise them.)

What makes the introductory paragraph such a special case is that it's so unpredictable. Let's examine the variables involved in producing this elusive part of a finished product:

1. Not everyone writes the introduction first. Many writers begin with only a topic or thesis statement, produce a draft, reread what they've written, then write a beginning that introduces what they already know is there. In this case the body of the paper generates the introduction (and probably the conclusion as well).

2. Some writers have to do the introduction first. They can't begin the body until the introduction is exactly as they want it. Writers like these usually do a great deal of prewriting. They are confident that they have discovered their thesis and purpose and, in general, know where they want their essays to go. In this case, the introduction generates the rest of the paper.

The way you approach the introduction might also vary from paper to paper. If you're writing on a subject you're unsure of, one you're still working through as you write, you would be more likely to do the introduction last. If the subject is one you've already worked through, then you might write the introduction first. Neither way is the "right" way; find the approach that works best for you.

In addition to when you write your introduction, there are other variables, such as what belongs in an introduction. Here are some possibilities:

1. Something to create audience interest

2. A presentation of the subject

3. A definite thesis statement

4. Something to show why your piece should be read

5. Something to establish a rapport between writer and reader

6. Something to establish the areas of disagreement between writer and reader

7. Something to establish the authority of the writer

At first this might seem to be an overly complicated list. However, stop to consider that your introduction presents your reader with the first impression of you and your ideas. You want your reader to feel that you have something important to say and that you are capable of saying it. If you don't succeed in the introduction, you are less likely to win an overall positive response—even if the rest of the paper is excellent. Consequently, your introduction deserves special care and handling.

One happy qualification: Not every introduction must contain all seven features. Some very good papers contain only one. There's no magic formula for the perfect introduction to every paper. Instead, think back to our earlier discussion about audience and purpose. Your introduction needs to promote the purpose and appeal to the audience of the piece. Simple advice, we know, but hard to follow. If you learn to become constantly aware of audience and purpose, your introductions should get better.

The Inverted Pyramid

There is a formula for writing introductions—it's not magic, however, and it's not terribly imaginative. But it can be helpful for pieces of writing you have to produce in short periods: in-class essays, exams, written proficiency tests, essays on job application forms. You may want to use it as a way to get started if you're stuck; when you revise the whole piece, you can revise the introduction as well. You may find that this formula—the inverted pyramid—works better than another type of introduction. If it suits your audience and purpose, then don't hesitate to use it.

As Figure 4–1 illustrates, the inverted pyramid introduction moves downward on the ladder of abstraction from a general statement toward a specific statement of your thesis. In the space between the general statement and the

FIGURE 4-1 The Inverted Pyramid

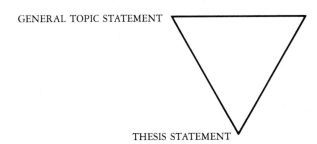

GENERAL TOPIC STATEMENT

THESIS STATEMENT

thesis you provide further restrictions of your topic or illustrations of it, or both. Here is one example of how it works.

> Over the years many changes have occurred to benefit the university. Research into the origins of these changes reveals that one incredible person played an important role. Helen Foreman Spencer invested her time, her interest, and her philanthropy to strengthen this and other institutions in the region. Mrs. Spencer, with her husband Kenneth, aided in the development of many worthwhile causes, individually as well as with the Kenneth A. and Helen F. Spencer Foundation. As we look at her contributions, we will discover that she was a woman with overwhelming concern and generosity.

Topic   Beneficial changes at the university

Specific Focus   Helen Spencer's concern and generosity led to significant contributions

The first sentence introduces the topic. The second sentence makes the topic more specific: It tells us that one person played an important role. The third and fourth sentences add even more detail: They name the benefactors and relate some of their characteristics. The last sentence completes the introduction by telling us that the essay will focus on elements of Mrs. Spencer's character. The paragraph starts from a general statement, then adds the specifics one by one until the reader has a picture complete enough to continue reading the piece.

There are some inherent dangers in the inverted pyramid formula. Look at the first paragraphs of the readings in this text. None of them follow this formula exactly. Why not? Because usually when we write we're saying something about ourselves and the way we feel about a subject; we don't want to sound just like everyone else. And readers don't want all writing to sound alike; formulaic writing can be boring and counterproductive—unless the formula serves a purpose, as in a lab report or a specialized business presentation. Although the sample follows the form correctly, it fails to be a particularly interesting introduction. In the revised version which follows, specific details add to the paragraph's interest and help establish the organization.

> In the last twenty years, the university's campus has changed considerably. Two major additions were the Spencer Chemistry Building and the Helen Foreman Spencer Theater. Research into the origin of these changes reveals that one incredible person played a major role in each. Helen Foreman Spencer invested her

time, her interest, and her philanthropy to strengthen
this and other institutions in the region. Mrs.
Spencer, with her husband Kenneth, aided in the
development of many worthwhile causes, individually as
well as through the Kenneth A. and Helen F. Spencer
Foundation. As we examine her contributions, we will
discover that she was a woman with overwhelming
concern and generosity.

Another danger of the inverted pyramid is that too often students begin too
high on the ladder of abstraction; that is, they begin with a generalization so
sweeping that it just can't lead to a statement specific enough. Many English
teachers have winced over introductions beginning something like, "Since the
beginning of time, mankind has . . . ."

If you're in a writing situation that prompts you to use the inverted pyramid,
avoid the first sentence so universally known to your readers that they don't
need to read it. Here are some sample overgeneralized opening sentences:

1. Suicide is a major problem in today's world.
2. Man has always been plagued by health problems.
3. Ever since the caveman days, finding suitable housing has been a problem.
4. Every family has its share of fights.
5. Pollution concerns us all.
6. Throughout your life you have made choices.
7. The American Dream began long ago.
8. As most teenagers know, life in high school can be difficult.
9. Television commercials are designed to make us buy products.
10. Nuclear warfare is a constant threat.
11. According to Webster, "abuse" is defined as . . .

EXERCISE 4–6

Using the same general topics, rewrite each of the sentences in the example
so they would make good first lines for potential themes. For example, number seven might be rewritten as "The spirit of today's American Dream set sail
with Columbus in 1492."

Variations on Beginnings

What, then, can you do in an introduction? Here are a few suggestions. But
remember, these suggestions may not be appropriate for every piece of writing. The introduction, like all parts of any piece of writing, must conform to

your purpose, audience, and message. And, as you can see from the following examples, introductions are frequently more than one paragraph.

1. Begin with a story, an anecdote, a little bit of narration. Most of us like a story, so a narrative closely connected to your subject may attract your readers, intriguing them so they want to learn more about your topic. The following paragraphs introduce an article on the stress and despair police officers live with.

It comes back to him in strange ways, at unexpected times. One day recently, Dean Nichols was driving down the street in Dallas, feeling very much like a normal person for the first time in years. Then he spotted the squad car in his rearview mirror.

Momentarily, he reacted as any normal person would: His adrenaline rose and his heartbeat accelerated. He ran through the litany of authorizations, stickers, and numbers that are the bane of any driver's existence—he'd forgotten to renew the plates. Should he pull over? Take the next right? Slow to a crawl and hope the squad car passed him? Speed up and try to lose it?

Dean suddenly found himself grinning. Pull over? Slow down? Speed up? What was he thinking? Those were the very actions guaranteed to arouse suspicion in even the most inexperienced cop. He knew. Only a few months before, he'd been the guy in the squad car, roaming the streets of Houston, looking for some poor fool ignorant enough to slow down at the sight of a cop in his rearview mirror. He was grateful for the chance to smile, because he was not usually amused by reminders of the five years he had spent as a cop. Most of his memories were unpleasant: bodies strewn across the Gulf Freeway; the stern eyes of a superior advising him he'd just received a complaint from some citizen Dean had thought he was helping; the putridness of the drunks on deep Main; the pungent smell of burnt gunpowder; the relentless crackle of the two-way radio.

(JIM ATKINSON, "The Ragged Edge," *Texas Monthly,* December 1982, pp. 137+.)

2. Start with a quotation that captures your topic, one that indicates the direction your essay is to take. The following introductory paragraph uses a quotation to describe the feeling created by relations between the U.S. and Russia.

"What is bewildering is the conviction—and it is becoming more and more general—that in all the perils that confront us, the direction of affairs is given over to a way of thinking that has no longer any understanding of itself. It is like being in a carriage, descending an increasingly precipitous slope, and suddenly realizing that there is no coachman on the box." The lines were written in 1854 by Fyoder Tiutchev, poet and diplomat, in a letter to his wife. The image is frightening and many seem to have experienced similar fears as the year 1983 drew to a close.

(WALTER LAQUEUR, "US-Soviet Relations," *Foreign Affairs,* Vol. 62, No. 3, 1984, pp. 561–586).

3. Begin by providing your readers with background information that helps them see your perspective. The following paragraph offers such background material while revealing the form of the essay's argument.

In recent years, a growing number of older students have begun or have returned to college. They include housewives, veterans, clerical workers, and professionals such as registered nurses, all of whom are seeking college credit and many of whom are seeking bachelor's degrees. Although there are a few special courses and programs for these students, most of them are mainstreamed at once into classes with students of traditional college age. The growing number of returning or older students in freshman composition courses, in particular, raises questions about whether they should be taught in the same way as their younger classmates.

(PATRICIA CONNORS, "Some Attitudes of Returning or Older Students of Composition," *College Composition and Communication,* October 1982, pp. 263–266.)

4. Begin with a piece of dialogue that both interests the reader and gives him or her some insight into how you are approaching your topic. In this example, the two sentences that follow the brief dialogue identify the discomfort the reader feels with the situation presented.

Years ago I called a college buddy I hadn't heard from in a while. He had divorced his first wife but had remarried. I asked him how many kids he had now.
    "Just the one."
    "One? I thought you had two."
    "Aw hell!" he snorted. "You're thinking of the ones I had with Judy. They don't count."
    A silence several seconds wide dropped between us while I pictured those two fatherless children drifting into space without a tether. How could a man discount his children's existence with the indifference of a claims adjuster?

(C. W. SMITH, "Uncle Dad," *Esquire,* March 1985, pp. 73–85.)

5. Begin with a description that both interests your reader and directly ties in with your topic. The following introductory paragraphs describe the sleepiness of a small town in Nebraska, a sleepiness that is contradicted as the town is revealed to be the home of a large number of Minuteman III Missiles.

The land around Kimball, a small farm town (pop. 3,120) and county seat in the southwestern corner of the Nebraska panhandle, is mostly treeless plain, high ground suitable for wheat and pasture. There is oil here and there, nothing like that to be found in Texas, but enough to have made a few men rich in the 1950s and to provide jobs today. Mostly, there is emptiness, space on the margin of Midwestern fertility.
    Like the land around it, Kimball has certain Western tendencies. From time to time Kimballites and their panhandle neighbors petition to secede from Nebraska (Lincoln, the capital, is more than 400 miles to the east) and join Wyoming, the ultimate cowboy state. The town has a lively honky-tonk bar life, owing in part to the presence of the oil-field workers, and there is the occasional historically preserved building—like the one that houses the Corner Bar—more suggestive of the Wild West than the Farm Belt. Originally, the town even had a Western-sounding name, Antelopeville, but in the 1880s this gave way to Kimball,

a bow to Thomas Kimball, general manager of the Union Pacific Railroad, whose barreling, seldom-stopping freights are still the principal source of local noise. For Kimball is, whatever its roots and it longings, a quiet, solid little town. The basic house is in friendly porch-and-dormers style, usually shaded by the standard deciduous mix: elms, oaks, walnuts. The churches, of which there are many, resemble the houses, as if in compliance with some smalltown-setting building code. The old residential district is bordered on the south by ranch-style homes and on the north by camps of trailers, which house the oil-field hands. Downtown boasts a Rexall, a Ben Franklin, and a single stoplight.

To drive into town from any direction, however, is to come to understand that Kimball is a very out-of-the-ordinary place. Along the farm roads and the interstate you see, from time to time, fenced-off areas of an acre or so that look at once very familiar and like nothing in particular—a few light poles, some antennae, a big slab of concrete on rails. These areas might have something to do with the phone company or a public utility. But they don't. Since 1964, the land surrounding Kimball has held powerful nuclear weapons. Two hundred Minuteman III rockets, the most advanced land-based nuclear missiles in the country's arsenal, are buried around Kimball at six-mile intervals. These missiles represent the largest concentration of Minuteman IIIs (there are currently 550 Minuteman IIIs spread along the Western missile belt) and nearly one-fifth of all land-based nuclear weapons in the United States.

(DAVID CHAMBERLAIN, "Missile Center–USA," *Harper's Magazine,* March 1985, pp. 61–67.)

6. Start with a definition that reinforces or contradicts your readers' expectations. The definition may promote the readers' understanding of your topic or it may dispel preconceptions and identify your approach. Beginning with a dictionary definition of a word or concept is usually not a good idea. Dictionary defintions have a general application and are accessible to your readers. Furthermore, your readers want to know how *you* define your ideas; after all, your ideas and intellectual constructs form the basis for your communication or its failure.

The next introduction offers various definitions that may fit our idea of "immigrant," but, as it isolates one particular immigrant group, it builds toward a definition that differs greatly from those offered earlier.

An immigrant may be the person who wades across the Rio Grande to pick vegetables or run a sewing machine. He may be a Russian Jew driving a taxi in Manhattan. If he's Chinese, he's in a kitchen 12 hours a day until enough is saved for a restaurant.

But this stereotype doesn't fit in Monterey Park, Calif., an eight-square-mile dot surrounded on three sides by thundering ten-lane freeways (that's prime property around Los Angeles), about fifteen miles east of Rodeo Drive and on the western edge of the San Gabriel Valley. The city of 59,000 is 40 percent Asian, and about three-fourths of those are Chinese. "Little Taipei" they call it in Hong Kong and Taiwan. Over there, Monterey Park is the place to go to, a mini–international financial and commercial center, a haven for flight capital. Combined deposits at the city's banks (38 at last count), mostly small and Chinese-run, are at least $1.5 billion, which works out to $25,000 for every man, woman and child in Little Taipei. But then Chinese are big savers, and even a modestly well-off immigrant brings in $50,000. Deposits also flow in from Chinese throughout southern California who consider Monterey Park their financial center.

"At first, the Chinese that settled in Monterey Park were not businessmen," recalls Wesley Ru, a prosperous auto parts manufacturer and importer. "They were mostly PhDs and engineer types who emigrated from Taiwan or Hong Kong, professionals, good neighbors who keep to themselves, high achievers.

"Then, in the last five, seven years, Taiwan and Hong Kong businessmen started to come. First it was the real estate people, and then trading companies, heavy investors, people that come with hundreds of thousands of dollars in cash, and their first stop would be the Mercedes dealer and the second stop would be the real estate broker. This group of businessmen—entrepreneurs—were bolder, more boisterous, more demanding and sometimes even cunning."

(ANDREW TANZEV, "Little Taipei," Forbes, May 6, 1985, pp. 68–71.)

7. Begin with a statement that challenges readers' beliefs. Are trees beautiful and desirable? Most of us think so; therefore when the author of the following piece tells us they aren't, he challenges us to read on.

Bynum, N. C.—This state is too beautiful. I want it to stop. I have about 75 pine trees in my yard, and I don't want them there anymore. After being surrounded by thousands of especially lovely pine trees for two years, it's making me crazy and I long to see something flat and desolate.

(JOHN WELTER, "My Kingdom for a View," Kansas City Star, Feb. 21, 1985.)

8. Start by establishing the writer's authority. The author of the following paragraph could have established his authority by mentioning his experience or academic credentials. Instead, he does it by showing his readers that he has read the pertinent background material against which he can judge his subject.

In December 1975 *Newsweek* told us that there was a "writing crisis." By the end of the 1970s, several books told us of the sinking literary skills of our students: *The Literacy Hoax* (1978), by Paul Copperman; *What's Happening to American English?* (1978), by Arn and Charlene Tibbetts; *The Great American Writing Block* (1979), by Thomas Wheeler; *Empty Pages* (1979), by Clifton Fadiman and James Howard; and *Less than Words Can Say* (1979), by Richard Mitchell.

It was never possible to know whether or not there actually was a writing crisis in 1975, because there was no accepted national writing test (there still isn't one), and writing is extremely difficult to measure in any case. However, enough people in education and the workplace were concerned about the quality of student writing for us to assume that a problem of some magnitude must have existed. And a solution of some magnitude is now in place; it is called the National Writing Project (NWP).

(MARK GOLDBERG, "An Update on the National Writing Project," Phi Delta Kappan, January
1984, pp. 356–357.)

Some Student Samples

The following first draft introduction is dull, lifeless. It is an example of the inverted pyramid type discussed earlier, but it does not work the way an introduction should. That is, it fails to spark interest and it gives no clear indication of how the essay will proceed. Most of its sentences are overgeneralized.

> Throughout your life you have made choices. Some more difficult than others and some having powerful consequences while others may not have any. No matter what your choice is, even if it proves to be a bad one, you feel good that you exercised your freedom to make your own decision. Usually the choices you make are conscious ones and so is your motivation, but there are some choices you have never really thought about. Mom and Dad made them for you in infancy or soon thereafter. If you take pride in making your own informed choices, if you question the choices made for you, maybe you should think about what you eat.

Despite our criticism of the paper, let's remind ourselves of what the author did well. She knew that a writer approaching a hostile topic needs to be won over or kept neutral if any real attempt at persuasion can be made. She tried in this introduction to establish a point of agreement between herself and her audience: Most of her audience believe that the freedom to choose is an important part of our individuality. Her introduction counts on this primary agreement to build enough of a bond of commonality to get her readers at least to delay their potentially hasty rejection.

Her strategy shows that she understands quite a bit about the writer's relationship to the reader. Unfortunately, she neglects the reader's need to become interested in the topic and thus begins with a series of sentences so vague, impersonal, and so universally true that they don't need to be written.

In a different paper, one written to teachers to encourage them to expand their definition of the idea of learning, this same student wrote the following introduction:

> I don't want to tell you how to do your job; too many people already have. I will, however, tell you how one teacher I had did his job, unconventionally, but effectively.

If we were to ask you which paper came earlier in the semester, you would probably guess the first one. Unfortunately it's the other way around. Learning to write more effectively is not a smooth steady progression from writing which is less good to writing which is good. Every assignment presents a new challenge, demands different thinking skills (see pp. 66–76), and calls for different writing strategies. Occasionally the topic itself is one that defies you to use your new talents. Such is the case with the first example. The student who wrote this introduction was generally writing good papers, but this particular paper caused her a great deal of trouble. She knew her classmates were not going to be sympathetic to a paper on vegetarianism, so she avoided the issue and tried to work herself up to the main point gradually.

Her second introduction, however, is much better. Once again she sees the need to establish a bond between herself and her audience. This time, however, her strategy is more effective. When she tells her teacher audience that too many people are telling teachers how to do their jobs, she strikes a responsive chord and helps guarantee that the initial part of her audience's reading will be friendly. Furthermore, she conveys her general subject matter and her attitude about it. Notice that she doesn't give a complete thesis statement or a detailed description of the subject. In this case, she knows that she has time for that later. (The full text of this essay is presented on p. 135.)

You can see that the possibilities for introductory paragraphs are myriad. No type is intrinsically better than the others; no type automatically guarantees your readers' acceptance of and interest in what follows. In constructing an introductory paragraph, as in constructing a thesis or an entire essay, you must consider purpose, audience, message, and forum, and then experiment with and eventually choose among options.

As you become more aware of your options and gain greater experience with forms and types of introductions, you become better able to make decisions that increase your effectiveness as a writer.

Exercise 4–7 gives you an opportunity to decide what constitutes a good—that is, an effective—introductory paragraph. Your revisions of the sample introductions cannot be right or wrong; they can only be more or less effective.

EXERCISE 4–7

Each of the following introductions contains the basic idea for developing an essay. Unfortunately, each of them also fails to take into account that a real person is going to be reading and responding to content, style, presentation, and mechanics.

A. Discuss what works about each of the following introductions. Use specific examples and refer to audience, purpose, and forum.

B. On the basis of the introduction, discuss what you think comes next in the paper. Compare your answers to those of your classmates. What accounts for the differences? Decide which of your versions would make the best essays. Why?

C. Rewrite each of the introductions using the advice we gave on writing introductions. Select a type or combination of types you think would be better suited to the audience, purpose, message, and forum.

D. In groups or as a class, read aloud the revised introductions and discuss their effectiveness.

1. **Audience:**   High school and college students
   Purpose: To persuade audience that part-time job is a good idea
   Forum: High school or college newspaper

There are many key advantages to a part-time job that are both highly educational and rewarding to the students' well-being. It is highly recommended, therefore, that the high school students take on part-time jobs while attending school. A part-time position is a way in which to gain extra spending money as well as a way to organize one's time. Its value, however, arises as an experience that teaches a student the values of establishing priorities and responsibilities. A job at this particular time may also help lead to a career in the future.

2. **Audience:**   Consumers
   Purpose: To make consumers wary of commercial jingles
   Forum: Magazine for general, nonprofessional readers

Music is defined by Webster as ''the art and science of combining vocal and or instrumental sounds or tones in varying melody, harmony, rhythm, and timbre, especially so as to form structurally complete and emotionally expressive compositions.'' If you were to add—to sell a product—you would have a commercial jingle.

I read an article the other day of parents complaining about the bad influence some songs could have on their children. They wanted to stop these songs from being broadcast on the radio. It makes me wonder what these parents think of commercials. Commercials are an influence on everyone's lives everyday. Commercials can make children want a new toy, teenagers want designer clothes, dad want a new car, and mom want the new perfume.

3. **Audience:**   Adults
   Purpose: To increase tolerance for content of song lyrics
   Forum: Any magazine read by adults who might be worried about lyrics

Drugs, alcohol, and sexual persuasion. This all seems so stereotypical of rock and roll. Why not? Since the 1950s when Elvis thrust his pelvis around, that's been the

story of rock and roll. Even today teens go to rock
concerts to see their famed band members jumping around on
stage advocating in their lyrics the use of marijuana.
They say, ''It sounds so good when you're high.'' Parents
are standing by quietly, listening to the words of their
teens' favorite songs. Pink Floyd sings about cocaine—how
it makes the user numb, no pain. What does this suggest to
a teen? That when life gets painful, cocaine is just
around the corner to take the pain away. It all sounds so
attractive. This celebration of drugs teaches, or at least
gives teens the idea, that coping with life by using drugs
is acceptable. To some this seems like nonsense, but there
are others who take this advice seriously. To them it
seems simple—not so complex.

4. **Audience:**   Teenagers who are considering becoming wait-
resses
   Purpose: To prepare them for the various traumas sure to
come
   Forum: High school newspaper

    Drunken men and anxious women who look for delight,
this is my story. I walked in with my best friend Tracy
for the ''Big'' job interview. My first job . . . I didn't
care what I had to do as long as I made the money. Perkins
was the name and waitressing was the game, and what a game
to play.

5. **Audience:**   Professor
   Purpose: To show understanding of the civil rights
issues involved in a court case
   Forum: Political science course paper

    As in George Orwell's novel *1984*, ''Big Brother is
watching you.'' How much control does the government have
over people's lives? The Federal Government filed suit to
force a hospital to turn over the medical records of an
11-day-old baby girl whose parents opposed surgery for her
severe birth defects.

EXERCISE 4–8

Now try writing an introductory paragraph of your own for each of the following situations.

1. **Audience:**   Parents of elementary school children in urban
area

| | Purpose: | To discuss advantages of extracurricular sports for this age group |
| | Forum: | Article in school district's monthly newsletter |

2. Audience: University's student government association
   Purpose: To congratulate members for their work in organizing a successful May Day fundraiser
   Forum: Formal letter

3. Audience: Teenage readers of a popular magazine
   Purpose: To report on the increasing number of teenage suicides, explore causes and solutions
   Forum: Article in a general-interest magazine

The Special Case of the Concluding Paragraph

Writing the Conclusion

The ending of a paper may also present writers with special problems. The most important task for an ending is to give the reader a sense of closure, a sense that the subject under discussion has been satisfactorily treated and properly concluded. The conclusion is the author's last chance to ensure that readers have understood, the last chance to appeal to the readers for action, agreement, or understanding.

Furthermore, the conclusion responds to the human need for a sense of closure. Most people are uncomfortable without this sense; for example, when friendships dissolve or fade, we try to find reasons for their dissolution. Indeed, many of our social customs have been derived, at least in part, from our need for a sense of closure—farewell and retirement parties, award banquets, funerals, graduations.

Readers also expect closure from writing. Closure can be achieved in several ways. A long or complicated piece may provide closure by restating major points. An argument may provide closure by strongly reiterating its major point—its assertion—or by calling for some action from the reader. Other types of writing may make predictions based on the evidence presented earlier in the paper. And others might end by referring to some information, a situation, or an anecdote first presented in the introductory paragraph(s). Another piece of writing may end with a quotation or dialogue that reinforces its thesis; it could also end by "re-viewing" the thesis in light of material presented in the body of the paper. In other words, there is no one clear formula for ending a piece of writing. Instead, the writer can only ask, "Does my conclusion work toward accomplishing my purposes?"

Before we examine some sample endings, we need to offer some cautions. Some endings don't work very well.

Ineffective Endings

1. Dissolving into general statements.

After building the momentum of your essay from a lively and specific introduction through the use of well-connected and well-supported major points, don't suddenly leap to broad generalizations. (See "The Abstraction Ladder," p. 39.) Don't make your concluding comments so general that they could be tacked to the end of any essay on the same topic.

2. Claiming to have found the ultimately workable solution or the completely defensible position.

After acknowledging opposing views or presenting sufficient support for your narrowed thesis, don't conclude by suddenly claiming that your position is the only correct one. Remember that in the conclusion, you are still attempting to engage your readers, not to alienate them. So maintain the voice of reason.

3. Raising additional or new issues.

The conclusion is no place to bring up a new point; new points demand new evidence and new support. Be careful to place all points and evidence in the body of the paper; the conclusion then brings these points together.

Variations on Endings

The following examples illustrate some of the kinds of conclusions which are generally effective. The final indication of effectiveness, of course, is your audience's response to your presentation. We've separated the conclusions into categories., so you can examine isolated approaches at work. Remember that conclusions frequently incorporate more than one approach.

1. Present a dialogue reinforcing the thesis.

The following paragraphs conclude C. W. Smith's "Uncle Dad," an article about divorced fathers. (The article's introductory paragraphs appear earlier in the text, p. 107.) In the article, Smith explores the pain that separation from their children may cause fathers and their attempts to ease this pain. He then moves to an explanation of the problems caused by his own divorce. In the conclusion he recounts a brief dialogue with his daughter that underscores the point that a father can never fully make up for the trauma of divorce.

> She gave that [picture] to me. The inscription reads, "To Dad, a very special person who helped me through a lot of hard times. I love you."

As proud as I am for having earned those words, and as much as I'd like to end on that upbeat note, the truth is that no trauma is altogether erasable. The other night Nicole and I were talking about her future as an adult; she couldn't decide between being an artist or a psychologist. Well, there's your love life to consider, too, I said. "Oh, I think I'll just live with somebody," she said. "I don't think I'll get married." Why not? "Because then I might have kids and just get divorced."

—C. W. SMITH

2. Recommend a course of action.

This type of conclusion is suitable for several types of essays. The following paragraph concludes a student's essay about Epperson House, a mansion on the University of Missouri—Kansas City (UMKC) campus purported to be the home of various ghosts and spirits. This whimsical conclusion is in keeping with the writer's account of the history of the mansion, but also addresses the forlorn nature of that history.

> I propose that UMKC turn Epperson House into a School for Occult Studies. With an in-house ghost, this seems a perfect opportunity to study the spirits. Maybe we could offer a B.A. in ghosts. Maybe even a Master's and a Ph.D. If our program were good enough, perhaps we could attract ghosts from all over the country. Surely the lonely spirit of Epperson House could use some company.
>
> —Jeri Hile

3. Ask your reader to share a belief.

Here is the conclusion of another student's paper. The paper examines, largely through exemplification, the changes in mission and life style that religious orders have experienced. Embracing these changes, the writer calls for others to accept and embrace them as well.

> Time does bring changes and changes, although often painful, may be life-producing. Religions have been called to change in the last fifteen years in order that they may better serve the needs of the Church and the needs of the day. The call to change is a call to life or death. Let's choose life and know the celebration that is sure to follow.
>
> —Mary Ljungdahl, C.S.J.

4. Use a quotation that illustrates your thesis.

Rachel Carson, marine biologist and science writer, argues against the increasing use of chemical pollutants in "The Obligation to Endure." The piece ends with a quotation. Notice that a context is built before the quotation; notice, too, that this conclusion contains a call to action.

> There is still very limited awareness of the nature of the threat. This is an era of specialists, each of whom sees his own problem and is unaware of or intolerant of the larger frame into which the right to make a dollar at whatever cost is seldom challenged. When the public protests, confronted with some obvious evidence of damaging results of pesticide applications, it is fed little tranquilizing pills of half truth. We urgently need an end to these false assurances, to the sugar coating of unpalatable facts. It is the public that is being asked to assume the risks that the insect controllers calculate. The public must decide whether it wishes to continue on the present road, and it can do so only when in full possession of the facts. In the words of Jean Rostand, "The obligation to endure gives us the right to know."
>
> —RACHEL CARSON

5. Make a prediction or forecast.

After examining the attitudes that often lead to divorce, the student writer of the next conclusion predicts that he and his fiancée will be able to stay married because they are devoted to making it work and are aware of the attitudes that could endanger their upcoming marriage.

```
        Saying these things requires courage on my part.
As I mentioned earlier, I have just gotten engaged. I
will be married next year. The statistics say that I
will be divorced by 1995 and remarried by 1998. My
wife-to-be and I, however, are of the opinion that the
statistics will not be true in our case. We're both
stubborn, in love, and don't need that tax break. We
might be an endangered species, but as Noah could tell
you, ''it only takes two, my friend, it only takes two
. . .''
```

> —David E. Long

6. Restate or summarize earlier points.

This type of conclusion usually works best if the paper has presented an involved argument or if its major purpose is to convey specific information. In either of these cases the audience may need a reminder, the reinforcement that a restatement or summary provides. The following paragraph concludes a paper comparing Socrates' beliefs about immortality as given in one work to modern Catholic beliefs about immortality. The major points made in the body of the paper are restated in the conclusion.

> Outwardly, there seems to be an insurmountable
> gap between Socratic and Catholic beliefs in the
> immortality of the soul. However, on closer
> examination, one finds fewer differences. First,
> Socrates preceded Jesus. Second, polytheism was
> prevalent during Socrates' lifetime. Finally, the most
> important similarity is their underlying belief that
> if one lived a good, just, and pure life, one should
> be rewarded.

—H. Lee Cronister III

7. Return to the opening scene or the introduction.

This type of conclusion works especially well if the paper began with an anecdote or some bit of narration. The following is the conclusion to a piece whose introduction was presented earlier. The last three paragraphs return to the story which opened the article.

> None of these changes would be meaningful, though, unless the public rethinks its attitudes toward the police. It's easy enough blithely to assume that everyone still supports the local police. But the sad fact is that civic responsibility has become little more than an empty slogan, associated with right-wing politics, the gun lobby, and other groups many citizens find distasteful. Nothing could be sillier; if there is one public concern citizens *can* agree on, it is the need for safe streets and the need for a dedicated, well-trained police force to make them that way. Those are not ideological issues. They are a matter of common sense. There is a single lesson to be learned from the crisis currently afflicting our police forces: Crime is not the police's problem alone. It's ours, too.
>
> After Dean Nichols resigned, he had another sleepless night or two. His first couple of months as a civilian went well. His progress at the Criswell Center for Biblical Studies in Dallas was steady, and he was able to support his family modestly with part-time work as a security consultant. But then the economy caught up with him; fewer and fewer companies wanted to pay for his services. He had to face the question squarely: Should he go back to police work to support his family?
>
> He didn't know. He certainly couldn't go back into a big-city police department, but he'd heard about an opening on a small suburban force near Dallas. Maybe he could handle that. The hours and pay would be good, the danger minimal.
>
> The drive to the Balch Springs Police Department was long, so he had a chance to ponder his problem further that morning. Suddenly he knew the answer. He couldn't do it. He'd dig ditches if he had to, or sell guns. He pulled off to the side of the road, made a U-turn, and drove back to Dallas. Anything would be better than living on the Ragged Edge.

(JIM ATKINSON, "The Ragged Edge," *Texas Monthly,* December 1982)

EXERCISE 4–9

Analyze the concluding paragraph or paragraphs of an essay in this text. Categorize it if you can—try to determine which of the conclusion techniques it uses. Then write a short paragraph evaluating its effectiveness. Does it provide you with a sense of closure?

EXERCISE 4–10

Write at least two conclusions for the paper on which you are now working. (Or choose an earlier paper.) Consciously try to write each of the two conclusions to conform to the types discussed. Your familiarity with the possibilities increases the likelihood that you can use the techniques effectively. Neither the introduction nor the conclusion needs to be perfect after the first draft. Frequently the process of rethinking and revising changes the body of a paper so much that the original introduction and conclusion must be rewritten. In these cases the introductions and conclusions are often the last parts of the paper to be finished. (See Chapters 5 and 6 on revision.)

This chapter has dealt with the tasks that concern you as you move through the process of shaping a piece of writing. Defining your purpose and audience helps direct this shaping; reviewing your prewriting and reconsidering your thesis helps you align preliminary intentions with those that develop as you draft.

Most likely you have been revising as you draft—changing a word, adding an example, rearranging sentences. The next chapter continues the shaping process, offering more specific ways to revise and refine your writing to make it achieve your purpose.

A Pause for Reflection

By now you've had practice with some of the approaches to prewriting and have finished a draft of your first essay. Most of the approaches you used were probably new to you and required you to approach writing in ways that you've never tried before. Because you've been writing for years, you've already established a definite set of writing behaviors, patterns you follow when faced with a writing task. We've asked you to examine these patterns and modify them to some degree—no easy job. You've had to break a number of very old habits.

Put simply, a brief introduction to new approaches and their application to the writing of one essay is not enough to ensure that these approaches become part of the way you write and the way you think about writing. You'll need to continue experimenting and practicing the new techniques and those to be brought out in upcoming chapters. Since this experimentation and practice takes time, we don't want to introduce any new approaches or techniques for a while. Instead, we'd like you to write your next paper, or even your next two papers, using the methods we've already suggested. We'd also like you to try them out in your other classes. Writing, after all, is not a skill created by English teachers to be taught and used only in English classes; rather, writing is part of your overall intellectual development.

EXERCISE 4–11

Before you begin your next paper, reflect on the experiences you had using these new approaches on your last theme. Write a brief, informal description of how you wrote your last paper. How did it feel to use the new techniques? Be sure to describe any problems or difficulties you had in the process. Bring this description to class for discussion.

EXERCISE 4–12

Reread the description of your writing process that you wrote earlier (see p. 6) How does that description differ from the one you wrote for Exercise 4–11? Write a brief, informal discussion of the differences between the two processes. Feel free to include your preferences, your doubts, and any modifications you've made or think should be made.

EXERCISE 4–13

Write a set of goals for yourself for the remainder of this class. Include how you would like to modify your writing behaviors and explain why. For example, you might want to quit writing while you're watching television because you become distracted. Or you might want to start keeping a journal so you have a record of this year and because you like the kind of writing practice a journal affords. Your list can also include areas of your finished product which you'd like to improve: grammar, paragraphing, logic, increased support, better ideas. Just make sure your list includes items you want to improve or modify— not just those that have been marked wrong on previous papers or those you think your instructor would like to see. This list is designed to help you derive the greatest possible benefit from the class. Keep the list in your writing folder so you can return to it periodically throughout the course.

EXERCISE 4–14

Write a letter to the imagined audience of one of the essays you have written for this class (or any other class, as long as the audience wasn't the teacher). Focus on how you wanted the reader to respond. Explain why you wanted to generate those particular responses and what you've done specifically to accomplish your goals.

CHAPTER FIVE

Revision: Early Stages

*And so I mark out these old words and write again. . . .
And again. All the while knowing that deeper meaning
will rise to the surface like the form in a piece of stone, or
the grain of a polished wood, if I have faith in this
knowledge inside me. If I keep working. And over and
over the words do not fail me. Over and over I come to a
clarifying end. A circle is made.—Susan Griffin*

Although we have titled this section "Revision," you know by now that writers revise during all stages of their writing. Many writers begin revising their original thoughts even before they put pen to paper or fingers to keyboard. They are constantly rethinking and replanning. During the initial stages of prewriting, ideas change shape, change direction, and sometimes even disappear—judged unworthy, inappropriate, or perhaps unworkable.

After the first draft, however, revision becomes the writer's main task. For many writers, this stage is the least enjoyable part of writing. Perhaps you share this feeling. You've waded through all the reluctance and insecurity of getting started. You've done your research, your reading, your prewriting. You've succeeded in sitting down and putting pen to paper for an extended period. You've written a first draft from that initial capital letter to the final period. You're relieved; you feel, quite rightly, as though you've finished a great task. Then that sinking feeling hits. You're not finished. You still have to take care of those notes you've written to yourself in the margin. You still have to deal with those checks and question marks. Even more important, you need to reread your work to make sure it says what you want it to say (see Chapter 4, pp. 91–92).

You probably don't want to do all this work after writing a complete draft. You want the process to be finished and ready to turn in. You might even resent having to do more. But writers who want to produce good work—and produce it within the time constraints they're given— know that, unless they rewrite, they cannot accomplish this goal; therefore revision becomes an integral part of their writing processes.

But note: *Revision is something you choose to do.* You have to prewrite—

even if it's just for a few seconds before you write or during a pause while you are writing. You have to write to get your words down on paper. But you don't have to revise. You can turn the first draft in to your teacher, your boss, your editor. "After all," you might say, "when I write letters I rarely revise, and very often the first draft I write has some of my most lively and entertaining prose in it. Why shouldn't I, then, submit the first draft of other kinds of writing?"

That's basically a question you have to answer for yourself. In general, however, the answer lies in your audience's expectations. The more they have in common with you, the more forgiving and tolerant your audience tends to be. Audiences of professionals tend to expect a high level of professionalism in materials written for them. You have to determine when your writing is polished enough to accomplish its purposes.

We've reached another one of those points which tests your dedication. Learning how to revise your papers more efficiently and more effectively helps you become a better writer. Some writers maintain that writing is actually 90 percent rewriting.

This chapter offers an overview of the processes inherent in revision and some practical advice on and examples of how you can make these processes your own. No one method guarantees to make you The Great Reviser. On the contrary, as we emphasized earlier, all writers shape their own versions of the writing process. Your challenge remains to discover what works for you and then to integrate it into your own writing process.

The Role of Reading

Almost without exception, good revisers are good readers. Writers with a good background in reading have the option of using suggestions from other authors. They can use ideas, sentence patterns, literary devices, and other elements of good writing found in books and articles, and modify them. Yes, writers do borrow ideas from one another. (For the difference between "influence" and "plagiarism" see Chapter 9.) This reading background affects each stage of the writing process. Writers with good reading backgrounds generate more ideas during prewriting; they come up with varied strategies during writing; they develop more wide-ranging options during revision; and they adhere to more specific standards during editing.

Good writers must also learn to become good readers of their own writing. This isn't easy. Very often after writing a first draft, a writer develops a strong sense of ownership and an understandable feeling of pride in the accomplishment of getting so many words on the same topic down on paper. Learning to become a surgeon—to operate on your own words, sentences, paragraphs, and ideas—demands a great deal of courage and confidence. On the other hand, rereading and revising can spare you a great deal of embarrassment.

The Nature of Revision

Fortunately, the actual ways of revising can be divided into five neat categories. Unfortunately, many possibilities exist within each category when you are in the process of revising. Before we tell you what we think the categories are, let's see what you can come up with on your own.

EXERCISE 5–1

Take out your last paper. Compare the rough drafts with the final copy. Describe on paper, as clearly as you can, any changes you made. Can you see any general categories beginning to emerge? Were there certain kinds of revisions that you made consistently? Try to label the categories into which these revisions fit. Compare your results with your classmates' and see if you can reach any consensus on categorizing the types of revising you do.

Doing Exercise 5–1 probably helped you discover that the revisions on your last paper shared many features. In general, we revise for only a few reasons: to make our ideas clearer (thesis), to explain what we've said in greater detail (development), to change our emphasis (development, organization, style), to make our ideas easier to follow (organization, transition), and finally, to establish correctness (editing). There are five basic operations we perform on our papers when we revise: *addition, deletion, substitution, combination, rearrangement.* There are also only four levels of revision beginning with the overall *theme* and moving through the *paragraph,* the *sentence,* and the *word.* Our aim in this text is to help you improve in an area you are already familiar with; you are already a reviser—we hope to help you become a better one.

Before you began a first draft, we suggested that you review your prewriting by rereading it to get a picture of the whole subject under examination. Similarly, your first task after writing the first draft is to reread it, but don't do it immediately unless you feel especially creative. Sometimes it's better to set the first draft aside for a while—a few hours, or even a day if you have time. When you come back to it, your sense of ownership won't be quite so strong. And in the interim, new ideas and suggestions for changes might come to you. This new influx of ideas, an extension of prewriting, is another example of the power of incubation and reflection.

Theme Revision

From First Draft to Response

When you reread the first draft, don't look for the small errors and problems— you'll have time for that later. Read instead for the overall impression your paper gives you. Decide what you like about the paper and what worries you about it. Respond to its content and overall shape. Most of all, pay attention to what the paper is really saying. Immediately after you finish rereading, sit down and write a quick response to it. Answer these questions:

1. What main ideas do you remember?
2. What do you think the content of the paper accomplishes for your reader?
3. Where were you most pleased?
4. Where were you least pleased?
5. What do you think needs to be changed?

Very often this immediate response to a piece of writing helps you step outside your role of writer and allows you to respond more successfully in the role of an active reader. From this immediate initial response you can get a general sense of what your paper accomplishes and what is needed to make it even more effective.

From Response to Intention

The next, and more difficult, step is to compare your initial response with the paper itself:

- Do the main ideas you noted during the freewriting exercise correspond to the one you intended when you wrote the first draft?
- If not, is there a problem with the paper or did you discover a new idea as you were drafting?
- Do you need to change the idea in the paper or the way it is presented to make it clearer?
- Does the paper accomplish what you intended?
- If not, where does it go wrong and how can you modify it to reach your original goal?
- What did you do well in the sections of the paper that pleased you most?
- How can you bolster the weaker sections?
- What preliminary ideas do you have about the changes that need to be made?

These questions are designed to help you focus your attention on theme-level revision, the most critical stage of revision. You can answer these questions in your head—experienced writers often do—but written answers help students more. You can also answer the questions by freewriting. You could write a formal plan or a simple list of planned revisions. No matter which of these ideas best suits the way you think and write, put your ideas on paper so you won't lose them.

One possible strategy at this stage is to make notes in the margin or on another sheet of paper. You don't want to lose these initial impressions of your paper or the ideas you have about changing it. If you begin to revise and copy the paper immediately, chances are good you will lose some good ideas.

In comparing your initial response with your paper, the framework of a plan for revision should emerge. At this stage, you are particularly interested in making sure your paper says and does exactly what you want it to. (You don't need to be overly concerned about finding exactly the right phrase or word because changes you make in the overall theme might result in the deletion or modification of words and phrases you have struggled over.)

Paragraph Revision

In the following sections, we focus on your paragraphs, the building blocks for structuring your ideas. To judge the effectiveness of your paragraphs, you should consider three questions:

1. Does each paragraph serve a useful purpose related to your thesis?

2. Do your paragraphs, taken together, provide sufficient support?

3. Are your paragraphs arranged properly to accomplish your goals?

Let's discuss each of them with an eye toward developing a set of strategies to help you determine answers to these questions.

Revising Your Thesis

Does each paragraph in your essay serve a useful purpose? Throughout this text you have been urged to record a statement of your developing intentions. We have asked you to develop an awareness of your thesis, your intended audience, your purpose, and the forum through which your writing reaches its audience. This is another stage in the writing process where such a record comes in handy. If you have such a statement of intention, you can use it now to perform the first check on your paragraphs.

Put the statement beside your essay. Reread the essay, then reread your paragraphs checking each of them against the statement. There's no guarantee that you will automatically discover every inappropriate paragraph, but this technique does call attention to how the parts of your essay work together to frame your ideas.

By checking your responses to your first draft against your original statement of intention, you might discover that your thesis comes through clearly, that it's supported effectively, and that the support is organized efficiently. Then you're off and running. On the other hand, if you find that the idea presented in the draft isn't the one you started with, there are two possibilities:

One, you've discovered a new aspect of your topic in the course of writing, and your intention has changed. No problem—substitute the new intention for the early statement. You created the early statement simply as a guideline. (Note: *Reread your introduction and conclusion. They often reflect your original intention despite the rest of the paper's divergence from it. Make sure they correspond with the new direction.*)

Two, somehow you strayed from that original intention and have not discovered a new thesis, or you've created a new thesis but it fails to accomplish your purpose. Now you do have a problem. You need to ask yourself some questions: Can the original idea somehow be combined with ideas from the draft and a new thesis created? (If so, then construct a new statement of intention and review the entire paper with the new intention in mind. The process moves in circles.) Can the paper be salvaged, or should it be relegated to the ash heap? (This is a tough question, and in answering it writers frequently decide that a piece of work does not deserve to be revised. Perhaps the subject is too complex, perhaps the writing fails to reach the audience, perhaps what you've written is not worth writing. This is a painful decision for a writer, but it's better than being rejected by an audience.)

While you're doing these checks to make sure all your paragraphs focus on your thesis, you should also be asking yourself about the function of each paragraph. (If you need to review the nature of the thesis and the thesis statement, turn to pp. 46–47 in Chapter 2.) What is it designed to do? Support the argument? Provide background? Serve as a transition between two main ideas? Serve as a point of dramatic emphasis? If you can clearly see the purpose for each paragraph, you are probably on the right track and none of your paragraphs need to be *deleted.*

To check each paragraph, write a short phrase stating the paragraph's *content* and *purpose* in the margin or on a separate sheet of paper. If you were to do a check of our last paragraph, for example, you might write "content = function of paragraph; purpose = ask questions to check each paragraph's function to see if it should be retained." In rereading your draft prior to editing, you can use these phrases to check each of your sentences. At first this technique might seem unwieldy; however, before long you do this kind of checking mostly in your head. If you often have problems with organization, this technique can help you grasp your essay's overall structure and see what each part is designed to do.

EXERCISE 5–2

Map the paragraphs in the following student essay. In the margin by each paragraph, write a short phrase describing the paragraph's content and one describing its purpose.

Commercial TV Sponsors Stereotype their Audience

Advertisers would love to create a world where real men don't eat quiche and a housewife's biggest concern is the wax buildup on the kitchen floor. I found this to be true when I watched, at random, a

one-hour sample of commercial TV. This sample was
taken from Channel 41 on Friday, February 2, 1984
between the hour of 3:30—4:30 p.m. On weekdays during
this time slot, programming consists of Bugs Bunny and
Pink Panther cartoons. These cartoons are primarily
watched by kids just getting home from school.

It should come as no surprise that the
commercials that appear during this time slot cater to
this type of audience. Of the fifteen commercials I
observed during this period, seven were for children's
products and of these seven, five were advertisements
for breakfast cereals. Because this was a local
station, the rest of the commercials were promotions
for TV programs later that evening as well as some
advertisements for local businesses and mail order
houses.

The local and mail order commercials were low-
budget and did not seem to have a specific audience in
mind. It was quite clear, however, as to whom the
cereal commercials were targeted for. Children are
known to have wild imaginations. After all, one must
be able to suspend disbelief if the Pink Panther is
going to go on with his daily activities after a 500-
pound weight has been dropped on his head. The
animated characters in cereal commercials cater to
children's fantasies. Take the example of Fred
Flintstone, prominent citizen of Bedrock and proud
spokesman for Cocoa Pebbles cereal. An adult would
find it hard to believe that Fred can start his car by
moving his feet rapidly. But kids are fascinated with
Fred and his stone-age world. So when Fred says that
Cocoa Pebbles are delicious, kids believe him.

The commercials which don't have animated
spokesmen usually depict children as young, full of
life, and having a good time without getting their
clothes dirty or annoying their parents. I find it
ironic that the kids who are watching these
commercials are not out at play, but vegetating in
front of the tube. These kids would not even notice a
cereal-bearing leprechaun popping from the shrub.
Mothers always get bombarded with requests for cereals
with names that describe the character on the box but
have no description of the cereal. Who knows what is
actually inside a box of ''Trix''?

Thus, I conclude that the cereal ads that have
the greatest effect on the child's imagination are the

```
ones which sell the best. So, if a cereal advertiser
can create an appealing spokesman from a child's world
of fantasy, the cereal maker will be rich no matter
how awful the cereal tastes.
```

Revising Your Development

Do the paragraphs in your essay, taken together, provide all the facts and support needed to ensure that your audience responds the way that you want them to? If not, you'll need to revise. Perhaps you need to elaborate on a point by adding more examples or explanations. Perhaps the arrangement of ideas within a paragraph is confusing and needs reorganizing or better transitions. Perhaps the support is too vague, too general—so details need to be added. At this stage, you want to make sure that each paragraph adequately conveys its intended message.

After you know that the idea you're presenting is the one you want to get across, your focus shifts to the development of your thesis. If rereading has shown that you have provided adequate explanations, illustrations, and support for your thesis, then you're ready to move on to questions of organization. On the other hand, if the notes you've written in the margins or your written responses show weaknesses in your development, then you still have work to do before proceeding. Generally there are two kinds of weaknesses at this stage: inappropriate and inadequate development.

Inappropriate development results when the points you make fail to support your thesis. Delete any paragraphs or sentences that do not actively work to accomplish your intentions. Add details and illustrations that support and clarify the point of the paragraph for your audience.

Except for transitional paragraphs (paragraphs, often very short, which introduce the following paragraph and connect it with the preceding one) or paragraphs of emphasis, does each of your paragraphs contain adequate and appropriate reasoning and/or support? If not, what needs to be *added?* Adequate reasoning and support—explanations, illustrations, examples—help the reader follow and understand the points you make.

The following paragraph is poorly developed. As you read it, make a note of all the questions it leaves unanswered, all the claims it leaves unsubstantiated.

```
    It's silly to pay full price for clothes. You
shouldn't do it. You don't have to do it, in fact.
People who pay full price for their clothes are just
throwing money away, giving it to the big department
stores whose prices reflect a mark-up of 1000 percent.
I think that stores charge too much for clothes, so I
hardly ever shop in big department stores unless they
are having a sale.
```

How is this paragraph inadequately developed? Its major point is that people shouldn't pay the prices regularly charged by major department stores. But why not? The writer gives one fact, or what she takes for a fact—1000 percent mark-up. But the reader has no way of knowing if that piece of evidence is true. The reader has no idea of the source and no other facts are provided, so the author has no credibility; she has given the reader no good reason to believe her statements.

The paragraph repeats itself. It simply restates one idea; it does not develop it. The author implies that she knows a better way to shop, but she doesn't explain what it is. She hasn't supported her main assertion or presented a clear picture of her solution to the problem. Compare the original paragraph to the one that follows. The second version is more fully developed and gives the reader both a clear idea of the author's assertion and the evidence on which it is based.

> Two weeks ago I waltzed out of Macy's carrying my newly purchased $350 suit, newly purchased for $60. True, I can't wear the suit tomorrow because it's not heavy enough to wear in the dead of winter, but in April or May when the snow has melted I'll certainly be wearing it. And I'll be wearing it for $290 less than anyone else in town, $290 less than if I had bought it in season. Such bargains are not difficult to find if one will buy end of the season clothing or search for clearance sales. Indeed, John Franklin, the head buyer at my Macy's store, told me that women's clothing is marked up anywhere from 300 to 1000 percent; however, to clear out inventory, Macy's will occasionally discount sale items almost to wholesale prices. Shopping the sales is a good way to get more for your money and is sometimes the only way a consumer can afford what she wants.

This paragraph is better developed because it follows one course and because it provides evidence—one narrative and two examples—to support the main idea. It also omits vague statements of opinion ("Department stores charge too much for clothes") which are superfluous to the topic. The *revised,* better developed paragraph gives the reader reason to agree with the writer. It allows the reader to see the evidence behind the author's assertion.

Revising Your Organization

You know that your organization works if each of your points leads naturally to the next, if a reader isn't forced to stop and ask "What's going on here? How did I get to this point?" To avoid these questions you have two central concerns: (1) making sure paragraphs are arranged in an order that helps accomplish your purpose; and (2) making sure each paragraph's content is clearly related to the ones preceding and following and that you've included enough signposts for the reader to move smoothly within and between paragraphs.

Arrangement

Are your paragraphs arranged in an order that best accomplishes your intentions? There are some traditional arrangements for essays: From least to most important, from general ideas toward specific details (after the deductive model of thinking), from specific details toward general ideas (after the inductive model), sequential (as in the narrative or the presentation of a process), spatial (as in a description). Generally, you do not choose a method or organization first. For example, you would rarely start thinking about a topic by deciding to write an essay ordered from the least to the most important points. Rather, through your prewriting, possibilities for arrangement emerge; you then choose which method of arrangement would be best for your particular writing occasion, based on context, audience, purpose. (For a review of patterns of thinking, see pp. 66–74.)

What factors come into play as you decide on arrangement? Let's consider the possibilities inherent in one topic. After prewriting, the writer rereads the information he's gathered and determines which forms of organization the information seems to suggest.

```
Topic: Computers and personal liberty

Brainstorm:

Everyone knows your credit rating—both bad and good—
could help prevent fraud and other kinds of loss
thereby perhaps reducing certain kinds of loss—but
what about personal liberty?— Should anyone have the
right to look at my personal finances without legal
permission being GRANTED?—computers might end up
freeing us from more mundane types of tasks thereby
giving us more free time thereby increasing personal
liberty—government could keep track of whereabouts of
all citizens through use of large computer banks—
European countries already have I.D. cards—maybe you
do too with SS #s (except that no one has to legally
obtain a SS card). On the other hand, it's hard to get
normal work or go to school without one. Is the SS
card your national ID?—Might be good for the
government to know where everyone is anyway. You could
really cut down on crime by having a computer and
allowing identity checks, and America has the highest
```

```
violent crime rate of any other country.—All this
would be ok as long as you have a government dedicated
to civil liberties, but what would happen if a more
totalitarian element took over? On the other hand, if
they took over they'd do it anyway.—computerized
national records would also help medically—think
about blood and organ donors. With a computer system
you could get instantaneous matching. It could even
help with unemployment if you had a national
computerized employment registry.

Tentative thesis: Although in many ways a centralized
national computer system could significantly improve
life in America, the issue of personal liberty makes
this goal one to be pursued with great caution.
```

Although a great deal more thought and research would have to be done before turning this prewriting into a successful essay, you have enough information to discern some possible methods of arrangement:

1. The essay could begin with a discussion of all the possible advantages. These could be arranged from the least significant to the most significant, leaving a stronger impression on the reader. The issue of personal liberty could then be introduced and explored, and a conclusion drawn.

2. The essay could begin with an assertion about the importance of privacy and civil liberty and the pros and cons of each possible use could be examined. Someone in favor of a centralized system would list cons first and then refute them with pros; someone against this use of computers would begin with the advantages and then refute them with the dangers. In both these arrangements the author could either examine all the arguments on one side, then—in the same order—all the arguments on the other side. Or the author could do a point-by-point comparison. Most likely, the key arguments would still be considered last.

3. The essay could begin with the hypothesis that a national computer system was now in place and could then explore each of the hypothetical effects. Cause and effect thinking would then control the organization as well as the content. Once again, the writer would probably save the most dramatic effects for last because that's where they make a greater impact on the reader.

EXERCISE 5–3

We have given you three possible organizational focuses; there are more. Following the pattern of the three examples, write three more possible methods of organization for this essay. (Again, you might want to review briefly the modes of thinking on pp. 66–74.)

Transition

A piece of writing can be viewed as a chunk of the writer's thinking worked out on paper so that it can be shared by a reader (or reflected on by the writer). To ensure that the reader understands that chunk of thought, the careful writer provides guides, signposts that indicate the direction the thinking is taking and how each portion of it relates to the others.

These signposts are transitional devices. Relationships that exist between and among words, phrases, sentences, and paragraphs are in part clarified through the writer's reasoning and illustration. But transitional devices further clarify and direct, putting words, sentences, phrases, and paragraphs into context and proper relation for the reader.

In writing initial drafts, most likely you insert transitional devices simply because they help guide your thinking and writing. They help you identify for yourself the relationships that exist between words and ideas. They help you to organize your writing and to clarify that organization for your readers. But while revising you should pay close attention to the transitions you've provided, consciously looking for places where your reader might go astray because a relationship isn't clear enough. (This paragraph contains several transitional devices: the deliberate repetition of "They help" for emphasis and to provide connections between sentences that explain why transitions are needed; the use of "But" to signal to readers that a contrast of some sort is next. In this case, the contrast is between using transitional devices when drafting and when revising.)

Smooth transitions provide coherence and aid in organization. Before we examine several categories of transitional devices, we'd like to remind you that while revising at each of the four levels—word, sentence, paragraph, theme— you should look actively for gaps that could be filled by transitions. But you don't want to overdo them, and no one can tell you exactly how many or what kind of transitional device is most appropriate.

The best advice here is to read your paper as you expect your audience will, and then try to clarify relationships that don't seem well connected.

Indirect Transitional Devices

One way of providing transition is by repeating a key word or phrase. Often, this method also serves to emphasize points:

> Almost every aspect of medieval *Western* life was influenced by Islamic civilization. *Western* farmers imitated the techniques of irrigation developed by the Muslims and learned to grow many new plants, such as rice, citrus fruits, and peaches. *Western* merchants adopted the system of numbers and probably some forms of business partnerships. *Western* scientists, philosophers, and theologians were influenced by Islamic scholars.
>
> (MORTIMER CHAMBERS ET AL., *The Western Experience*)

You may also provide transitions by using pronouns and adjectives. Words like *it, this, that, these, those,* and *such* refer to a word or phrase used earlier.

You must be careful, though, that the antecedent of the pronoun (the word it refers to) is clear.

> In the British Museum Library today can be seen an ancient manuscript, the edges of whose pages are charred and flaked so that the endings of many lines are virtually indecipherable, if, indeed, they survive at all. Obviously, *it* not only is of extreme age but has been through harrowing vicissitudes. If *it* could speak, *its* narrative of adventures would equal in excitement those melodramatic episodes which were set down, ten centuries ago, on *its* own vellum leaves.
>
> (RICHARD ALTICK, *The Scholar Adventurers*)

One final type of indirect transitional device is the use of synonyms (words that share the same meaning) or synonymous phrases (phrases that share the same meaning):

> Long before children speak or understand language, they speak and understand a powerful *language of the face*. While working on her doctoral thesis several years ago, Denver psychologist Mary Klinnert discovered a process now known as "social referencing." Watching a session in a camera-lined laboratory-play-room, she noticed how strongly the mother's *facial expressions* influenced the baby's actions. So she invited toddlers, 12 and 18 months old, to play with scary toys like the Incredible Hulk and a remote-controlled spiderlike robot. Before making a beeline for the toy, some children hesitated and checked the mother's *face* for guidance. Klinnert had carefully trained the mothers in the *expressions* of approval or apprehension. When the mother smiled serenely, the child went ahead and played. But when the mother grimaced or showed fear, most children backed off and some cried. Not a word was required to keep the dubious infant away from uncertainty. All it took was a *convincing expression on the mother's face*. Klinnert explains: "The child learns ways of seeing the world from other people's expressions."
>
> (JEANNE MCDERMOTT, "Face to Face, It's the Expression That Bears The Message")

Direct Transitions

The other category of transitional devices is composed of words and phrases that signal a transition more directly than indirect devices do. But like indirect devices, the direct ones can also be used to show relationships between words, between and within sentences, between and within paragraphs.

The following list groups these words and phrases according to what kind of relationship they signal. It is by no means complete, but becoming familiar with it may help you include transitional expressions when they're needed to clarify a relationship or to signal your readers.

Addition or Enumeration (connects opposing items)

additionally, again, also, and, as well, besides, beyond that, equally important, finally, first (second, third, fourth), for one thing, further, furthermore, in addition, last, likewise, moreover, next, nor, now, or, similarly.

Contrast (connects opposing items)

after all, although, although this may be true, and yet, but, by contrast, despite, even though, however, in contrast, in spite of, nonetheless, nor, on the contrary, on the other hand, or, otherwise, still, though, yet.

Emphasis (emphasizes connecting items)

above all, certainly, especially, in any event, in fact, in particular, indeed, most important, surely.

Exemplification (connects item to example)

as an example, as an illustration, especially, for example, for instance, in other words, in particular, namely, that is, thus, to illustrate.

Chronological and Spatial Relationships (items related in time or space)

after a while, afterward, at last, at length, at once, briefly, by degrees, earlier, eventually, finally, first (second, third, etc.), formerly, gradually, immediately, in a short time, in the future, in the meantime, instantaneously, later, meanwhile, promptly, simultaneously, soon, subsequently, suddenly this time, until now.

above that, at this point, below that, beyond that, elsewhere, here, nearby, next to that, on the other side, outside, there, within.

Causal Relationships (items connected to show cause or effect)

accordingly, as a consequence, as a result, because, consequently, for, for this reason, hence, inevitably, necessarily, since, then, therefore, thus.

Summary (items connected to recapitulate)

as mentioned earlier, finally, in brief, in conclusion, in other words, in short, in sum.

EXERCISE 5–4

Read the following paragraph, taken from a letter, and underline each transitional device you come across. Then, as a class or in groups, discuss how the devices clarify relationships.

I've been trying to think of activities for you and Nicholas if you decide to come this June. I've enclosed a brochure about our local historical farm. Also on campus is the Recreation Building, which has a couple of swimming pools plus the usual racquetball courts; in addition, our lab school library stays open during the summer. All this is convenient, since you'll be staying at the University Inn, which is adjacent to our Student Center. In town, there is the Willow Park Zoo and the local library, which do children's programs in the summer. I think we may have activities for children on campus, too, but that information is not published yet. Farther out is Crystal Hot Springs—about 20 miles to the west—and to the east is Logan Canyon, a great place for hikes and such. Bear Lake is only 40 miles away, but it will just be thawing during early June (the water becomes semi-accessible in August).

EXERCISE 5–5

After reading the following paragraphs, list the transitional devices you see at work. Then write an analysis of how those devices function.

It ought to feel as if you are entering a new era. The building should be shiny, sleek, and low, with rounded corners and muted lighting and the soft sigh of automatic doors. But no: The rebirth of the computer age is taking place in a monstrous, red brick relic from the age of the slide rule; in its center is a three-story-high machine used to test the strength of nuclear reactor parts, and the like, by crushing them. Last spring, as the crusher was gearing up to pulverize man-sized pillars of concrete for the folks at the annual engineering open house, University of Illinois computer scientist David Kuck and his colleagues moved into the crusher's home. Amid piles of boxes and rounds of cables strewn through their new quarters, they embarked on a project they hope will change the face of computing.

Actually, it's fitting that the computer scientists and the crusher—electronic finesse and brute force—should share the Theoretical and Applied Mechanics building. For the scientific leap that Kuck's team wants to make is as far from current computing as computers are from the pulverizer. Kuck and his coworkers, as well as many other researchers in this country, want to recreate the computer.

(Susan West, "Beyond the One-Track Mind")

Sample Essays

Before we ask you to work directly with your own writing, we're going to give you some experience with pieces others have written. When you read each of the following first drafts, avoid the microscope approach, reading instead to gain an overall impression.

Paper #1: Student Draft

The Choice

Throughout your life you have made choices. Some more difficult than others and some having more powerful consequences, while others may not have any. No matter what your choice is, even if it proves to be a bad one, you feel good you exercised your freedom to make your own decision.

Usually the choices you make are conscious ones
and so is your motivation but there are some choices
you have never really thought about. Mom and dad made
them for you in infancy or soon after. If you take
pride in making your own informed choices, if you
question the choices made for you, maybe you should
think about what you eat.

Eating is a need but what you eat is a habit most
likely started by whoever fed you as an infant. You
may have consciously changed your eating habits
through dieting or cutting down on certain substances,
like salt or sugar. Most people never ponder the
choice they have between carnivorousness and
herbivorousness. You may think sitting down in a
restaurant and deciding to order fried chicken is a
choice for carnivorousness. I say it is not. It is an
unconscious choice to keep the same eating patterns of
your parents and that same choice they made for you.

If, after reading this paper you think about your
eating choices and choose to stay carnivorous, then
sit down in a restaurant and order fried chicken, I
would have accomplished my purpose and you would have
made your OWN CHOICE.

Obviously I am not writing this paper so you will
decide to stay carnivorous. I am writing this paper so
you will decide. I think your decision is important
not only because it will help you establish some
autonomy from parental decisions about eating but you
should think about what you eat and why you eat it.
Especially when what you eat involves the death of
another life, as is the case in carnivorousness.

I'm not going to scare you with statistics and
research on meat eating and its relation to heart
disease and other problems. I will only challenge you
to do one thing. Next time you eat a steak or chicken
leg, look at it. Closely. Think back to where it came
from and what was done to that cow or chicken to get
your dinner in its present state. Ask yourself if your
meal is worth the death of another animal or bird. If
you answer yes, at least you pondered the choice and
your decision is worth respect. If you answer no, then
you must have the strength to follow through on your
choice.

Common sense tells us that we do not need to eat
other species to live and live healthy. There are
vegetarian alternatives to hamburgers and hot dogs,

fish patties and other meat products. They are usually more expensive and inconvenient.

If you are willing to make a small sacrifice for the many animals you will save in your lifetime by not eating them, then maintain your integrity. It's not going to be easy. There are no more trips to McDonald's drive thru for a fast hamburger. You may have to invent a new dish at a restaurant by requesting the meat be left out. Don't worry, you will get used to it. Now you can feel good about what you eat.

Whatever your choice, what you lose is nothing to what you gain.

EXERCISE 5–6

Write a five-minute response, without going back to the paper, which answers the following questions:

A. What was the main idea?

B. What does the paper accomplish? (Its purpose?)

C. Where was your strongest positive response?

D. Where was your most negative response?

E. What is the major change that needs to be made?

EXERCISE 5–7

Repeat the directions in Exercise 5–6 for the following paper.

PAPER #2: Student Draft

The American Dream

What is the American Dream? Is it a large family? A better education? Success? Money? Or is it the betterment of yourself? Most people would say one of the first four, but the truth is that each generation has, while fulfilling one of the first four, also fulfilled the last one, making life easier and better for the generations to follow.

One facet of the American Dream is the family. Many people would like to have a large and loving family. These people have family-based tendencies and are usually very good parents. Sometimes they get their wish. Sometimes they don't.

Their dream family is loving and caring and

resembles the Cunningham family of TV's <u>Happy Days</u>.
Their husband or wife is successful, a hard worker,
and tries to fulfill their spouse's wishes. Their son
is intelligent. He makes A's in school and always
makes the Dean's List. He is a great athlete, being
the captain of the football team and a star on the
baseball team. He is handsome and dates quite often.
Their daughter, too, is very bright. She also makes
A's and the Dean's List. She is very beautiful and has
many boys vying for her attentions. She was also
Homecoming Queen. The cat and dog get along well and
both are extremely intelligent.

This dream family is what the person wants, but
what he or she gets is something very different. It
may be a mixture of this dream and their worst
nightmares. Every family, even my own, has its
problems. Their spouse's job may cause family
troubles. Their children may not be the most
beautiful, handsome, or intelligent. And to top it all
off, the dog and cat hate each other and constantly
break things in their attempts to kill one another.

Doesn't bettering yourself follow along the
family lines at the same time? If the father was a
high school graduate, the son wants to graduate from
college. This kind of betterment is unconscious, but
is present in almost everyone.

In some instances, this betterment comes in the
same job area. My great-grandfather was a farmer with
just a few acres. My grandfather was a farmer too, but
he owned over eighty acres. A father may be a doctor.
His son may want to be a doctor too, but in a
different field of medicine.

At other times, though, this betterment comes in
a different field altogether. My grandfather was a
farmer, my father is an autoworker, and I want to be a
pharmacist. This is merely an example of a growing
trend in families as the children try to get jobs
completely different from those of their parents.

Money can sometimes become a factor in this want
for betterment, but it is not always the case. My
father, while he continues to work, will make just as
much, and maybe more, money than I will. I will have a
college education and he has a simple high school
education. I am going to college so I will have a
better job than my father, not more money.

Even though people dream of having a ''perfect''

```
family, they realize they aren't going to get it. All
they can do is hope and try. They try to better
themselves in relation to their parents so they can
come closer to their idea of the ''perfect'' family.
This process is carried on by their children, whose
children do the same thing. The bottom line is, they
want to have it better for their children than they
did when they were children. Each generation has tried
and will try to raise its standard of living for its
children. That is part of the American Dream.
```

EXERCISE 5–8

Now we'd like you to practice comparing your response as a reader with a written text which is being revised. The first step is to compare your response to the written text's statement of intention. (We realize that since you didn't write the originals you weren't privileged to know the authors' original intentions. Therefore, we have provided you with the two authors' statements of audience, purpose, and context.)

Author Intention Statement, Paper #1. `To deal with, up front, the reasons why we eat meat and why we shouldn't. To convince readers to make their choices consciously rather than through habit.`

Author Intention Statement, Paper #2. `To show people that the American Dream is not as money-centered and the U.S. is not as materialistic as its critics maintain.`

Compare your written response to both the student papers and the corresponding intention statements. Provide written answers for the following questions on each paper:

A. Does the author's statement of intended thesis correspond with the one in your freewriting? If not, discuss the differences.

B. Does the paper accomplish what the author intended? If not, where does the paper go wrong?

C. Which needs more work, the quality of the main idea or the manner in which it is presented?

D. How would you suggest that the author revise this paper?

EXERCISE 5–9

Using the response you wrote in Exercise 5–7 and the comparison you wrote for Exercise 5–8, develop a revision plan for one of the sample student first drafts. You may choose freewriting, a sequential list, or you can write a formal explanation of your plan. Be as specific as possible. Remember that at this stage of revision we are most interested in assuring that the main idea grasped from reading the paper corresponds with the writer's intention, that the paper is adequately and appropriately developed, and that the paper is organized effectively. (*Hint:* In your plan for revision, you are working to make the draft correspond to the stated intention. You have the option to review and modify the original intention. What should be *added, deleted, substituted, combined, or rearranged?*)

Developing a Reader's Eye

The procedures you've just practiced for reviewing your first draft will help you develop new eyes to see your own paper. One of the major obstacles in revision—besides the urge to have a paper finished—is writers' inability to see their work with a critical eye. As writers we become possessive of what we have written; therefore, we are reluctant to open ourselves to the possibility of major revision. Furthermore, our minds often trick us both in simple and complicated ways. It's easy to leave out a word in sentence because when we create the sentences in our heads, write them, and then reread them, our mind often fills in the missing word, so we don't even notice its absence. The same applies to an entire paper. (In the rough draft of this text, we accidentally left out a word in the sentence before last. We left it out in the final copy as well. Did you notice?)

Most writing teachers have observed this phenomenon more than once: A student comes in for a conference about a paper and tells the teacher what the paper says. The teacher asks exactly where in the paper this particular meaning is developed. The student searches fruitlessly. Why? Because while writing the paper, the student was coming up with more thoughts about the paper than physically could be recorded. Memory told him the paper included some of those thoughts. One of our challenges as revisers, then, is to shift from the role of author to that of helpful editor.

Distance helps us make the shift. If we try to revise too close to the first drafting, we're still author/owners. We've said what we wanted to say at the moment, and everything looks fine—or we simply can't figure out how to make the writing more effective. The best thing to do at this stage is to put the piece down for a while and come back to it later. Sometimes fifteen minutes is enough. Overnight generally works best for us. *One warning:* Don't wait too long. Occasionally you can get so far away from a piece that recapturing the original spirit and intention becomes difficult.

Working with Groups

Another way to get the practice you need to become a successful reviser is to work with rough drafts your classmates have written. Many students discover that group work helps them learn how to write better. If your instructor uses groups, we encourage you to participate actively. The experiences that other writers have in solving their writing problems may help you learn how to solve yours. Furthermore, working in groups allows you to get the kind of immediate response usually available only in a face-to-face conversation. If your teacher doesn't use groups, then you might want to establish your own independent study groups, following the Guidelines for Group Collaboration. Even if you do form writing groups in class, you might consider extending these groups beyond the classroom.

Any writing group needs a set of rules or procedures for working sympathetically with the rough drafts of its members. There is no one standard all groups adopt, so here we present some general guidelines that can be modified for your own use.

Guidelines for Group Collaboration

1. *Be sympathetic to the efforts of others.*

They've devoted the same effort, time, and energy that you have. Begin each discussion with a remark or observation that shows the writer you appreciate the effort expended so far. You might comment on how well you like the choice of subject, on a particularly interesting passage or example, on a series of vivid images, on the amount and quality of detail used in support, on the way the paper begins or ends. In other words, writers like to know what they've done right as well as what they've done wrong.

2. *Be an active listener and reader.*

Unless you've given your full attention to the paper and its arguments, you won't be any help. You might even want to begin the discussion by asking the author to say a few words about the paper: what she likes best about the paper's accomplishments, what difficulties she encountered, how she solved or tried to solve the problems, where she feels the paper still needs attention. If you listen carefully, you might learn something to help with your paper, and you will also be better prepared to offer valuable suggestions to the author.

3. *Go through the paper at least twice.*

The first time you hear or read a piece, try to respond to the whole as it affects you as an audience; the next time through you will be better prepared to make suggestions. Take notes. Ask questions. Become an active participant in shaping the paper.

4. *Remember that you are working together.*

You are working not only to help create better finished products, but also to help each other learn *ways* to improve future efforts. Asking one another "why" and "how" particular points are made is very important. Why did you use that particular example? How did you go about solving the problem of tying up all the loose ends? What were you hoping to accomplish by using that comparison? How did you decide to organize your paper in that way? We could provide dozens of examples of possible questions—you can even use the questions on revision in this text. You will soon discover, however, that the exact wording of the questions is not as important as the kind of question you ask. Ask the kinds of questions that would help you write your own papers better.

The Individual Nature of Revision

In the next few pages, we present a wide variety of guides to revision. Choose one that either works for you as is or can be modified to suit your needs. Experiment with each of them; develop an approach to reseeing your initial drafts.

We designed this first guide to explore message, audience, and purpose. It focuses on the overall *theme* level and can be used effectively in the early stages of revision. Although it's designed for use by the individual writer, it can also be used in groups.

Guide #1: Author's Whole Paper Revision Catalog

1. Have I decided what my main idea is?

2. Do I know why I'm writing about this idea? What do I hope to accomplish?

3. Do I have an idea of my general or specific audience? Which forum?

4. Have I designed my paper with the answers to the following questions in mind?

   - Is it clear from my opening what my general subject is and how I feel about it?
   - If I've written a thesis statement, does it accurately and adequately state my meaning?
   - Have I designed my opening to catch my audience's attention, develop its interest?
   - Have I worked to sustain this interest throughout the paper?

The following guide offers direction for collaborating on initial drafts. Like the previous guide, it focuses on the overall *theme* level of revision; however, it is more complete and divides the consideration of the paper into three parts.

This guide can be used most effectively on an intermediate draft, although it could also be used on the first draft.

Guide #2: Complete Peer Revision Guide

INTRODUCTION

What strategies has the author used to create reader interest?
What strategies has the author used to involve the audience with the problem?
How would you summarize the paper's topic?
How would you paraphrase the thesis statement? (*Remember:* Not all papers have a thesis statement in the introduction. If the paper you are reading doesn't have one, then come back to this question after you have read the entire paper.)

BODY

Did the author anticipate any lack of background you might have had?
Did the author provide you with enough concrete support of the main point?
Are all the ideas arranged and connected so they flow together well?

CONCLUSION

What strategies has the author used to maintain the audience's interest?
Is the conclusion more than just a summary? Or, if it is a summary, were the paper's contents complicated enough to warrant a summary?
How has the author reinforced the main point?
Are the conclusion and the introduction connected in any way? How?

Use the following revision chart after you're satisfied that your thesis is the one you want to keep. Before you use this checklist, reread your thesis.

Guide #3: Revision Checklist

1. Does my paper need *added* support? Examples? Full paragraphs?

2. Are there parts of may paper which need to be *deleted* because they are weak or do not support the development of my thesis? Examples? Full paragraphs?

3. Have I arranged my ideas so the reader can follow them easily, or should I experiment with *rearrangement?*

4. Are there any examples or points which I could *substitute* for the weakest parts of my paper?

5. Are any of my points so similar that my paper would be more concise if I *combined* them?

Finally, we offer the following ten pieces of advice to remember as you're revising your material. The first few times you revise work in this class, you might want to copy this guide and keep it on your desk while you work.

Guide #4: An Author's Guide to Revision

1. Put some distance between yourself and your first draft. Don't start revising immediately after finishing it.

2. Reread your draft for its overall effect. Don't be too concerned about word-level or sentence-level problems.

3. Immediately after rereading, write a summary statement of the paper's thesis and purpose.

4. Check the summary statement with the one you used for your rough draft.

5. If these two statements are different, return to the paper to see where the changes occurred and whether you need to reconcile the differences.

6. Make a note of the sections of the paper which did not please you.

7. Have a friend or fellow student follow steps 2–6 for your paper.

8. Return to the parts of the paper that failed to please you. In the margins or on another sheet of paper, make notes about what you could do to make these parts more satisfactory.

9. Read your paper through aloud, or have someone else read it to you. Make notes of any places that don't seem "right" as you hear them.

10. Remember that most editing decisions can be made after major revisions have been completed.

CHAPTER SIX

Revision: Later Stages, Editing

All I know about grammar is its infinite power. To shift the structure of a sentence alters the meaning of the sentence, as definitely and inflexibly as the position of a camera alters the meaning of the object photographed.
—Joan Didion

After attending to the larger concerns of revision covered in the preceding chapter, you are probably finding that what you have written has changed—changed scope, focus, direction, thesis, or method of providing evidence and support. Now we'll look at other kinds of changes, changes that do occur throughout the writing process but which require special attention as you near the end of a writing task: sentence- and word-level revisions.

The Sentence

Revising for Topicality

When you're revising sentences at this stage, you're trying to make sure that each of your sentences helps to develop your thesis. Your first concern therefore is topicality—whether the sentence relates properly to your topic. If you have done a good job rethinking and revising your paragraphs, you don't need to check individual sentences for thesis topicality because you have already done this while reconsidering your paragraphs. Occasionally, however, the broader focus on paragraphing allows a nonessential or unclear sentence to slip through. To guard against this, you can map your paragraphs so you catch these errant sentences before they find their way into your final draft. This technique can also serve as a final check of your overall scheme of organization.

Revising for Meaning and Correctness

Although we discuss the various acts of composing as though they were sequential, that is simply so they can be ordered for placement in a textbook. We realize that you do some of your editing and text revision during your first drafts. Sometimes ideas about style and mechanics and grammar come to you during these drafts, and the process of writing is hard enough without denying inspiration merely for the sake of following the steps in a textbook. However, most of the revisions in your earlier drafts should be aimed at making your writing correspond with your purposes. Once you identify your intentions and figure out how to develop them in your writing, you can concentrate more of your energy on stylistic, grammatical, and mechanical improvements.*

Making these improvements can also spare you some painful embarrassment. In California the Memorandum Club awards certificates for pieces of public writing submitted in the following categories: Most Wordy, Most Confusing, Most "Is This for Real?", Most Bureaucratic Jargon, Most Pointless, Most Uncommunicative, Biggest Copout, Most Contradictory, Most Ticklish, Worst Timed, and Worst Typographical Error. One 1985 winner:

> While gathering for the penultimate meeting of our Governing Board, it was randomly observed that the Bulletin Board was not accomplishing its predetermined mission of clearly conveying communication.

John Ehrman, a San Jose, California, computer professional, has collected over 1600 bloopers from speeches and memos by professionals. Enjoy the following five examples:

1. To be a leader, you have to develop a spear de corps.
2. He likes sitting there in his big executive shrivel chair.
3. Things were all up in a heaval.
4. That needs some thinking about; let me go away and regurgitate for a couple of hours.
5. I wish someone would make a decision; I'm tired of hanging in libido.

And a headline from the *Kansas City Times:*

> Coach Marv Harshman of Washington has the gaul to speak his mind and the victories to back it up.

Some teachers collect examples of student writing in which the failure to reread and revise has created some unintentionally humorous reading for the

---

*We do not attempt in this text to provide you with a complete handbook of grammar and mechanics. If you discover that you need more intense help in these areas, we suggest that you ask your instructor to recommend a good handbook; every college student should have a complete handbook of grammar, usage, and mechanics to use as a reference. If a writing lab is available, use it; individual instruction can help eliminate any of the surface errors in your writing. *One caution:* Your grammar and mechanics will not improve significantly unless you commit yourself to improvement.

audience. Teachers collect these "slips" largely out of frustration; they want their students to succeed, to become caring writers. A reader who is laughing over an inadvertent pun or puzzling over an apparently nonsensical sentence might have difficulty taking that author's ideas seriously. To ensure that your meaning is not obscured, you need to keep a "reader's eye" functioning through all stages of revision.

Sentence Beginnings

Often writers concentrate so hard on creating overall meaning that they de-velop unconscious habits on the sentence level—habits which detract both from meaning and the overall effect. One of these habits is beginning sen-tences in ways which distract, rather than engage, the reader. Checking each sentence can help you avoid negative reader responses.

One habit which can irritate your reader is *beginning too many of your sentences in the same way*. To guard against this stylistic irritation, underline the first word in each of your sentences on a draft in progress. Do you notice a pattern? Are there one or more words that appear with great frequency? If so, is there a purpose for this repetition?

Sometimes writers begin several of their sentences with the same word for emphasis, but unless you can be sure the reader will see repetition as an effective stylistic device, vary the beginnings of your sentences.

Beginning sentences with "it" when there are other options may also irritate an active reader. In speaking we frequently begin a sentence with "it" because the word serves as a convenient filler, allowing us time to prepare the rest of the sentence.

It's a beautiful day out there.

It's been a long time since I've seen you.

Such constructions are neither grammatically nor stylistically wrong. The ques-tion a writer must ask is whether the construction best involves the reader with the writing. A speaker doesn't have the opportunity to revise; a writer does. How can the two previous sentences be made more pleasing to a reader? The context controls the possibilities, but here are some examples:

The sun's shining and the wind's blowing 15 knots. *(Good news to a sailor.)*

I haven't seen you since the first week of the semester. *(Bad news to a student.)*

These two revisions not only delete the meaningless "it," but also add concrete meaning to the sentences.

Writers also begin sentences with "it" to refer to something in the previous sentence. But sometimes *beginning a sentence with "it" used as a referant is confusing* because it refers to too much in the previous sentence.

```
Each time Tippy had a litter of puppies, my
father would wait until they were weaned and we had
```

```
grown attached to them before taking them to the
pound. It was a ritual, usually set off by one of them
chewing up a piece of furniture.
```

The second sentence could be rewritten in this way:

```
Taking the puppies to the pound was a ritual,
usually set off by one of them chewing up a piece of
furniture.
```

The revision eliminates the "it" and, in repeating the word "pound," creates a more obvious transition between the two sentences. But the revision also creates a slightly different meaning; in the first version the "it" includes not only taking the puppies to the pound but also the weaning and the attachment. You must make sure the reader clearly understands the meaning represented by this pronoun. In other words, sometimes you choose to use the pronoun because it best suits your purpose. For our purposes, we hope you become aware that the choice exists and know why you decide which structure to use.

EXERCISE 6–1

Rewrite the sentences (taken largely from papers written in a graduate class on the teaching of writing) in the following passages to eliminate the "it." You may decide not to make the deletion. For each case, explain your choice.

A. How did that limb survive all those years of mischievous school boys passing by? It's too late now because, although it's just the right height to be ripped off, the muscle connecting it to the trunk is now four inches by fourteen inches.

B. It was just the kind of weather to be outdoors in.

C. It is nearing noon and my vigil is coming to an end.

D. A sign reads, "Unsafe for Boating or Swimming." Water activities are reserved for nature's creatures. It's as if nature were given front-stage privileges.

E. The wind blows the water in the pond. It blows the clouds, the trees, the ducks' feathers and makes the flowers sway.

F. The pond itself is surrounded by a walkway that seduces the walker into strolling along its winding paths. It is shored up by a picturesque retaining wall of wooden pilings stood on end and cemented in place. Part of the bank above is bounded by a large rock retaining wall which is wide enough to perch upon if you are agile enough to make the leap up to it. It is reminiscent of a young cavalier sweeping his lady fair in voluminously long skirts up to sit beside him. As a matter of fact, there are several couples doing just that—courting in the same old traditional style.

Beginning sentences frequently with "There are" and "There is" can be the sign of a lazy writer at work. At the very least, you should be aware of your options. Consider the following sentence: "There are three major causes for divorce: money, sex, and boredom." While there is nothing stylistically or grammatically incorrect about that sentence, other ways to present the same idea might come to mind:

1. Money, sex, and boredom are the three major causes for divorce.

2. The three major causes for divorce are money, sex, and boredom.

3. Of the causes of divorce, money, sex, and boredom are the major three.

4. Money, sex, and boredom cause more divorces than any other factors.

Which of these sentences is best? The answer can be found only in the rest of your essay. How many times do you use the "there are" construction in the essay? If you use the construction too frequently, you run the risk of boring your reader. What are you trying to emphasize? Each of the sentence variations provides a slightly different emphasis and changes the meaning a reader derives from your writing.

EXERCISE 6–2

Copy each of the sentences about divorce, including the first. After each, write a sentence focusing on how the emphasis of the sentence affects a reader.

EXERCISE 6–3

Read the following two paragraphs and underline the words beginning each sentence. Using the freewriting technique, discuss whether the underlined sentence beginnings are designed for a purpose or whether they are merely unconscious and irritating repetitions.

```
        There once was a young man who was accepted into
a Midwestern medical school. He had to leave behind
all of the things he had learned to love over the past
eighteen years. It hurt and he hated it. Needless to
say, he had a tough freshman year. Luckily he made it.
Most in his situation don't. The reason it was so
tough for him to adjust wasn't the change from country
life to the city life. It wasn't that the kids in his
class hated him. The reason he didn't like college
could be put into three words. He was scared. He was
scared to death of leaving the security of his home
and going off away from his family and friends. It
```

doesn't have to be this way. Students can learn to
adjust to college life. It's better if they make these
adjustments as early as possible. Believe me, because
I'm the medical student who survived.

The biggest adjustment usually occurs fifteen
minutes after the new medical students arrive at
school. They sit on their beds in a building with
brick walls like a penitentiary. They then look around
and start to smile. They see no parents, no warden, no
one to tell them what to do. They realize that they
are free. This is the beginning of the bad things
bound to happen during the first few months. They wake
up at midterm to the realization that they're flunking
out. They may have been free, but they had forgotten
something. With freedom comes responsibility. It
should be made clear to all freshmen that enrolling in
college is only the first big step toward their
careers. Studying and good grades are necessary from
the first day until the last final exam—if they want
to succeed in college.

Let's list the first words.

Paragraph 1. There—He—It—Needless—Luckily—Most—The (reason)—
It—The (reason)—He—He—It—Students—It—Believe

Paragraph 2. The (biggest)—They—They—They—This—They—They—
With—It—Studying

Now let's discuss your freewriting for Exercise 6–3. Because we are now
examining elements of style, we are touching on questions of taste and preferences rather than right or wrong, so be prepared for some differences of
opinion. We only ask that you explain the reasons for your decisions. Here's
one possible response:

The writer begins with a ''There are''
construction because he wants to imitate the fairy
tale opening—OK. The sentences which begin with ''It''
can all be rewritten. The repetition of ''The reason''
is done to provide the reader with a transition
between ideas—OK. The repetition of ''He'' keeps the
focus on the example and helps provide transition—OK.
The repetition of ''They'' works well because it
emphasizes the shift from ''He'' and also emphasizes
the sequence of actions students experience.

EXERCISE 6–4

> Using your own freewriting, or a combination of yours and that of your class-mates, rewrite the passage.

Verbs

Sometimes writers neglect their verbs despite the verb's role as meaning-maker and meaning-connector. They repeat one verb frequently or use verbs that bring few images to mind.

"To Be" Forms

> Sometimes writers habitually use forms of the verb ''to be'' to carry the weight of their sentences' meaning. ''To be'' forms—*is, am, are, was, were,* and *been*—are abstract equal signs which add no nuance of meaning to your ideas. They are ''correct'' but they are also easy, and if used too frequently throughout a piece of writing, especially when attractive options are available, give rise to an abstract, depersonalized feeling about your ideas. Sometimes writers use them because they choose to do so; no alternative accomplishes the same purpose. At other times, however, writers use these forms unconsciously, instead of seeking alternatives.

The paragraph you have just read was our first draft. We chose, if that's the right word, forms of "to use" for four of our verbs. We also selected "are" as our verb four times. The paragraph violates its own advice. Thanks to revision and helpful suggestions from other writers who read our rough drafts, we made some changes. In the following paragraph, we have consciously decided to retain "are" twice and "use" twice; however, we made other changes. Compare the two paragraphs for effect. (We changed the underlined verbs.)

> Sometimes writers habitually allow forms of the verb ''to be'' to carry the weight of their sentences' meaning. ''To be'' forms—*is, am, are, was, were,* and *been*—function as abstract equal signs which add no nuance of meaning or life to your writing. They are ''correct'' but they are also easy, and if you use them too frequently throughout your writing, especially when you have attractive options, they give rise to an abstract, depersonalized feeling about your ideas. Sometimes writers choose them because they need

```
to do so; no alternative accomplishes the same
purpose. At other times, however, writers use these
forms unconsciously, instead of seeking alternatives.
```

In the context of one paragraph these changes may seem trivial; however, through the pages of an almost 600-page manuscript the number of repetitions becomes significant.

EXERCISE 6–5

Reread the paragraph about the pond reprinted below. Notice that the author has relied almost entirely on the verb form "is" to connect the details in the paragraph. Using the version you created after eliminating the "its," rewrite the passage again; this time eliminating the "to be" forms. Compare your version with those of your classmates. Discuss the choices you made and, if possible, decide on one or more versions you feel are now powerful examples of good writing.

```
      The pond itself is surrounded by a walkway that
seduces the walker into strolling along its winding
paths. It is shored up by a picturesque retaining wall
of wooden pilings stood on end and cemented in place.
Part of the bank above is bounded by a large rock
retaining wall which is wide enough to perch on if you
are agile enough to make the leap up to it. It is
reminiscent of a young cavalier sweeping his lady fair
in voluminously long skirts up to sit beside him. As a
matter of fact, there are several couples doing just
that—courting in the same old traditional style.
```

EXERCISE 6–6

Take out copies of the essays you've written for this class. Put brackets around each of your verbs. Have you created a pattern of using abstract "to be" verbs? Pick out at least five sentences formed with these verbs and rewrite them. Which versions are more interesting and carry more meaning?

Passive Construction. Related to the "to be" construction is the passive construction. The passive is created by combining a verb form of the infinitive "to be" with a participle. The passive is often used in technical writing and in cases which do not call for a subject to be identified. The three sentences immediately above and the sentences in the following list are in the passive voice:

1. It was decided that you will not receive the promotion.
2. The dog was being walked when it was stolen by the dognappers.

3. Your memorandum was received and acted on immediately after its receipt.

4. The accident was investigated by both state and county officials.

The passive construction is another example of a grammatically correct form which can nevertheless prompt negative audience responses. The reasons are twofold. Sometimes the passive is a convenient way to avoid assigning responsibility. For example, *who* was it who decided that "you will not receive the promotion" and *who* "received . . . and acted on the memo"? Unfortunately this form is used widely in bureaucracies. We say "unfortunately" because the use of the passive often obscures meaning, actually interfering with the communication process. Another problem with the passive is implicit in its name; the form is "passive" because it deletes the central actor from the sentence and because it generally makes for a longer sentence than its active counterpart.

Let's consider the sentences as they might appear in the active voice.

1. *The manager decided that you will not receive the promotion.* (Now the responsibility is clear and you know whom to see.)

2. *John was walking the dog when the dognappers stole it.* (In the first case it probably wasn't a denial of responsibility to say that the dog was being walked, but the first version has twelve words, the second ten. Two words might not sound like much of a difference, but when you consider that a 750-word essay might have about 70 sentences, you could add an extra 140 words—almost 20 percent—to your essay. These are not powerful words which carry significant meaning but rather form words which help complete a grammatical construction.)

3. *Both county and state officials investigated the accident.* (This version emphasizes the actors—the officials—in a way passive voice doesn't. The passive denies responsibility by emphasizing the accident; if the officials did not conduct the investigation properly, there's probably good reason for using the passive.)

4. *Purchasing received your memorandum and acted on it immediately.* (Now, should you have problems, you know which department to contact. Knowing who to see could save you time and frustration.)

Although these second sentences are not "more correct" than the first ones, they have the advantage of being less likely to create problems for your readers or to irritate them. Sentences couched in the active voice are less likely to hinder communication between writer and reader.

Tense. Another problem some writers run into between their initial drafts and their final draft is verb tense. Quite often the writing of an essay extends over a fairly long period and takes place at several different sittings. As a result, writers occasionally mix their verb tenses. Read the following short selection.

①I used to be a procrastinator.
②''Tomorrow'' was my favorite word.③I have no

trouble agreeing to take on projects—it's the follow-through that's difficult.④My mother would ask me to do something.⑤I said yes and then put the project off until I conveniently forgot about it.⑥I had some terrible experiences as a result of this habit: I almost flunked art because my project was a week late.⑦I wasn't accepted by my favorite college because I missed the sign-up date for the ACT.⑧My girl friend and I were late to the prom dinner because I had put off getting the car filled up.⑨But I changed.⑩How?⑪The first three weeks of college did it.⑫In these three weeks I turned in a late paper to my English professor; he took two grades off.⑬I put off studying for my math test until the last night only to discover that I have no grasp of differential equations; I got a 62 on the test. ⑭I put off buying my parking sticker; I got a $25 parking ticket.⑮No one is letting me skate by here; I had to change to survive.

Although this piece has many positive attributes—a sense of humor, good examples, stylistic variety—it suffers because it forces the reader to hopscotch through the verb tenses. The selection combines the past, the present, and the habitual past, jarring the reader at each shift.

No simple rule helps you avoid this problem. We could advise you to keep your tenses consistent. We could give you a series of grammar handbook rules, but you would still have to depend on your own awareness of the way the verbs work in your essay. We have already suggested that you bracket all the verbs in your draft before you begin the final draft. When you review these verbs, note the tenses. If you discover that you are using different tenses, then review the flow of your essay to ensure that your reader can follow your time sequence. [*Note:* You can, of course, have more than one tense in your essay— if they follow logically.]

Let's review the previous selection to see where its writer went wrong. In the third sentence the writer makes a personal observation in the present tense—perhaps because he was vividly reliving the past as he wrote. Nevertheless, this shift jars the reader because the first sentence implies that the writer has changed. The fourth sentence takes the reader back to habitual past action—no problem because we're reading about how he used to be. The fifth sentence, however, presents a simple past action which relates to the habitual action of the fourth sentence. This shift causes the reader to ask if the writer is referring to a specific example or to a series of examples; the answer is unclear. The paper's tenses follow consistently until the second clause of the thirteenth sentence. Once again the writer shifts to the present tense—probably because he's still struggling with differential equations. However, in this paper he is referring to a specific time in the past; his present state is not relevant in the context of this paper. The same problem recurs in the last sentence. The writer makes a comment about his current state although the focus of the paper is the past.

EXERCISE 6–7

Using the preceding discussion, rewrite the paragraph on procrastination, appropriately adjusting the tenses.

Sentence Fragments

The sentence fragment is an old nemesis for many student writers. Simply put, the fragment is a group of words, beginning with a capital letter and ending with a period, which fails to follow the rule that calls for an independent subject and verb. "John walks" is a grammatically complete sentence because it forges subject and verb into an independent clause. "That he would have to hurry to the library and check out the books he needed before closing time" is a fragment because, although the clause abounds with subjects and verbs, it lacks the merger of an independent subject and verb. All the subjects and verbs which follow the "that" are dependent on the clause which should precede the "that" for their meaning. Why all this fuss over sentence fragments anyway? First, teachers and other professionals consider the fragment an error which marks the careless or, even worse, uneducated writer. Second, fragments make the reader break the smooth flow of reading to figure out just what the writer is doing. Since most of us need all the help we can get when we're writing, we don't want to put any unnecessary barriers between us and our readers.

If you often write fragments, the best thing we can do for you is help you become aware of the most common reasons fragments occur. With this awareness, you can begin to eliminate accidental fragments from your writing.

Fragments most commonly occur when the writer fails to connect a trailing dependent clause to the main part of the sentence as in the following example: "Fred pulled down, almost over his eyes, a sweat-stained Stetson. *Which saved him from being recognized by the man who had bought his horse.*" As a general rule, check those sentences—which are not questions—that begin with "Who," "What," "Whose," "Which," "When," and "That." Chances are they're fragments.

Sometimes the writer fails to connect an introductory clause to the main clause which follows, as in "Although Fred managed to avoid him that night in the bar and for the next week. He couldn't avoid him when the day of the rodeo arrived." Whenever you have sentences which begin with words such as "Although," "Because," "As," "Unless," "Whenever," "How," and "Since," make sure these words introduce clauses which are connected to a following main clause.

Sometimes writers even choose to write fragments. And for good reason.

Fragments provide an effective means of calling attention to a particular part of your writing, of creating emphasis, of varying sentence length. In the following example, the author, a high school English teacher, uses fragments for a definite purpose:

```
    I was once big enough that I wore only overalls,
gray T-shirts and turf shoes for an entire school
year. . . . But now I care to be average. And own a
Calvin Klein Shirt. That fits.
```

In this case he uses fragments to call attention to his change in size. The fragments add pieces of emphatic detail to show just how much he's changed and how significant these changes are.

EXERCISE 6–8

Label the sentences in each of the following five examples as fragments or nonfragments. Either rewrite each of the fragments, or write a sentence explaining why you would leave the fragment for effect.

1. He came to school all right. Whenever and only whenever he had the urge.

2. Such was Christopher's life. A series of disappointments followed by unexpected success.

3. Since he was expected to be dressed exactly right for the part, which really wasn't very large. He had to spend hours finding just the perfect combination of clothes for his costume.

4. The fish was a behemoth. When it broke water, a fountain cascaded over the boat. That was the one that got away.

5. I absolutely won't do it. Unless, of course, you tell me to.

Run-on Sentences

As noted in the previous section on sentence fragments, a sentence forges subject and verb into an independent clause. Independent clauses can be joined in certain ways to reflect relationships between the ideas they express (see Sentence Types, p. 159). A run-on sentence, though, joins two or more independent clauses without punctuation or subordinators. Here's a run-on sentence:

```
    Howard was supposed to sail on the Queen Mary on
the first of March however the Queen Mary was forced
into dry dock.
```

As the sentence is written, a reader can't tell what was supposed to happen on the first of March. Was Howard to sail that day or was the ship forced into dry dock on that day? The revised sentence clarifies the matter.

```
    Howard was supposed to sail on the Queen Mary;
on the first of March, however, the Queen Mary was
forced into dry dock.
```

Although the following run-on sentence does not confuse meaning, it does fail to meet the reader's expectations of what a sentence should do.

```
    When we were children we liked to spend Friday
nights with Inez she let us walk to the store on
Saturday mornings to buy soda and cookies she told us
stories later as we all sat on the front porch.
```

If you read the above sentence aloud, you find yourself stopping or pausing at certain points because you pick up clues in the sentence about which portions of it hang together. That's a good way to check for run-ons. To revise, add the necessary punctuation or change the structure of the sentence:

```
    When we were children, we liked to spend Friday
nights with Inez because she let us walk to the store
on Saturday mornings to buy soda and cookies. Then she
would tell us stories as we all sat on the front
porch.
```

If you have a tendency to write run-on sentences, you need to check each sentence of your draft, looking closely at the way you've joined independent clauses.

Subject-Verb Agreement

None of us need to be told that the subject and verb need to be in agreement, that if you have a singular subject you should have a singular verb. Since we were small children we have learned to avoid saying things like "They was certain that the bus would never come" or "She eat ice cream." Nevertheless, composition teachers continue to read papers which contain errors in subject-verb agreement. Why? Most often these errors appear through simple carelessness; when we're writing we're concentrating so hard on getting our ideas on paper that our mind short-circuits and we slip up. Occasionally we write a sentence that is so complicated we get lost in its grammatical forms and lose sight of what our subject was. The real question is not why these errors occur but rather how they find their way into final drafts. The answer is usually careless proofreading.

You can improve your proofreading skills greatly by being aware of the kinds of errors you make. We've already suggested bracketing your verbs before you complete your final draft. Bracketing focuses your attention on the verbs; to check for agreement errors, match each verb with its subject. Matching them doesn't take long, and catching these errors before someone reads them eliminates some of that reader irritation we've been warning you about. And if your readers include your instructor, chances are great that irritation will be expressed in a lower grade.

If you need intensive work with subject-verb agreement, seek some help from your instructor, a handbook, a learning center, or writing lab. If you need a brief reminder, the following list of rules and examples should help increase your awareness.

Compound subjects. Most compound subjects clearly call for a plural verb.

Going to school and working at the same time *complicate* my life.

However, compound subjects joined by the words *or, either–or,* or *neither–nor* call for the verb to agree with the subject closest to it.

The dog or the cats *have* to be taken to the vet today.

Either the Volkswagon bus or one of the new American mini-vans *is* the best deal on the market. *(Notice that the closest subject is "one"–not "vans.")*

Neither the Volkswagon bus nor the American mini-vans *compare* favorably with the new Japanese imports. *(Now the closest subject is "mini-vans," so the verb is plural.)*

Collective nouns. When you use a collective noun (administration, team, faculty, class, band, etc.) as your subject, you have a choice to make. If you are referring to the group acting as a whole, your verb is singular.

The administration *has decided* that, unfortunately, another tuition increase is likely.

If, however, you are referring to the actions of the individuals of the group, then you might want to use a plural verb.

The administration *stroll* into the meeting at different times without apologizing for the disruption.

Many of your readers might feel the previous sentence is awkward—even though it is grammatically correct. You can make an easy modification that solves the problem.

Members of the administration stroll into the meeting at different times without apologizing for the disruption.

Quantities. Subjects which are quantities also call for you to make a decision. With words like "some," "none," "all," "part" you have to look at the context of your text. "All" of what? If your answer is singular, so is your verb. If your answer is plural, so is your verb.

Some of the students in a writing class *struggle* with paragraphing. *(plural)*

Part of the shoe's sole *is caught* in the escalator. *(singular)*

All the dog's feet *are* white. *(plural)*

Other subjects referring to quantities, such as "majority," "minority," "amount," numbers, and fractions are singular or plural depending on the context.

The majority of Republicans *vote* a straight party ticket. *(The sentence refers to individual actions, so it takes a plural verb.)*

The Senate Republican majority *is facing* a rules challenge from the Democrats. *(The sentence refers to a challenge the group as a whole is facing, so it takes a singular verb.)*

Twenty-nine Senators *vote* together 95 percent of the time. *(Although they vote together, the sentence refers to their individual actions.)*

Fifty-one percent of the votes cast constitutes a majority. *(The sentence refers to one concept.)*

Indefinite pronouns. These subjects (each, everyone, one, no one, everybody, nobody, neither, either, somebody) always call for a singular verb no matter what qualifiers follow them.

Each of America's newborn babies *has* the right to expect the opportunity to succeed.

Either of the two boys *mows* the lawn each week.

Plural nouns with a singular meaning. These subjects, although they look plural (electronics, mathematics, gymnastics, politics, etc.), take a singular verb.

Gymnastics *was* a favorite at the 1984 Olympics.

Sentence Types

The English language contains four sentence types: simple, compound, complex, and compound-complex.

The *simple sentence* consists of one subject and one verb with no subordinate clauses and forms one main independent clause.

The street light shone on the brass number of his collar.

The *compound sentence* contains at least two main independent clauses connected by a coordinating conjunction ("and," "or," "but," "for," "nor," "so," "yet") or a punctuation mark (comma, semicolon, or colon.)

"I have never had confidence and *I am not young."*

He would lie in the bed and finally, with daylight, *he would go to sleep.*

The *complex sentence* contains one main independent clause and one or more subordinate dependent clauses.

'Each night I am reluctant to close up *because there may be someone who needs the care.'*

The *compound-complex sentence* contains at least two main independent clauses and at least one subordinate dependent clause.

The two waiters inside the cafe knew that the old man was a little drunk, and *while he was a good client* they knew *that if he became too drunk* he would leave without paying, *so they kept watch on him.*

Most writers naturally use a variety of these sentence types simply because we use them in our conversation. The old-fashioned reading book which presented the "See Jane run" view of a child's language did not take into account the vast linguistic repertoire a child develops before entering school. The freewriting of students at all ages confirms the almost universal ability to use each of these basic sentence types. Despite this, many writers who are not comfortable with their writing or their subject matter fall back on simple and compound sentences for the majority of their writing. Why? Because these forms are the easiest to use to transmit information; they cause the fewest difficulties in understanding, mechanics, and grammar. The insecure writer has enough problems getting started, generating ideas, and organizing; difficult sentence constructions would only add another level of interference.

Nevertheless, to become successful a writer must learn to vary the type and length of sentences to increase stylistic effectiveness. The wider a writer's stylistic range, the wider the range of subject matters he can tackle and the wider the range of audiences he can reach. Fortunately, a writer does not have to write with the complexity of a William Faulkner or a Henry James to present stylistic variety. The examples of simple, compound, complex, and compound-complex sentences presented here come from Ernest Hemingway's short story "A Clean, Well-Lighted Place," and Hemingway is famous for his terse, spare style.

What does this mean for you as a writer? After all, we don't expect you to aspire to become Ernest Hemingways. Stylistic variety means avoiding a dull, repetitious reliance on one sentence pattern throughout your writing. It also means being able to draw on various sentence patterns to make your writing more effective. Read the following excerpt from a student paper we used earlier in the text.

```
    One facet of the American Dream is the family.
Many people would like to have a large and loving
family. These people have family-based tendencies and
usually are very good parents. Sometimes they get
```

their wish. Sometimes they don't. Their dream family
is loving and caring, much like the Cunningham family
of TV's *Happy Days*. Their husband or wife is
successful, a hard worker, and tries to fulfill their
spouse's wishes. Their son is intelligent. He makes
A's in his classes and makes the Dean's list. He is a
great athlete, being captain of the football team and
a star on the baseball team. He is handsome and has a
very active social life. Their daughter, too, is very
bright. She also makes A's and the Dean's list. She is
very beautiful and has many boys vying for her
attention. She was also the Prom Queen. The family's
cat and dog also get along very well and both are
extremely intelligent and obedient.

This excerpt displays many positive features. Examples are plentiful. It uses analogy, allusion, and a touch of humor. Its sentences vary considerably in length (9-11-11-5-3-16-11-4-11-19-10-6-8-12-5-17 words). The writer uses variety in length both to shift focus and to provide emphasis. Reread each of the short sentences and notice each of their functions.

The piece, however, lacks sentence variety. Every sentence, with the exception of the last one, is a simple sentence. Maintaining this pattern throughout an entire paper runs the risk of both irritating and boring the reader, counteracting the advantages of its positive features. Simple sentences often mask or do not effectively communicate the relations among the ideas each contains, leaving the reader responsible for figuring out how the sentences in a paragraph relate. The excerpt also contains a few other problems we have noted in this chapter: repetitious abstract verbs, sentences which deviate from the paragraph's focus. Let's consider a version revised with sentence variety and these other criticisms in mind.

Many people dream the American Dream of the large
and loving family. The members of their dream family
love and care for one another in much the same way
that the Cunninghams do on *Happy Days*. The husband and
wife are successful, hard workers, and each tries to
filfill the other spouse's wishes. Their son is
intelligent. In addition to earning A's in his classes
and making the Dean's list, he also captains the
football team and stars on the baseball team. Very
handsome, he has an active social life. Their
daughter, too, is very bright; she also makes A's and
the Dean's list. And because she is very beautiful—she
was even named Prom Queen—she has many boys vying for
her attention. Even the family's cat and dog get along
well, and both are extremely intelligent and obedient.

EXERCISE 6–9

   A. Analyze the revision above for the following:
   - sentence types
   - use of verbs
   - deleted content
   - number of words in each sentence
   - other revisions

   B. In a well-organized paragraph or two, explain why the second version is better than the first. Be sure to consider its effect on a potential reader.

   C. We left several "to be" forms in the revision. Rewrite those sentences using more active, concrete verbs.

Sentence Variety

Perhaps you noticed that in the revision, some of the most successful changes had nothing to do with changing sentence types but rather with changing the ways in which information was presented within sentence types. From this observation you could rightly conclude that varying sentence types is not the only way to achieve sentence variety. In fact, just because you use the four types of sentences throughout an essay does not guarantee that your sentences will hold your audience's interest. The following, slightly exaggerated example illustrates this point.

```
     I walked to the store. My brother walked with me,
and my dog walked with me. My brother was two. I
pulled my wagon while I walked. While I pulled my
wagon, I talked with my brother, and I played with my
dog.
```

Four sentences, all four sentences types. Obviously the paragraph is one that none of us ever has to claim. But its monotony illustrates several points about interesting writing: Sentence variety alone is not enough; good writing has to have concrete detail to interest us; sentence structure also plays a role in developing an interesting style.

Let's play with this paragraph a little using five familiar questions: Who? When? What? Where? Why?

Who?   I walked to the store with my two-year-old brother and my St. Bernard.

When?   When I was five, I walked to the store every afternoon with my two-year-old brother and my St. Bernard.

What?   I pulled my rusted red wagon which had only three wheels.

Where?   When I was five and living in a shack in the desert outside Las

Vegas, I walked a mile through the cactus to the store with my brother and my dog.

Why?   We went to the store to buy jawbreakers.

We still haven't dealt with the playing and the talking yet, but the paragraph has changed considerably already. Now let's see how the paragraph looks:

```
When I was five and living in a shack in the
desert outside Las Vegas, my two-year-old brother, my
St. Bernard, and I walked a mile through the cactus to
the store to buy jawbreakers. I pulled my rusted red
wagon which had only three wheels. While I pulled my
wagon, I talked to my brother, and I played with my
dog.
```

You surely want to know more about this amazing little boy and his trip to the store. But, you say, anyone would because now there's more detail. Let's take another look at how this detail could be arranged:

```
I was five, and I lived in a shack. The shack was
outside Las Vegas. It was in the desert. I walked to
the store. I walked to the store everyday. My brother
walked to the store with me. He was two. My dog walked
with us. It was a St. Bernard. . . .
```

We could go on, but we'll spare you. The details remain specific; only the sentence structure has changed. The narrative, however, is excruciatingly tedious. Few students write like this, but many suffer from similar tendencies. They present sentence after sentence with the same subject-verb-object pattern and ignore the possibilities of presenting the same information in a more interesting style.

The most interesting version of this paragraph is the second one, because it uses a variety of sentence styles to capture the reader's interest and attention. The variety also helps the reader connect the ideas and images, to understand how they relate. The variety of prepositional phrases, modifiers, and clauses makes this version more readable, more understandable, and more interesting. Here's how the changes were made to create the second version:

- We added a compound adverbial clause containing three prepositional phrases to tell "when" and "where." (When I was five and living in a shack in the desert outside Las Vegas . . .)

- We modified "brother" in order to define more clearly "who." ("two-year-old")

- We substituted "St. Bernard" for "dog," telling more specifically "what."

- We added an adverbial and prepositional phrase to tell more specifically "where." ("a mile through the cactus")

- We added a prepositional phrase and an infinitive to tell more specifically "why." ("to the store to buy jawbreakers")

- We added two modifiers to "wagon" to tell more specifically "what." ("rusted red")

- We added a clause to tell even more specifically "what." ("which had only three wheels")

EXERCISE 6–10

What follows are the details of a story in *Sports Illustrated* about the first woman to win the 1,135-mile Iditarod Trail Sled Dog Race. Using the information you've gained from this chapter, rewrite the paragraph to create a stylistically interesting version.

```
     Libby Riddles lives in Teller, Alaska. She is 28.
It was night. It wasn't fit out for man; it wasn't fit
out for beast. She made her way across the sea of ice,
and her dogs made their way across the sea of ice. It
was called Norton Sound. It was the fifteenth day of
the race. The race was the 1,135-mile Iditarod Trail
Sled Dog Race. The race was from Anchorage to Nome. A
blizzard was fierce; it was blinding. The blizzard was
whipped by winds. They were at 70 knots. Duane
Halverson, Lavon Barve, and John Cooper were the other
leaders. The blizzard pinned them down. They were in
the village; it was called Shaktoolik. It was 229
miles from Nome. Riddles decided to forge on through
the storm. She was alone. The male mushers said it was
silly. But it was a move. It separated the women from
the boys. It separated the winner from the losers.
Riddles mushed across the finish line. It was two days
later. She was 2½ hours ahead of Halverson. She was
the first woman to win the Iditarod. The Iditarod is
supermacho. ''I left those guys in my dust,'' she
chortled.
```

The Word

Syllables govern the world.—John Selden

Most of the *word-level* revision you do is during the editing process. Occasionally, however, you encounter a word so obscure or so obviously out of place that it interferes with the reader's ability to understand the idea.

Homonyms

Homonyms are words which sound alike but are spelled differently. Unfortunately, these are also the kinds of errors that cause major irritation for readers. The following list is probably all too familiar. (On the first draft, written late at night long after the point when effective writing was possible, one of us wrote "to familiar.")

their—there—they're
to—two—too
waive—wave
prey—pray
elicit—illicit
piece—peace
rein—rain—reign
passed—past
principle—principal
cite—site—sight

Most of the time you clearly know the difference between the two words; your mind just plays tricks on you. Nevertheless, you should learn to catch these kinds of errors before they appear in your final draft. How? Know your own weaknesses and be on the lookout for errors you regularly make. You might even place a written list of your most frequent errors on the desk while you're proofreading. (If you use a word processor with a spell check feature, make sure you have the homonyms listed in your private dictionary.)

EXERCISE 6–11

A. Look up any of the words on the homonyms list whose meanings you aren't absolutely sure of.

B. Write a sentence using each of them to help fix the word's meaning in your mind.

C. As a group, make a list of other homonyms you know.

Common Misspellings

You might be thrilled to know that even some very good writers have trouble spelling. Unfortunately, spelling problems cannot be vanquished by a set of spelling rules or a list of commonly misspelled words. As with other types of editing errors, misspelled words can be eliminated from your final drafts most efficiently by becoming aware of your own deficiencies as a speller. Start keeping a list of words you regularly misspell. Classify the errors into types. For example, your categories might include homonym mistakes, *ie/ei* mistakes (achieve/weird seize/siege), *e/a* mistakes (desperate/separate), double-letter mistakes (occurred, embarrass, jotting, accommodate, accumulate), letter-change mistakes (beaugiful), sound mistakes (complection).

EXERCISE 6–12

Compile a list of all the common spelling errors members of your class make. As a group, create a classification system for all these errors. Design a chart to place in your notebook. List each of your mistakes in the appropriate place on the chart.

This chart should give you a good idea what kinds of spelling errors to watch for as you prepare your final drafts. Look for patterns of mistakes, and when you come across these kinds of words while you're editing, use your dictionary.

EXERCISE 6–13

By this time, you've probably written several essays which have been marked for editing errors. To avoid these errors in future essays you need to recognize the patterns of mistakes you make. Knowing your weaknesses helps you begin to make improvements. Design a chart to record the progress of your own editing skills.

Words with an Apostrophe

Be especially thorough as you edit or proofread your final draft that you use an apostrophe wherever needed. The lack of an apostrophe, though a relatively minor error, still can irritate or confuse your readers. Be sure that any contractions you use include an apostrophe where needed; the apostrophe in a contraction substitutes for the missing letter or letters:

can't	wasn't	it's*
won't	doesn't	would've
didn't	wouldn't	don't

The apostrophe can also indicate omissions of other elements:

o'clock	Spirit of '76
class of '89	Superbowl '86

From time to time, an apostrophe is used to form the plural of a number.

The temperature was in the 90's.
He shoots in the low 70's.

(Apostrophes are optional in these cases—the 90s is also correct.)
Apostrophes are also used with letters and words when they are referred to as words:

Annie is awfully proud of all those *A's.*
I counted at least seventeen *moreover's* in this paper.

---

*The word *it's* always means "it is" or "it has."

Forming Possessives

A more difficult problem in using an apostrophe involves forming possessives. In general, the possessive case of a noun or pronoun that doesn't already end in *s* is formed by adding an apostrophe and *s*.

everyone's favorite	Stephen's yell
somebody else's project	children's books
Grandpa's teasing	daddy's eyes
the team's strength	mother's laugh
the group's belief	the article's thesis

When you join two or more names and wish to indicate joint ownership, only the last name takes an *'s*.

Kathy and Michelle's sisters
Hargrove, Morrell, and Grant's new business

If you want to indicate separate ownership, use *'s* after each name. But if the construction becomes too cumbersome, rewriting the sentence might be better.

Kathy's and Michelle's sisters
Their new business

If you wish to form the possessive of a singular noun that already ends in *s*, add *'s* unless the extra *s* makes the possessive form hard to pronounce.

James's property
Hess's idea
Socrates' point
for goodness' sake

Finally, form the possessive of a plural noun that already ends in *s* by adding an apostrophe:

four days' work	the cars' permits
the speakers' conclusions	the owners' bankruptcy
the artists' representations	the employees' demands

Pronoun Agreement

Another error that can cause your readers problems involves pronoun agreement. By "agreement" we mean that a pronoun should be consistent in number, gender, and person with the word or words to which it refers. The word or words to which the pronoun refers is called an antecedent.

What are the antecedents of the italicized pronouns in the following sentences?

Eventually she will make *her* decision.

The other members have already made *their* decision.

When you use a pronoun to refer back to an antecedent, you must be sure that the pronoun and antecedent agree. The most bothersome agreement problem occurs when the pronoun and its antecedent do not agree in number. In other words, the pronoun and its antecedent must both be either singular or plural. If the antecedent is plural, the pronoun must also be plural. And if the antecedent is singular, the pronoun must be singular. Here are some sentences in which the antecedent and pronoun are in agreement:

Beth drove over in her new truck. *(Both "Beth" and "her" are singular.)*

Members must present their cards at the door. *(Both "members" and "their" are plural.)*

But the pronoun and antecedent in the following sentence are not in agreement:

Each member must present their card at the door. *("Each member" is singular; "their" is plural.)*

You may correct the agreement problem in a couple of ways. First, you can rewrite the sentence:

Members must present their cards at the door.

Another method of correction presents other problems:

Each member must present his card at the door.

Now the pronoun and antecedent agree—both are singular. But this correction isn't really accurate if some members are female. If they are, this correction works.

Each member must present his or her card at the door.

Constructions like this one, however, sometimes get very awkward. When they do, it's usually better to reconstruct the sentence using the plural—then gender agreement isn't a problem. You are likely to run into problems like these when your antecedent is a word such as *anybody, anyone, everyone, everybody, nobody, no one, somebody, someone, a person.*

Collective nouns also present problems in this area. A collective noun is one which, although singular, represents a group of several members. Some collective nouns: *group, team, family, class, public, committee.*

In determining whether to use a plural or singular pronoun with a collective pronoun, you must first decide whether the collective noun is referring to the group as a whole or to the individual members of the group. If the collective noun refers to the group as a whole, then the collective noun may be treated as singular.

The committee will announce its selection at noon. *(Both "committee" and "its" are singular.)*

The public neglected its responsibility. *(Both "public" and "its" are singular.)*

But if you are referring to the individual members of the group, the collective noun may be treated as plural.

The family appreciated their shared interests. *(Both "family" and "their" are plural.)*
The class presented their proposals at the meeting. *(Both "class" and "their" are plural.)*

Most of all, be consistent when dealing with a collective noun. If the noun appears several times in a piece of writing, any pronouns which refer to it should be uniformly singular or plural. Remember, too, that the verb indicates number (plural or singular). Make sure that it, too, agrees.

EXERCISE 6–14

Rewrite the following sentences to eliminate errors in words with apostrophes and pronoun agreement.

A. Its finally time to pay the piper.

B. Im pretty sure that this is someone elses paper.

C. Sometimes when I least expect it, I hear Alices words coming out of my mouth.

D. Every person in the building had to show their identification to the detectives.

E. The legislature is making their last effort to win public approval.

F. Nobody in their right mind would agree to those conditions.

G. The committee is making their own appointments.

H. Someone left their car in our driveway.

I. The audience will have to make up its own minds.

J. Everybody likes to see the results of his or her own hard work, especially when he or she is looking for some incentive to continue his or her efforts.

A Special Note—The Role of the Word in Shaping Thought: The Issue of Gender

The actual world we live in shapes our language. For example, if we examine a particular culture's language and find there is no word for "war," we will probably also find that the concept of war has no reality in that culture's experience. A culture with a wide variety of words for "snow" is probably one in which being able to differentiate between types of snow is important. Most midwesterners see only two types of snow: "snow" and "sleet." Skiers, however, might see "powder," "ice," or "corn." To them the different kinds of snow are important, so they have developed a language that allows them to differentiate. Mario Pei reports in his book *The Story of Language* (New York:

Mentor, rev. ed. 1965) that the inhabitants of the South Sea island of Ponape have five words for "brother" but none for "father." In all probability theirs is a matriarchal society. Neither their culture nor their language allows them to experience the relationship typical in American society between a child and his or her father.

Linguists like Pei and Benjamin Whorf also maintain that the nature of our language colors the way we think about the world. Our concern here is with the way our language shapes our perception of the roles men and women play in society. Simply stated, the question is: does the nature of our language make us think about males and females in such a way that each is rigidly assigned a particular set of societal roles?

To gain some perspective, consider for a moment the Romance languages. They distinguish between genders in the plural, while English does not. In French one refers to a group of females as *elles,* a group of males as *ils.* In English we use *they* in both instances. However, to refer to a group of mixed or unknown gender, French automatically resorts to the masculine *ils.* Similarly, in Spanish one may refer to *mis hijos* (my sons) or *mis hijas* (my daughters); but when the group is of mixed gender, one again uses the masculine *mis hijos* (my children).

Moving closer to home, we should ask ourselves what we are telling children about social roles when we teach them words like "chairman," "policeman," "congressman," "salesgirl," "stewardess," "meter maid," or "manpower." Are we saying that particular professional roles should be associated with a particular gender? In the recent past we called married women who did not earn salaries and stayed at home "housewives." We had no word for men who stayed at home without jobs; perhaps they would have been called "bums." The newly coined word "househusband" perhaps helps us to accept a practice once rejected.

Many educators and other concerned citizens consider these problems with language and gender important enough that they have taken strong stands against what they call "sexist" language: language that perpetuates sexual stereotypes. True, the effort to purge our language of sexism has led to some awkward new terms such as "person-hole cover" and "personkind." But fortunately these examples do not characterize the majority of the changes recommended and taking place in our language today.

A thoughtful writer must decide how to deal with the problem of sexist language. In the previous sentence, for instance, we wrote "a *writer* must decide." If we want to refer to the "writer" in a subsequent sentence or clause, what pronoun should we use? In the past there would have been no problem. Following the practice of the Romance languages, we would have automatically used the masculine "he." Today, however, such usage is considered unacceptable because it tends to reinforce, even if unintentionally, the idea that all writers are male.

Similarly the following sentence is undesirable: "*Each* of them did *his* homework on time." One solution to the problem is to use the plural pronouns "they" or "their" as both plural and singular. Thus we would have: "*Each* of them did *their* homework on time."

Although this usage is common, it is not widely accepted in academic and professional communities since it violates the principles of pronoun agreement we discussed in the previous section. There are better solutions. Throughout this text we have tried to avoid using singular nouns when referring to generic categories, choosing instead the plural. If, for example, we write "writers must decide," then we don't have to deal with the gender issue in choosing a pronoun. When we do use singular nouns, we alternate between masculine and feminine pronouns, or we simply say "he or she."

Our purpose, of course, is not to eliminate gender but rather to eliminate it as an issue. We want to become conscious of how the decisions we make as writers affect the perceptions of our audience. Consequently we do not refer to grown women as "girls." We do not see the need to call attention purposelessly to the gender of a professional—as in "male nurse" or "female astronaut." We do not automatically employ a male usage in cases of collective or unknown gender. Neither do we, however, resort to such unfortunate creations as "first baseperson."

Our goal should be to become aware of how the words we choose reflect our vision of the nature of the world around us. Becoming aware of the different layers of meaning and the shaping power of language takes us a step closer to this goal.

Revision Checklist: Editing

PARAGRAPHS

1. Check each paragraph for correlation to thesis statement.
2. Check each paragraph for supporting detail (where appropriate).
3. Check organization. Make a map of the essay—outline, cluster, or structure.

SENTENCES

1. Check beginnings. Underline the first word of each sentence.
   - Look for frequent repetitions. Do they serve a purpose?
   - Should sentences beginning with "it" be rewritten?
   - Should sentences beginning with a "there are" construction be rewritten?
2. Check your verbs. Bracket the verbs.
   - Should forms of "to be" be replaced with more concrete, descriptive verbs?
   - Should passive constructions be replaced with the active voice?
   - Are your tenses consistent? If not, review the time flow of your essay for logical sequence.

3. Make sure all verbs have subjects that form complete grammatical sentences.

- Do any fragments you find add an emphasis that contributes to the reader's appreciation of your essay? If not, rewrite them as complete grammatical sentences.
- Are there any sentences without verbs? Are they intentional? If not, check their potential effect on your reader.

4. Check your verbs for agreement with their subjects.

WORDS

1. Check for correct use of homonyms from your personal error list.

2. Review your personal spelling chart and check for common errors.

3. Check each use of the possessive to make sure the form is correct.

4. Circle each pronoun and locate its antecedent. Do the two agree? If not, change the pronoun or the antecedent or reconstruct the sentence to eliminate the error.

5. Check to see that you are not using sexist language.

Proofreading Suggestions

Many writers have difficulty proofreading their own work both because of their sense of ownership and because our normal reading habits make proofreading difficult. Since the writer created the piece being proofread, the writer's brain reads faster than the eye, often filling in omitted details and correcting grammatical errors automatically. This process is so natural that the errors are not communicated to the writer. Also, readers normally do not read every word and complete sentence of a text. They usually read groups of words as their eyes quickly scan the page. Consequently even obvious errors are often missed. Changing this behavior is difficult. If you know that you have difficulty proofing your essays and you occasionally make mistakes which should be edited, then the following suggestions might help you prepare a more polished final draft.

1. Word-level editing. Read your essay backwards, from the last word to the first. Use two 3 × 5 notecards to cover up the words before and after the one you are reading. Whenever you come to a word which you do not use frequently or which you occasionally misspell, check the spelling and, if appropriate, the word's meaning. Whenever you encounter a possessive or an apostrophe, stop to make sure you've used the correct form.

2. Sentence-level editing. Once again, read your essay backwards, this time using the notecards to cover the sentences on either side of the one receiving your attention. In this step you are looking for appropriate sentence structure, punctuation, active verbs, subject-verb agreement, and general stylistic effect.

3. Read your essay aloud, slowly. Listen for errors. Sometimes you hear the omitted words, the shifted tenses, the lack of agreement between subject and verb, the shift in pronoun reference that you did not catch reading silently.

4. Finally, if your instructor permits, form an editing group and check each other's essays before your complete the final draft. Professional writers often get assistance from their editors.

The following Final Revision and Editing Checklist reminds you of the possible ways to think about revising your paper. Check each box after you've performed that particular phase of revision or editing. Begin with ideas and work your way toward words. The chart alone can't help you revise, but it should focus your attention and give you a logical sequence for proceeding.

Final Revision and Editing Checklist

	ADD	DELETE	SUBSTI-TUTE	COMBINE	REOR-GANIZE
IDEAS					
PARA-GRAPHS					
SENTENCES					
WORDS					

Sample Student Paper

In the next pages we present a sample student paper as it progresses from prewriting through editing. As you read it, look for the following:

1. The movement in prewriting down the ladder of abstraction, the final topic emerging in the last brainstorm.
2. The different kinds of revision which took place in the first draft.
3. The use of prewriting during the drafting to solve a problem.
4. The importance of editing to the success of the final draft.

Prewriting

1.	New York (Manhatten) K.C.—people rude	Big City. Difference from
2.	Lake of the Ozarks	
3.	The Zoo	
4.	House (Mine)	
5.	Hutchinson, Kansas	Fun, people nice, relaxing
6.	Colorado Beautiful, smells good, moutains, nature	
7.	Cliff Springs Camp	
8.	Benjamin Stables	
9.	Steve's House	
10.	Cresant Hills, Iowa	

In this stage the author is looking for a topic.

Second Prewriting

New York
Manhatten
Bridge
Taxis
Fast, get in wreck
Streets
Cement everywhere
Tall buildings
Hard to see sky
People everywhere
(like a flow of
traffic during rush
hour)
Bums
Bag Ladies
Trash
Smells
Busy at night

China Town
Empire State Bldg
World Trade Center
Beach
Laguardia Airport
(land in ocean)
Dance
Dancers serious
Everyone good
Chorus Line

Radio City Music Hall
Fame
Toe shoes
Sore throat
Aching body

She's found her topic and begins to narrow by first expanding.

She now knows that she could write about her dance experience

All the lights
Big signs and
advertisements
Two story restaurants
(Mc D)
Eleven story (Macys')
Shopping
Bloomingdales
Sacs
Gimbles

Lincoln Center
Statue of Liberty

Sights Streets (City)
Manhatten Bridge
*Times Square
Bloomingdales
Saks 5th Avenue

Gimbles
Macys
Lincoln Center

Statue of Liberty
China Town
Empire State Building
World Trade Center
*Wall Street
Laquardia Airport

Radio City Music Hall
*Broadway
Broadway Shows
(Chorus Line)
Central Park

Beach Musicians on
corners
Horse Buggies
People out all hours
People rude—will run
you over

Famous Restaurants
New York Deli
Mamma Leoni's

Losing weight
Leotards, tights

Sweat

Piano, wooden floor
Third—floor studio
David Howard
People so rude
Serious about
themselves
Hot, sweaty, smelly
Ballet shoes

Taxis (Yellow) Fast
Cement
Skinny streets
Tall buildings on
both sides
(hard to see sky)
people everywhere
people jam—traffic
jam
bums
bag ladies
trash
smelly
(Night—fully lit)
Big signs and
billboards
Stores—two stories
Everything built up
Delis and Corner
Markets
*little vending
stands

The student continues prewriting to generate ideas, details, images as quickly as possible. At this point she is not concerned with spelling, usage, grammar. Her task is to get these ideas on paper.

Tavern on the Green
Russian Tea Room
Lindy's

Third Prewriting

Dance

People are serious about—make a career
Everyone is really   People are strong
good   Muscels toned
Chorus Line   *Metal bars
Fame   *Room crowded
*Kansas City Ballet   No demonstration
Toe shoes   *Told and Do
Sore feet   Hot studio
Aching Body   Lose weight
Wooden floor   Cover up's
Leotards, tights   pants, sweaters
little skirts   Sweat
big, old T-shirts   Covered with Rosin
White cover   David Howard—teacher
Piano—music live   Dancers rude—con-
Third-floor studio   cerned with them-
Ballet shoes   selves
Mirrors across front   Humid—rain makes
of room   floor stickier

She has her
focus and
begins to
generate
details.

Note that
not all of
these items
find their
way into the
essay.

First Draft

In July of 1985 I made a trip to New York. Manhatten Island, Midtown Manhatten. I went to dance, and dance was what I went to do. I had high expectations of my abilities, but they were soon shot down when I walked in the studio on the third floor of a building on 62nd and Eighth Streets. A small room it was. Not what I was used to. There was a little walkway with worn red carpet. Dancers

The author has done such a good job with her prewriting that most of the revisions in the following draft are on the paragraph, sentence and word levels. Notice how many of the various kinds of revision the author uses.

deletion

where *~~located~~* in every space possible. All

~~strattaling~~ strattling each other to get

stretched out. They were all waiting for

~~other~~ the people on the dance floor to fin-

rearrangement ish class.[*The desk to sign in was way back

in the corner*] The dance floor was elevated a   move down

little from the walkway and a metal bar sep-

erated them. Metal bars surrounded the room

and there were more stacked in the corner to

be pulled out to the middle of the room when

bar work was being done. The front wall *~~the~~

~~one that~~* was covered with mirrors, just like

any dance studio. The wall to the left was

all windows. Of course they were always shut

so there would be no possible

~~to keep the heat in even though it was~~

relief from the smeltering heat

substitution *~~probably~~ ~~about 95 degrees F outside~~* In the

front right corner of the dance floor was the

Everything was done to piano music

addition piano.∧ *~~so there was no stopping.~~* *~~I really~~

~~enjoyed it, feeling that music~~* _____. *

off-white ? over it.

substitution The floor was wooden with a∧ *~~cover over it~~*.

?

The *~~cover~~* was covered with rosin, which

was great to turn on except for when

~~when~~ * * it rained and the humidity was

Then it became

high *~~was~~ very sticky and difficult to dance

on.

This
section
causes
problems
throughout

I walked in trying to look confident,
even though I felt sick to my stomach with
nervousness and wanted to go home. The reception desk was back in the back right corner.
From where I was it looked miles away. I

substitution *~~started~~* ^{made} my way through the sea of legs,

arms, and trim bodies. At the desk I intro-

addition duced myself and got *~~a~~* ^{an ever popular} ''who cares'' re-

sponse. Get dressed and stretch ^^{out} was what I

was told. I soon discovered that what I was
going to wear~~ing~~*, the common thing at our
studio in Kansas City, looked really out of
place in New York. I had just some tights and
a leotard, colors pink and black. Everyone
else was wearing all different colors of layered clothing. Like they would start with the

substitution basic leotard and tights, *~~although~~* ^{except} they

would be like, blue and green, or *~~maroon~~*

marroon and yellow, *~~all different colors~~* ^{some really crazy colors}

Then over those they would wear sweats, cut
off, and a short chiffon (sp?) skirt and then
maybe a big, holey(sp?), see-through T-shirt.

substitution *~~I felt almost naked without a couple layers~~* ^{They gave me a feeling of being almost}

~~of clothes~~.* ^{naked}

Time came to take the floor and I

found a place on the bar. The room, being

small anyway, was extremely crowded. It

didn't take me long to see how good everyone

was and the frightful feeling of not belong-

rearrangement ing to come over me now. ¶*Everyone was there

for a career, this was serious and there was

no time for socializing with others. I had

hoped to make some friends up there, but no

one had the time to talk, let alone get to be

friends. ¶*Everyone there was really strong

and had great muscle tone. I was really im-

pressed with the skill these people pos-

sessed. One guy I stood next to, the third

day I was there, was starring in Chorus Line,

the one on Broadway at the time, and was also

doing background work on the T.V. show *~~fame~~*

Fame. He was really good, and I enjoyed

seeing him dance. I found out that other peo-

ple in the class were from New York City Bal-

rearrangement let, *~~taking classes to keep in shape, and~~ Joffrey Ballet, and even K.C. Ballet

~~some were from the Kansas City Ballet also.~~ All were there for the summer to keep in shape

~~Keeping in shape was the main reason all of~~

~~those people where there for the summer.~~* Of

coarse none of them needed it, from my point

of view. On top of being good they *~~were~~* all

had perfect figures. Real skinny and *~~pitite~~*

~~petete~~ petite(sp?), the typical *ballerina ~~ballarina~~*.

This made me even more self-conscious(sp?).

I made it through class, not feeling

too well in the end. My body ws aching from

pushing it so hard to keep up. My feet felt

like lead weights as I tried to walk off of

the floor. I was soaking wet from perspria-

tion. There was no way I had ever sweated

that much before. The only thing that kept

going through my head was, ''Will I return

tomorrow?'' But in the back of my head I knew

I would. For the love of dance and the one

time of performing something correct kept

calling me back.

**The author realized during the first draft that she needed more
detail about the rigor of the studio if she hoped to make her audience empathize.**

Return to Prewriting

Bar Work

Never the same	Tried to follow person in front
Snap, snap, snap	Tell and Do
No demostration	Words different
Floor work	Best in toe shoes

```
Others in ballet    Thrived on challenges
Faster and harder   With live music keep going
                    until stopped
With record, stop when each piece is over
Felt lost    Didn't belong
```

Resume Drafting

This feeling increased as class went

on. The teacher would snap out the words and

then you did them. There was no demonstra-

tion, no time to rehearse, pysically or men-

tally. I kept to the back trying to follow

the people in front of me. Everything was

done over and over and over again, with in-

creasing speed and difficulty. *~~That~~* The piano

never stopped. I was used to a record that

would stop after each peice and give me some

time for rest . There was no time for rest

here.

Here she turns the prewriting above into draft form

Editing

In July of 1985, I made a trip to New

York. Manhatten Island, Midtown Manhatten. I

went to dance, and dance was what I went to

do. I had high expectations of my ablities,

but they were soon shot down when I walked in

the studio, on the third floor of a building

In this section the author integrates the above draft into her essay, makes the revisions she noted on her first draft, and begins to work more on style.

on sixty second and eighth streets. A small

room it |was|. Not what I |was| used to. [There

was] a little walkway with worn red carpet.

Dancers |were| in every space possible. All

strattling each other to get stretched out.

They |were| all waiting for the people on the

dance floor to finish class. The dance floor

|was| elevated a little from the walkway and a

metal bar seperated them. Metal bars sur-

rounded the room and there |were| more stacked

in the corner to be pulled out to the middle

of the room when bar work |was being| done. The

front wall |was| covered with mirrors, just

like any dance studio. The wall to the left

|was| all windows. Of course they |were| always

shut so there would be no possible relief

from the smoltering heat in that studio.

Dancers |were| suppose to sweat. In the front

right corner of the dance floor |was| the

piano. Everything |was| done with live piano

music. *The floor *was wooden* with an off-
                    covered

white canvas over it. The canvas |was| covered

with rosin, which |was| great for turns, except

for when it rained and the humidity |was| high.

When she
checked her
verbs, she
discovered
that she had
overused
"to be"
forms,
repeated
other verbs
that
brought no
images to
mind, and
depended
too heavily
on passive
construction

~~Then it became sticky and difficult to dance~~ ~~on.~~ *

I walked in trying to look confident, even though I felt sick to my stomach with nervousness and wanted to go home. The reception desk was back in the back right corner. From where I was the sea of legs, arms, and trim bodies. After reaching the desk I introduced myself and got an ever popular, ''who cares'' response. Get dressed and stretch out, was what I was told. I soon discovered that what I was going to wear, the common thing at our studio in Kansas City, looked really out of place in New York. I had some tights and a leotard, colors pink and black. Everyone else was wearing all different colors of layered clothing. They would have the basic leotard and tights except in all kinds of crazy color combination. Over those they would wear sweats, cut off, and a short chiffon skirt, and maybe a big, holey, see through T-shirt. They gave me a feeling of being almost naked.

Time came to take the floor and I

She also begins to check for meaningless intensifiers.

found a place on the bar. The room, being

small anyway, was extremely crowded. It

didn't take me long to see how good everyone

was and the frightful feeling of not belong-

ing to come over me. This feeling increased

as class went on. The teacher would snap out

the words and then you did them. There was no

demonstration, no time to rehearse, physi-

cally or mentally. I kept to the back, trying

to follow the people in front of me. Every-

thing was done over and over and over again,

with increasing speed and difficulty. The

piano never stopped. I was used to a record

that would stop after each peice and give

some time for rest. It was easy to see, there

was no time for rest there. Everyone was

there for a career, this was serious and

there was no time for socializing either. I

had hoped to make some freinds up there, but

no one had time to talk, let alone get to be

friends.

Everyone there was really strong and

had great muscel tone. I was *really* im-

pressed with the skill these people possessed. One guy I stood next to, the third day I was there, was staring in Chorus Line, the one on Broadway at the time, and was also doing background work on the television show Fame. He was really good, and I enjoyed watching him dance. I found that other people in the class were from New York City Ballet, Joffry Ballet, and even Kansas City Ballet. All were there for the summer to keep in shape. Of course none of them needed it, from my point of view. On top of being good, they all had perfect figures. Real skinny and petite, the typical ballerina. This made me feel even more self conscience.

   I made it through class, not feeling too well in the end. My body was aching from pushing it so hard to keep up. My feet felt like lead weights as I tried to walk off of the floor. I was soaking wet from perspiration. There was no way I had ever sweat that much before. The only thing that kept going through my head was, ''Will I return tomorrow?'' But in the back corner of my mind, something told me I would For the love of dance and *that* the feeling of performing

something correctly, just that one time;

would call me back.

Although this version is better than the first, it lacks the force that more active verbs could have given it.

Editing

In July of 1985, I made a trip to New

York. Manhattan Island, Midtown Manhattan. I

went to dance and dance is what I did. I had

spelling corrected

high expectations of my abilities, but they

were soon shot down when I walked in the stu-

dio, on the third floor of a building, on

sixty second and eight streets. *A small room

it was, not like my studio in Kansas City.

You walked in through a little walkway with

worn red carpet. Dancers were everywhere.*

next page

*The small room, not like what I was used to,

surprised me. [Walking in through the little

walkway with worn red carpet, all that could

Here she has problems with a dangling modifier.

be seen was dancers. They were everywhere.*]

spelling corrected

all straddling each other to get stretched

out. They were waiting for the people on the

dance floor to finish class. A metal bar was

all that seperated the elevated dance floor

from the walkway. Bars just like it surrounded the room, with others stacked back in

the corner to be pulled to the middle *~~for~~* during

bar work. Just like any dance studio, mirrors

covered the front wall. The wall to the left

had windows, never to be opened for relief

from the smoltering heat. Dancers needed to

sweat. In the front right corner of the dance

floor, the piano sat, and it was played for

every excercise all through class. The

∧*floor* wooden had a rosin-coated, off-white canvas

over it, which made turns easier. Then if it

rained and the humidity rose, the rosin be-

came sticky and made dancing that much more

difficult.

insert above ⌐ The small room, not like what I was used to,

surprised me. Walking through the little

walkway with worn red carpet, I ran into a

⌐ mass of bodies. Dancers were everywhere

She could still make more of her expectations of a N. Y. dance studio.

    I walked in trying to look confident,

even though I felt sick to my stomach with

nervousness and wanted to go home. The recep-

tion desk, in the back right coner, looked

miles away. *~~I made~~* After making my way through the sea

of legs, arms, and trim bodies, I reached the

desk and introduced myself. I got an every

popular, who cares, response of, ''Get

dressed and stretch out.'' I did exactly that

and then discovered how out of place I

looked. The common dress at our studio in

Kansas City was quite different from that in

New York. I had on leotard and tights, colors

black and pink. Everyone else wore the mulit-

colored layered look. For example they would

start with the basic leotard and tights and

add a pair of cut off sweats, a chiffon

skirt, and a big, holey T-shirt. They gave me

a feeling of being naked.

Sentence
construction
is still weak   The outstanding strength and muscel

tone, along with the skill of these dancers

really impressed me. One guy I stood next to,

the third day I [was] there, was starring in A

Chorus Line, the one on Broadway at the time,

and also doing background work in the televi-

sion show Fame. I enjoyed watching him dance.

Some other people in the class [were] from the

New York City Ballet and even a few from the

Kansas City Ballet. During summertime they

all took extra classes to keep in shape. From

my point of view, none of them needed it.
They all had perfect figures, on top of being
good. Their skinny, petite bodies made me
feel even more self-conscious.

I made it through class, not feeling
well in the end. Soaked from perspiration, my
body was aching from pushing it so hard to
keep up. My feet felt like lead as I tried to
walk off the floor. The only thing that kept
going through my head was, ''Will I return
tomorrow?'' But in the corner of my mind,
something told me I would. For the love of
dance and the *feeling of performing something correctly, just that one time, would
call me back.

Internal Rewrite

She has separated this paragraph during the rewrite. Why do you think she did so?

Time came to take the floor and I
found a place on the bar. It did not take me
long to see how good everyone was and the
frightful feeling of not belonging to increase. The teacher snapped out the words and
you were expected to do as she said. No demonstration, no time to rehearse, physically
or mentally, was allowed. I kept to the back,

Once again she rewrites for a purpose—to intensify the perception the audience has of the rigor of the dance studio.

trying to follow the people in front of me.
We kept doing everything over and over and
over again, increasing speed and difficulty
everytime. The piano music never seemed to
stop. In Kansas City, we used a record that
stopped after each piece, which gave little
rest periods. In New York, there was no time
for rest. The serious matter of making it or
failing rode on every dancer's shoulders. The
dream that dance would become their career
filled everyone's head. Every spare minute
had to be spent in practice. I had hoped to
make some friends, but no one had time to
talk, let alone make friends.

Purpose: Sharing and describing an experience
not many other people get to have. To let
others know what it is really like at a dance
school in New York.

Audience: Others, mainly students in the
classroom. I know they would be reading it.
It would be more appealing to those with some
dance experience.

Reread the
statements
of audience
and
purpose
before you
read the
final draft.
What
further
changes
would you
make?

Final Draft of Student Paper

In July of 1985, I took a trip to New
York. Manhattan Island, Midtown Manhattan. I
went on a dance scholarship and dance is what
I did. I had high expectations of my abilities, but they diminished almost the minute I

added detail walked in the studio on the third floor <u>of a
loft</u> on 62nd and 8th. The small room, not
like what I was used to, surprised me. Walking through the little walkway with worn red
carpet, I ran into a mass of bodies. Dancers
were everywhere, all straddling each other to
get stretched out, waiting for the people on
the dance floor to finish class. Only a metal
bar separated the elevated dance floor from
the walkway. Bars just like it surrounded the
room, with others stacked back in the corner
to be pulled to the middle during bar work.
Just like any dance studio, mirrors covered
the front wall. The wall to the left had windows, never to be opened for relief from the
smoldering heat. Dancers needed to sweat. In
the front right corner of the dance floor,
the piano sat, and it was played for every

**Reread the
first version
of this
paragraph.
Notice how
much
stronger the
active verbs
make this
version.**

exercise all through class. The wooden floor
had a rosin-coated, off-white canvas over it
to make turns easier. [But if it rained and
the humidity rose, the rosin became sticky
and made dancing that much more difficult.]

Is this better than the last version?

    I walked in trying to look confident,
even though I felt sick to my stomach with
nervousness and wanted to go home. The reception desk was in the far back right corner,
miles away. After making my way through the
sea of legs, arms, and trim bodies, I reached
the desk and introduced myself. I got an
ever-popular, who-cares, response of ''Get
dressed and stretch out.'' I did exactly that
and then discovered how out of place I
looked. The common dress at our studio in
Kansas City was quite different from that in
New York. I wore a leotard and tights, colors
black and pink. Everyone else wore the multi-
colored, layered look. For example, starting
with the basic leotard and tights, they added
cut-off sweats, a chiffon skirt, and a big,
holey T-shirt. [Next to them, I felt naked.]

This works much better. Emphasis

Time came to take the floor and I found a place at the bar. It did not take long for me to see how good everyone was and for the frightful feeling of not belonging to increase. The teacher snapped out words, expecting the dancers to do as she said. [No demonstration, no time to rehearse, either physically or mentally.] I kept to the back, trying to follow the people in front of me. We kept doing everything over and over again, increasing speed and difficulty each time. The piano music never seemed to stop. In Kansas City, we used a record that stopped after each piece, allowing us little rest periods. In New York, there was no time for rest. The serious matter of succeeding or failing rode on every dancer's shoulders. The dream that dance would become a career filled everyone's head. Every spare minute had to be spent in practice. I had hoped to make some friends, but no one had time to talk, let alone make friends.

A fragment used for emphasis

corrected spelling

The outstanding strength and <u>muscle</u> tone

as well as the skill of these dancers really

impressed me. One male dancer I stood next to

corrected spelling my third day was starring in A Chorus Line,

the one on Broadway at that time, and also

doing background work in the television show

''Fame.'' I enjoyed watching him dance. Some

other people in the class were from the New

The Joffrey Ballet has dropped out. What effect does this change have?

York City Ballet and even a few from the Kan-

sas City Ballet. During summertime they all

took extra classes to keep in shape. From my

point of view, none of them needed it. They

all had perfect figures, on top of being good

dancers. Their skinny, petite bodies made me

feel even more self-conscious.

I made it through class, not feeling

well in the end. Soaked from perspiration, my

body ached from pushing it so hard to keep

up. My feet felt like lead as I tried to walk

off the floor. The only thing that kept going

through my head was, ''Will I return tomor-

row?'' But in the corner of my mind, some-

thing told me I would. For the love of dance

and the happy, satisfied feeling of perform-

```
ing something correctly, just that one time,

would call me back.
```

Deborah Gregory

Another Pause for Reflection: Three Possible Essay Topics

Before we move on to Chapter 7, here are some general topics you might find interesting as subjects for essays to write for this class. Under each topic we've provided a series of prewriting exercises and some possible specific assignments.

Topic #1

We use language in three distinct ways: to present facts or to make an accurate representation of our observed world; to state an opinion or to create an opinion; to create metaphors for our world. Language used factually attempts to provide a one-to-one correspondence to the world we see.

The Language of Fact

Factual language is essential to scientific observation, to business and financial reports, to plans for physical action. When the Reader's Digest *Fix-It-Yourself Manual* tells you how to repair a broken fuse box, your safety depends on the accuracy of the book's language. When the business analyst writes a company report upon which next year's marketing strategies are based, the company's financial health depends on how closely the report corresponds to reality. When the federal government prepares a report on another country's military strength, future Congressional action and our very welfare may depend on how accurately the authors of the report shape their words to present the truth.

The Language of Opinion

The language of opinion is designed to recreate a different kind of reality; it attempts to translate the writer's beliefs or opinions into acceptance by the reader. This reality cannot be verified in the same way that the language of fact can. For example, if the author of the financial analysis wrote that the company's earnings in New York were $1.2 million, a decrease of 16.9 percent, the reader could verify the accuracy of the report. If the writer went on to say that these figures would spell financial disaster unless the company's marketing plans were changed, the reader could not verify the statement. The reader has now entered the realm of inference and opinion and can only agree or disagree with the author's assessment. In questions of belief and opinion, agreement replaces verification as the measure of "truth."

The Language of Metaphor

Although we commonly associate metaphor with literature, metaphor permeates our language. When we say that someone is a star or that he couldn't fight his way out of a paper bag, we have entered the world of metaphor. In the first we are comparing the shining brightness of a star with the success someone has achieved, in the second we are comparing the relative weakness of a paper bag with someone's physical ability. Metaphor allows us to use features from two apparently dissimilar items in order to make a statement about one of the items. Metaphor is therefore similar to the language of opinion because the reader has to agree that the comparison is valid to accept the metaphor.

On the surface, the topic of George Gurley's article on page 15 is the junkyard dog. Gurley, however, focuses on the dog as a means of examining some of the ways we use language.

One usage he explores is the euphemism, the attempt to replace a concrete term tainted by a potentially negative connotation with a more neutral or positive term. A "garbage collector" might hold a dirty, low-status job; a "sanitation engineer," however, has a clean, middle-class occupation.

He also reminds his readers that when they create metaphors—describing something in terms of something else—they'd better make sure their audience understands both parts of the comparison. For example, if a sportswriter tells you that a runner is a flash-in-the-pan, what is she? Like a grease fire—blazing up and then slowly fading away? Like a nugget of gold in a miner's pan—a find in otherwise mediocre company? Like the flash in the pan of a flintlock rifle—lots of fire and noise but no action?

1. Bring to class at least three examples of euphemisms, unspecified contexts (consider ads and commericals), and failed metaphors. Be prepared to explain your examples.

2. Rock. Tree. Cloud. Vine. These four elements of nature are common to your experience. Which of these do you most resemble? Write your choice on a piece of paper, fold it, and exchange it with a classmate. Then interview your partner. Ask five questions to help you ascertain which metaphor your classmate has chosen to describe himself. After you've finished, take a guess and then compare it with what's written on the folded paper. Discuss the accuracy of your guesses. One of the difficulties of attaching a label to someone is that language is symbolic, not representational. A person may be like a cloud; but a person is not a cloud. Write for five minutes, speculating about the difficulties the symbolic nature of language presents to communication. Think especially about words like "Freedom," "Democrat," "American."

Follow this with a longer piece focusing on how language has caused you problems or difficulties in previous attempts at communication.

3. Song lyrics use all three types of language. Review the lyrics of some currently popular music or any other music you are familiar with—hymns, for example. Choose one lyric that predominantly uses one type of language

and bring it to class for discussion. Write a short analysis of each lyric, explaining with examples why you have assigned each lyric to its category.

4. Choose a song lyric which presents an opinion or belief. Write a paper stating the belief the lyric is advocating and explain how the lyric goes about developing this belief.

5(a). Choose a song lyric that either fails to accurately use the language of fact—perhaps it pretends to be "factual," while actually advocating a belief about the world—or one which presents an opinion or belief you cannot accept. What kind of world does it describe? How do the people in this world act? What moral and ethical view of the world do the lyrics convey? Is this world view similar to or different from your own? Specifically where and how in the lyric does its author create what you have just described? After discussion, pick one lyric—either your own or one chosen by a classmate—that creates a strong sense of agreement, or one that you find upsetting. For the next class, bring in at least one full page of prewriting; you may use any of the techniques you've learned thus far. In addition, write at least four statements of opinion (tentative thesis statements) about the lyric which you develop as a result of studying it. For example: I believe this song encourages its listeners to take an active role in protesting government inaction in South Africa; I believe this song describes a kind of love which doesn't really exist; I believe this song encourages irresponsible behavior with sex and drugs.

5(b). Discuss in class or write an analysis of one of your four statements which would make a good starting point for a longer paper. Ask yourself the following questions: Why is it worth writing about this topic? Do I have any reservations about it as a topic? Who would be interested in reading this paper? Why? Where would I be likely to reach this audience? What kinds of written forms (think about the grid) might be appropriate for this topic? Which would help me best accomplish my purpose? How can I write the essay to appeal to my readers? How do I establish contact with them? Would it be more effective to consider this topic in the past, the present, or the future?

5(c). Choose one of the prewriting techniques and do a complete prewrite for your topic. Then reread your prewrite. Use some method—underlining, cutting and pasting, gridding, outlining—to sort your material. Revise your initial assertion. Expand on your current prewrite by at least half a page. Ask yourself the following questions: Is there anything I don't know about this topic which I need to know? Where can I find the necessary information? Should any of my information be deleted? Does it need to be rearranged or combined? Now write your rough draft.

5(d). After rereading your rough draft, revise it. Bring it to class. Answer in writing the following questions:

• What kind of relationship have you tried to establish with your reader? Bracket those sections of your paper which helped you answer this question.

- What have you assumed your selected audience knows about your topic?
- Have you given concrete examples, illustrations, or reasons to convince your reader of the probability of your opinions? Note in the margins the purpose of each of your supporting arguments.

Be prepared to discuss these questions in class before you begin your next draft. [This assignment was based on readings presented in Susan Wittig, Franklin Holcomb, and Anne Dunn, *The Participating Reader* (Englewood Cliffs, N.J.: Prentice-Hall, 1978).]

Topic #2

For years English teachers have travelled across the United States incognito. Whenever asked by a travelling companion, "What do you do?" the English teacher has learned to reply swiftly, "I'm a census taker." Anything but the truth. Why? Because if the truth were given, the travelling companion would reply one of two ways: either "Oh, that was my worst subject!" or "Oh-Oh. Now I'll have to watch what I say!"

To ascertain why the English teacher is so universally maligned, the National Council of Teachers of English is soliciting manuscripts for a collection of student-written essays which examine responses to English classes. The tentative title of the collection is *In and Out of the Trenches: The Students' Stories.* (This apocryphal assignment is a modification of one Dick Luckert uses with teachers in the Greater Kansas City Writing Project.)

1 (a). Write five sentences, each recalling one of your most memorable positive experiences in an English class.

1 (b). Write five sentences, each recalling one of your most memorable negative experiences in an English class.

2 (a). Pick one of the five sentences from 1(a) above and write on it *nonstop* for five to ten minutes.

2 (b). Do the same thing for 1(b).

3. Complete the following phrase three different ways: "Upon completing years of taking English classes . . . "

4. Review the first three prewriting assignments. Write an extended paragraph in which you describe the essay you would like to write. Describe the subject, what you would like the focus to be, why you chose this particular subject, and what strategies you might use to develop your essay. Bring a copy of your rough draft to class and discuss it with a classmate before revising.

Topic #3

Write an essay in which you follow the career of your favorite actor, singer, artist, politician, athlete, musician. Notice that the basic nature of this assignment is process—you are describing the process of change. Notice also, however, that there are other ways of thinking about the topic. Perhaps in reviewing the person's career you notice that there are four distinct stages which you can label, for example, "struggling unknown"; "alcohol, drugs, and honky tonks"; "success and stardom"; "conversion to humanitarianism." If you followed this pattern, you would be using classification/division. Perhaps you see as your main focus the dramatic difference in the person's personal life after achieving success—comparison/contrast. Perhaps you feel that the person you chose is an exemplar of religious spirit; in this case you might want to focus your paper on definition, using religious spirit as your focal point.

CHAPTER SEVEN

Convincing Others: Argument and Persuasion

Those who corrupt the public mind are just as evil as those who steal from the public purse.—Adlai Stevenson

Defining "Argument"

Although argument appears here in a separate chapter, you should be encouraged to know that you will continue to use those processes and skills you've been refining throughout the text. You still need to use prewriting devices to help generate ideas and shape your thoughts. You still need to go through the processes of rereading and reconsidering your ideas and your support. You still need to consider purpose and audience. What you write still needs to go through all the stages of revision from global considerations through editing.

What, then, makes the process of convincing others different enough from other kinds of writing to merit its own chapter? The answer lies in resistance. When you anticipate that your audience will resist your ideas, you are forced, if you want to be successful, to adopt some specific strategies to temper or overcome this resistance.

When you try to convince someone that your position on an issue is the correct one, that it is closer to the truth than other positions, you are arguing. An argument is a logical presentation of points designed to make your audience agree with you, or at least accept the validity of your position. No matter how forcefully an argument is presented, it may fail to change the reader's mind if the issue is one about which he or she feels strongly. But a well-planned argument should at least lead the reader to accept and understand the writer's point of view. In other words, you may not change a mind that is completely decided, but you can demonstrate that your position rests on logical, solid, and acceptable grounds.

The word "argument" is not new to you. Unless you are an extremely even-tempered person, you've "argued" before. You've argued with siblings about which TV program to watch. You've argued with parents about an activity or a curfew. You've argued with a friend or classmate about current events or ideas presented in a lecture.

EXERCISE 7–1

List three arguments you've had with somebody and the issue each involved (you may not want to get too personal, for you'll be sharing your responses with your classmates.) Then discuss, in a group or as a class, how you and your opponent each presented your view of the issue. Was there a clear "winner"? That is, did the argument result in a change of behavior or point of view for either of you? What emotions were displayed? Anger, sorrow, frustration? Gladness? Humor?

Most of the arguments you've had were probably somewhat emotional. You've probably even won some arguments on the basis of emotion, not reason. That is, if your parents initially refuse to allow you to take a week-long ski trip, they may eventually give in because the trip seems so important to you, because they feel guilty, because they love you and want you to be happy. You may have prompted a friend to change plans or gotten a friend to lend you a jacket because of your friendship. But depending upon such emotional appeals is risky, for with many of the people whose views differ from yours you share no emotional bond upon which you can depend to get your way. For these people, and for many of those you have as friends or relatives, you need to appeal to reason rather than emotion if your position is to stand any chance of acceptance.

Appealing to reason is fairer in a way, for the issue itself receives the emphasis. Your argument must still be planned with your audience in mind, of course. But by focusing on the *issue* instead of the emotions associated with it, both you and your opponent are more likely to stay calm, to listen well, to be objective, and to discuss the matter reasonably rather than hurling insults.

As we discuss it in this chapter, *argument is a logical process of presenting one's position on a clearly stated issue.* The issue to be argued must meet certain requirements, and the manner of presenting your position is more logical than emotional. In an argument, the writer appeals to the audience's reason by presenting the reasoning that led to his or her position.

Such appeals to reason are not new to you, either. At times when asking your parents or a friend for something, you've presented your case logically, relying little, if at all, on emotion to sway them. You've also listened to a good many arguments, not only by parents and friends but by politicians, supervisors, co-workers, university officials, and teachers. In school now, and later as you pursue a profession, you are obliged both to present and hear arguments on a variety of issues. As a student, you may find it necessary to argue for a change in course requirements or student services. You may argue with another student or with a professor about a view presented in a textbook.

Attorneys argue cases. People in business argue about budgets, policy changes, personnel matters. Nurses, doctors, and medical technicians argue about treatment, diagnoses, ethical responsibilities. Teachers argue about effective methods, curriculum design, and placement procedures. Scholars argue about themes and significance. Construction workers and architects argue about design, strength, and placement. When a controversy arises, anyone who works must argue about how best to accomplish a task, how best to solve a problem, how best to resolve some troubling situation. We undertake such arguments in order to convince someone that our position is the one closest to the truth.

EXERCISE 7–2

Look through the professional journals in the library until you find one of interest. It can focus on any area—medicine, psychology, architecture, personnel management, literature, education, economics, business, agriculture. After skimming several articles, select one whose argument you can readily identify. Bring to class bibliographical information and write a paragraph explaining what issue is being argued and the author's position on that issue.

Forming Beliefs and Opinions

In arguing issues in writing, you anticipate some measure of doubt and disbelief toward your position. Therefore, you must analyze your audience carefully, assess the assumptions they may hold as they read, and then attempt to show them, step by step, the reasoning underlying your position. If the steps are well reasoned, if each can be regarded as true, your conclusion—your position—follows logically from that reasoning. Remember, though, that even a well-executed argument may fail to change your reader's mind, for the reader's belief may rest on reasoning as valid as your own but different, or the reader's beliefs, like many of your own, may be based on something other than reason.

EXERCISE 7–3

List several issues about which you feel so strongly that no argument could change your beliefs. Then write a paragraph explaining why your beliefs couldn't be changed. What is the basis for these beliefs? Emotion? Reason? Faith? Tradition?

EXERCISE 7–4

In your journal or a short paper, explore more fully one of the issues you listed in Exercise 7–3, tracing the origin of your position on the issue. Summarize the opposing view as well, exploring what you believe to be the basis of the opposing view. Then present the line of reasoning someone with the opposing view would take.

EXERCISE 7–5

1. Write a sentence that expresses your position on each of the general issues listed below:

abortion   gun control
capital punishment   the national deficit
drunk driving laws   nuclear power
euthanasia   prison reform

2. Now, go back through your statements, this time indicating the strength of your belief by labeling each with a number from 1 to 5. Number one indicates a weak belief, number five a strong, adamant belief.

3. Next, pick the *three* statements from above that you rated highest, those you believe most strongly. Then, for each of the three, explain in a one-to-two-page paper how you came to hold that belief, how it was formed, what led you to adopt your position.

Where do your beliefs and opinions come from? Many beliefs are shaped by religion—because your church does not condemn abortion, neither do you. Other beliefs are formed by personal or family tradition—because your family has always owned guns and used them responsibly, you are opposed to gun control. Still others are based on experience—because an acquaintance was killed last year by an intoxicated driver, you believe that no law about drunk driving could be too harsh. And some are based on reason—after considering arguments on both sides of the issue, you decide that euthanasia is a completely moral and ethical choice for the terminally ill.

But beliefs are also formed through "public wisdom." You develop many emotional or logical beliefs from articles in newspapers and magazines, stories repeated on the TV news and in TV documentaries, and ideas picked up from family, friends, teachers, employers, and acquaintances. A series of articles in a weekly magazine denounces drunk driving laws as harsh, so you do as well. Or a well-researched documentary outlines a plan for prison reform, a plan to which you quickly subscribe. A family member whom you admire supports a certain political candidate, so you endorse the candidate as your own.

We are all influenced to some degree by what we read and hear. The media may be our only sources of information about issues with which we've had little direct experience. But when we begin simply to parrot the opinions of others, to adopt lines of reasoning without examining them, we do ourselves and our writing an injustice.

As you work on an argument for this class and others, take yourself out of the realm of public wisdom as much as possible. Although you'll have to rely on experts' opinions for some facts or data, deal with an issue honestly—as yourself, not as your favorite columnist or news commentator. This may automatically put some topics out of bounds. If the only arguments you can muster on an issue are those that you've heard repeated constantly, it's probably best to select another topic. If you've heard all the arguments, chances are your reader has heard them as well. (Most writing teachers flinch at the prospect of reading still more papers on gun control, abortion, euthanasia, etc.) This caution is not meant to denigrate the strength of your beliefs but to suggest that some topics have received such close scrutiny from so many experts over such a long period of time that few people could design a fresh argument about them. And you may have such deep-rooted beliefs about some topics that you're unable to view them with the objectivity that constructing an argument requires.

Choosing Arguable Topics

What sorts of topics, then, are suitable for argument? First, while practicing the prewriting techniques for selecting and developing a topic, keep in mind that your topic should be one that allows you more room for thought than many "public wisdom" topics allow. You may be able to find a fresh approach to one of those topics, but if not, avoid them.

Second, the point you choose to argue must be one about which some doubt exists. There must be at least two possible views on the topic; it must be a matter of some dispute, some debate, some doubt. It must be an issue about which some question exists. It must be *arguable.*

What isn't arguable? Primarily, topics which concern facts and tastes or those about which no doubt exists.

Facts are facts. One may doubt the source of a fact, of course, and if the source is found faulty then there is no fact. Facts are statements that can easily be proven true; thus the element of doubt needed for an arguable point does not exist. The following are facts:

- Jerry Mathers played the part of Theodore Cleaver on TV's *Leave It to Beaver.*

- The 39 hostages remaining in Beirut after TWA flight 847 was hijacked were released June 30, 1985.

- As of 1984, no woman had ever been elected President of the United States.

- The San Marcos River originates from springs in San Marcos, Texas.

These statements are not arguable, for they can be verified easily.

Matters of personal taste or opinion are not arguable either, for they allow no room for doubt. Your tastes and opinions are your own and do not rely on any objective standard for their validity. Thus the following statements cannot be argued:

- I prefer Tom Waits to all other singers and songwriters.

- Manicotti is better than lasagna.
- I have always liked short skirts.
- Our softball team, the Disoriented Austinites, had the most fun during the playoffs.

Any of these statements or the factual ones presented earlier might be suitable for expository essays—essays whose purpose is to inform or to explain—but they are not suitable for argumentation because they are not subject to doubt. (Some of the statements could be made arguable if an element of doubt were introduced, if they were phrased less as personal opinions.)

One final category of topics not suitable for argumentation comprises matters whose truth can be readily established; their points are so general that no opposing view can be taken. Here again, these issues could possibly be handled in an expository form, but because no doubt exists they could not be developed in an argument.

- Some universities have divested themselves of their South African investments.
- Computer literacy is becoming a part of public education at all levels.
- Violence and sex play a part in the plots of many soap operas.
- Consumers must be aware and informed if they are to select the telephone service best suited to their needs.

In short, then, when developing a topic for argument, you must avoid matters of fact and taste as well as those whose truth is instantly apparent.

An arguable topic is one with which you are familiar enough to present your own viewpoint but about which other viewpoints exist. Your view can be proven neither true nor false—you can only establish a good case for its truth. You establish your case by presenting the reasoning and support on which your view rests. Such a presentation may not prove conclusively that your position is the correct one, for controversial issues are seldom absolutely settled, but it does establish the validity of your position. The following statements contain points that can be argued:

- An analysis of his work and life suggests that Nathaniel Hawthorne was deeply concerned about incestuous relationships and their effects.
- Computers in the English classroom can be used successfully for invention and revision as well as for grammar instruction.
- *The Breakfast Club* is one of the few "teen exploitation" films to portray teenagers in a sensitive and realistic manner.

These statements can be argued because their claims cannot be accepted as true; one may doubt their veracity. You could argue for or against them, and your success in getting your reader to accept your position depends on the reasoning and support you offer.

EXERCISE 7–6

Individually or in groups, decide which of the following statements are arguable. Write a few sentences for each explaining your decision.

1. The U.S. government should not restrict the importation of Italian shoes.

2. Pierced ears are not attractive.

3. Halfway houses for drug abusers should not be operated in residential areas.

4. It is better to have loved and lost than never to have loved at all.

5. The United States has no effective means of identifying and punishing terrorists.

6. Rocky Road ice cream tastes better than Butter Brickle.

7. Women are vain.

8. Mothers should not work outside the home until their children are at least five years old.

9. Men are better cooks than women.

10. Parents should not be permitted to keep their children with them in "survivalist" camps.

11. Poor inner-city children benefit from organizations that provide them with a week or two of summer camp in the country.

12. All high school students should study at least three novels before graduating.

In explaining your reasons for believing that some of the statements are arguable and others are not, you came very close to argumentation. You took a position—"Number nine is not arguable," for example, and then explained why your position was closer to the truth than its opposite. You may have said the statement concerns a matter of personal opinion, a matter which depends on no objective standard, and therefore cannot be argued. Or perhaps you said that the statement *could* be argued because at least two views exist and evidence could be offered on both sides.

EXERCISE 7–7

For the next week, make regular entries in your reading and media logs responding to issues that are suitable for argumentation. Use the log to explore possibilities raised by what you've seen in newspapers, magazines, or on television.

EXERCISE 7–8

Use at least three of the prewriting techniques we've discussed to do some preliminary work for an argument paper. Take as a general subject any of those issues in which you have a special interest, or use topics raised in other classes. *Your paper will be easier and more personal, however, if you steer clear of those issues around which so much "public wisdom" is floating—abortion, gun control, capital punishment, and so on.* Brainstorm, freewrite, cluster, and use the grid or other prewriting methods to find arguable topics.

EXERCISE 7–9

After prewriting to discover possible arguable topics (Exercise 7–8), choose four you are most interested in writing about. Then discuss each with a partner or in a group to discover various viewpoints that could be taken toward each topic. Be especially attentive to opposing views.

EXERCISE 7–10

For the next class period, construct a thesis sentence (or two) for each of the four topics you explored in Exercise 7–9. You should now have at least one thesis sentence for each of the four topics. In your group or as a class check each thesis sentence to see if it contains an arguable point. Remember that to be arguable, the thesis

1. cannot be a matter of fact.
2. cannot be a matter of personal taste or opinion.
3. cannot be a matter universally accepted or rejected.

The thesis of an argument *must* address a matter about which some doubt remains. It must be a matter of judgment, so that as a writer your task is to present your position as the most reasonable one.

Audience in Argument

In order to argue effectively, you need to anticipate the views your audience holds and determine how strongly they can be expected to adhere to their views. Because effective argumentation depends on reasoning, you need to know as much as possible about how the audience reasons.

To draw conclusions about the position you expect your audience to hold, you need to know something about their background, their interests, and concerns. Knowing something about their background—age, gender, socioeconomic level, occupation—helps you select and present the points that will appeal to them most effectively. Determining beforehand how well informed your readers are about the issue you are arguing also helps you construct your argument. If they are very familiar with the issue, then you can refer briefly to some basic facts or information. But if the issue is one about which they are relatively uninformed, more background and more explanation are required.

As you analyze your audience, you are attempting to define common ground, to identify views you both hold and experiences you've both had. For example, if you are arguing about a change in office policy, referring to daily office routines may establish common ground from which your side of the issue may be argued. So could common attitudes. Religious, socioeconomic, ethnic, or professional background might also be areas where you and your audience can meet. If, as an accountant, you are concerned that the members of your firm are composing engagement letters that could lead to lawsuits against the firm, it's likely that other members share your concern. After establishing that concern, you can then argue for what you believe is the best solution to the problem.

Without some common ground, no argument can take place. Although you and members of your audience may disagree on the issue, you must assume that you both work through problems logically, that reason is an acceptable method by which to resolve your differing views. If this willingness is not present, nothing can be argued.

Beyond this acceptance of reason, you must ascertain the assumptions both you and the audience hold and how they differ. Working from your common ground, you can then argue points concerning your differences.

Suppose, for example, that your social organization has asked you to write a proposal to be read by the university's Alumni Association, its Parents Organization, and various members of the university administration. The proposal asks for an exception to a longstanding rule that prevents all campus organizations from holding parties Sunday through Thursday nights. Your organization will be celebrating its twenty-fifth anniversary in the coming year and would like to begin festivities on a Tuesday night. So you are proposing that an exception be made to the rule.

What can you assume about the audience? You may assume that the administration are reluctant to grant exceptions to rules. You may also assume that they may be subject to pressure from the Alumni Association and the Parents Organization because the administration generally likes to keep happy those who are likely to support the university.

About the Alumni and Parents groups you may assume that they share your pride in your organization and would like to see a successful anniversary celebration. Many members of both organizations will be attending the festivities; many will also be involved in planning and operations.

The members of all three groups are older than you; most have been out of school for a while and have been working in various professions and occupations. Most retain an interest in your organization—some more strongly than others—and most look at the celebration as a justified event.

The difficulty, however, is to convince the administration and some members of the other two groups that an exception to a rule—a rule designed to prevent extracurricular activities from interfering with studying—is warranted. To assure your audience that you are aware of their position and to respond to their objections with solid reasoning, you must anticipate the objections your audience may have and answer those objections point by point.

EXERCISE 7–11

For each of the following writing situations, list assumptions you could make about the audience that would help you in determining their position. What is your common ground? Also list the objections you'd expect the audience to have or the reasons they would agree with the stated position.

1. Fourth of July Festival

Argument

Each July 4, your city holds a festival featuring music, food, a carnival, and other activities. At this year's festival you were dismayed to discover that the carnival rides were very expensive; children's rides cost $1.50 and adult rides $2.00. You've decided to write a letter of protest to the organizers of the event and to city officials, and to address the public through newspaper editorials. The festival is a fund-raising event, but you think that high prices deter many people from participating. So you want the volunteer organizers to set lower prices next year.

Audience

Organizers—people in the business and professional community who volunteer their time to organize the festival.

Mayor and City Council—people who help in organizing the event and who must approve all festival plans.

Public—other residents of your city, some of whom attended the festival and others who did not.

2. Day-care Center

Argument

Your university runs a day-care program for the children of students, faculty, and the community at large. The weekly charges are identical for all children, a practice you'd like to see changed. The university does make a small profit from its day-care center, and you think the profit should be used for operating costs so students could be charged less than the other two groups. Students, after all, generally have less money than faculty members or workers in the community, and good, reasonably priced day care is essential for students who have children. You decide to write letters to the administration, the faculty, the student newspaper, the city's daily newspaper, and the directors of the day-care center arguing for reduced rates for students.

Audience

Administration—university officials who are concerned about retention and costs.

Faculty—instructors who may or may not have children in day care. Those who do are likely to be fairly young or new to their professions.

Students—some who are parents; most who are not. For most, it's a financial strain to pay tuition, buy books, and meet living expenses.

Community members—some who have children in this center; most who do not.

Day-care center directors—officials who are primarily concerned with good care for the children, but who are also concerned about covering operating costs.

3. Transferring to Another University

Argument

You have decided to transfer to another university next fall because most of your friends go there. It also has a slightly better Communication Studies Department—your major—so you'd benefit academically as well as socially. Costs are about the same. But the university you are attending now is your parents' and sisters' alma mater, and the whole family was counting on you to graduate from there as well. You write a letter presenting your argument in favor of a transfer to your parents and to each of your two sisters.

Audience

Parents—active in University Alumni Association, strong supporters of and believers in their alma mater.

Sisters—also support the alma mater but not as strongly as your parents. Both were happy there and never considered another college.

When you construct an argument, it's important to analyze the audience just as you've done in Exercise 7–11. Noting who they are, their position on the issue, and the objections they may make to your argument helps you decide how to structure the argument, what points to include, and how to answer the objections they might have.

People who do a great deal of public speaking know the importance of audience analysis. If you follow a politician on the campaign trail, you'll see that his or her speech is tailored to each particular audience. This is not to say that politicians or other public speakers simply tell the audience what they want to hear—although some may—but that the manner in which the speech is written changes to make the message more acceptable to each audience.

EXERCISE 7–12

In exercises 7–7 through 7–10 you worked on finding a subject for an argument. You did some prewriting, wrote preliminary thesis sentences, and explored the possibilities each presented as a topic for argument. Select one of the thesis sentences for a paper (this may require additional prewriting or discussion). Then analyze the audience for your argument using the guide that follows.

Audience for Argument

1. General characteristics:
   - age
   - gender
   - economic background
   - educational background
   - ethnic background
2. Probable common ground
3. Their knowledge of the topic
4. My assumptions about them
5. Their assumptions about me
6. Their objections to my position
7. Overall, this audience is
   - against my view of the issue
   - indifferent to my view
   - in agreement with my view

Structuring an Argument

An argument, like other essays, can be divided into an introduction, a body, and a conclusion. It is worth noting again that an introduction may be one paragraph or several, as may the conclusion, and that each supporting point of your argument may take one or more paragraphs for proper development.

In addition to the regular functions of interesting your readers in your topic and providing signals of what is to follow, the introduction should also appeal to the common ground you have found with your audience. It might contain broad references to the opposing argument, references acknowledging the validity of an opposing point, qualifying the point, or attempting to refute it. References to common ground and opposing arguments might also be used as transitions between paragraphs or points. An entire argument, in fact, may be structured by the opposing argument as you reveal the flaws in each opposing point or show how the points of your argument add up to a more valid position than those of the opposition.

No single structure exists for all arguments. If you've taken speech or communication classes, however, you may be familiar with the following pattern. The pattern consists of eight parts, but as you structure your own argument or read those of other writers, you quickly see that the pattern is adaptable to a writer's purpose. You need not include all steps, nor must you follow the pattern in a set order.

1. Introduction: In the introduction, the writer tries to gain the audience's attention and establish his or her own credibility. Some of the ideas discussed in the section on introductory paragraphs (pp. 102–114) might be suitable here.

2. Exposition: In this section, the writer provides any background information that may be necessary to the argument.

3. Proposition: Here the thesis or major point is stated.

4. Arrangement: In this section, the writer states the divisions or categories by which the paper has been organized. George Hanford's essay at the end of this chapter follows a statement of his thesis *(proposition)* with an *arrangement* section in which he states the three points he considers in his essay.

5. Evidence: This part presents support for the major point or thesis, including proof, evidence, examples, and illustrations.

6. Confutation: In this section, the writer acknowledges opposing arguments. The writer may refute or qualify opposing views, trying to show the error of the opposing argument.

7. Digression: Here the writer does *not* wander from the issue, as the term implies. Rather, the writer points up parallels or analogies or refers to related issues that support the argument.

8. Conclusion: Depending on audience and purpose, the conclusion may summarize the argument, emphasize the major point, suggest action, or consider future ramifications of the topic.

An effective argument contains some of these parts, but it need not contain them all. The *exposition* for example, might be omitted if your audience is familiar with the background of the issue you are arguing. *Exposition* could serve as the *introduction*. You might want to move the *confutation* to an early part of the paper if you suspect that you wouldn't get your readers' attention until you established that certain views were unsupportable. The *evidence* section is generally the lengthiest. In a short or uncomplicated argument, you may have no need for the *arrangement* section. You can structure an argument simply by using *introduction, evidence,* and *conclusion.*

The argumentative pieces you write find their own form based upon your audience, purpose, and subject. Chances are that form is some variation of this eight-part pattern. Use the pattern to help you find the form, but don't feel compelled to force your points into this structure.

EXERCISE 7–13

Read George Hanford's essay, "An Educational System that Has No Losers" at the end of this chapter. Then, in groups, go back through it, trying to identify the eight parts just described.

EXERCISE 7–14

For the argumentative paper you have been developing in the previous exercises, list the points comprising the opposing argument. Then answer each point, acknowledging those that are valid but finding some way to diminish their importance, qualifying those whose validity holds up only under certain circumstances, and refuting those that are invalid.

EXERCISE 7–15

Now write a draft of your paper. You must juggle lots of considerations—audience, opposition, the topic of your own argument. As you write, keep in mind that most likely you will need to revise all or parts of your paper. Right now, though, you need to get a completed draft on paper so you'll have some material to revise. If you have difficulty getting started, follow the eight-part pattern presented earlier.

Supporting Your Argument

As in any other essay, the thesis of your argument must be supported by reasons, explanations, illustrations, and examples. Because an argument is an appeal to reason, however, you can expect your audience to be especially wary of the evidence you offer in support of your main and subordinate points. They will scrutinize your argument and evidence for its logic and validity. A hostile audience—one which opposes your view—may be especially eager to note distortions of fact and breaks in logic.

How, then, can you assure the validity of your evidence?

First of all, you must choose reliable, authoritative sources. Your sources may be gleaned from newspapers, magazines, books, articles, television, movies, interviews, or experience, but in every instance you must make sure the evidence is reliable, reputable, authoritative, and unbiased.

Let's start with your own experience. You may certainly use your own experiences as evidence in favor of your argument, but you must be careful not to generalize too much from them. Your experience may not be representative; thus you may not assume that just because your own experience supports an argument that the experiences of others will. You may use it as part of your evidence but not as the sole basis for your argument.

You must also be careful about the evidence you gather from your reading and viewing. Your sources should be the most current ones available and the most respected. Thus a report in *Redbook* on the advantages of a low-fat diet would be more credible than one in *The National Enquirer* but less credible than a study published in the *Journal of the American Medical Association*. The reputation of the source affects the measure of validity your audience assigns to the evidence.

The same is true of evidence you gather from interviews with experts. The expert must indeed be knowledgeable about the subject of your argument. The opinions expressed by a sociology professor about a particular urban renewal project may not be as reliable as an interview with a city council member. Here again you must consider what your audience will accept as expert and informed.

Be aware, too, of possible bias on the part of an expert, bias which could be embedded in views expressed both orally and in writing. Examine the reasoning that leads to those views as closely as possible; try to determine whether the view is based on solid reasoning. Even if the reasoning appears sound, examine the view with a critical eye and use it accordingly.

Facts and Opinions

The more you can base your argument on factual evidence, the sounder it is, for facts are verifiable. When you use opinions—opinions of an authority, for example—be as sure as possible that the expert's opinion rests on fact. An expert opinion should be objective; it should have been reached after a careful examination of fact.

You must also interpret facts and opinions fairly. If the registrar of your university tells you, for example, that minority enrollment is lower than what one would expect given the population of the school, you are not justified in claiming that the university actively practices discrimination. Minority enrollment could be low for a number of reasons—an ineffective recruitment policy, intensive recruitment efforts in cities with low minority populations, a lack of programs attractive to minority students. Combined with other evidence, low minority enrollment might indeed indicate discriminatory practices, but alone such evidence is weak.

Logical Reasoning

Induction. Because argument is based on logic and appeals to reason, you need to become familiar with two types of logic—induction and deduction. When you use induction, you observe instances or facts and draw a general conclusion from them. You reason, then, from the specific to the general. You use this type of reasoning often—perhaps daily—as you make decisions or form opinions.

Suppose you have been asked to babysit again by a neighborhood couple. Trying to decide whether to accept, you review these facts:

- The couple pays less than others for whom you babysit.
- The children are wild and rowdy.
- There are no good reading lamps; television reception is poor.
- You're expected to entertain the children until they want to go to sleep.
- Often the people don't have the cash to pay you, so you have to go back to collect your earnings.
- Their house is a disgusting mess.

From the evidence you've gathered—evidence gathered from your own experience—you conclude that working for this couple again will be a miserable and unrewarding experience.

The thesis of the following student essay was reached through induction. The student was asked to view one television program, keeping notes of the number and types of commercials aired during that program. Based on her observations, then, she was to make some point about the program, the audience, or the advertisers' conception of the audience.

As you read the essay, note the kind of support she draws from her observations.

The Drudge

Advertisers know who their audience is and what types of items it will buy. Thus different types of commercials are shown at times and during programs expected to attract the target audience. Advertisers stereotype this audience, believing that commercials which feature the stereotype will appeal to the viewers. During soap operas the main stereotype is the housewife. And, although most housewives are concerned with keeping their homes relatively neat and inhabitable and their families happy and safe, commercials shown during soap operas depict the housewife as a plain woman whose only concerns are cooking, cleaning, and taking care of her family.

The women who portray housewives in these commercials are just about always made to look plain and unattractive. Their hairstyles are conservative—ponytails held by navy ribbons or modified curly tops—and their make-up minimal. No red lipstick, no heavy mascara or blue eyeshadow. They are dressed in dark polyester pleated pants and plaid shirts buttoned to the neck. The image suggests that housewives are neat and practical, plain, and unfashionable. The image is degrading.

A recent episode of The Guiding Light was interrupted by nineteen commercials. They varied in type but were all directed to the housewife. The greatest number of the commercials—ten—advertised food or cooking products. The usual slogan was that the product featured was best for a family or a husband. Crisco Oil, for example, ''doesn't leave your chicken greasy'' so it is guaranteed to keep the cook's family healthy and happy.

Other food commercials were aimed at the mother who wanted to please her children. In one Kraft ad, the kids would only eat Kraft macaroni and cheese, or ''cheese and macaroni,'' as the darling children preferred to say it. The implication was that good mothers buy Kraft because their children like it and because its increased cheese levels are more nutritious.

A commercial for Skippy Peanut Butter urged mothers who care about their children to buy Skippy because it has ''no added sugars.'' The mothers in the commercial, dressed in polyester pants and cardigans, discussed the sugar consumption of their kids while at a picnic table spread with cakes and cookies.

Other commericals shown during this soap opera urged housewives to purchase particular cold medicines. Most of these featured sick children or ailing husbands; after all, mothers never get sick. All of these showed the housewife administering the cold remedy and then being instantly rewarded by the immediate recovery of the child or husband. The housewife's joy at the recovery implies that she has once again been recognized as a good mother or wife because she selected the right cold medicine.

A commercial for Chloraseptic followed this pattern. A very conscientious wife cured her husband's cough and sore throat using the product; her concern for his health led her to the right decision.

The last major type of product advertised was the dreaded household products—detergent, wax, soap, cleaners. These commercials portray the housewife as someone who cleans all day and is never discouraged when one of the children messes something up. These commercials show the housewife as striving for the cleanest clothes, floors, dishes, and toilet bowls as if her life depended on their sterility. Often these commercials show a family member getting something dirty and the housewife coming to the rescue to get it clean again. In the Tide commercial, the children get their favorite clothes filthy and the mother comes along with Tide and saves the day by getting the clothes sparkling clean again.

Advertisers often depend upon stereotypes to reach different types of people. The housewife stereotype is generally disturbing, for it depicts housewives as women whose sense of their own value lives and dies with the strength of their detergent or cold capsule. This image is far from glamorous and at times insulting. But what is most disturbing is that it must sell products, for if it weren't effective, it wouldn't be used.

EXERCISE 7–16

In groups or as a class, evaluate the essay above, answering the following questions:

1. What did the writer do well?

2. What is the thesis of the essay?

3. On what specific observations does the writer base generalizations?

4. What generalizations does the writer make?

5. Is the writer justified in making those generalizations? That is, do the number and quality of the observations support the generalizations?

6. Can you present any evidence, gathered from your own experience, that would weaken or contradict the writer's generalizations?

EXERCISE 7–17

Conduct an inductive experiment and write a paper using the results. You may follow the television commercial example above or create one of your own.

Deduction. Deductive reasoning works from the general to the specific. Taking a generalization that can be accepted as true, one applies it to a specific instance. If the generalization is true, then any instance included in it must also be true. Thus a conclusion is reached. In the babysitting example, then, you may conclude deductively, working from the generalization reached by induction, that you should not accept the babysitting job because

Babysitters for that household are treated and paid poorly.
I am a babysitter for that household.
I will be treated and paid poorly.

Based on this conclusion you decide to refuse the babysitting job.

You use both deduction and induction often in your personal and professional life. Following are more examples of deductive reasoning, reasoning which goes from a generalization to a specific instance to a conclusion:

Major Premise	The lowest bidder is always hired by Company Co.
Minor Premise	We are the lowest bidder.
Conclusion	We will be hired by Company Co.
Major Premise	The July accounting printouts are always inaccurate.
Minor Premise	This is the July printout.
Conclusion	This is inaccurate.
Major Premise	Anyone who fails the Departmental exam fails the course.
Minor Premise	André failed the Departmental exam.
Conclusion	André will fail the course.

In each of these bits of reasoning—called *syllogisms*—the first or major premise is a generalization that must be accepted as true if the reasoning and conclusion are to be accepted. Each generalization was reached inductively—by years of noticing that July printouts are often wrong because the fiscal year ends June 30, because workers take vacations, because summer is a busy season. That generalization then becomes the starting point for deductive reasoning. In other words, to say that because this year's printout was inaccurate all July printouts are inaccurate is probably faulty logic. Once is not enough. But if you can reach a generalization based on several specific instances, your generalization is more likely to be accepted as true.

In a syllogism, the major premise states a generalization that can be accepted as true and the minor premise states a specific instance of that generalization. If either can be proven untrue, the conclusion cannot be true.

One of the main reasons a syllogism can be found untrue is that the generalization, the major premise, cannot be accepted as true. Exceptions to the generalization may abound, or the generalization may rest on weak support.

Major Premise   People who own Mercedes are rich.

Minor Premise   Emmett owns a Mercedes.

Conclusion   Emmett is rich.

Emmett might well be rich. But he might also be overspent, living on credit, and on the verge of filing for bankruptcy. Or, Emmett may be paying for a Mercedes with money allocated for repayment of a student loan. Or he may have won the car in a lottery or drawing.

Students who pass Freshman English know how to write well.
Terry passed Freshman English.
Terry knows how to write well.

But passing Freshman English does not necessarily mean that Terry can write well. Terry may have passed with a D. Or the class may have not been very demanding and was easy to pass regardless of one's writing skills.

Generalizations rest on evidence, on inductive examination of facts and instances. If the support is faulty or if exceptions exist, the resulting deductive argument is not true. Some faulty generalizations can be corrected by making them less inclusive, more realistic. Consider this one:

Retired people like to travel.
June is retired.
June likes to travel.

As stated, this deductive argument is too inclusive, for it implies that *all* retired people like to travel. Common sense, and perhaps experience, tells you that not *all* retired people enjoy travelling. Some like to stay home, reading, pursuing hobbies, completing projects, visiting friends. But the argument works if the generalization is qualified:

Many retired people like to travel.
June is retired.
June probably likes to travel.

You can sometimes make a generalization work if you make it less sweeping. Words such as *usually, sometimes, most, often, some, frequently, occasionally, few, much,* and *many* may be used to qualify generalizations.

Quite often in conversation and writing, generalizations (major premises) are not stated. Instead, they are implied; from the minor premise and conclusion, the reader or listener infers the major premise.

> My father was a college student in the '60s, so he was against the Vietnam War. *(Unstated generalization: All college students in the '60s were against the Vietnam War.)*

> That book was on the best-seller list for ten weeks; it must really be good. *(Unstated generalization: All books that remain on the best-seller list for ten weeks must be good.)*

> Professor Campbell is an English teacher, so she knows about figures of speech. *(Unstated generalization: All English teachers are familiar with figures of speech.)*

Such a shortened syllogism is called an *enthymeme*. As with a full syllogism, the generalization on which an enthymeme is based must be examined to determine whether it can be accepted. In the examples just given, the first two unstated generalizations are probably not acceptable; therefore, the syllogism's reasoning is faulty. Not all college students in the 1960s were against the Vietnam War, so one cannot assume that a particular student during that time was against the war. Nor is it true that only good books remain on the best-seller list for weeks; it's possible that a mediocre book could hold its position there for a long time. The best-seller list is not a standard of worth but a measure of popularity.

The third enthymeme is probably acceptable, for its generalization—its major premise—appears true. All English teachers are familiar with figures of speech, at least to some degree, for in their study of the language and literature they have worked with metaphor, simile, alliteration, and other figures of speech. Because she is included among those who have studied figures of speech, Professor Campbell, too, knows about them.

EXERCISE 7–18

Supply the unstated generalization for each of the following enthymemes. Then decide whether the generalization is acceptable or faulty.

1. Of course I make mistakes. I'm only human.
2. She'll have her pick of graduate schools. Her grade-point average is 4.0.
3. Peter Gent is a former football player, so people buy his books.
4. They are both members of Students Against Drunk Driving, so they never drink at parties.
5. He is from Georgia, so he has a southern accent.

EXERCISE 7–19

Using one of the generalizations below, write a paragraph based on deductive reasoning. The generalization should serve as the topic sentence of your paragraph, and from it you need to develop a minor premise and conclusion. Draw support from your experiences and reading.

1. Students often hate reading.
2. Students are responsible for their own education.
3. People who don't know enough about themselves are doomed to repeat their mistakes.
4. High-pressure sales persons often lose customers.
5. Assertive people often get what they want.

Breaks in Logic

Whether you are scrutinizing evidence in order to reason inductively or working deductively from a generalization, you must be aware of faulty reasoning, those breaks in logic that weaken if not destroy your argument. As you construct arguments or study the arguments others present, watch for the fallacies presented in the next few pages. Should they appear in your argument, your audience has a clearly defined point to use in refuting your argument and is less likely to accept your overall reasoning.

Faulty Generalizations

The generalization you form inductively after observing facts and instances as well as the generalization you use as the major premise in a syllogism may be faulty if it has been too hastily drawn or is too sweeping.

A hasty generalization is one based on too little evidence or evidence that is insufficient or irrelevant. One cannot generalize from too small a sample. If, for instance, you notice on two consecutive Mondays that one-fourth of the students in your calculus class are wearing Hawaiian shirts, do you have enough evidence to assert that college students wear Hawaiian shirts on Mondays? Probably not.

A sweeping generalization is one that is too broad, one that does not allow for exceptions. Stereotypes are often little more than sweeping generalizations, for a stereotype ascribes identical characteristics to all members of a certain group. Because stereotypes often reinforce or grow out of prejudices, a writer who wants to be accepted as reasonable and responsible avoids them.

That is also why you should avoid hasty and sweeping generalizations in any argument you construct. You are appealing to reason and logic in an argument, and including hasty or sweeping generalizations automatically predisposes your reader to reject your argument. How might an audience respond to these faulty generalizations?

Accounting majors are always boring and dull.

Tall men and women are infinitely more graceful than shorter ones.

Humanities professors are more understanding and kind than those in the sciences.

People who dine at Mario's are better dressed than those who dine at Harry Starker's.

Students at this college prefer "All My Children" to "General Hospital."

Oversimplified Causes

Another type of fallacy to avoid involves oversimplifying a causal relation. When you are examining a cause-and-effect relationship, you must remember that a cause may have more than one effect and that an effect could be the result of several causes.

You oversimplify a causal relation when you assume that an effect is the result of only one cause.

Kevin does well in school because his parents tutor him at home. *(His parents' assistance may improve his work at school, but Kevin may also be intelligent and motivated, and he may concentrate during class and study hard—all of which contribute to his good performance.)*

Faulty causal argument also occurs if you ignore some cause or emphasize the wrong one.

Stephani made cheerleader because she has such a great smile. *(But she's also very athletic and graceful, can project her voice, and has the infectious personality needed to motivate the crowd.)*

In another type of faulty causal argument, you assert that one event caused another simply because one followed the other. This type is called *post hoc ergo propter hoc,* a delightfully rhythmic way of saying "after this, therefore because of this":

Of course it's raining—I just washed my car. *(The rain was caused by meteorological conditions, not the fact that I washed my car.)*

Either/Or Fallacy

If you present a complex issue as having only two sides, when other sides or positions exist, you are engaging in faulty reasoning. Most issues are complex enough that they can't be reduced to two extremes:

America, love it or leave it. *(Perhaps it's possible to change what isn't lovable.)*

Either we spend more money on public education or we will see public education deteriorate completely. *(Perhaps spending more wisely is a possibility; perhaps leaving things as they are will not lead to complete deterioration.)*

As a politician, she's either stupid or naive. *(Perhaps she just sees things differently or is operating under assumptions the writer is unaware of.)*

Personal Attacks

A fallacy that occurs when you attack the opposition by calling names or insulting someone's character, the *ad hominem* fallacy avoids the primary issue by focusing on personalities—real or imagined.

> Why anyone should trust such a slick-talking New Yorker is beyond me. *("Slick-talking" is name calling, and being from New York could not possibly have much bearing on the issue.)*

> Those who call for censorship are dangerous religious fanatics. *(Who they are or the opinion one has of them should not affect the argument presented.)*

> I'm opposed to anything which that crook Allen supports. *(Emphasis should be on the issue, not on who supports it; and using the word "crook," of course, is name calling.)*

Begging the Question

If you assume that the premise or premises on which you base your argument have already been proven, but make no attempt to prove them, you are begging the question. Since argument is based on acceptable or valid premises, you must prove that the premises are true rather than expecting your reader to assume their truth.

> Self-serving policies such as the one proposed by Representative Vader should be rejected outright. *(The argument should establish that the policy is self-serving, not merely assume that it is.)*

> The destructive and decadent lyrics of the songs recorded by these two rock stars are contributing to the moral decay of an entire generation.*(The lyrics must be proven destructive and decadent; an entire generation must be proven to be in a state of moral decay.)*

> The testimony of a person who dresses as distastefully as he surely cannot be trusted. *(One's fashion sense or lack thereof is no indication of one's trustworthiness.)*

Red Herring

This fallacy occurs when a side issue is introduced that diverts attention from the central issue.

> He may indeed have failed to perform some of his duties properly, but no one else who works there has performed theirs properly either. *(The issue here is whether he has done his job. The job performance of co-workers is not at issue.)*

> Enough of this discussion about whether this tax plan should be approved; the real question is whether taxation is fair at all. *(The question of whether taxation is fair has no bearing on whether this tax plan should be approved.)*

Appeal to Ignorance

This fallacy cites the lack of conclusive evidence on an issue to advance an alternative. It is used to argue for one position because no evidence is available to support the opposing view.

> Children with AIDS should not be allowed in the schools because we don't know just how contagious they are or in what ways their disease can be spread. (*Existing information about the disease and its method of infection should be used to support a position instead of an appeal to what isn't known. Notice that this fallacy can be used to deny evidence—to say that whatever evidence exists is not conclusive enough.*)

> We believe our current Senator should be re-elected because we know her; we know her record and her performance as a public servant. But we can't be sure of her opponent; he has no history of public service, so he's an unknown quantity. (*The opponent may turn out to be a better public servant than the incumbent. This argument appeals to what is* not *known about the opponent to support the candidacy of the incumbent. Basing an argument on the incumbent's record would make the support stronger.*)

Appeals to Emotion

Another category of logical fallacies avoids the issue being argued by appealing to emotions. Writers who emphasize irrelevant matters through fallacies such as the following obscure the real issue of their argument.

Appeal to Flattery

A person with a family as lovely as yours will surely want to purchase our complete family portrait package. (*The loveliness of one's family has nothing to do with the family's inclination to purchase the portrait package.*)

Appeal to Fear

This all-inclusive life insurance policy will protect your family completely from poverty should you meet an untimely death. (*Plays on fears for one's family but ignores the merits of the policy as compared to others.*)

Appeal to Pity

He really should get the award this year; after all, he's been nominated three times and has never won. (*Ignores his qualifications for the award and how he compares with other nominees.*)

Appeal to Authority

General Chuck Yeager, the pilot with the right stuff, is the spokesperson for this line of auto parts, so it is the best. (*Ignores quality and price of auto parts; and Yeager, though well known, may not be an expert on cars.*)

Appeal to Identification Needs

Caring, loving fathers will protect their families with a piece of the rock. *(Plays on parents' sense of responsibility and their love for their children; seeks to get those who believe or want to believe they are caring and loving to purchase insurance as evidence of their love. Ignores questions of personal situation or circumstance.)*

True Texans know there's nothing like a Longneck beer. *(Plays on desires to belong to a particular group or on one's identification with that group.)*

Successful executives rate the Gold Cit Card as a money card guaranteed to win instant acceptance at millions of stores and restaurants worldwide. *(Plays on one's desire to be considered successful.)*

Appeals to Quantity (The Bandwagon Appeal)

Rosie's Boutique is the shop most favored by the elegant and extravagant. *(Plays on one's desire to be part of the crowd of elegant and extravagant shoppers.)*

Thousands have already switched to Poly-Citrus Fruit Drink! Don't be left behind! *(Encourages consumers to join the numbers that have switched simply because so many have switched. Ignores the merits of the drink.)*

We want a 100 percent contribution rate in this year's Charity Campaign—don't keep us from reaching our goal. *(Encourages prospective contributors to become part of the group of actual contributors regardless of the merits of the charities benefiting from the drive.)*

EXERCISE 7–20

Identify the fallacy or describe the flaw in each of the following statements. Then rewrite the statement to eliminate the fallacy.

Example

Original   Any business would be glad to hire liberal arts majors because they are so smart. *(Sweeping generalization; oversimplification)*

Revised   Many businesses like hiring liberal arts major because students who complete a liberal arts curriculum are generally quite skilled in communciation and logical thought.

1. These knee-jerk liberals are more concerned with clean air than with our nation's prosperity.

2. Only greedy and capitalistic property owners support that law.

3. Only a fool would travel to a country so torn by civil war and political unrest.

4. Jane Fonda's workout video is the best-selling one, so it's probably the best.

5. That poor guy wouldn't have done it if he had had a better life—he was an orphan who grew up on the streets, soon resorting to drugs and alcohol to escape his painful past.

6. If you're not part of the solution, you're part of the problem.

7. News reporters are a callous lot, sniffing after pain to make it public.

8. Parents who do not assure that their children are computer literate are dooming their children to failure.

9. MTV videos are sick.

10. Children are just natural troublemakers.

11. M. J. Wilder, a leading child development specialist, endorses this toy line.

12. A man as intelligent and fit as you certainly realizes the importance of continued weight training.

13. City building inspectors can be bribed easily.

14. This chance to vacation in Jamaica will never come again.

15. Incompetent and dumb public officials like her should be removed from office.

Many of the fallacious statements in the preceding exercise could be matters of personal taste or opinion. As such, they are not arguable. Your revision of them, however, should have transformed them into statements suitable for argumentation—statements that can be proved more or less true and whose validity can be supported objectively.

Remember that when you argue, you must focus your attention on the issue being considered, seeking to establish the probable truth of your position. Thus you must rely on reasoning—the selection, presentation, and support of points that lead to your conclusion. For your readers to understand your argument, you must guide them through your reasoning process. And for them to take you seriously, you must avoid fallacious argumentation.

EXERCISE 7–21

Exchange the draft of your argumentation paper (Exercise 7–15) with a partner. Then check to see if the draft you are examining contains any logical fallacies. Underline or bracket the sentences which appear to use fallacious reasoning.

When your own paper is returned, check the sentences that your partner indicated might contain faulty reasoning. Revise them to eliminate the fallacy or explain why the statements are valid.

Argument or Persuasion?

The body of an argument presents the reasoning that leads you to offer your position as the most valid one or the one most closely allied to the truth. Argument makes an appeal to reason, so emotional appeals have little part in an argument. An emotional appeal may be appropriate in the introduction or conclusion of an argument as long as the appeal is muted and does not interfere with the logic of your case. Other acceptable emotional appeals are discussed in the nest section.

As noted earlier, the emphasis in argument rests on the subject itself, and the aim of argument is to establish truth. Truth, absolute truth, may be elusive, for controversial issues are rarely simple and seldom completely resolved. Any resolution is often a result of finding one view more probable than the other, of finding one view closer to the truth than another.

Persuasion, however, has little to do with finding truth. The aim of persuasion is to win the assent of your audience; thus persuasive writing centers on the audience rather than on the subject. And because persuasion centers on the audience, emotional appeals are acceptable, though they may not always be ethical.

Persuading Others

As noted in the preceding section, the difference between argument and persuasion is primarily one of focus. Argument focuses on the issue; persuasion on the audience. Quite often an argument includes some persuasive devices. Their inclusion in an argument is acceptable as long as their use is ethical.

Presenting logical fallacies is not ethical because such fallacies prey on the weaknesses, the insecurities, the fears, and the prejudices of the audience or attempt to abuse their trust. By preying on one's desire to belong, for example, an emotional appeal may divert attention from a product's merits to a consumer's personal need that may or may not be satisfied by purchasing the product. An advocate of one political candidate may attack an opposing one by name-calling, thus obscuring the real issue of the position and commitment of each. Such tactics are sometimes successful with an audience, especially if the audience is already inclined to agree with you.

But those same tactics weaken your position with those who oppose your point of view. Since argument aims to present one position as the most valid, using such tactics decidedly weakens your ability to win over your opponent.

Persuasion has little to do with trust. Because the aim of persuasion is to win the assent of the audience, much of the persuasive writing you encounter centers on the audience, attempting to move them in one direction or another. Persuasion may be used in conjunction with argument, of course, for winning the assent of the audience is sometimes crucial in winning its acceptance of an argument.

Thus, linking some persuasive techniques to logical reasoning may contribute to the success of your argument. Establishing common ground and acknowledging your opponent's viewpoint, both discussed earlier in this chapter, are two methods of strengthening your audience's identification with you and the position you are arguing. The stronger such identification is, the more likely it is that you will win the assent of your audience.

Emotional appeals which engage the audience's sense of fairness or justice, address their desire to see an unjust situation corrected, or demonstrate understanding and empathy for their position can often convince the audience to accept your argument. But such emotional appeals should be linked with argument; alone they are apt to be viewed as manipulative devices whose purpose is to deceive the audience into agreement by ignoring reasoning processes.

In addition to establishing common ground with your audience and acknowledging opposing views, you may use the following persuasive techniques in your efforts to strengthen your argument.

Engaging "Respectable" Emotions

Appeals to emotions may ethically be made when accompanied by argument, if those emotions are respectable or justified and if the appeal steers clear of fallacious reasoning. Appealing to someone's sense of guilt, for example, may be justified if the person has good cause to feel guilty. Appeals to an audience's sense of justice or fair play may be an effective method of laying the groundwork for your argument. As you read the following argument, notice which emotions the writer is appealing to:

```
Dear Mal,
        It is unfortunate that our staff can't all be
assigned separate offices, but space at the university
is limited and student organizations like the
newspaper staff just have to cope. I want to propose a
solution for our problem of sharing the desk we've
both been assigned.
        We are both subject to the same pressures and
deadlines. When I am unable to use the desk and office
equipment, I am unable to meet those deadlines and the
pressure increases. I certainly don't want to
monopolize facilities we must both share, but I would
like to work out a mutually agreeable schedule so that
we can both have equal access to our working space.
Below is my first effort at a schedule; I've tried to
take into account class meetings and other
responsibilities we both must meet.
```

The introductory paragraphs of the argument above appeal to the reader's sense of what is fair and assume that the reader wants to work toward a solution to avoid further unfairness. Without becoming accusatory, the writer suggests that the current situation is unjust and that the reader is at least partially responsible for the unjustice. By bringing in the reader's sense of responsibility for the situation, the writer hopes to enlist the reader's help in working out a solution.

Demonstrating Understanding or Empathy

Demonstrating to your readers that you understand their plight or their position or that you identify with their feelings and desires may make them more inclined to accept, or at least consider, the merits of your argument.

This strategy goes a long way toward reducing any hostility that may arise when opposing views clash. If you can show your readers, both in the introduction and the body of your argument, that you recognize their position, that you understand it, and that you are aware of its merits, you add significantly to your own credibility.

Likewise, if you can show your readers that you empathize with them, you can expand your common ground, even though you arrive at a conclusion they may be expected to reject at first. The broader your common ground, the more likely it is that they will find your argument convincing. Notice how the writer of the following example shows an understanding of the audience's position:

> Dear Mom and Dad,
>   I wasn't quite expecting the volcano that erupted last night when Frankie and I told you that we had decided to get married next summer. I know we're young, we're still in school, marriages take work, money will be short. You're right on all counts; there's no denying that. But we've considered these obstacles or conditions and we have a pretty good idea of what to expect. We've considered them, believe me. And here's what we've come up with:

This writer demonstrates early and completely an understanding of the opposing position and its merits. Such a demonstration is bound to get the readers' attention and to show them that the writer is focusing clearly on the issue. Thus they will be more inclined to accept for consideration the argument being offered—in this case, a qualification of all the points that have been acknowledged.

Adjusting Your Tone

You may also increase your chances of successfully persuading your audience if you adjust your tone to make it compatible with your audience's inclinations and beliefs. By tone, we mean everything in your writing that reveals the attitude you are taking toward your subject and your readers. Thus through word choice, the selection and arrangement of points and support, and your awareness of common ground, you demonstrate to your readers how you feel about them and about your subject.

Most often, the tone you are striving for is calm, balanced, and moderate rather than extreme. Because you want to appear to be a reasonable and intelligent human being, you acknowledge opposing views. You do not exaggerate or overstate the importance of your points or support. You avoid fallacious reasoning because the use of fallacies quickly destroys the reasonable image you want to project. Fallacious reasoning may also make you appear bitter or hostile, impressions that generally hamper your audience's willingness to be persuaded.

Thus no matter how strongly you feel about the point you are arguing, your writing is more effective if you maintain a reasonable and moderate tone and avoid name-calling and emotionally loaded words; using either may alienate your audience.

Instead, balance your tone. Pay close attention to the connotations of the words you use. What is the difference between a "teacher" and an "educator"? A "politician" and a "statesman"? Be alert to the language preferences your audience are likely to hold. Will the word "businessmen" irritate an audience composed partially of women? Do owners of funeral homes prefer to be referred to as "funeral directors," "morticians," or "undertakers"? A very casual tone comprising slang and colloquialisms would most likely be inappropriate in an argument directed toward the board members of a large company; likewise, an elevated and formal tone would be out of place in an argument about who among your co-workers should purchase next month's coffee supplies. Such incongruities between purpose and tone are likely to be humorous.

At times, humor may strike just the tone you need in an argument. It may, as in George Hanford's argument, provide a moment in which both reader and writer recognize their common goals or backgrounds. Humor may make a weighty argument less burdensome or reduce an audience's hostility. Humor may also reduce an audience's defensiveness about certain topics. Humor generates good feelings; that's probably why so many public speakers begin their talks with a few jokes.

We are not encouraging you to spend hours researching jokes in the library. But if a humorous (and nonmaligning) comment or anecdote occurs to you as you plan or write an argument or persuasive piece, consider leaving it in the final draft. You have to decide whether the humorous bit is appropriate and whether it serves your purpose and tone.

Look back at the two letters earlier—the one to Mal and the one from the daughter. The tone in each is balanced, calm. Both situations could conceivably be hostile and nasty, but the writer's tone in each helps focus attention on the issue involved. Compare the following versions with the originals:

```
Mal,
          I'm sick of you hogging the phone, the
desk, the typewriter. I've got stories to do, too, and
my work is as important as yours if not more so. Quit
being such an egomaniac, such a clod; your selfishness
is ruining my work. I'm using the desk every morning
from now on, so you can just buzz off.
```

Dear Mom and Dad,

         Why'd you have to yell so much? There's nothing you can do. Frankie and I are old enough to get married, so if you don't like it, that's just too bad. Don't come to the wedding if you don't approve, and don't come visit us. You can't stop us. We're not children.

EXERCISE 7–22

Examine the following short paragraph, then answer the following questions about its strength and tone.

1. What point is being argued? Is it an arguable point?
2. Where has the writer demonstrated knowledge of the opposing view?
3. How would you state the opposing view?
4. What fallacies has the writer used in the argument? How do they affect you as a reader?
5. How would you describe the tone the writer has used? How—in what words, phrases, or points—is it conveyed?
6. Does the argument use humor? Is it effective?

         I'm sick of being called unpatriotic because I drive a foreign car. You know, unpatriotic as in the bumper sticker: ''Hungry? Eat your import.'' Those tobacco-chewing, cowboy-hatted rednecks drive around in pick-em-up trucks that get about 7.5 miles to the gallon. Who is being unpatriotic? *Me* in my 27-mile-per-gallon small import which conserves our nation's energy or the loudmouth who thinks he can herd cows in a truck?

         The price I paid for my car included a $2,000 import tax. That's $2,000 that the government sucks up somewhere in its elephantine structure that I paid for the privilege of buying the car that I wanted. I'm patriotic. I'm contributing to the American economy all right. At least $2,000 worth. And I'm conserving our fuel as well. This is America, land of the Freedom of Choice. So I wish those chauvinistic, pseudo-patriotic, frustrated John Waynes would get off my back (bumper).

EXERCISE 7–23

Rewrite the argument above. In your revision, balance the tone, eliminate the fallacies, and strengthen the support as needed. As with any revision, you may rearrange, combine, substitute, delete, and add material to achieve your purpose.

EXERCISE 7–24

Select one or two newspaper or magazine advertisements that you find especially appealing or persuasive. Then analyze it (or them) to discover what makes it so persuasive, paying close attention to the way it uses appeals to reason and appeals to emotion.

EXERCISE 7–25

Take your argumentation paper (last seen in Exercise 7–21) through one more draft, this time incorporating persuasive techniques where needed. Consider ways to recognize common ground, acknowledge opposing views, engage respectable emotions, demonstrate understanding or empathy, and adjust your tone.

EXERCISE 7–26

In Exercise 7-13 you were asked to read the following argument by George Hanford, dividing it into the eight sections described in classical rhetoric.

Read the essay again, using the notes you took earlier, and this time evaluate the tone and persuasiveness of the argument. To help shape your evaluation, record your responses to the following questions:

1. What is the background of the writer of this argument?
2. What is his major point?
3. What is his persuasive purpose? That is, why is he advocating this position? What would he like his audience to do?
4. Who is the audience? How would you characterize its members?
5. Is the writer's evidence sufficient to support his major points?
6. Are the major points argued well enough to justify his conclusion?
7. To what emotions does the author appeal? Are the emotional appeals warranted?
8. How does the writer demonstrate his understanding of the audience's position or his empathy with the audience?
9. What is the author's tone? In what words, phrases, or points is the tone conveyed?
10. How has the writer used humor in his argument? Why has he used humor? That is, what effect do you think the writer's use of humor has on the audience?

The following is the text of a speech delivered by George Hanford, who was then President of the College Board, at the City Club in Cleveland, Ohio, on May 31, 1985.

An Educational System
That Has No Losers:
Academic Preparation for All

George Hanford

Among his many other wise observations Aristotle, we are told, once remarked that education is " . . . an ornament in prosperity, but a refuge in adversity." That principle certainly seems to apply to American education, which is left pretty much to itself when times are good, but becomes a major source of concern when things are not going so well.

Consider, for example, the wave of public concern that swept the country not long ago, about the quality, the problems, and the role in our national life of education and the schools.

Just two years ago last month, the Secretary of Education's National Commission on Excellence in Education proclaimed that we were "a nation at risk . . . threatened by a rising tide of mediocrity," and called for a major new national agenda of educational reform.

Hard upon the Bell Commission Report came no less than 36 others, sponsored by national educational bodies both great and small, each with its own version of the lament.

So many reports, in fact, that one wit wisecracked, "It isn't so much a rising tide of mediocrity that threatens the nation, as it is a rising tide of reports."

It was all reminiscent of the late 1950s, the sputnik era, when Russia's sudden sprint ahead in the space race left many Americans concerned about whether we were losing our edge in know-how, creativity, technology.

This time, however, it was a combination of economic reverses at home and a looming specter of industrial and technological competition from abroad that caused the concern.

In both circumstances, there was a broad consensus that we needed to improve the quality of American education, particularly in science and technology.

There was a renewed concern about education's connection to the practical worlds of our domestic economy, our world leadership, our national security . . . in short, our country's overall health and vitality.

And, there were plenty of prescriptions: "more homework" . . . "harder courses" . . . "better teachers" . . . "a longer school day (or years)" . . . "eliminate frills" . . . "get back to basics."

Then, suddenly we heard just last fall that SAT scores had stopped going down—in fact, went up a bit—that high school students are studying more academic courses, and doing better in other ways.

Secretary Bell held a press conference to say that the news was a sign that the Educational Excellence Movement was sweeping the nation. And President Reagan mentioned it in his State of the Union Message.

What were we to believe? Clearly, a case of what we in education would call "cognitive dissonance." You know about cognitive dissonance. It's like the boy who went to summer camp, and after the first week wrote home to say, "The food is awful, and besides the helpings are too small." In other words, apparent contradiction in the facts.

That's not all that is confusing about the current attitudes about education. Despite all the concern over educational quality, education issues in last year's presidential campaign pretty much boiled down to school prayer, and how much the federal government should contribute to educational costs—in other words, "Who prays and who pays?"

The debate is far from over, and I don't mean to make light of religious conviction, but school prayer is not an issue: As long as there are students taking the scholastic aptitude test, there surely will be prayer in the schools.

Who pays is a more complicated issue. My thesis today is that in the long run, if our educational system does not do its job, we all pay. In that connection, I hope I can make three points to you:

1. American education did and does, as all those reports told us, need improvement and revitalization if it is to measure up to the needs of the nation. But the turnaround has begun, on the initiative of educators, who welcome the recent flush of attention to the quality of our schools. The ground is fertile for additional effort and the prospects for large results are good.

2. The good news, the signs of improvement, should not lull us into a foolish complacency about the issue of educational quality, nor should the fact that times are getting a little better make us think that we can get along without a major retooling of our nation's schools. The reform effort is at its most dangerous stage . . . if constant vigilance is the price of liberty, then constant effort is the price of quality, and the job is far from done.

3. Private enterprise and the professions have a major stake in the turnaround, because it is cheaper to do the job right the first time, and because the students involved are their future employees, customers, and fellow taxpayers. They are already involved in helping the schools, but can make an important *additional* contribution (and serve their own best interests even better) in some critical areas where the payout may take longer, but the implications even more important.

In support of point one—that things are getting better—consider the following from the world of the college board:

Exhibit A—Output indicators are improving markedly.

National average scores on the scholastic aptitude test seem to be stabilizing, after a decline that began in 1963, and continued without interruption for seventeen years—a decline that was among the most-often-cited pieces of evidence that something was wrong with the nation's schools.

The scores hit their all-time low in 1980, then held steady in 1981.

In 1982 the verbal average went up two points and the math average went up one point. In 1983, math went up one point but verbal went down a point.

In 1984, the verbal average rose a point, from 425 to 426, and the math average went up three points, from 468 to 471. We will not know the results for the academic year just ending until late summer, but I predict that the trend will continue.

Why are these modest changes significant?

First, because they represent scores of about a million high school seniors—a third of all high school graduates, and two-thirds of those who go right on to college. Even a small change over such a large population is real and meaningful. The odds against these changes occurring by accident are more than a million to one.

Second, and more importantly, they are not the result of quick fixes, or short-run changes in student or school performance. The SAT does not measure short-run changes. It measures student abilities that are developed over years of learning experiences both in and out of the classroom.

In other words, these youngsters are showing the result of real improvement in the instruction they are getting, the motivation they are receiving, and their own efforts . . . improvement at every stage in their schooling, from the time they began school a dozen years ago.

And please remember: The SAT score decline was first noted as a long-term trend just over a dozen years ago, in 1972, as those very young people were getting under way in elementary school. Back then, educators began to get the message, and began to take action that is now showing results in the senior tests. I do.

Other improved output indicators:

These seniors reported taking more solid, academic courses than their predecessors—continuing a seven-year trend.

The proportion of students scoring in the highest ranks, which had been shrinking, has increased slightly.

And finally, the advanced placement program, which enables high school students to take college-level courses and earn credit for them in high school, is growing at a record pace, this year alone involving more than 6,200 high schools and 177,000 students—and it is growing in schools of every description serving students of every socioeconomic level.

All of which means that students and schools are getting more serious, and doing better.

Exhibit B—The schools are ready and willing to improve even more. Again, from the world of the college board:

Two years ago this month, we published a little booklet with a big idea. Called *Academic Preparation for College,* it is the result of more than two years of deliberation among high schools and college teachers, subject specialists, administrators, community leaders and policymakers nationally. It represents their consensus on what high schools should equip, and colleges should expect, high school students to know and be able to do—the subject matter they should know and the academic skills they should have—in order to succeed in college.

No such description of preparation in high school for college had existed for nearly two generations, and the response was electric. Within weeks, requests from all over the nation exhausted the first printing of 150,000 copies. They came from teachers, administrators, parents, students, board members, government officials, and legislators. The demand was so great, that we reprinted twice. Today there are nearly 350,000 copies in print and, we have continual evidence, in use.

The secret of this success is simply that unlike the other reports that merely described our educational problems, our little book offered strategies for a solution, and the schools were eager and ready to move.

Am I trying to tell you that improving SAT scores, more serious students, schools hastening to reform, mean that the battle for educational excellence is won, and we don't have to worry any more? Not a bit of it.

Educational reform is just beginning to take hold at the college level and in our schools. We still have too many dropouts, too many students taking junk food courses, too many remedial courses in colleges and universities to make up for what students didn't learn in high school.

At the same time, we are doing less well in educating the very students who are a growing proportion of our school population, and will be a growing proportion of the workforce of the future—minority students.

The number of 18-year-olds is declining, but both the number and the proportion of minority students is increasing. Already, in 35 of the nation's largest inner-city school districts, nearly three-fourths of the students are minority.

Functional illiteracy is about three times as prevalent among minority youth as among all youth. College-bound minority students average almost 50 points less on SAT verbal and math scores than all students.

It has been said that ignorance is the only thing that is more expensive than education, and the Carnegie Foundation recently offered us the perfect illustration of that: They found that business and industry are currently spending some $40 billion a year—nearly as much as is spent on all higher education in the nation—in training for their employees. Some of it goes for specialized or advanced training specific to the corporate need, but a lot of it goes for remedial education that should have been done in the schools.

No, I am not saying that reform is accomplished. I am saying . . . and here I come to my second message . . . that reform has begun, on the initiative of educators, that they welcome the broader attention now being given to educational problems and that they need the support for reform that has just begun to take hold.

I say "should" because the history of American education is littered with the pages of reports that never bore fruit in the form of true reform. Unless we can maintain concern, support and action by those outside of education who have an interest, including employers, the momentum for reform can swiftly dissipate.

For it is just when the situation is turning around that the risk is highest. The hardest part is the gritty task of keeping the reform trend going.

So it is an ideal time, I think, for the private sector to put their influence behind some educational reforms which hold promise for long range payoff in areas not now being addressed adequately.

Now, I am aware that Cleveland has an extensive program of school-business partnerships, involving all of your senior and junior high schools with some fifty companies, including some of the top names in the Fortune 500. And they include several postsecondary institutions, among them Case Western Reserve, Cleveland State, the University of Akron, and Cuyahoga Community College.

Civic groups and hospitals also cooperate in these efforts, which are at the forefront of a long and honorable tradition. The first work-study program started in the New York City schools in 1915. Especially during the past fifteen years there has been a tremendous increase in school-business alliances nationally, through programs like Adopt-A-School.

And they produce worthwhile results for many youngsters. They motivate them to stay in school and attend classes. They provide a clear goal—a job at the end of the line—to prove the connection between schooling and employment. They provide material resources and expertise schools desperately need. And they release employees to spend time in volunteer activities which range from tutoring in basic subjects to helping create college-level computer courses.

Good? Of course. Good enough? Well . . . most of these efforts have relatively short-term goals: the immediate problems of youth unemployment, improving skills and attitudes of entry-level workers, and greater opportunities for disadvantaged and minority youngsters to learn about and gain access to careers upon graduation from high school.

In general they steer clear of the academic core of the curriculum, which is of course the part most critical for the success of students who are going to go on to college, the future pool of professional and managerial talent.

Why hasn't more attention been given to our future professionals and managers in efforts of this kind? Can it be that there is a common assumption, by educators and businessmen alike, that kids bright enough to go to college can fend for themselves educationally? If so, that assumption is just plain wrong.

It is wrong because kids "bright enough to go to college" are made, not born. There is a direct relationship between the quality of education a child receives and later educational attainment.

If we are going to meet the challenge of a post-industrial, service society, a society where the manufacturing jobs have moved offshore to cheaper labor markets, and a society where know-how with ideas, people, problems will be the currency of employment and success, then it seems abundantly clear that Americans are going to have to be educated both better and differently.

We are going to have to find ways to enable the growing proportion of minority students in our schools to achieve at a level equivalent to their non-minority peers. And, we are going to have to enable an ever-growing proportion of all students to progress further in the higher-order mental activities—the knowing, the understanding, the reasoning—that a new era will require of them.

In the past it's been all too easy to adopt high standards and blame the students for their failure. Today we cannot afford to do that. We waste too many brains, and we do nothing to cause reform in the system. And this, it seems to me, is something in which business, industry and the professions should have great interest, and to which they can contribute much. I am, in short, suggesting a strong new emphasis in their aid to the schools which focuses on the academic component.

And I am proposing that organizations like this, and their individual members, should become active in pressing for such an emphasis.

"But," you may say, "those of us who are not educators don't know what to push for." Maybe so. But here let me recommend to you the little booklet I mentioned earlier. *Academic Preparation for College* is the centerpiece of what we at the college board call our educational EQuality project. Capital E for equality because expanding access to educational opportunity is a major goal of our organization, and capital Q for the quality that makes the opportunity meaningful.

In that project, we are encouraging schools and colleges to work together . . . in their communities, with the private sector . . . to adopt and implement the outcomers described in that booklet as standards of performance—for the schools in preparing students, and for the students in entering college.

We are conducting pilot projects to demonstrate how this can be accomplished in the context of local means and needs. And we are working to have them recognized and endorsed by local and state educational systems, and major national education organizations.

And I am happy to say that one of those pilot projects is underway here in Cleveland, involving Cuyahoga Community College and the Cleveland public schools. We understand that they have independently received support from the Cleveland Foundation and the Ford Foundation to initiate joint curriculum planning along the lines suggested by the EQ Project.

Endorsement and support by professional groups and by business and industry is absolutely essential to the success of those efforts.

Now, there appears to be another fallacy afoot: that academic preparation in high school is important *only* for the college-bound. Again, not so. As we worked on the statements in the green book, we reviewed them intensively in a series of dialogues between school people and business and industry leaders. The business people told us what we already suspected—that with only slight modification, the skills set forth there are every bit as applicable and important to students going directly from high school to work as they are to students going from high school to college.

They indicated that the ability of their entry-level employees to read, write, speak and listen, do mathematics, reason, and learn effectively—in short, the abilities developed in academic courses, are much more important to business and industry than school people have assumed they are.

So it is not really an either-or proposition. I am not suggesting that business and industry abandon their present efforts to help students who are not assumed to be college bound, just to add a new dimension, a new level of commitment.

In a way that I am talking about is imbedded in a story that one of my predecessors at the board, Sidney P. Marland, liked to tell.

It took place while he was superintendent of schools in Winnetka, a prosperous north shore suburb of Chicago, and involved an irate father, an MIT graduate, who complained that his son's school counselor was giving him bad advice. "My son wants to go to MIT, and the counselor said he shouldn't try," the father said.

Sid looked up the boy's record. "I'm sorry to say I have to agree with the counselor," he told the father. "Your son's grades are just not good enough. He's in the bottom half of his class. He'd never have a chance."

"Bottom half of the class," the father said. "Why that's just ridiculous. With the school taxes we pay here, nobody should be in the bottom half of the class."

In a way, that expectation is what I suggest we need to work toward: an educational system and program that has no losers. It may be statistically impossible to put everyone in the top half of the class, but we strive to make sure that those in the bottom half still have what they need to succeed.

It's been said that the trouble today is that the future isn't what is used to be. That may be true, but we can change it. We have the opportunity today to educate the ones who will determine the future of this country in the twenty-first century. Let's make the most of it.

EXERCISE 7–27

Return to page 26. Reread the newspaper article on the University of Kansas apartheid protester, as well as your log entry responding to the article.

1. Write an analysis of the possible reasons why the university loan officer felt justified in saying, " 'We can put whatever we want in our files.' "

2. Write an analysis of the possible reasons the student felt her rights had been violated.

3. Write an editorial for a university newspaper either arguing in favor of the student's point of view or justifying the loan officer's point of view.

4. Write a letter to the Board of Regents either recommending that the university establish a policy against keeping such information in student files or supporting the university's right to do so.

EXERCISE 7–28

Read the following text of the Declaration of Independence. Then complete the next two activities.

1. Divide the text into *introduction, exposition, proposition, arrangement, evidence, confutation, digression,* and *conclusion.*

2. Evaluate the text by using the questions listed in Exercise 7–26.

The Declaration of Independence

When in the Course of human events, it becomes necessary for one people to dissolve the political bands which have connected them with another, and to assume among the powers of the earth, the separate and equal station to which the Laws of Nature and of Nature's God entitle them, a decent respect to the opinions of mankind requires that they should declare the causes which impel them to the separation.

We hold these truths to be self-evident, that all men are created equal, that they are endowed by their Creator with certain unalienable Rights, that among these are Life, Liberty, and the pursuit of Happiness. That to secure these rights, Governments are instituted among Men, deriving their just powers from the consent of the governed, That whenever any Form of Government becomes destructive of these ends, it is the Right of the People to alter or to abolish it, and to institute new Government, laying its foundation on such principles and organizing its powers in such form, as to them shall seem most likely to effect their Safety and Happiness. Prudence, indeed, will dictate that Governments long established should not be changed for light and transient causes; and accordingly all experience hath shewn that mankind are more disposed to suffer, while evils are sufferable, than to right themselves by abolishing the forms to which they are accustomed. But when a long train of abuses and usurpations, pursuing invariably the same Object evinces a design to reduce them under absolute Despotism, it is their right, it is their duty, to throw off such Government, and to provide new Guards for their future security. Such has been the patient sufferance of these Colonies; and such is now the necessity which constrains them to alter their former Systems of Government. The history of the present King of Great Britain is a history of repeated injuries and usurpations, all having in direct object the establishment of an absolute Tyranny over these States. To prove this, let Facts be submitted to a candid world.

He has refused his Assent to Laws, the most wholesome and necessary for the public good.

He has forbidden his Governors to pass Laws of immediate and pressing importance, unless suspended in their operation till his Assent should be obtained; and when so suspended, he has utterly neglected to attend to them.

He has refused to pass other Laws for the accommodation of large districts of people, unless those people would relinquish the right of Representation in the Legislature, a right inestimable to them and formidable to tyrants only.

He has called together legislative bodies at places unusual, uncomfortable, and distant from the depository of their public Records, for the sole purpose of fatiguing them into compliance with his measures.

He has dissolved Representative Houses repeatedly, for opposing with manly firmness his invasions on the rights of the people.

He has refused for a long time, after such dissolutions, to cause others to be elected; whereby the Legislative powers, incapable of Annihilation, have returned to the People at large for their exercise; the State remaining in the mean time exposed to all the dangers of invasion from without, and convulsions within.

He has endeavoured to prevent the population of these States; for that purpose obstructing the Laws for Naturalization of Foreigners; refusing to pass others to encourage their migration hither, and raising the conditions of new Appropriations of Lands.

He has obstructed the Administration of Justice, by refusing his Assent to Laws for establishing Judiciary powers.

He has made Judges dependent on his Will alone, for the tenure of their offices, and the amount and payment of their salaries.

He has erected a multitude of New Offices, and sent hither swarms of Officers to harass our people, and eat out their substance.

He has kept among us in times of peace, Standing Armies without the Consent of our legislatures.

He has affected to render the Military independent of and superior to the Civil power.

He has combined with others to subject us to a jurisdiction foreign to our constitution, and unacknowledged by our laws; giving his Assent to their Acts of pretended Legislation:

For quartering large bodies of armed troops among us;

For protecting them, by a mock Trial, from punishment for any Murders which they should commit on the Inhabitants of these States;

For cutting off our Trade with all parts of the world;

For imposing Taxes on us without our Consent;

For depriving us in many cases, of the benefits of Trial by Jury;

For transporting us beyond Seas to be tried for pretended offences;

For abolishing the free System of English Laws in a neighboring Province, establishing therein an Arbitrary government, and enlarging its Boundaries, so as to render it at once an example and fit instrument for introducing the same absolute rule into these Colonies;

For taking away our Charters, abolishing our most valuable Laws, and altering fundamentally the Forms of our Governments;

For suspending our own Legislatures, and declaring themselves invested with power to legislate for us in all cases whatsoever.

He has abdicated Government here, by declaring us out of his Protection and waging War against us.

He has plundered our seas, ravaged our Coasts, burnt our towns, and destroyed the lives of our people.

He is at this time transporting large Armies of foreign Mercenaries to compleat the works of death, desolation and tyranny, already begun with circumstances of Cruelty & perfidy scarcely paralleled in the most barbarous ages, and totally unworthy the Head of a civilized nation.

He has constrained our fellow Citizens taken Captive on the high Seas to bear Arms against their Country, to become the executioners of their friends and Brethren, or to fall themselves by their Hands.

He has excited domestic insurrections amongst us, and has endeavoured to bring on the inhabitants of our frontiers, the merciless Indian Savages, whose known rule of warfare is an undistinguished destruction of all ages, sexes, and conditions.

In every stage of these Oppressions We have Petitioned for Redress in the most humble terms: Our repeated Petitions have been answered only by repeated injury. A Prince, whose character is thus marked by every act which may define a Tyrant, is unfit to be the ruler of a free people.

Nor have We been wanting in attentions to our British Brethren. We have warned them from time to time of attempts by their legislature to extend an unwarrantable jurisdiction over us. We have reminded them of the circumstances of our emigration and settlement here. We have appealed to their native justice and magnanimity, and we have conjured them by the ties of our common kindred, to disavow these usurpations, which would inevitably interrupt our connections and correspondence. They, too have been deaf to the voice of justice and of consanguinity. We must, therefore, acquiesce in the necessity, which denounces our Separation, and hold them, as we hold the rest of mankind. Enemies in War, in Peace Friends.

We, therefore, the Representatives of the United States of America, in General Congress, Assembled, appealing to the Supreme Judge of the World for the rectitude of our intentions, do, in the Name, and by authority of the good People of these Colonies, solemnly publish and declare, That these United Colonies are, and of Right ought to be Free and Independent States; that they are Absolved from all Allegiance to the British Crown, and that all political connection between them and the State of Great Britain, is and ought to be totally dissolved; and that as Free and Independent States, they have full Power to levy War, conclude Peace, contract Alliances, establish Commerce, and to do all other Acts and Things which Independent States may of right do. And for the support of this Declaration, with a firm reliance on the protection of Devine Providence, we mutually pledge to each other our Lives, our Fortunes and our sacred Honor.

CHAPTER EIGHT

Writing About Literature

*For men and women are not only themselves; they are
also the region in which they were born, the city,
apartment or farm in which they learnt to walk, the
games they played as children, the old wives' tales they
overheard, the food they ate, the schools they attended, the
sports they followed, the poets they read, and the God they
believed in. It is all these things that have made them
what they are . . . —W. Somerset Maugham,* The Razor's
Edge.

If Maugham is right, then every moment of your life and the experience of
each of these moments have made you what you are. But even before your
personal past is a historical past that has also helped to shape you—the lives
of your parents and of their parents, the culture and history of your country
and others. So when you take some action, make some decision, think some
thought, you bring yourself to that act—a self of which you are aware but also
one formed in part by forces and circumstances long past and perhaps never
recognized.

When you read, you are also affected by both your personal and historical
pasts. Your responses—how you react, think, understand, and feel—are shaped
by who you are. The best readers are those most conscious of the interplay
between the reader's aggregate past and the piece of writing being read. They
are aware of words and their meanings, of their rhythms, of the images they
create in your mind. As they read, they form connections—connections between words and what they represent in the physical world, connections between events and ideas in the piece being read, connections between the ver-

sion of reality on the printed page and the version comprising all the reader is and all the reader has done. Reading literature requires an awareness of these connections; that awareness, as well, is one of the first joys of literature. By being aware of those connections, one can recreate the text—in other words, take the text of a story, a novel, an essay, or any other piece of writing and make sense of it. Understanding a piece of writing is largely a matter of making connections, connections among its parts and connections to one's own experience and imagination.

To write about a piece of literature, you must first read it well. So before discussing the relationship between reading literature and writing about it, we will focus on how to make the reading process more productive. That productivity depends in part on preliminary writing.

Audience and Purpose

Why Do You Write About Literature? Who Reads What You Write and Why?

Sometimes, of course, literary scholars write about literature because they have new insights they would like to convey to their colleagues; they have something original to contribute to the world of literary scholarship. To accomplish this goal may take years of education and practice; graduate students learn this craft by writing innumerable term papers. Reviewers write about literature to help potential readers decide which new books to read. Other essayists write about literature to offer a general audience their interpretations of culture.

In your composition class you might read examples of these kinds of writing, but your goal should not be to duplicate work written by experts, especially the kind written for other experts. In most of your writing, you generally write from the point of view of a neophyte demonstrating levels of proficiency to an initiate. In other words, when college students write about literature, generally they are demonstrating to their professors, in lucid writing, that they have an understanding of a piece or pieces of literature. In this situation you are clearly writing to be evaluated.

Throughout this chapter, we address these writing situations, but first we'd like to introduce you to another way to write about literature, one that's less public but extremely useful.

Writing as Discovery

Interestingly, one of the main purposes of writing about literature—and this is true for neophytes and famous scholars alike—is to discover meaning. Many literature teachers have experienced the following process: The teacher assigns a group of poems to be read. One of the poems the teacher has never taught before, and during the preparation the teacher discovers that clear, cohesive interpretation of the poem is elusive. The teacher begins the class with a certain amount of trepidation; after all, isn't the teacher supposed to know everything? The teacher reads the elusive poem to the class and asks for questions. The first question triggers a series of responses, and the teacher begins to understand how the poem works. As the discussion progresses the teacher develops a more thorough understanding of the poem. Sometimes this same process works on a poem which has been taught before—except this time the teacher gains new insights and either modifies or perhaps even discards a previous interpretation.

Similar discoveries are common to graduate students. Almost every graduate student has experienced the horror of being assigned to interpret in writing a seemingly incomprehensible piece of literature. Frequently these students are forced to begin writing before they come up with any solid understanding; amazingly, the act of writing often opens up ideas and usually leads to some level of understanding.

From these two generalized examples we can make several observations. First, being forced to shape information into a piece of writing often stimulates our minds to make discoveries we are unable to make when our only audience is ourselves. Writing, then, is more than just telling someone what we know or how we think; it is also a way of discovering meaning or making meaning for ourselves so that we can then communicate that meaning to others. Also, teachers and graduate students are not led to make these discoveries only because of a need to communicate. Their abilities to discover meaning are enhanced by their wealth of "funding"—by all their previous experience reading literature, by their previous experience in life, and by their previous education. The need to communicate serves as a catalyst for understanding, not as a magic wand for comprehension.

You already have certain characteristics in common with these teachers and students of literature. You have already accumulated a store of life experience. You have each known a certain amount of pain and suffering, have experienced loss, have loved and been loved, have celebrated joy and elation. You have already been exposed to a wide variety of literature. You have heard fairy tales and nursery rhymes, read stories and seen dramas; at some time in your life you have probably even experimented with writing your own poetry and fiction. You have also gained some insights into how to read literature. Your teachers have introduced you to some of the formal definitions of literary criticism. They have discussed concepts such as plot, character, theme, rhyme scheme, symbolism, tragedy. In other words, even though you may not have already done much writing about literature, you are not a beginner; you bring a substantial background to this class.

You might well be asking yourself why, if you already have so much background, you are still being taught how to read and write about literature. The answer is that literature, like life, is rich, complex, filled with ambiguities, sometimes defying comprehension. But like life, it also yields understanding in some proportion to the experience we have with it. We offer you more experience to increase the funding which you bring to your reading.

The Discovery Process

Prereading

Your first task is to learn to become a more active reader. One place to begin is with what you already know. Remember, you are not a beginner. You bring a store of experience to the act at hand—use it. Begin with the obvious. What do you know about the piece you are reading? Is it a poem, a short story, a novel, or a play? Who wrote it? Do you know anything about the author, or have you read any other works that he or she has written? Look at its form before you start reading. Is there anything that sets this apart from other works of literature in the same category? If your memory is not too reliable, write brief answers to these questions. They might suggest an approach when you begin writing later.

Look at the title. Write down the expectations you develop from the title. If you have read pieces with similar titles, make a list of them. Perhaps this list suggests some interesting comparisons you could use to further your understanding or to write an essay. These preliminary notes also form the basis for a study guide for exams in the course.

Using prereading questions to become familiar with some of the surface features of a text can be productive in several ways. First, they help you develop a set of expectations about the text, expectations that may guide your reading. If your expectations are fulfilled—that is, if the text does indeed unfold as you predict—understanding may come more quickly. But it's also fine if the text develops in another way because preliminary expectations are constantly modified during the reading process. Even if your expectations are not met, they focus your attention on your reading, helping to make you an active reader.

The prereading questions also help you make some of those connections that are so necessary to understanding. The questions *force* some connection; with the first connection you make, you begin to form an understanding of the work.

But that first connection also helps you establish a personal interest in the literary piece. Because the questions ask you, as a reader, to respond, you begin interacting with the text, bringing your sum of experience to the words on the page. That interaction in itself creates more of an interest than reading passively does.

Prereading Fiction

Short Stories

Reading short stories comes easily to most people because the short story's narrative structure is familiar at once; it's the same narrative structure that dominates popular American movies and novels. The short story's length gives it the additional advantage of brevity. Like a movie, a short story can be experienced, appreciated, and interpreted in one continuous sitting.

Before you begin reading any piece of literature, it's a good idea to become familiar with some of its surface features. Look it over, make some observations. Notice the title and the author. Thumb through the pages, briefly noting the shape of the paragraphs and the sentences. This preliminary examination should take only a few minutes, but it might give you some initial insights with which to begin your reading. Then take a few brief notes. Below is a list of useful questions to answer before reading a short story:

1. How do you respond to the title?

2. Who wrote the work?

3. What do you know about the author?

4. What do you know about the author's work?

5. What is the story's form? How does the story look on the page? (Like other stories you've read?)

6. Does anything else about this story immediately catch your attention? (i.e., unusual sentences, headings, lots of dialogue, inventions)

The following comments are a response to the prereading questions; responding to those questions helped the writer make some connections, form some expectations, and frame some questions that increase his interest in the story. This sample prereading is for the short story "Young Goodman Brown" (found on pp. 247–256):

> This story was written by Hawthorne (middle 19th century?). He also wrote The Scarlet Letter which was about sin and guilt in Puritan New England. I remember that he's called a writer of romances and that he's sometimes mysterious. The title of this story makes it sound like another Puritan story—Young Goodman Brown. I wonder if everyone called him *Goodman* because that's his name or because he really is a good-man?
>
> The story isn't divided up into parts. I noticed some dialogue—Goodman's wife's name is Faith. Now I know we're going to have a Puritan story. I'm also going to watch to see if his wife really is Faith-ful. Name symbolism?

Notice that the author of this prereading didn't follow our steps in order. He chose to begin with the author because he knew something about Hawthorne which influenced the way he responded to the title. Although the prereading questions are numbered, they are not designed as a sequence but rather as a free-flowing set of suggestions to focus your attention.

Young Goodman Brown

Nathaniel Hawthorne
1804–1864

Young Goodman Brown came forth at sunset into the street at Salem village; but put his head back, after crossing the threshold, to exchange a parting kiss with his young wife. And Faith, as the wife was aptly named, thrust her own pretty head into the street, letting the wind play with the pink ribbons of her cap while she called to Goodman Brown.

"Dearest heart," whispered she, softly and rather sadly, when her lips were close to his ear, "prithee put off your journey until sunrise and sleep in your own bed to-night. A lone woman is troubled with such dreams and such thoughts that she's afeard of herself sometimes. Pray tarry with me this night, dear husband, of all nights in the year."

"My love and my Faith," replied young Goodman Brown, "of all nights in the year, this one night must I tarry away from thee. My journey, as thou callest it, forth and back again, must needs be done 'twixt now and sunrise. What, my sweet, pretty wife, dost thou doubt me already, and we but three months married?"

"Then God bless you!" said Faith, with the pink ribbons; "and may you find all well when you come back."

"Amen!" cried Goodman Brown. "Say thy prayers, dear Faith, and go to bed at dusk, and no harm will come to thee."

So they parted; and the young man pursued his way until, being about to turn the corner by the meeting-house, he looked back and saw the head of Faith still peeping after him with a melancholy air, in spite of her pink ribbons.

"Poor little Faith!" thought he, for his heart smote him. "What a wretch am I to leave her on such an errand! She talks of dreams, too. Methought as she spoke there was trouble in her face, as if a dream had warned her what work is to be done to-night. But no, no; 'twould kill her to think it. Well, she's a blessed angel on earth; and after this one night I'll cling to her skirts and follow her to heaven."

With this excellent resolve for the future, Goodman Brown felt himself justified in making more haste on his present evil purpose. He had taken a dreary road, darkened by all the gloomiest trees of the forest, which barely stood aside to let the narrow path creep through, and closed immediately behind. It was all as lonely as could be; and there is this peculiarity in such a solitude, that the traveller knows not who may be concealed by the innumerable trunks and the thick boughs overhead; so that with lonely footsteps he may yet be passing through an unseen multitude.

"There may be a devilish Indian behind every tree," said Goodman Brown to himself; and he glanced fearfully behind him as he added, "What if the devil himself should be at my very elbow!"

His head being turned back, he passed a crook of the road, and, looking forward again, beheld the figure of a man, in grave and decent attire, seated at the foot of an old tree. He arose at Goodman Brown's approach and walked onward side by side with him.

"You are late, Goodman Brown," said he. "The clock of the Old South was striking as I came through Boston, and that is full fifteen minutes agone."

"Faith kept me back a while," replied the young man, with a tremor in his voice, caused by the sudden appearance of his companion, though not wholly unexpected.

It was now deep dusk in the forest, and deepest in that part of it where these two were journeying. As nearly as could be discerned, the second traveller was about fifty years old, apparently in the same rank of life as Goodman Brown, and bearing a considerable resemblance to him, though perhaps more in expression than features. Still they might have been taken for father and son. And yet, though the elder person was as simply clad as the younger, and as simple in manner too, he had an indescribable air of one who knew the world, and who would not have felt abashed at the governor's dinner table or in King William's court, were it possible that his affairs should call him thither. But the only thing about him that could be fixed upon as remarkable was his staff, which bore the likeness of a great black snake, so curiously wrought that it might almost be seen to twist and wriggle itself like a living serpent. This, of course, must have been an ocular deception, assisted by the uncertain light.

"Come, Goodman Brown," cried his fellow-traveller, "this is a dull pace for the beginning of a journey. Take my staff, if you are so soon weary."

"Friend," said the other, exchanging his slow pace for a full stop, "having kept covenant by meeting thee here, it is my purpose now to return whence I came. I have scruples touching the matter thou wot'st of."

"Sayest thou so?" replied he of the serpent, smiling apart. "Let us walk on, nevertheless, reasoning as we go; and if I convince thee not thou shalt turn back. We are but a little way in the forest yet."

"Too far! too far!" exclaimed the good man, unconsciously resuming his walk. "My father never went into the woods on such an errand, nor his father before him. We have been a race of honest men and good Christians since the days of the martyrs; and shall I be the first of the name of Brown that ever took this path and kept—"

"Such company, thou wouldst say," observed the elder person, interpreting his pause. "Well said, Goodman Brown! I have been as well acquainted with your family as with ever a one among the Puritans; and that's no trifle to say. I helped your grandfather, the constable, when he lashed the Quaker woman so smartly through the streets of Salem; and it was I that brought your father a pitch-pine knot, kindled at my own hearth, to set fire to an Indian village, in King Philip's war. They were my good friends, both; and many a pleasant walk have we had along this path, and returned merrily after midnight. I would fain be friends with you for their sake."

"If it be as thou sayest," replied Goodman Brown, "I marvel they never spoke of these matters; or, verily, I marvel not, seeing that the least rumor of the sort would have driven them from New England. We are a people of prayer, and good works to boot, and abide no such wickedness."

"Wickedness or not," said the traveller with the twisted staff, "I have a very general acquaintance here in New England. The deacons of many a church have drunk the communion wine with me; the selectmen of divers towns make me their chairman; and a majority of the Great and General Court are firm supporters of my interest. The governor and I, too—But these are state secrets."

"Can this be so?" cried Goodman Brown, with a stare of amazement at his undisturbed companion. "Howbeit, I have nothing to do with the governor and council; they have their own ways, and are no rule for a simple husbandman like me. But, were I to go on with thee, how should I meet the eye of that good old man, our minister, at Salem village? Oh, his voice would make me tremble both Sabbath day and lecture day."

Thus far the elder traveller had listened with due gravity; but now burst into a fit of irrepressible mirth, shaking himself so violently that his snake-like staff actually seemed to wriggle in sympathy.

"Ha! ha! ha!" shouted he again and again; then composing himself, "Well, go on, Goodman Brown, go on; but, prithee, don't kill me with laughing."

"Well, then, to end the matter at once," said Goodman Brown, considerably nettled, "there is my wife, Faith. It would break her dear little heart; and I'd rather break my own."

"Nay, if that be the case," answered the other, "e'en go thy ways, Goodman Brown. I would not for twenty old women like the one hobbling before us that Faith should come to any harm."

As he spoke he pointed his staff at a female figure on the path, in whom Goodman Brown recognized a very pious and exemplary dame, who had taught him his catechism in youth, and was still his moral and spiritual adviser, jointly with the minister and Deacon Gookin.

"A marvel, truly, that Goody Cloyse should be so far in the wilderness at nightfall," said he. "But with your leave, friend, I shall take a cut through the woods until we have left this Christian woman behind. Being a stranger to you, she might ask whom I was consorting with and whither I was going."

"Be it so," said his fellow-traveller. "Betake you to the woods, and let me keep the path."

Accordingly the young man turned aside, but took care to watch his companion, who advanced softly along the road until he had come within a staff's length of the old dame. She, meanwhile, was making the best of her way, with singular speed for so aged a woman, and mumbling some indistinct words—a prayer, doubtless—as she went. The traveller put forth his staff and touched her withered neck with what seemed the serpent's tail.

"The devil!" screamed the pious old lady.

"Then Goody Cloyse knows her old friend?" observed the traveller, confronting her and leaning on his writhing stick.

"Ah, forsooth, and is it your worship indeed?" cried the good dame. "Yea, truly is it, and in the very image of my old gossip, Goodman Brown, the grandfather of the silly fellow that now is. But—would your worship believe it?—my broomstick hath strangely disappeared, stolen, as I suspect, by that unhanged witch, Goody Cory, and that, too, when I was all anointed with the juice of smallage, and cinquefoil, and wolf's bane—"

"Mingled with fine wheat and the fat of a new-born babe," said the shape of old Goodman Brown.

"Ah, your worship knows the recipe," cried the old lady, cackling aloud. "So, as I was saying, being all ready for the meeting, and no horse to ride on, I made up my mind to foot it; for they tell me there is a nice young man to be taken into communion to-night. But now your good worship will lend me your arm, and we shall be there in a twinkling."

"That can hardly be," answered her friend. "I may not spare you my arm, Goody Cloyse; but here is my staff, if you will."

So saying, he threw it down at her feet, where, perhaps, it assumed life, being one of the rods which its owner had formerly lent to the Egyptian magi. Of this fact, however, Goodman Brown could not take cognizance. He had cast up his eyes in astonishment, and, looking down again, beheld neither Goody Cloyse nor the serpentine staff, but his fellow traveller alone, who waited for him as calmly as if nothing had happened.

"That old woman taught me my catechism," said the young man; and there was a world of meaning in this simple comment.

They continued to walk onward, while the elder traveller exhorted his companion to make good speed and persevere in the path, discoursing so aptly that his arguments seemed rather to spring up in the bosom of his auditor than to be suggested by himself. As they went, he plucked a branch of maple to serve for a walking stick, and began to strip it of the twigs and little boughs, which were wet with evening dew. The moment his fingers touched them they became strangely withered and dried up as with a week's sunshine. Thus the pair proceeded, at a good free pace, until suddenly, in a gloomy hollow of the road, Goodman Brown sat himself down on the stump of a tree and refused to go any farther.

"Friend," said he stubbornly, "my mind is made up. Not another step will I budge on this errand. What if a wretched old woman do choose to go to the devil when I thought she was going to heaven: is that any reason why I should quit my dear Faith and go after her?"

"You will think better of this by and by," said his acquaintance, composedly. "Sit here and rest yourself a while; and when you feel like moving again, there is my staff to help you along."

Without more words, he threw his companion the maple stick, and was as speedily out of sight as if he had vanished into the deepening gloom. The young man sat a few moments by the roadside, applauding himself greatly, and thinking with how clear a conscience he should meet the minister in his morning walk, nor shrink from the eye of good old Deacon Gookin. And what calm sleep would be his that very night, which was to have been spent so wickedly, but so purely and sweetly now, in the arms of Faith! Amidst these pleasant and praise-worthy meditations, Goodman Brown heard the tramp of horses along the road, and deemed it advisable to conceal himself within the verge of the forest, conscious of the guilty purpose that had brought him thither, though now so happily turned from it.

On came the hoof tramps and the voices of the riders, two grave old voices, conversing soberly as they drew near. These mingled sounds appeared to pass along the road, within a few yards of the young man's hiding-place; but, owing doubtless to the depth of the gloom at that particular spot, neither the travellers nor their steeds were visible. Though their figures brushed the small boughs by the wayside, it could not be seen that they intercepted, even for a moment, the faint gleam from the strip of bright sky athwart which they must have passed. Goodman Brown alternately crouched and stood on tiptoe, pulling aside the branches and thrusting forth his head as far as he durst without discerning so much as a shadow. It vexed him the more, because he could have sworn, were such a thing possible, that he recognized the voices of the minister and Deacon Gookin, jogging along quietly, as they were wont to do, when bound to some ordination of ecclesiastical council. While yet within hearing, one of the riders stopped to pluck a switch.

"Of the two, reverend sir," said the voice like the deacon's, "I had rather miss an ordination dinner than to-night's meeting. They tell me that some of our community are to be here from Falmouth and beyond, and others from Connecticut and Rhode Island, besides several of the Indian powwows, who, after their fashion, know almost as much deviltry as the best of us. Moreover, there is a goodly young woman to be taken into communion."

"Mighty well, Deacon Gookin!" replied the solemn old tones of the minister. "Spur up, or we shall be late. Nothing can be done, you know, until I get on the ground."

The hoofs clattered again; and the voices, talking so strangely in the empty air, passed on through the forest, where no church had ever been gathered or solitary Christian prayed. Whither, then, could these holy men be journeying so deep into the heathen wilderness? Young Goodman Brown caught hold of a tree for support, being ready to sink down to the ground, faint and overburdened with the heavy sickness of his heart. He looked up to the sky, doubting whether there really was a heaven above him. Yet there was the blue arch, and the stars brightening in it.

"With heaven above and Faith below, I will yet stand firm against the devil!" cried Goodman Brown.

While he still gazed upward into the deep arch of the firmament and had lifted his hands to pray, a cloud, though no wind was stirring, hurried across the zenith and hid the brightening stars. The blue sky was still visible, except directly overhead, where this black mass of cloud was sweeping swiftly northward. Aloft in the air, as if from the depths of the cloud, came a confused and doubtful sound of voices. Once the listener fancied that he could distinguish the accents of townspeople of his own, men and women, both pious and ungodly, many of whom he had met at the communion table, and had seen others rioting at the tavern. The next moment, so indistinct were the sounds, he doubted whether he had heard aught but the murmur of the old forest, whispering without a wind. Then came a stronger swell of those familiar tones, heard daily in the sunshine at Salem village, but never until now from a cloud of night. There was one voice, of a young woman, uttering lamentations, yet with an uncertain sorrow, and entreating for some favor, which, perhaps it would grieve her to obtain; and all the unseen multitude, both saints and sinners, seemed to encourage her onward.

"Faith!" shouted Goodman Brown, in a voice of agony and desperation; and the echoes of the forest mocked him, crying, "Faith! Faith!" as if bewildered wretches were seeking her all through the wilderness.

The cry of grief, rage, and terror was yet piercing the night, when the unhappy husband held his breath for a response. There was a scream, drowned immediately in a louder murmur of voices, fading into far-off laughter, as the dark cloud swept away, leaving the clear and silent sky above Goodman Brown. But something fluttered lightly down through the air and caught on the branch of a tree. The young man seized it, and beheld a pink ribbon.

"My Faith is gone!" cried he, after one stupefied moment. "There is no good on earth; and sin is but a name. Come, devil; for to thee is this world given."

And, maddened with despair, so that he laughed loud and long, did Goodman Brown grasp his staff and set forth again, at such a rate that he seemed to fly along the forest path rather than to walk or run. The road grew wilder and drearier and more faintly traced, and vanished at length, leaving him in the heart of the dark wilderness, still rushing onward with the instinct that guides mortal man to evil. The whole forest was peopled with frightful sounds—the creaking of the trees, the howling of wild beasts, and the yell of Indians; while sometimes the wind tolled like a distant church bell, and sometimes gave a broad roar around the traveller, as if all Nature were laughing him to scorn. But he was himself the chief horror of the scene, and shrank not from its other horrors.

"Ha! ha! ha!" roared Goodman Brown when the wind laughed at him. "Let us hear which will laugh loudest. Think not to frighten me with your deviltry. Come witch, come wizard, come Indian pow-wow, come devil himself, and here comes Goodman Brown. You may as well fear him as he fear you."

In truth, all through the haunted forest there could be nothing more frightful than the figure of Goodman Brown. On he flew among the black pines, brandishing his staff with frenzied gestures, now giving vent to an inspiration of horrid blasphemy, and now shouting forth such laughter as set all the echoes of the forest laughing like demons around him. The fiend in his own shape is less hideous than when he rages in the breast of man. Thus sped the demoniac on his course, until, quivering among the trees, he saw a red light before him, as when the felled trunks and branches of a clearing have been set on fire, and throw up their lurid blaze against the sky, at the hour of midnight. He paused, in a lull of the tempest that had driven him onward, and heard the swell of what seemed a hymn, rolling solemnly from a distance with the weight of many voices. He knew the tune; it was a familiar one in the choir of the village meeting-house. The verse died heavily away, and was lengthened by a chorus, not of human voices, but of all the sounds of the benighted wilderness pealing in awful harmony together. Goodman Brown cried out, and his cry was lost to his own ear by its unison with the cry of the desert.

In the interval of silence he stole forward until the light glared full upon his eyes. At one extremity of an open space, hemmed in by the dark wall of the forest, arose a rock, bearing some rude, natural resemblance to an altar or a pulpit, and surrounded by four blazing pines, their tops aflame, their stems untouched, like candles at an evening meeting. The mass of foliage that had overgrown the summit of the rock was all on fire, blazing high into the night and fitfully illuminating the whole field. Each pendent twig and leafy festoon was in a blaze. As the red light arose and fell, a numerous congregation alternately shone forth, then disappeared in shadow, and again grew, as it were, out of the darkness, peopling the heart of the solitary woods at once.

"A grave and dark-clad company," quoth Goodman Brown.

In truth they were such. Among them, quivering to and fro between gloom and splendor, appeared faces that would be seen next day at the council board of the province, and others which, Sabbath after Sabbath, looked devoutly heavenward, and benignantly over the crowded pews, from the holiest pulpits in the land. Some affirm that the lady of the governor was there. At least there were high dames well known to her, and wives of honored husbands, and widows, a great multitude, and ancient maidens, all of excellent repute, and fair young girls, who trembled lest their mothers should espy them. Either the sudden gleams of light flashing over the obscure field bedazzled Goodman Brown, or he recognized a score of the church members of Salem village famous for their especial sanctity. Good old Deacon Gookin had arrived, and waited at the skirts of that venerable saint, his revered pastor. But, irreverently consorting with these grave, reputable, and pious people, these elders of the church, these chaste dames and dewy virgins, there were men of dissolute lives and women of spotted fame, wretches given over to all mean and filthy vice, and suspected even of horrid crimes. It was strange to see that the good shrank not from the wicked, nor were the sinners abashed by the saints. Scattered also among their palefaced enemies were the Indian priests, or powwows, who had often scared their native forest with more hideous incantations than any known to English witchcraft.

"But where is Faith?" thought Goodman Brown; and, as hope came into his heart, he trembled.

Another verse of the hymn arose, a slow and mournful strain, such as the pious love, but joined to words which expressed all that our nature can conceive of sin, and darkly hinted at far more. Unfathomable to mere mortals is the lore of fiends. Verse after verse was sung; and still the chorus of the desert swelled between like the deepest tone of a mighty organ; and with the final peal of that dreadful anthem there came a sound, as if the roaring wind, the rushing streams, the howling beasts, and every other voice of the unconcerted wilderness were mingling and according with the voice of guilty man in homage to the prince of all. The four blazing pines threw up a loftier flame, and obscurely discovered shapes and visages of horror on the smoke wreaths above the impious assembly. At the same moment the fire on the rock shot redly forth and formed a glowing arch above its base, where now appeared a figure. With reverence be it spoken, the figure bore no slight similitude, both in garb and manner, to some grave divine of the New England churches.

"Bring forth the converts!" cried a voice that echoed through the field and rolled into the forest.

At the word, Goodman Brown stepped forth from the shadow of the trees and approached the congregation, with whom he felt a loathful brotherhood by the sympathy of all that was wicked in his heart. He could have well-nigh sworn that the shape of his own dead father beckoned him to advance, looking downward from a smoke wreath, while a woman, with dim features of despair, threw out her hand to warn him back. Was it his mother? But he had no power to retreat one step, nor to resist, even in thought, when the minister and good old Deacon Gookin seized his arms and led him to the blazing rock. Thither came also the slender form of a veiled female, led between Goody Cloyse, that pious teacher of the catechism, and Martha Carrier, who had received the devil's promise to be queen of hell. A rampant hag was she. And there stood the proselytes beneath the canopy of fire.

"Welcome, my children," said the dark figure, "to the communion of your race. Ye have found thus young your nature and your destiny. My children, look behind you!"

They turned; and flashing forth, as it were, in a sheet of flame, the fiend worshippers were seen; the smile of welcome gleamed darkly on every visage.

"There," resumed the sable form, "are all whom ye have reverenced from youth. Ye deemed them holier than yourselves, and shrank from your own sin, contrasting it with their lives of righteousness and prayerful aspirations heavenward. Yet here are they all in my worshipping assembly. This night it shall be granted you to know their secret deeds: how hoary-bearded elders of the church have whispered wanton words to the young maids of their households; how many a woman, eager for widows' weeds, has given her husband a drink at bedtime and let him sleep his last sleep in her bosom; how beardless youths have made haste to inherit their fathers' wealth; and how fair damsels—blush not, sweet ones—have dug little graves in the garden, and bidden me, the sole guest, to an infant's funeral. By the sympathy of your human hearts for sin ye shall scent out all the places—whether in church, bedchamber, street, field, or forest—where crime has been committed, and shall exult to behold the whole earth one stain of guilt, one mighty blood spot. Far more than this. It shall be yours to penetrate, in every bosom, the deep mystery of sin, the fountain of all wicked arts, and which inexhaustibly supplies more evil impulses than human power—than my power at its utmost—can make manifest in deeds. And now, my children, look upon each other."

They did so; and, by the blaze of the hell-kindled torches, the wretched man beheld his Faith, and the wife her husband, trembling before that unhallowed altar.

"Lo, there ye stand, my children," said the figure, in a deep and solemn tone, almost sad with its despairing awfulness, as if his once angelic nature could yet mourn for our miserable race. "Depending upon one another's hearts, ye had still hoped that virtue were not all a dream. Now are ye undeceived. Evil is the nature of mankind. Evil must be your only happiness. Welcome again, my children, to the communion of your race."

"Welcome," repeated the fiend worshippers, in one cry of despair and triumph.

And there they stood, the only pair, as it seemed, who were yet hesitating on the verge of wickedness in this dark world. A basin was hollowed, naturally, in the rock. Did it contain water, reddened by the lurid light? or was it blood? or, perchance, a liquid flame? Herein did the shape of evil dip his hand and prepare to lay the mark of baptism upon their foreheads, that they might be partakers of the mystery of sin, more conscious of the secret guilt of others, both in deed and thought, than they could now be of their own. The husband cast one look at his pale wife, and Faith at him. What polluted wretches would the next glance show them to each other, shuddering alike at what they disclosed and what they saw!

"Faith! Faith!" cried the husband, "look up to heaven, and resist the wicked one."

Whether Faith obeyed he knew not. Hardly had he spoken when he found himself amid calm night and solitude, listening to a roar of the wind which died heavily away through the forest. He staggered against the rock, and felt it chill and damp; while a hanging twig, that had been all on fire, besprinkled his cheek with the coldest dew.

The next morning young Goodman Brown came slowly into the street of Salem village, staring around him like a bewildered man. The good old minister was taking a walk along the graveyard to get an appetite for breakfast and meditate his sermon, and bestowed a blessing, as he passed, on Goodman Brown. He shrank from the venerable saint is if to avoid an anathema. Old Deacon Gookin was at domestic worship, and the holy words of his prayer were heard through the open window. "What God doth the wizard pray to?" quoth Goodman Brown. Goody Cloyse, that excellent old Christian, stood in the early sunshine at her own lattice, catechizing a little girl who had brought her a pint of morning's milk. Goodman Brown snatched away the child as from the grasp of the fiend himself. Turning the corner by the meeting-house, he spied the head of Faith, with the pink ribbons, gazing anxiously forth, and bursting into such joy at sight of him that she skipped along the street and almost kissed her husband before the whole village. But Goodman Brown looked sternly and sadly into her face, and passed on without a greeting.

Had Goodman Brown fallen asleep in the forest and only dreamed a wild dream of a witch-meeting?

Be it so if you will; but, alas! it was a dream of evil omen for young Goodman Brown. A stern, a sad, a darkly meditative, a distrustful, if not a desperate man did he become from the night of that fearful dream. On the Sabbath day, when the congregation were singing a holy psalm, he could not listen because an anthem of sin rushed loudly upon his ear and drowned all the blessed strain. When the minister spoke from the pulpit with power and fervid eloquence, and, with his hand on the open Bible, of the sacred truths of our religion, and of saint-like lives and triumphant deaths, and of future bliss or misery unutterable, then did Goodman Brown turn pale, dreading lest the roof should thunder down upon the gray blasphemer and his hearers. Often, awaking suddenly at midnight, he shrank from the bosom of Faith; and at morning or eventide, when the family knelt down at prayer, he scowled and muttered to himself, and gazed sternly at his wife, and turned away. And when he had lived long, and was borne to his grave a hoary corpse, followed by Faith, an aged woman, and children and grandchildren, a goodly procession, besides neighbors not a few, they carved no hopeful verse upon his tombstone, for his dying hour was gloom.

EXERCISE 8–1

Follow the six prereading steps for the following story. Record your responses and bring them to class for discussion.

The Coup de Grâce

Ambrose Bierce
1842–1914?

The fighting had been hard and continuous; that was attested by all the senses. The very taste of battle was in the air. All was now over; it remained only to succor the wounded and bury the dead—to "tidy up a bit," as the humorist of a burial squad put it. A good deal of "tidying up" was required. As far as one could see through the forests, among the splintered trees, lay wrecks of men and horses. Among them moved the stretcher-bearers, gathering and carrying away the few who showed signs of life. Most of the wounded had died of neglect while the right to minister to their wants was in dispute. It is an army regulation that the wounded must wait; the best way to care for them is to win the battle. It must be confessed that victory is a distinct advantage to a man requiring attention, but many do not live to avail themselves of it.

The dead were collected in groups of a dozen or a score and laid side by side in rows while the trenches were dug to receive them. Some, found at too great a distance from these rallying points, were buried where they lay. There was little attempt at identification, though in most cases, the burial parties being detailed to glean the same ground which they had assisted to reap, the names of the victorious dead were known and listed. The enemy's fallen had to be content with counting. But of that they got enough:

many of them were counted several times, and the total, as given afterward in the official report of the victorious commander, denoted rather a hope than a result.

At some little distance from the spot where one of the burial parties had established its "bivouac of the dead," a man in the uniform of a Federal officer stood leaning against a tree. From his feet upward to his neck his attitude was that of weariness reposing; but he turned his head uneasily from side to side; his mind was apparently not at rest. He was perhaps undertain in which direction to go; he was not likely to remain long where he was, for already the level rays of the setting sun straggled redly through the open spaces of the wood and the weary soldiers were quitting their task for the day. He would hardly make a night of it alone there among the dead. Nine men in ten whom you meet after a battle inquire the way to some fraction of the army—as if any one could know. Doubtless this officer was lost. After resting himself a moment he would presumably follow one of the retiring burial squads.

When all were gone he walked straight away into the forest toward the red west, its light staining his face like blood. The air of confidence with which he now strode along showed that he was on familiar ground; he had recovered his bearings. The dead on his right and on his left were unregarded as he passed. An occasional low moan from some sorely stricken wretch whom the relief-parties had not reached, and who would have to pass a comfortless night beneath the stars with his thirst to keep him company, was equally unheeded. What, indeed, could the officer have done, being no surgeon and having no water?

At the head of a shallow ravine, a mere depression of the ground, lay a small group of bodies. He saw, and swerving suddenly from his course walked rapidly toward them. Scanning each one sharply as he passed, he stopped at last above one which lay at a slight remove from the others, near a clump of small trees. He looked at it narrowly. It seemed to stir. He stooped and laid his hand upon its face. It screamed.

The officer was Captain Downing Madwell, of a Massachusetts regiment of infantry, a daring and intelligent soldier, an honorable man.

In the regiment were two brothers named Halcrow—Caffal and Creede Halcrow. Caffal Halcrow was a sergeant in Captain Madwell's company, and these two men, the sergeant and the captain, were devoted friends. In so far as disparity of rank, differences in duties and considerations of military discipline would permit they were commonly together. They had, indeed, grown up together from childhood. A habit of the heart is not easily broken off. Caffal Halcrow had nothing military in his taste nor disposition, but the thought of separation from his friend was disagreeable; he enlisted in the company in which Madwell was second-lieutenant. Each had taken two steps upward in rank, but between the highest non-commissioned and the lowest commissioned officer the gulf is deep and wide and the old relation was maintained with difficulty and a difference.

Creede Halcrow, the brother of Caffal, was the major of the regiment—a cynical, saturnine man, between whom and Captain Madwell there was a natural antipathy which circumstances had nourished and strengthened to an active animosity. But for the restraining influence of their mutual relation to Caffal these two patriots would doubtless have endeavored to deprive their country of each other's services.

At the opening of the battle that morning the regiment was performing outpost duty a mile away from the main army. It was attacked and nearly surrounded in the forest, but stubbornly held its ground. During a lull in the fighting, Major Halcrow came to Captain Madwell. The two exchanged formal salutes, and the major said: "Captain, the colonel directs that you push your company to the head of this ravine and hold your place there until recalled. I need hardly apprise you of the dangerous character of the movement, but if you wish, you can, I suppose, turn over the command to your first-lieutenant. I was not, however, directed to authorize the substitution; it is merely a suggestion of my own, unofficially made."

To this deadly insult Captain Madwell coolly replied:

"Sir, I invite you to accompany the movement. A mounted officer would be a conspicuous mark, and I have long held the opinion that it would be better if you were dead."

The art of repartee was cultivated in military circles as early as 1862.

A half-hour later Captain Madwell's company was driven from its position at the head of the ravine, with a loss of one-third its number. Among the fallen was Sergeant Halcrow. The regiment was soon afterward forced back to the main line, and at the close of the battle was miles away. The captain was now standing at the side of his subordinate and friend.

Sergeant Halcrow was mortally hurt. His clothing was deranged; it seemed to have been violently torn apart, exposing the abdomen. Some of the buttons of his jacket had been pulled off and lay on the ground beside him and fragments of his other garments were strewn about. His leather belt was parted and had apparently been dragged from beneath him as he lay. There had been no great effusion of blood. The only visible wound was a wide, ragged opening in the abdomen. It was defiled with earth and dead leaves. Protruding from it was a loop of small intestine. In all his experience Captain Madwell had not seen a wound like this. He could neither conjecture how it was made nor explain the attendant circumstances—the strangely torn clothing, the parted belt, the besmirching of the white skin. He knelt and made a closer examination. When he rose to his feet, he turned his eyes in different directions as if looking for an enemy. Fifty yards away, on the crest of a low, thinly wooded hill, he saw several dark objects moving about among the fallen men—a herd of swine. One stood with its back to him, its shoulders sharply elevated. Its forefeet were upon a human body, its head was depressed and invisible. The bristly ridge of its chine showed black against the red west. Captain Madwell drew away his eyes and fixed them again upon the thing which had been his friend.

The man who had suffered these monstrous mutilations was alive. At intervals he moved his limbs; he moaned at every breath. He stared blankly into the face of his friend and if touched screamed. In his giant agony he had torn up the ground on which he lay; his clenched hands were full of leaves and twigs and earth. Articulate speech was beyond his power; it was impossible to know if he were sensible to anything but pain. The expression of his face was an appeal; his eyes were full of prayer. For what?

There was no misreading that look; the captain had too frequently seen it in eyes of those whose lips had still the power to formulate it by an entreaty for death. Consciously or unconsciously, this writhing fragment of humanity, this type and example of acute sensation, this handiwork of man and beast, this humble, unheroic Prometheus, was imploring everything, all, the whole non-ego, for the boon of oblivion. To the earth and the sky alike, to the trees, to the man, to whatever took form in sense or consciousness, this incarnate suffering addressed that silent plea.

For what, indeed? For that which we accord to even the meanest creature without sense to demand it, denying it only to the wretched of our own race: for the blessed release, the rite of uttermost compassion, the *coup de grâce.*

Captain Madwell spoke the name of his friend. He repeated it over and over without effect until emotion choked his utterance. His tears splashed upon the livid face beneath his own and blinded himself. He saw nothing but a blurred and moving object, but the moans were more distinct than ever, interrupted at briefer intervals by sharper shrieks. He turned away, struck his hand upon his forehead, and strode from the spot. The swine, catching sight of him, threw up their crimson muzzles, regarding him suspiciously a second, and then with a gruff, concerted grunt, raced away out of sight. A horse, its foreleg splintered by a cannonshot, lifted its head sidewise from the ground and neighed piteously. Madwell stepped forward, drew his revolver and shot the poor beast between the eyes, narrowly observing its death-struggle, which, contrary to his expectation, was violent and long; but at last it lay still. The tense muscles of its lips, which had uncovered the teeth in a horrible grin, relaxed; the sharp, clean-cut profile took on a look of profound peace and rest.

Along the distant, thinly wooded crest to westward the fringe of sunset fire had now nearly burned itself out. The light upon the trunks of the trees had faded to a tender gray; shadows were in their tops, like great dark birds aperch. Night was coming and there were miles of haunted forest between Captain Madwell and camp. Yet he stood there at the side of the dead animal, apparently lost to all sense of his surroundings. His eyes were bent upon the earth at his feet; his left hand hung loosely at his side, his right still held the pistol. Presently he lifted his face, turned it toward his dying friend and walked rapidly back to his side. He knelt upon one knee, cocked the weapon, placed the muzzle against the man's forehead, and turning away his eyes pulled the trigger. There was no report. He had used his last cartridge for the horse.

The sufferer moaned and his lips moved convulsively. The froth that ran from them had a tinge of blood.

Captain Madwell rose to his feet and drew his sword from the scabbard. He passed the fingers of his left hand along the edge from hilt to point. He held it out straight before him, as if to test his nerves. There was no visible tremor of the blade; the ray of bleak skylight that it reflected was steady and true. He stooped and with his left hand tore away the dying man's shirt, rose and placed the point of the sword just over the heart. This time he did not withdraw his eyes. Grasping the hilt with both hands, he thrust downward with all his strength and weight. The blade sank into the man's body— through his body into the earth; Captain Madwell came near falling forward upon his work. The dying man drew up his knees and at the same time threw his right arm across his breast and grasped the steel so tightly that the knuckles of the hand visibly whitened. By a violent but vain effort to withdraw the blade the wound was enlarged; a rill of blood escaped, running sinuously down into the deranged clothing. At that moment three men stepped silently forward from behind the clump of young trees which had concealed their approach. Two were hospital attendants and carried a stretcher.

The third was Major Creede Halcrow.

Novels

The novel is the most popular literary form of the twentieth century. The popular novel shares with the short story its familiar narrative structure; however, its extended length demands a reading over a longer period of time and therefore makes more demands on a reader's attention. Here are some prereading suggestions:

1. How do you respond to the title?
2. Who wrote the work?
3. What do you know about the author?
4. What do you know about the author's works?
5. What is the novel's form? (Like other novels you've read?) How many chapters are there? Are the chapters titled?
6. Does anything else about this novel immediately catch your attention? (i.e., unusual sentences, chapters, drawings, obvious divisions)

Prereading Poetry

Although the poem shares with the short story the value of brevity, students usually find it a more difficult form. Since a poet compresses meaning and experience, interpretation of even the smallest details is essential to even a minimum level of understanding. And poems often explore the ambiguities of life; consequently any student who treats a poem as a puzzle with one distinct hidden meaning faces certain frustration. Rather, what a literature teacher seeks from students is an interpretation which can be supported by the physical features of the poem.

The first step before reading a poem is simply to look at it and make some observations:

1. How do you respond to the title?

2. Who wrote the poem?

3. What do you know about the author?

4. What do you know about the author's works?

5. What is the poem's form? How many lines are there? Do they rhyme? How does the poem look on the page? (Like other poems you've read?)

6. Does anything else about this poem immediately catch your attention? (i.e., unusual lines, names, stanza form)

This preliminary exploration need not be a microscopic examination. Your purpose is simply to get an initial feel for the poem and to identify any expectations you might reasonably have about your reading. Briefly record your initial reactions; they might come in handy later. Remember that all you are doing now is getting ready to read. The success of the writing you do later depends on the quality of your reading.

Here's a sample of a prereading notation for "Alabama Poem" by Nikki Giovanni (p. 262):

```
    1.   This poem is probably about how the author
makes poetry out of Alabama, or it's an attempt to
translate Alabama into poetry. I expect that it will
be ''countrified.''

    2.   Nikki Giovanni

    3.   She's a black, woman poet

    4.   I've heard that she's political both about
women's issues and black problems. I've read a poem
she wrote about love. It was sensual, frank, and
beautiful. I remember that I liked the language so
much that I read it to my girl friend; she liked it
too.

    5.   The poem has thirty-seven lines, none of
which seem to rhyme. It looks like a contemporary
poem: There aren't any regular stanzas although four
of the lines start at the left margin and the other
thirty-three are indented. That could mean that
there are four parts of the poem--I'll have to look
for transitions in the poem's subject matter. The
```

poem looks like ones I've read by Ferlinghetti and e.e. cummings--I'd be surprised if she has anything in common with them!

6. There aren't any capital letters. There are some quotations marks so maybe there's some dialogue in the poem. That means that there might be some characters in the poem, so I should check to see.

Alabama Poem

NIKKI GIOVANNI 1943–

if trees could talk
    wonder what they'd say
met an old man
    on the road late afternoon
hat pulled over to shade
his eyes
jacket slumped over his
shoulders
told me "girl! my hands seen
more than all
them books they got
at tuskegee"
smiled at me
half waved his hand
walked on down the dusty road
met an old woman
    with a corncob pipe
    sitting and rocking
    on a spring evening
"sista" she called to me
"let me tell you—my feet
seen more than yo eyes
ever gonna read"
smiled at her and kept
on moving
gave it a thought and went
back to the porch
"i say gal" she called down
"you a student at the institute?
better come here and study
these feet
i'm gonna cut a bunion off

soons i gets up"
i looked at her
she laughed at me
if trees would talk
wonder what they'd say

EXERCISE 8–2

Answer the six prereading questions for the following poems. Record your responses and bring them to class for discussion. Notice that poems frequently have no formal titles. In those cases, use the first line.

The Boys Across the Street Are Driving My Young Daughter Mad

RAY BRADBURY 1920–

The boys across the street are driving my young daughter mad.
The boys are only seventeen,
My daughter one year less,
And all that these boys do is jump up in the sky
and
beautifully
finesse
a basketball into a hoop;
But take forever coming down,
Their long legs brown and cleaving on the air
As if it were a rare and warm summer water.
The boys across the street are maddening my daughter.
And all they do is ride by on their shining bikes,
Ashout with insults, trading lumps,
Oblivious of the way they tread their pedals
Churning Time with long tan legs
And easing upthrust seat with downward orchard rumps;
Their faces neither glad nor sad, but calm;
The boys across the street toss back their hair and
Heedless
Drive my daughter mad.
They jog around the block and loosen up their knees.
They wrestle like a summer breeze upon the lawn.
Oh, how I wish they would not wrestle sweating on the green
All groans,
Until my daughter moans and goes to stand beneath her shower,
So her own cries are all she hears,
And feels but her own tears mixed with the water.
Thus it has been all summer with these boys and my mad daughter.

Great God, what must I do?
Steal their fine bikes, deflate their basketballs?
Their tennis shoes, their skin-tight swimming togs,
Their svelte gymnasium suits sink deep in bogs?
Then, wall up all our windows?
To what use?
The boys would still laugh wild awrestle
On that lawn.
Our shower would run all night until the dawn.
How can I raise my daughter as a Saint,
When some small part of me grows faint
Remembering a girl long years ago who by the hour
Jumped rope
Jumped rope
Jumped rope
And sent *me* weeping to the shower.

Sonnet XVI

WILLIAM SHAKESPEARE 1564–1616

But wherefore do not you a mightier way
Make war upon this bloody tyrant Time?
And fortify yourself in your decay
With means more blessed than my barren rhyme?
Now stand you on the top of happy hours,
And many maiden gardens, yet unset,
With virtuous wish would bear your living flowers,
Much liker than your painted counterfeit.
So should the lines of life that life repair,
Which this times's pencil, or my pupil pen,
Neither in inward worth nor outward fair
Can make you live yourself in eyes of men.
        To give away yourself keeps yourself still,
        And you must live, drawn by your own sweet skill.

To His Coy Mistress

ANDREW MARVELL (1621–1678)

Had we but world enough, and time,
This coyness, Lady, were no crime.
We would sit down and think which way
To walk and pass our long love's day.

Thou by the Indian Ganges' side
Shouldst rubies find; I by the tide
Of Humber would complain. I would
Love you ten years before the Flood,
And you should, if you please, refuse
Till the conversion of the Jews.
My vegetable love would grow
Vaster than empires, and more slow;
An hundred years would go to praise

Thine eyes and on thy forehead gaze;
Two hundred to adore each breast,
But thirty thousand to the rest;
An age at least to every part,
And the last age should show your heart.
For, Lady, you deserve this state,
Nor would I love at lower rate.

But at my back I always hear
Time's winged chariot hurrying near;
And yonder all before us lie
Deserts of vast eternity.
Thy beauty shall no more be found,
Nor, in thy marble vault, shall sound
My echoing song; then worms shall try
That long preserved virginity,
And your quaint honor turn to dust,
And into ashes all my lust:
The grave's a fine and private place,
But none, I think, do there embrace.

Now therefore, while the youthful hue
Sits on thy skin like morning dew,
And while thy willing soul transpires
At every pore with instant fires,
Now let us sport us while we may,
And now, like amorous birds of prey,
Rather at once our time devour
Than languish in his slow-chapped power.
Let us role all our strength and all
Our sweetness up into one ball,
And tear our pleasures with rough strife
Through the iron gates of life:
Thus, though we cannot make our sun
Stand still, yet we will make him run.

Manifesto: The Mad Farmer Liberation Front

WENDELL BERRY 1934–

Love the quick profit, the annual raise,
vacation with pay. Want more
of everything ready made. Be afraid
to know your neighbors and to die.
And you will have a window in your head.
Not even your future will be a mystery
any more. Your mind will be punched in a card
and shut away in a little drawer.
When they want you to buy something
they will call you. When they want you
to die for profit they will let you know.
So, friends, every day do something
that won't compute. Love the Lord.
Love the world. Work for nothing.
Take all that you have and be poor.
Love someone who does not deserve it.
Denounce the government and embrace
the flag. Hope to live in that free
republic for which it stands.
Give your approval to all you cannot
understand. Praise ignorance, for what man
has not encountered he has not destroyed.
Ask the questions that have no answers.
Invest in the millennium. Plant sequoias.
Say that your main crop is the forest
that you did not plant,
that you will not live to harvest.
Say that the leaves are harvested
when they have rotted into the mold.
Call that profit. Prophesy such returns.
Put your faith in the two inches of humus
that will build under the trees
every thousand years.
Listen to carrion—put your ear
close, and hear the faint chattering
of the songs that are to come.
Expect the end of the world. Laugh.
Laughter is immeasurable. Be joyful
though you have considered all the facts.
So long as women do not go cheap

for power, please women more than men.
Ask yourself: Will this satisfy
a woman satisfied to bear a child?
Will this disturb the sleep
of a woman near to giving birth?
Go with your love to the fields.
Lie easy in the shade. Rest your head
in her lap. Swear allegiance
to what is nighest your thoughts.
As soon as the generals and the politicos
can predict the motions of your mind,
lose it. Leave it as a sign
to mark the false trail, the way
you didn't go. Be like the fox
who makes more tracks than necessary,
some in the wrong direction.
Practice resurrection.

Prereading Drama

Although the structure of drama is similar to that of both movies and television programs, to most college students drama is the most alien literary form. The twentieth-century viewer has grown accustomed to the distancing effect of the screen intervening between art and audience. Drama on stage demands a greater suspension of disbelief than any medium that relies on a screen. The audience watches real reople, in physical proximity, perform. Compared to the screen arts, there are fewer visual effects and this makes stage performance seem less real than performance on screen which is actually the greater artifice. The following prereading questions will help you become familiar with a piece of drama before you read it:

1. How do you respond to the title?

2. Who wrote the play?

3. What do you know about the author?

4. What do you know about the author's works?

5. What is the play's form? How many acts are there? How does the play look on the page? (Like other plays you've read or seen?)

6. Does anything else about this play immediately catch your attention? (i.e., unusual sentences, characters' names, setting)

EXERCISE 8–3

Do the prereading for the following play:

Fat Lucy*

Frank Higgins
1953–

Cast

Lucy—the Fat Lady in a circus freak show
Moskowitz—the owner of the circus
Slade—the manager of the freak show

Set

The inside of Lucy's trailer.
A cheap chair. A cheap table.

Time

Now

(FAT LUCY, a 500-pound circus fat lady, sits and looks contentedly off into the distance. We hear a ruckus offstage as two men shout at each other. Lucy looks frightened, then vows not to be frightened.
SLADE, the man who runs the sideshow, enters and stands at the side of the playing area.)

SLADE: C'mon c'mon would you come on?
MOSKOWITZ: I'm coming!
SLADE: Well then come on!

(MOSKOWITZ, the owner of the circus, enters)

MOSKOWITZ: Dammit this better be important.
    The dancing pig's got loose.
SLADE: Big deal.
MOSKOWITZ: This is the Ozarks. One of the locals shoots the dancing pig, we don't got a second act.
SLADE: You can always find a dancing pig.
MOSKOWITZ: Not foxtrot.
SLADE: Yeah well get a load of this.

(the men come centerstage and are now in Lucy's trailer)

MOSKOWITZ: What?

SLADE: Look.

MOSKOWITZ: Nothing.

SLADE: No eyes.

MOSKOWITZ: Air conditioner?

SLADE: Her!

MOSKOWITZ: Sick? Luce? Got that killer diarrhea?

(he feels her forehead)

       Doesn't feel like diarrhea.

SLADE: She won't talk.

MOSKOWITZ: The dancing pig runs wild.

SLADE: Now you listen . . .

MOSKOWITZ: People pay to *look*.

SLADE: Look close.

MOSKOWITZ: No problem here!

SLADE: This is your circus . . .

MOSKOWITZ: You own the freaks.

  Somebody doesn't want to talk I can't be bothered.

  I gotta catch a pig, I gotta plan Missouri, I gotta count receipts.

SLADE: You gotta stop this now or there won't be receipts.

MOSKOWITZ: She won't talk, big deal.

SLADE: Keep your lion tamer away from my fat lady.

MOSKOWITZ: What's Valencia doing?

SLADE: In here every day.

MOSKOWITZ: Love under the big top.

SLADE: No joke.

MOSKOWITZ: Lucy and Valencia want to get it on, it's natural.

SLADE: This ain't natural.

MOSKOWITZ: Don't you talk about what's natural.

SLADE: Your lion tamer's doing things what's gonna change everything.

MOSKOWITZ: Two of you really in love? A thought.

  Last week the wirewalkers got married up on the wire; special admission, best take yet.

SLADE: No ears.

MOSKOWITZ: Top dollar see a lion tamer hook up with a fat lady.

  Network news. Human interest.

SLADE: Look at her! She's not eating!

MOSKOWITZ: She's sick today. Scarf up some extra jelly rolls tomorrow.

SLADE: She's not eating *period*. Damn lion tamer's messing her mind.

  She's losing weight!

MOSKOWITZ: . . . Sure?

SLADE: Neck bone's showing.

MOSKOWITZ *(looking)*: Damn.

SLADE: Missing a chin.

MOSKOWITZ: You got eat something, baby.

SLADE: Lettuce. You got to stop her, Moskowitz:
    she's my main attraction,
    customers say my Snakeskin Boy's a bad rash,
    I lose her, freak show's a fat zero.
MOSKOWITZ: Calm down.
SLADE: People aren't coming to your circus if they're not entertained!
MOSKOWITZ: Alright.
SLADE: I go broke, you go broke.
MOSKOWITZ: Can it.

(Moskowitz motions Slade away)

MOSKOWITZ: Lucy honey, this true?
SLADE: She don't eat nothing, eats lettuce.
MOSKOWITZ: What's going on?
SLADE: When I think how easy other guys got it.
    Brewer with Sullivan Brothers, killer rats.
    One man operation, rats made him rich.
MOSKOWITZ: Slade.
SLADE: Should be my rats.
MOSKOWITZ: Slade.
SLADE: Well fat ladies are like winos; wino might quit,
    but get that first shot in him and he's off.
    Cheesecake down your throat . . .
MOSKOWITZ: Leave her alone.
SLADE: Cheesecake you can't stop, you'll be laying it on!
MOSKOWITZ: Dammit!
SLADE: Hear me lady?!

(the men struggle)

VOICE: Su-ey! Su-ey! Come to papa, where are ya, baby? Su-ey!
MOSKOWITZ: Why don't you do something useful?
SLADE: I'm not looking no pig.

(Moskowitz takes out some money and whispers to Slade)

VOICE: Su-ey! You're breaking my heart baby! Su-ey!
    You could help me, Moskowitz!
MOSKOWITZ: In a minute!

(Moskowitz finishes with Slade and Slade exits)

MOSKOWITZ: Now what's going on?

(silence)

MOSKOWITZ: Buddies aren't we?

(silence)

MOSKOWITZ: Last year you were down with diarrhea, who sat up with you
    all night?

. . . When you needed root canal, who brought in the best root canal guy in Kentucky?

. . . Who is it every time he goes in a store buys you a movie star magazine?

. . . You owe me one answer.

Ever been a time I haven't been kind to you?

(Lucy shakes her head)

MOSKOWITZ: So talk.

So Valencia's coming around every day.

LUCY: Fernando.

MOSKOWITZ: What's Fernando done to you?

. . . Must of done something.

Coz here you are taking a chance on getting sick.

LUCY: I'm getting well.

MOSKOWITZ: Didn't you hear 'bout Big Bertha with Sullivan Brothers?

LUCY: What?

MOSKOWITZ: Last year some cult got their hooks in her.

LUCY: Baptists.

MOSKOWITZ: Right. She had her jaws wired shut for Jesus.

Pancreas cramps pretty near put her away.

LUCY: Lie.

MOSKOWITZ: Call.

LUCY: Will.

MOSKOWITZ: I'll give you the number.

(pause)

MOSKOWITZ: He's hurt your feelings, and now you're too depressed to eat.

I knew it, I'll kill him.

LUCY: Don't blame Fernando.

MOSKOWITZ: He's trouble.

LUCY: He only talks.

MOSKOWITZ: He only talks you won't eat? . . . You're on strike. I knew it.
Listen little lady we're on the edge no light at the end of the tunnel less it's a long tunnel which means no extra money we could close next week I don't want him giving you any political crap.

LUCY: We don't talk politics.

MOSKOWITZ: . . . Then what's he telling you?

LUCY: Tells me 'bout the ancient Inca empire.

Tells me 'bout the beautiful Andes Mountains in his Peru.

Tells me 'bout the lost city of Machu Picchu.

MOSKOWITZ: Good stuff to know. Useful too.

But nothing to change your life over.

LUCY: Tells me there's nothing wrong with my glands.

MOSKOWITZ: He's got no medical training.

LUCY: Tells me I eat too much.

MOSKOWITZ: One man's opinion.

LUCY: Fernando asked me what I eat, three cheesecakes, two dozen jelly doughnuts, six pack of cola, a German chocolate cake, and then for lunch . . .

MOSKOWITZ: Circus has got a hard schedule, shows every night, you got to keep your strength up.

LUCY: Fernando says I have a beautiful soul.

MOSKOWITZ: I told you you had a beautiful soul before he did.

LUCY: Fernando says I'm contaminating my temple.

MOSKOWITZ: What?

LUCY: Fernando says the body is the temple of the soul.

He says nature has evolved for us these wonderful bodies to travel in the spiritual world.

MOSKOWITZ: He's drunk.

LUCY: Doesn't drink.

MOSKOWITZ: Wacked on dope.

LUCY: Doesn't do dope.

Fernando says our bodies are miraculous events.

MOSKOWITZ: You are the miraculous event.

LUCY: I am not contaminating my soul no more.

VOICE: Su-ey! Come to papa, please.

Whatta you gonna do, Moskowitz?!

MOSKOWITZ: When your daddy dropped you off to the circus in his U-Haul he said all you did was watch TV.

Now Fernando's telling you what he thinks is best for you.

Think that makes you special?

Fernando tells everybody what's best for them.

But you look real serious and listen,

and all the time you're looking into his movie-star blue eyes.

. . . Lucy fell in love with the lion tamer.

That's why Lucy's losing weight.

She's not thinking about her temple.

She's thinking about Fernando's temple.

She's thinking she loses enough weight,

Fernando falls in love with Lucy.

(pause)

Has Fernando ever said he had romantic feelings for you?

(silence)

Has Fernando ever indicated you lost weight you would be a couple?

(silence)

No.

LUCY: Fernando will fall in love with me.

MOSKOWITZ: You hope.

LUCY: I have faith.

MOSKOWITZ: Faith screws people up.
  I've seen people from *your* Ozarks handle rattlesnakes
  to prove they had *faith*, they got their face bitten off.
LUCY: I . . . have . . . faith.
MOSKOWITZ: . . . Say you lose four hundred pounds,
  you don't die of cramps in the pancreas by going against
  your glands,
  Fernando falls in love with you.
  What then?
LUCY: Get married.
MOSKOWITZ: What then?

(Silence)

MOSKOWITZ: Let's say you stay with the circus.
  You and Fernando live in this trailer,
  but still one-night stands nine months a year.
  What do you do every night?
  Sit in the stands?
LUCY: Have a baby.
MOSKOWITZ: Lug a baby.
LUCY: For awhile.
MOSKOWITZ: Raise a child in this environment?
LUCY: No way.
MOSKOWITZ: Quit the circus?
LUCY: You got it . . . I want a house.
MOSKOWITZ: . . . And how will the greatest lion tamer of the 20th century
  make a living then?

(silence. Moskowitz plays an interviewer with an employment agency)

MOSKOWITZ: "Well Mr Valencia, so you want our agency to help
  find you a job.
  Hmmm, you put your head in lions' mouths.
  Not much call for that.
  What? Oh, you've cracked a whip.
  Well I don't think we can make you a foreman for that.
  There's a much bigger call for cracking *metaphorical* whips.
  I have a question about your references. They're all geeks."

  So the Fabulous Fernando, vacuum cleaners door to door.
LUCY: No.
MOSKOWITZ: Then what?
VOICE: Su-ey! Where's my precious? Pig pig pig pig pig!
MOSKOWITZ: What is it with women?
  All they want is the merging of their souls in front of a fireplace that
  doesn't smoke too much with a partner who is perfect in a time that never
  ends in a world that never was.
  Some of these women are not hot to look at, but they got beautiful souls,

and you'd think they'd a learned by now they should be looking for a guy who's got a beautiful soul but who is probly not gonna have a movie-star kisser.

But no, when the women want somebody always Mr. America, Clark Gable, Superman they want.

And these women have faith.

. . . I'm going to hurt you.

Coz I like you.

We go around different towns, who you think all the women fall in love with?

LUCY: Trapeze.

MOSKOWITZ: Too far away tell if he's cute.

Uses a net. No danger.

LUCY: Ringmaster.

MOSKOWITZ: Old man.

LUCY: Juggler.

MOSKOWITZ: Boy.

LUCY: Clown.

MOSKOWITZ: Lion tamer.

Danger, domination, tight pants.

Women eat it up.

And Fernando likes to be eaten up.

You think you the only one ever noticed Fernando's cute?

A discovery?

Fernando nails down three hundred women a year.

And these are not one-night stands.

Three- or four- five-minute stands back to back.

You never wondered why Fernando doesn't see you right after the show?

LUCY: Feeds the animals.

(Moskowitz shakes his head)

LUCY: Has a drink.

MOSKOWITZ: Doesn't drink.

LUCY: Juice.

MOSKOWITZ: No juice.

LUCY: Changes clothes.

MOSKOWITZ: Two minutes.

LUCY: Unwinds.

MOSKOWITZ: Ah! How?

LUCY: Meditates.

MOSKOWITZ: Makes a deposit.

(pause)

MOSKOWITZ: And you think four hundred pounds will change that.

Oh yes, wipe the little tear, the little tear that shows I'm right.

Slink off four hundred and you'll be like every other woman he porks.

Lion can't change his spots.
And a lion does not get tied up with one lionness.
He learned from the lions.

(Lucy wipes more tears away)

MOSKOWITZ: See what I mean, honey?
LUCY: . . . Maybe.

(Slade enters with a box)

SLADE: How's it going?
MOSKOWITZ: Fine.
SLADE: Eating?
MOSKOWITZ: (taking the box)
                    Talking.
SLADE: God you can't do anything.
   We get her down on the ground stick a funnel in her face.
MOSKOWITZ: Get out of here.
SLADE: Hear me?
MOSKOWITZ: Help find that dancing pig!
SLADE: I'm getting a funnel!
MOSKOWITZ: Find the pig!
SLADE: I'm gonna find the pig and roast it and it's gonna dance down your
   throat.

(Slade exits but we hear him outside)

                    Here pig pig pig pig! Delicious pig.
MOSKOWITZ: . . . So.
LUCY: Maybe I can't keep Fernando . . .
MOSKOWITZ: No maybe.
LUCY: But I'll always have him for a friend.
MOSKOWITZ: Stop being the fat lady, have to leave the circus.
LUCY: You got other jobs.
MOSKOWITZ: Can you walk a highwire?
   Swallow swords?
   Juggle five balls your feet?
   Triple somersault?
   . . . Bye bye, Fernando.
LUCY: After all the money I brought you?
MOSKOWITZ: This operation is hand to mouth.

*(Moskowitz opens the box to reveal gigantic jelly doughnuts. As things go
on, he eats and licks oozing jelly.)*

LUCY: . . . If I can't keep Fernando, maybe I can keep somebody else.
MOSKOWITZ: Who?
LUCY: . . . Don't know.
MOSKOWITZ: Dreamer.

LUCY: Other fish in the sea.

MOSKOWITZ: Fish in the sea don't talk about Macho Picchu.

Fish in the sea find the Incas uninteresting.

Fish are interested in beer and bowling, fish argue what year they come out with four-wheel disc brakes.

No fish like Fernando Valencia.

. . . Your problem is you want everything.

LUCY: All I want is somebody I love and who loves me.

MOSKOWITZ: You want everything.

LUCY: I'll find that somebody just for me somewhere.

MOSKOWITZ: Coz you got faith?

Women get old waiting.

. . . What are you going to do for a living?

LUCY: Typing lessons.

MOSKOWITZ: Secretary?

LUCY: Other people do it.

MOSKOWITZ: You rise above *other people.*

You got a gift.

LUCY: I'm ugly.

MOSKOWITZ: Beauty is the beholder.

Glamor magazines *sexy women.* But to the natural person, ugh.

LUCY: I'm fat.

MOSKOWITZ: You're not fat.

LUCY: I'm disgusting.

MOSKOWITZ: Old time chinawomen: wrapped little feet.

To us: disgusting. Rich chinamen: *alright.*

LUCY: I want a house.

I want a white picket fence.

MOSKOWITZ: And you think losing weight gets you a white picket fence?

LUCY: Yes.

MOSKOWITZ: Nice husband.

LUCY: Yes.

MOSKOWITZ: And things'll be great.

LUCY: Yes.

MOSKOWITZ: Things'll be normal.

LUCY: Yes.

MOSKOWITZ: Be like they are.

MOSKOWITZ: Happy.

LUCY: Yes!

MOSKOWITZ: Then why do people have to see Fat Lucy?

Why do the secretaries, why do the foremen, why do the people at the employment agency every night leave their little houses and white picket fences and come to the sideshow and plunk down two bucks to see the Goatfoot Boy, the Snakeskin Boy, and to see Lucy?

Especially Lucy?

Always Lucy?

They come because they're bored! Miserable!
They come because the only way they can feel better is to find somebody they think who's got it worse!
Wake up!
You make good money, good friends, good conversation, good trailer, no rent, you travel, see the country, plenty to eat, wake up!

(pause)

MOSKOWITZ: If you leave, people like me and Fernando will miss you very much.

(pause)

MOSKOWITZ: Well.
 You're a big girl.
 You can make up your own mind what to do.
 Do what makes you happy, I'll be happy.

(Moskowitz finishes the doughnut.
He leaves the box open with other doughnuts visible and exits.
Lucy looks at the doughnuts.
She reaches for one, then pulls back.
She reaches again and picks a doughnut up.
She brings the doughnut to her mouth, she takes a bite.
She chews.)

(the lights fade)

(the end)

Reading For Discovery

Some ways of reading literature are more productive than others. For example, some students read passively. The words on the page pass before their eyes but fail to register in their minds. These students don't pause for reflection or contemplation. They frequently discover that they've been reading for ten or fifteen minutes but can't remember what they've just read. When they finish reading, they have only a vague recollection of the whole, recalling perhaps a few details but having little idea of how things fit together and experiencing only a fuzzy emotional response to the literature. This is the kind of reading more practically saved for the Sunday comics or for the baseball box scores.

Active readers, however, are engaged with words and images before them. They read with two minds, one processing the words on the page and one relating these words to ideas, emotions, experiences, and to other works of literature they've read. They read with curiosity. They sometimes pause, returning to earlier words or passages to look for connections. They make notes to themselves. They note places where they have questions; they look up words they don't know.

The next stage in the process of writing about literature is reading the text. You approach literature with an inquiring mind, observant and open to suggestion. Although our goal in this chapter is to help you learn how to write about literature, we hope you don't lose sight of the underlying purposes for reading literature of all kinds: pleasure, knowledge, and the expansion of your awareness of what it means to be a human being. Literature helps you attain these goals; that's why it's taught in schools. We ask you to write about literature because writing is the most powerful way to make what you've read your own. In addition, reading literature and writing about it can help improve your ability to analyze and to think critically about your world.

So as you read, be aware of the connections between you and the text. Try to make those connections actively, reviewing your own experience to see whether you have felt an emotion similar to one appearing in the text, whether you've known someone like one of the characters, whether you resemble any of the characters, whether you have been to or read about a place mentioned in the text. Look also for connections between what you are reading and other works of literature—similarities of plot, theme, imagery, characterization, style.

Furthermore, it's a good idea to begin your reading far enough in advance to allow for a second or subsequent readings. Scheduling enough time to read a short story more than once should not be difficult, but if you are assigned a novel you have to be careful to leave enough time for rereading or to read carefully and thoroughly the first time through. Just as revision often clarifies your writing, rereading often clarifies what you read.

Literary Features: Considerations for Reading

After a preliminary look at the work using the prereading techniques, you are ready to read. But first we'd like to remind you of some of the components of literature, some of the features that give literature its grace and beauty.

Each of these components works not only to shape the text but, along with your active reading, to shape your understanding of it.

1. Plot. The plot is what happens; it is the series of events that occur in a piece, story, drama, or novel. A thorough understanding of the plot is necessary—you need to know who did what or what happened—for much of your understanding depends on the basic action of the piece you are reading.

But it's also useful to think of plot when you read a poem. Many poems do not have plots per se, but they do have some sort of situation or circumstance that indirectly forms a plot. That is, the poem may not be a narrative—a story—but forming some idea of what is happening gives you a sound base for other connections you make as you read.

2. Setting. The setting is where and when the work takes place. Recognizing the setting and the assumptions you have about that setting increases the number and quality of the connections you make. What would you expect of a story set in a classroom? On a large Long Island estate? In a backwoods Southern town? As you read, try to determine how the setting fits with the other elements to form a unified piece.

As an extension of setting, you might also consider the period when the author is writing. This consideration might be especially helpful if the piece provides no inherent clues to setting. A poem, for example, might seem to evoke no particular time or place.

Look for clues about the setting. Descriptions of houses, clothes, people, scenes may point to time and place. The language of the story or the dialogue may also offer clues.

3. Character. This refers both to the people who appear in a work and to whatever attributes, qualities, and personalities these people possess. As you meet each character in a literary work you immediately begin to form an impression of him or her, an impression based both on what the author tells or implies and on what you know about life and people. The characters move the plot or, in some cases, are moved by it. As you read, consider the expectations you have about the characters, expectations created by your own knowledge as you fit the characters into the elements of the literary work.

4. Language. Language is another component of a literary work that demands the reader's attention. First of all, words have both denotative and connotative meanings. Denotative meanings are the conventional definitions, the sort of definition you might find in a dictionary. But words also have connotations—associations we make according to our own experience. Some connotations are shared. We may associate the word "apple," for example, with school teachers or the Garden of Eden or New York City. But some connotations may be individual; "apple" may suggest a crisp November night in a city backstreet where a lone apple tree grows behind a furniture store. Use the connotations—those the author intended as well as your own—to help you make meaning. (What you eventually write about a literary work must be solidly connected to the text itself, but considering various connotations helps you make the necessary connections.)

Be aware, too, of your general impression of the language. The language may be formal, elevated, consisting of long words and complicated sentence patterns. Or it could be short and simple. It may mimic a certain style of speech—a Southern drawl, an educated cadence, Western slang, or a visitor's foreign accent.

Another important language consideration is imagery—the language in a piece of literature that makes it concrete rather than abstract. Imagery consists of those objects or qualities which can be perceived by the five senses. In the following lines from Ezra Pound's *Canto I*, for example, the reader sees a ship loaded with sheep, the sail filling in the wind; hears the sounds of weeping, the sail flapping. The senses participate so actively that the smell of salt air and the touch of the wind become part of the experience even though they are only implied.

> We set up mast and sail on that swart ship,
> Bore sheep aboard her, and our bodies also
> Heavy with weeping, and winds from sternward
> Bore us out onward with bellying canvas,
> Circe's this craft, the trim-coiffed goddess.

Images—in all kinds of literature—contribute to the piece's mood, its overall feeling, and ultimately add thematic significance.

5. Symbolism. A symbol is something that stands for or represents something else. Thus "word" is a symbol for the dark little marks grouped across this page. We are all familiar with symbols, for we use them daily to organize and understand our world. Clothing, for example, may be a symbol of status, wealth, good taste, one's concept of one's self. But clothing may also be a symbol of ostentation, nonconformity, propriety or its lack. The meaning we attach to clothing as a symbol—the way we connect it to what it symbolizes—depends on our own system of deciphering symbols as well as the assumptions we make about how others use and interpret symbols.

The same is true of the symbols in a literary work. A writer uses a word, an event, an image to capture and evoke the various levels of meaning a symbol may hold. These various levels of meanings do lead to ambiguity, but ambiguity allows readers to explore a literary work, to connect it to their own lives and experiences.

Symbols allow the writer to say more than is literally written on the page. They condense meaning, encouraging readers to sift through possibilities, thoughtfully connecting their own ideas and associations to the concepts in the literary work.

So as you read, watch for words, images, events, descriptions that are repeated, that seem to be significant to the development of the text. You may not immediately grasp what a symbol represents, but by being alert for symbols you can begin to structure a meaning that makes sense when it is considered in relation to the work's other components. Be aware, too, that various readers interpret symbols differently, just as various readers see the characters in the work differently. Such differences are fine as long as readers can clearly present the reasons behind their interpretation and illustrate those reasons by referring to specifics from the text itself.

6. Metaphor. A metaphor is a figure of speech; that is, it's a way using language in a nonliteral sense. When you use a metaphor, you call one thing another. A metaphor is a way of comparing, of equating one thing to another. By doing so, the first thing assumes some of the qualities of the second or is associated with it. Here's a metaphor from e. e. cummings:

after which our separating selves become museums
filled with skilfully stuffed memories
("it is so long since my heart has been with yours," *is 5*).

Here the writer equates himself and another with museums, museums preserving memories. A person cannot literally be a museum, but the metaphor ascribes to a person many of the characteristics of a museum—a place in which items of value and beauty are carefully stored. The metaphor evokes various associations, associations vital to understanding the writing.

A simile is much like a metaphor; however, it's a little weaker because it uses the words "like" or "as." So in working out a metaphor or simile you once again need to make connections with your own life and experience, with other works you have read, with the various meanings and connotations a series of words suggests.

7. *Irony.* Irony is a stylistic device; it refers to a situation in which a real circumstance or event is presented as its opposite. Thus when a friend growls and grumps at you and you reply, "Awfully nice to see you," your reply is ironic, for it probably isn't very nice to see someone who is growling and grumpy. When you read a text in which what is said is the oppostie of what is meant, you are reading something ironic. Likewise, if the characters in a text seem to be unaware of the full meaning of what they are doing or saying, the meaning of which the reader can perceive, you are also dealing with irony.

At the end of Hemingway's *The Sun Also Rises*, Lady Brett says to Jake Barnes, "We could have had such a damned good time together." He replies, "Yes. . . . Isn't it pretty to think so?" His reply—appropriately phrased as a question—contains a good deal of irony, because the reader knows that what has gone on between them hasn't been "pretty" at all. The ironic contrast between what they say and the reality of what they have done forces the reader to come to a conclusion about the nature of their relationship.

In T. S. Eliot's "The Love Song of J. Alfred Prufrock," we read that

In the room the women come and go
Talking of Michelangelo.

The irony in this couplet stems from the contrast between the shallow social life of Prufrock and his friends and the elevated, magnificient subject—Michelangelo—they discuss. The irony encourages the reader to judge the world in which Prufrock moves against the world of Michelangelo.

8. *Point of View.* Every piece of literature has a point of view, a way in which the writer tells a story or looks at a subject. A story can be told or a subject can be viewed by one of its characters or by someone unnamed. If the point of view is omniscient, then whoever is telling the story or viewing the subject has complete access to all information related to the story. The omniscient viewer knows everything about characters—what they have done and what they will do, what they think and what they have thought. But the person telling the story could have a limited viewpoint—that is, only partial access to informaton. The point of view could be first person, told by "I," or third-person, told by another person.

9. Theme. Another element of a literary work that can help your interpretation is theme. The theme is the central idea of a work, an idea around which all portions of the work cluster, an idea that identifies the work. A work may have more than one theme; several smaller themes may exist as well as a major one. And the theme could be explicitly stated; you may find a passage within the text that states it. But the theme may also be implicit; it may be one you form as you arrange the connections you have made about the text.

Read with a pencil, highlighter, or pen in hand. (If you don't own the book you're reading, record page numbers, quotations, and reactions on other paper.) In the margins, record your thoughts and reactions. When you notice that a particular idea, image, event, or symbol seems to recur in the work, start a category for it at the front or back of the piece where you can list the page numbers on which it appears. Be alert for the nine elements mentioned previously, and try to form some impression of how they interact in the piece you are reading.

If you notice that the author spends more time developing one or more of these elements than the others, then be aware as you read of how the element(s) is being used. As you read, the elements of the piece lead you to responses; you develop ideas, see comparisons, raise questions. Record them all, for they may be crucial to your understanding of the piece and valuable in communicating your understanding in writing of your own.

Remember: *No matter what kind of literature you are reading, annotate.* That's what margins —or extra paper—are for. If you annotate as you read, you have a record of your responses, your questions about the text, your observations. All these notes serve as resource material and suggest direction when you begin to write. A sample annotation of "Alabama Poem" follows.

Alabama Poem

narrator

NIKKI GIOVANNI

If <u>trees</u> could talk   *Been around a long time –*
    wonder what they'd say   *have seen a lot*
met an old man
    on the road late afternoon
    hat pulled over to shade
    his eyes
    jacket slumped over his
    shoulders
old man told me "girl! my hands <u>seen</u>   *like the trees*

more than all
them books they got || experience as knowledge
at tuskegee"
* smiled at me
half waved his hand
walked on down the dusty road
met an old woman
with a corncob pipe
sitting and rocking
on a spring evening
"sista" she called to me
"let me tell you—my feet
old woman seen more than yo eyes   trees || experience again
ever gonna read"
* smiled at her and kept
on moving
gave it a thought and went
back to the porch
old woman "I say gal" she called down
"you a student at the institute?
better come here and study
these feet
why important? ||I'm gonna cut a bunion off   practical knowledge
||soons I get up"
I looked at her
* she laughed at me
if trees would talk
wonder what they'd tell me | repeat, almost refrain
friendly environment
tuskegee institute = Black college

Reading Fiction: Special Considerations

When you read fiction, the central literary elements are plot, character, setting, and point of view. As you read, pay careful attention to how the author develops each of these and how they interrelate. In particular, determine who's telling the story. The nature of the narrator gives the piece its slant, its particular angle on the world. How you respond to the narrator determines, in large part, how you respond to the other elements. In some cases there is no perceptible narrator; you respond to the events as though you are seeing them through the lens of a camera. This appearance, however, can be deceptive because there is still an author who has chosen what to let you know of the events, the characters, and the setting.

When you are reading longer, more complicated fiction—a Russian novel, for instance—you should make lists of the characters, the settings, and the main plot events. This helps you keep everything straight.

Also keep in mind that while plot, setting, characterization, and point of view are the central elements of fiction, the other literary elements also play important roles. In Charles Dickens' *Bleak House*, for example, the pervasive fog and the Court of Chancery (probate court) function as symbols. Donald Barthelme's *Snow White* relies heavily on imagery to convey meaning. Hemingway and F. Scott Fitzgerald are masters of irony.

Reading Poetry: Special Considerations

Most poems are written to be read aloud. Poets take great care to create sounds and rhythms that contribute to the overall effect of their poems. Our first suggestion, then, is to read any poem you're working on aloud. Then read it again silently. This second reading involves examination, interpretation, response, and reflection. Then read the poem aloud again. This time try to interpret the poem through your reading. Don't be afraid to ham it up; sometimes you gain new insights into a poem by trying to match your dramatic interpretation of the poem to what you think the poem's meaning is.

We believe in annotating during the second reading of poems. We should clarify that by "second reading" we mean you should read it again as many times as necessary to arrive at a cogent interpretation of the poem. Some poems demand more readings than others. Through making notes to yourself and writing down questions, you become actively involved in making meaning.

Reading Drama: Special Considerations

Reading drama is also difficult. In some ways a drama is like an extended, more highly structured narrative poem. Generally shorter than a novel, drama relies heavily on visual image to complement the words spoken by the characters. These images are frequently supplied in sketchy stage directions. The playwright relies heavily on the abilities of actors and directors to interpret the drama successfully. Students, who almost always read the drama rather than seeing it performed, therefore play the roles of both actor and director. They must visualize the various stage settings, imagine the characters in action on the stage, and create the voices and intonations of the characters in their heads. You must not skip the author's stage directions. When you read in italics that *The sky above boils with raw, red energy,* you should know that the author is providing the director with an important element in the play's interpretation. In plays like *Death of a Salesman*, the setting itself evokes a presence that sheds light on the play's action and is central to the play's interpretation.

Drama, like poetry, condenses meaning. You must stay attuned to nuances in the dialogue—without hearing the characters' voices. Since drama is usually more compact than long fiction, you may also expect that dramatists rely heavily on the power of metaphorical language. Some drama is written in verse, so when you read it you are reading both poetry and drama.

When you read drama, you can also rely in part, on your experience interpreting fiction. In general, however, the drama of an age is spartan in comparison to its long fiction. You can still watch to see what the author does with character, setting, plot, and theme. Now, however, you must read differently.

There are no longer long paragraphs and sections of background and explanation; long descriptions are rare. You have to discover most of the background material by paying close attention to the characters' dialogue where this kind of information is usually presented.

Drama, like poetry, combines sight and sound. In addition, since drama is written to be performed, a silent reader toils alone. A member of an audience shares the artistic experience with other members of the audience, and the experience is enhanced by the audience's responses. At the university, we read drama because through reading and discussing it—its nature, its history, its artifices, its literary beauty—we come to understand it better. Thus, the academic experience contributes not only to your cultural background and understanding—to your funding—but also to your development as a member of the audience.

Writing for Discovery

We'd like to open this section by repeating an assumption from this chapter's introduction: When writing about literature, most of you begin before you have worked out exactly what you want to say. When this happens, the techniques we introduce below may not only help you discover what you want to say, but may also help you understand the piece of literature you're writing about. Some of the techniques should seem familiar to you; they are derivatives of techniques you applied in earlier sections of the text.

The writing that you do at this stage has only one audience—yourself. You are writing to discover the meaning you've derived from your reading and to continue exploring possibilities for writing. You already have resources from which to draw: your prereading notes, your reading notes, and your annotations. Although there are an infinite number of ways to proceed, we present approaches that work for our students and ourselves when we write about literature. Experiment with our suggestions and those your instructor makes. After you've tried them all, choose the ones you feel most comfortable with. If you've developed an effective approach of your own, continue to use it—but give ours a try first. They might add something to your own.

The Response Log

Immediately after reading the piece or pieces you have been working on, record your responses in a log. (With something lengthy, stop to record your responses when something interests or puzzles you.) If you keep a response log for each piece you read, you are better prepared for class lectures and discussion, examinations, and formal papers. Furthermore, a piece you have written about becomes more completely yours. By recreating a piece of literature using your own varied experience as the impetus, you enter more fully into the writer's circle.

No formula exists for a response log. The log serves as a place for you to experiment with your ideas and interpretations. The writing can be formal or informal; you may use notes, fragments, or complete sentences. Since you are the audience, you design the log to suit your own needs. You know that soon you will either be tested on the material or you will have to write a paper on it. Your need is to understand and to translate this understanding into communication acceptable and intelligible to someone else. The response log gives you a starting point.

Here are some suggestions for possible focuses for a log:

1. How you felt about the piece. What you liked most. Least. What specifically made you feel this way.

2. A brief summary of what you read. Summarizing helps fix the piece in your memory and provides you with review material when you are preparing for an examination.

3. Parts of the piece you didn't understand. Any specific or general questions you have.

4. A statement of what you think the author was trying to say. You might find more than one theme.

5. A list of other works you've read that remind you of this piece in some way. You might want to include a brief description of the similarities you see. Relying on memory is often dangerous.

6. A list of possible topics for papers which occurred to you in the previous process.

7. A notation about any research you would have to do to write a paper on this piece.

- On the author.
- On the author's other works and general themes.
- On the work itself.
- On the author's period and his or her contemporaries.
- On works that appear on your list of similarities.

8. Notes to yourself about any literary characteristics (images, characterizations, symbols, setting, irony, etc.) which you found striking and might be worth pursuing later in greater detail. (If you are not familiar with these terms of literary criticism, see pp. 278–282.)

We have presented these suggestions in the order we feel is most productive for generating ideas. If you modify this list or change the order, and it works for you, then use it. We are not trying to dictate a rigid set of procedures for writing, but rather we are trying to help you develop your own effective ways of approaching writing assignments you may face in your first year of college.

The following sample response to "Alabama Poem" follows the general format given above. Notice that it doesn't follow all the suggestions but rather uses what the writer found valuable.

''Alabama Poem''/ May 26, 1985

I liked this poem although it seems pretty simple. The poem gives a value to all kinds of experience and people--even simple experience worthy of dignity. Not very ''poetic,'' however. The characters--old man/woman--poke fun at the narrator's ''book learning'' but they seem friendly and goodhearted. The narrator seems to respect them--she listens to them, gives them value. Comes back to listen to the old woman. The people who have lived life seem to have some special knowledge like the trees do: the old man's hands have ''seen''; the old woman's feet have ''seen.'' So have the trees but they don't talk.

I'm not sure there's any special meaning to the bunions. Is she cutting off some of her knowledge, or is she applying some practical knowledge of the world? Maybe G put this in simply to add to the folksy touch.

What's the theme? Kinds of learning? The dignity and value of life lived? A personal reminder to put formal education in its proper prospective. The poem sort of reminds me of Alice Walker's *The Color Purple*; dignity of life was an issue in it too. Wonder if all of G's poems are this simple in language and meaning?

Paper topic: My education, value of life? Ways to ''see'' the world? (Did G. attend Tuskegee Institute?) Might check and see if there's anything comparing G and Walker. Maybe I'll read some more G poetry and see if I find similar themes or maybe I could even do something with innovative use of forms. Maybe she did read e.e. cummings!

EXERCISE 8-4

Pick one of the poems from Exercise 8-2. Reread your notes from prereading, read the poem, then write a response log entry. Do the same for either "Young Goodman Brown" (p. 247) or "The Coup de Grâce" (p. 256).

The Cluster

Earlier in the text we suggested that clustering ideas was an effective way both to explore a topic and to develop some ideas about potential organization. Clustering can also be effective when writing about literature. To do a cluster about a piece of literature, first you choose one word that captures your emotional or intellectual response to the poem. Frequently more than one word comes to mind. That's fine. Simply write the other words down and cluster them as well. Follow the same tentacle techniques you used earlier in the text. When you're finished, you should have the foundation for several possible essays.

The cluster on "Alabama Poem" (Figure 8–1) illustrates one writer's process in moving toward an essay on the poem. Notice that the cluster not only generates ideas but also forms some tentative organizational connections. The writer connects the author's use of the tree to both the narrator's curiosity and openness and to the ways the old people "see" the world.

FIGURE 8-1

Pick any of the poems from Exercise 8–2, except the one you did for 8–4. Reread what you wrote for your prereading, read the poem, then do a cluster responding to it.

Other Ways of Responding to Literature

In earlier chapters we encouraged you to use brainstorming and freewriting as ways of prewriting. They are also useful postreading techniques. Both have the capacity to open your mind to new ideas about what you have just read. Furthermore, they often help you isolate the points in the work that left the most vivid impression. Also they frequently identify questions you have about what you've read. Occasionally these two techniques surprise you by providing some tentative answers to questions that were troubling you during your first reading.

Pick any of the poems from Exercise 8–2 you have not yet responded to. Re-read your prewriting, read the poem, then respond to it using brainstorming or freewriting.

Try the prereading exercises for the following story. Read it; then use any of the techniques for responding to literature we have presented in this chapter.

The King of Jazz

Well I'm the king of jazz now, thought Hokie Mokie to himself as he oiled the slide on his trombone. Hasn't been a 'bone man been king of jazz for many years. But now that Spicy MacLammermoor, the old king, is dead, I guess I'm it. Maybe I better play a few notes out of this window here, to reassure myself.

"Wow!" said somebody standing on the sidewalk. "Did you hear that?"

"I did," said his companion.

"Can you distinguish our great home-made American jazz performers, each from the other?"

"Used to could."

"Then who was that playing?"

"Sounds like Hokie Mokie to me. Those few but perfectly selected notes have the real epiphanic glow."

"The what?"

"The real epiphanic glow, such as is obtained only by artists of the caliber of Hokie Mokie, who's from Pass Christian, Mississippi. He's the king of jazz, now that Spicy MacLammermoor is gone."

Hokie Mokie put his trombone in its trombone case and went to a gig. At the gig everyone fell back before him, bowing.

"Hi Bucky! Hi Boot! Hi Freddie! Hi George! Hi Thad! Hi Roy! Hi Dexter! Hi Jo! Hi Willie! Hi Greens!"

"What we gonna play, Hokie? You the king of jazz now, you gotta decide."

"How 'bout 'Smoke'?"

"Wow!" everybody said. "Did you hear that? Hokie Mokie can just knock a fella out, just the way he pronounces a word. What a intonation on that boy! God Almight!"

"I don't want to play 'Smoke,'" somebody said.

"Would you repeat that, stranger?"

"I don't want to play 'Smoke.' 'Smoke' is dull. I don't like the changes. I refuse to play 'Smoke.'"

"He refuses to play 'Smoke'! But Hokie Mokie is the king of jazz and he says 'Smoke'!"

"Man, you from outa town or something? What do you mean you refuse to play 'Smoke'? How'd you get on this gig anyhow? Who hired you?"

"I am Hideo Yamaguchi, from Tokyo, Japan."

"Oh you're one of those Japanese cats, eh?"

"Yes I'm the top trombone man in all of Japan."

"Well you're welcome here until we hear you play. Tell me, is the Tennessee Tea Room still the top jazz place in Tokyo?"

"No, the top jazz place in Tokyo is the Square Box now."

"That's nice, O.K., now we gonna play 'Smoke' just like Hokie said. You ready, Hokie? O.K., give you four for nothin'. One! Two! Three! Four!"

The two men who had been standing under Hokie's window had followed him to the club. Now they said:

"Good God!"

"Yes, that's Hokie's famous 'English sunrise' way of playing. Playing with lots of rays coming out of it, some red rays, some blue rays, some green rays, some green stemming from a violet center, some olive stemming from a tan center—"

"That young Japanese fellow is pretty good, too."

"Yes, he is pretty good. And he holds his horn in a peculiar way. That's frequently the mark of a superior player."

"Bent over like that with his head between his knees—good God, he's sensational!"

He's sensational, Hokie thought. Maybe I ought to kill him.

But at that moment somebody came in the door pushing in front of him a four-and-one-half-octave marimba. Yes, it was Fat Man Jones, and he began to play even before he was fully in the door.

"What're we playing?"

"'Billie's Bounce.'"

"That's what I thought it was. What're we in?"

"F."

"That's what I thought we were in. Didn't you use to play with Maynard?"

"Yeah I was on that band for a while until I was in the hospital.

"What for?"

"I was tired."

"What can we add to Hokie's fantastic playing?"

"How 'bout some rain or stars?"

"Maybe that's presumptuous?"

"Ask him if he'd mind."

"You ask him, I'm scared. You don't fool around with the king of jazz. That young Japanese guy's pretty good, too."

"He's sensational."

"You think he's playing in Japanese?"

"Well I don't think it's English."

This trombone's been makin' my neck green for thirty-five years, Hokie thought. How come I got to stand up to yet another challenge, this late in life?

"Well, Hideo—"

"Yes, Mr. Mokie?"

"You did well on both 'Smoke' and 'Billie's Bounce.' You're just about as good as me, I regret to say. In fact, I've decided you're better than me. It's a hideous thing to contemplate, but there it is. I have only been the king of jazz for twenty-four hours, but the unforgiving logic of this art demands we bow to Truth, when we hear it."

"Maybe you're mistaken?"

"No, I got ears. I'm not mistaken. Hideo Yamaguchi is the new king of jazz."

"You want to be king emeritus?"

"No, I'm just going to fold up my horn and steal away. This gig is yours, Hideo. You can pick the next tune."

"How 'bout 'Cream'?"

"O.K., you heard what Hideo said, it's 'Cream' You ready, Hideo?"

"Hokie, you don't have to leave. You can play too. Just move a little over to the side there—"

"Thank you, Hideo, that's very gracious of you. I guess I will play a little, since I'm still here. Sotto Voce, of course."

"Hideo is wonderful on 'Cream'!"

"Yes, I imagine it's his best tune."

'What's that sound coming in from the side there?"

"Which side?"

"The left."

"You mean that sound that sounds like the cutting edge of life? That sounds like polar bears crossing Arctic ice pans? That sounds like a herd of musk ox in full flight? That sounds like male walruses diving to the bottom of the sea? That sounds like fumaroles smoking on the slopes of Mt. Katmai? That sounds like the wild turkey walking through the deep, soft forest? That sounds like beavers chewing trees in an Appalachian marsh? That sounds like an oyster fungus growing on an aspen trunk? That sounds like a mule deer wandering a montane of the Sierra Nevada? That sounds like prairie dogs kissing? That sounds like witchgrass tumbling or a river meandering? That sounds like manatees munching seaweed at Cape Sable? That sounds like coatimundis moving in packs across the face of Arkansas? That sounds like—"

"Good God, It's Hokie! Even with a cup mute on, he's blowing Hideo right off the stand!"

"Hideo's playing on his knees now! Good God, he's reaching into his belt for a large steel sword—Stop him!"

"Wow! That was the most exciting 'Cream' ever played! Is Hideo all right?"

"Yes, somebody is getting him a glass of water."

"You're my man, Hokie! That was the dadblangedest thing I ever saw!"

"You're the king of jazz once again!"

"Hokie Mokie is the most happening thing there is!"

"Yes, Mr. Hokie sir, I have to admit it, you blew me right off the stand. I see I have many years of work and study before me still."

"That's O.K. son. Don't think a thing about it. It happens to the best of us. Or it almost happens to the best of us. Now I want everybody to have a good time because we're gonna play 'Flats.' 'Flats' is next."

"With your permission, sir, I will return to my hotel and pack. I am most grateful for everything I have learned here."

"That's O.K., Hideo. Have a nice day. He-he. Now, 'Flats.' "

Determining Purpose and Finding a Topic

Earlier in this chapter we stated that one of your aims in writing about literature in a class is to demonstrate your ability to relate your understanding of a literary work to an experienced reader for the purpose of evaluation. We hope that the stories, poems, and plays presented here have shown you that the very practical concern with evaluation does not diminish the powerful role writing can have in improving your ability to read literature. The next step, of course, is demonstrating that ability, through writing, to an audience.

Common Purposes for Writing about Literature

Even if your aim is to demonstrate your ability to understand literature, there are a variety of purposes you may choose from which could accomplish your goals.

Occasionally your instructor assigns you a purpose—especially on essay exams, but usually you have to select your own. The first step is to review your prereading notes, your reading notes, and your postreading notes. (All these now become your prewriting.) Often several possible topics are already apparent to you. In those cases, you only have to select the one that interests you the most and for which you see a clear pattern of support within the literature. The support for your thesis must come from the literature; it must be generated by the literature and it must be supported by references to and examples from the literature.

Ultimately, you recreate your own version of the work you've read. You do this by interacting with the text: by responding, questioning, interpreting, applying your own set of experiences. You convince your reader of the validity of your interpretation largely by how well you show this interaction in your own writing. Your ideas must be shown to relate to ideas which actually appear in the text.

The purposes for writing about literature listed here are presented in order of complexity—least demanding first. Although this list is not complete—the more one reads literature and writes about it, the more complex one's topics can become—any one of these purposes provides a suitable focus for an essay or a longer research paper.

1. To present information:
   - About an author's life.
   - About the social milieu of an author.
   - About the critical reception of a work or works.
   - About how critics have responded to a work or works.
   - About a literary tradition.
   - About literary definitions.

2. To examine an author's use of one or more literary devices (for example, image, symbol, rhyme scheme, etc.) in a work or works.

3. To develop an interpretation of a single work or part of a work. (This involves demonstrating how a work's artistic features contribute to meaning.)

4. To compare two or more works to illustrate the theme or artistic process of one or more of the works in the comparison. (This can involve an investigation of patterns of meanings.)

5. To show the place of a particular work among other works by the same writer.

6. To show the place of a particular work among other works with similar themes.

7. To show the place of a particular work among others with similar literary features.

8. To show how the author's life, the history of his or her time, contributes to a work's meaning.

Purposes as Prewriting

The common purposes listed on page 293 can also serve as devices to generate ideas for writing. We derived the questions below by applying the list of purposes to earlier activities with "Alabama Poem." The answer to each question could lead to an essay.

1. How does the poem reflect Giovanni's own experiences?
2. How have critics responded to this poem?
3. Into what literary tradition does this poem fit?
4. What does the poem "mean" and why?
5. Why does she use trees at the beginning and the end?
6. What point of view of knowledge does the poem present?
7. How are the old people and the trees related?
8. How is the conflict between "book learning" and experience presented?
9. How do hands, feet, and trees fit together?
10. What motivates the narrator on her journey?
11. How does this poem compare to e. e. cummings' poetry?
12 Was the poet influenced by him? If so, how?
13. How does my definition of knowledge correspond to the poem's?
14. What makes this a "black" poem?
15. How does this compare with other poems Giovanni has written?
16. How is this an "Alabama Poem"?
17. How does Giovanni compare with other writers like herself? Who are they?
18. Is this a "good" poem? In comparison to others she's written?
19. Is this poem meant to be read alone, or was it published with companion pieces?
20. What do the bunions mean?

Narrowing Your Focus

Thus far we have taken you through some initial steps in preparing to write about literature. You've completed at least two readings, annotated or taken notes, done some discovery writing, and reviewed some of the common purposes for writing about literature. You should now be ready to pick a topic and develop a tentative thesis. The complexity of your topic and your thesis depends largely on your previous life experience and your previous experience writing about literature.

· Let's review some of our prewriting to see how topics can be developed and narrowed. In the next section we present the draft of an essay written from the prereading, the annotation, the cluster, and the response to Nikki Giovanni's "Alabama Poem." We have annotated the essay with comments about how it follows the processes described in this chapter.

Draft

When I was in the 8th grade, my teachers assigned us a research paper. I didn't know what to write about, so I read through the encyclopedia until I stumbled on the entry for ''technology.'' I was so fascinated by the pictures of the future that I knew I had found my topic. I spent most of a week condensing and paraphrasing the encyclopedia entry. My teacher was pleased with my efforts; I was pleased with my A.

The writer begins with a personal response. He suggested this as a possible topic in the response he wrote on page 287.

He uses examples in his introduction which should engage the interests of his audience (peers and teacher).

In my sociology class and my biology class I soon discovered that I didn't have to think about the relationship of the material to anything else: read—memorize—answer the multiple choice questions. No need to go to class; we just heard the book covered and re-covered. As a result I've begun to ask what it means to get an education. Is it knowledge I'm here for?

Thesis related to poem's meaning.

The narrator of Nikki Giovanni's ''Alabama Poem'' asks a similar question when she questions at both the beginning and end of the poem ''if trees could talk/wonder what they'd say.'' As the poem progresses the reader watches the narrator converse with an old man and an old woman. The subject of both conversations centers on a comparison between ''book learning'' and the kind of ''seeing'' (knowledge) which can only come through firsthand physical experience.

Paragraph includes evidence from text.

Suggested in cluster on page 288.

The old man and the old woman gently poke fun at the narrator's method of learning—reading books—at the Tuskegee Institute. The old man says that his '' 'hands seen/more than all/them books' ''; the old woman says '' 'my feet/seen more than yo eyes/ever gonna read.''

Evidence from text, direct quotation.

Suggested in annotation on page 283.

Annotation
page 282–3.

The girl makes no response, but since
the poem begins and ends with the question of
the trees, one must assume that she does not
immediately reject the contentions of the two
old people. The narrator, and ultimately the
reader, are led to the same questions I asked
myself: ''What is knowledge? How does one obtain it?''

Because Giovanni remains neutral and repeats the question at the poem's end, it
would be difficult to claim that either
knowledge from education or knowledge from
experience is given the edge. However, one
could assert that Giovanni at the very least
implies that, whatever the judgment on college education, knowledge from experience
should not be overlooked.

She does other things in the poem which
support the concept of gaining knowledge from
experience. The poem has no capitalization or
formal punctuation marks (beyond quotation
marks). Even the narrator, who's getting the
formal education, doesn't speak in complete
sentences. She often leaves out the subject
as in ''smiled at her and kept/on moving)/
gave it a thought and went/back to the porch.

The author herself also seems to avoid
the more formal kinds of poetic structures
which might mark a poet with considerable
''book learning.'' The poem has neither formal rhyme scheme nor a patterned rhythm. The
poem works through the images of the old people, the colloquial nature of the dialogue,
and the gentle, natural—indeed the couple
are compared to trees—quality with which
Giovanni characterizes them.

Giovanni in the end, however, won't let
her reader fully identify with the old couple. As noted earlier, the poem ends with a
question. Even more important, the narrator
herself remains on a journey seeking knowledge; whereas the old man and the old woman
are complacent with what they know. When the
narrator returns to the question, I feel that
she has expanded her definition of knowledge
beyond college to include experience but she

Refers to formal elements of literature.

Refers to formal elements of literature.

Writer reaches his own conclusion as to the meaning of the poem. He has used his own experience and an analysis of

Commented on in the response log on page 287.

Suggested in cluster.

This idea was suggested in the cluster on page 288.

the text to
develop an
interpretation.
He also
used
questions
#4, 5, 6, 7,
8, 9, and 10
from page
294.

has not limited herself to either. The question, however, remains unanswered.
    Perhaps for both the narrator and for
me, the answer to the question matters less
than the impulse which led to framing it.
Only through embarking on the pursuit of
knowledge can one hope to learn anything valuable.

The Nature of Proof

In many ways writing about literature shares characteristics with other kinds of writing. The advice given in Chapter 2, on narrowing topics serves equally well here. If you have found methods of approaching an essay that work for your other papers, you should try them while writing about literature. The modes of thinking are powerful aids in any endeavor involving writing.

In writing about literature, however, the nature of the proof you use differs from that in other kinds of writing. Here you are writing about a piece of writing, a task which focuses much of your attention on language and literary techniques. Your concerns become metaphor, simile, irony, symbol, allegory, schemes, rhythm, images, characterization, setting, plot, theme, conflict . . .

One final caution: Don't try to account for all the elements of literature in on essay—unless you are working on a brief poem. If you try to do too much, your essay becomes confusing and your arguments are impossible to discern.

EXERCISE 8–8

- Follow the reading procedures we've suggested in this chapter for "Sonnet XVI" (p. 264), and "To His Coy Mistress" (264). Then respond to each or use a response you've written already for an earlier exercise.

- Using the Thinking Grid (p. 75) and the nine elements of literature presented in this chapter, list as many topics as you can. Try for at least five. For example, you might consider comparing what the poems say about time; you could isolate the effects that time has on us or deal with the reasons time has certain effects on us; you could construct a definition of time; you could analyze the problems time causes and how each poet addresses those problems.

- Continue working with these poems through drafting, revising, and editing an essay.

EXERCISE 8–9

Write an essay on "Manifesto: The Mad Farmer Liberation Front" (pp. 266–67). (One possibility would be to examine the social conditions that produced this poem. You might be able to use this as a topic for research. See Chapter 9.)

EXERCISE 8–10

> The author of "Fat Lucy" is considering changing the play's ending. In the draft you read, Lucy eats the doughnut. Higgins is contemplating ending the play with Lucy resisting the doughnuts. Write an essay exploring how this different ending would affect the play's interpretation. Use techniques you've learned from this and earlier chapters to write a rough draft. Use the revision chapter to prepare your final draft.

EXERCISE 8–11

> Write an essay on one of the short stories in this chapter. Use the techniques you've learned to work your way through the writing processes to a final draft.

Sample Student Papers

> In the paper which follows, Donna Segroves used Donald Barthelme's short stories "The King of Jazz" (pp. 289–92), "Can We Talk", and "The Phantom of the Opera's Friend" as well as some of Barthelme's comments on his writing as the basis for an analysis of his style. She focuses on setting, plot, and characterization to provide the organization and support for her analysis.

A Style All His Own

One of the principal tools of a writer is style. Ranging from journalistic to abstract, style encompasses the use of narration, dialogue, vocabulary, sentence structure and the use of all other tools of writing; it is the overall aspect of writing—the manner in which the author guides his reader through the literary piece. Many writers take the reader by the hand and guide him through every step and obstacle, but Donald Barthelme is one of those unique authors who will push you out of the nest telling you to go fly on your own.

Typically a reader first looks for the setting in a story to help orient himself and create a better picture. But this aspect of writing is absent from Barthelme's writing. He jumps right into the story, leaving the reader floundering. The reader must infer from the content—the dialect, subject matter and people mentioned—exactly where and when the tale occurs. In one of his works, ''The King of Jazz,'' the name Maynard is mentioned. The reader can assume that Barthelme is referring to Maynard Ferguson, and thus place the story in the 1970's. From the language—

''What we gonna play, Hokie? You the king of jazz now, you gotta decide''——it can be assumed that the characters are black, and from the overall story one might infer that the characters are in a cafe or jazz joint. Barthelme makes the reader work to sort out the facts that other writers hand to the audience.

After orienting the reader in respect to time and place, most authors paint pictures of their characters, but Barthelme merely draws a chalk outline and then takes the audience beyond those lines and delves into the mind of the character. Many of his stories consist almost entirely of the first person. His short story ''Can We Talk'' consists entirely of the jumbled-up thoughts of a love-lorn man, so lost that he does not know or care what to think. By deleting the third and second person, Barthelme eliminates exterior stereotyping and exposes the true person. But he does not, however, disregard that some stereotyped traits can reveal information about the character. He employs dialogue to help classify the social and educational background. With this stereotype, however, the reader must acquaint himself with the character to some extent before passing judgment.

Like the setting and characters, the plot must be deciphered from indirect, obscure information. Once again the reader may be found frantically flapping to stay adrift until he can begin to fit together bits and pieces. Barthelme creates a puzzle, giving the reader a fragmented thought at one place and later perhaps an incomplete idea that ties into the first. Current Biography 1976 quotes Barthelme as saying, ''The principle of collage is the central principle of all art in the twentieth century in all media'' and writes that he ''believes that contemporary art must be built of fragments or else it falsifies the reality it reports.'' In ''The Phantom of the Opera's Friend,'' the reader can deduce that the Phantom of the Opera suffered an accident that maimed him from a line saying that new techniques in plastic surgery could make a normal life among society possible again. Later a fragmented thought, ''The acid . . .'' implies that he was severely burned. Barthelme said, ''I try to avoid saying anything directly and just hope that something emerges from what has been written,'' according to Contemporary Authors. The storyline may

not be realized until the final sentence or even the
second or third reading. Barthelme buries the plot
amongst scattered thoughts and phrases, and it is the
job of the reader to nurture it with brain power to
cause it to sprout forth.

Dialogue is one of the tools, if not the most
important one, Barthelme uses to lead the reader to
his conclusions about the setting, plot and
characters. His literature lacks the narration that
readily hands this information to the audience. His
writing is often entirely composed of conversations
between characters and internal monologues. In order
to enable the dialogue to convey the information he
desires, Barthelme must create it as realistically as
possible--full of colloquialisms, partial thoughts and
even gaps. These are the pieces of the puzzle that
create the collage and eventually unscramble it.

Donald Barthelme defies convention and refuses to
allow the reader to lapse into a state of oblivion.
Anyone looking for a story to read that will allow the
mind to relax should not pick up one of his pieces. If
someone is going to pursue his literature, he should
be prepared for ruffled feathers, multiple readings
and possible second opinions before understanding is
achieved. Barthelme makes the mind work and the wings
flap vigorously before the feet safely touch ground.

Mark Freeman's paper on Thoreau offers a general overview of the relationship among Thoreau's life, his convictions, his society, and his works. References to Thoreau's works and his life form the basis of the essay's support.
The paper was prompted by Freeman's reading of "Thinking Like a Bream."
Although the paper was well received in class, the students judged that it
would have presented a stronger case had Freeman also used direct quotations
from Thoreau's works rather than citing others quoting Thoreau.

Thoreau: His Sole Experience

With the nineteenth century came the Industrial
Revolution, the growth of cities, and the start of the
influence of organized labor on the social system. It
was also in this period, barely over one hundred years
ago, that the institution of slavery was questioned,
tenaciously fought over, and finally ended in America.
This age of change helped cultivate some of the great
minds of the social sciences and humanities, such as
Edgar Allan Poe and Sigmund Freud. Karl Marx and the

social philosophy he presented in his <u>Communist</u>
<u>Manifesto</u> reflected the worldwide unrest of the times.
It was also within this century that a boy was raised
in a small town in Massachusetts, grew up never to
marry, never to pay a tax, and never once to vote.
Nevertheless, Henry David Thoreau has become a
prominent force in social thought since his time. The
source of Thoreau's creativity? His perception of a
nation refusing the freedom and glory of individual
existence.

The son of a pencil maker, Thoreau's personal
appearance was not extraordinary. Said Robert Louis
Stevenson, ''He was not easy, not ample, not urbane;
not even kind; his enjoyment was hardly
smiling. . . .'' To those around him, he appeared
nothing more than a useless skulker. It appeared as
though he never worked. His baggy, dusty clothes
insulted the people of Concord. He never fit in with
the ''proper'' world around him. He frequently turned
down social gatherings because, ''<u>Such are my</u>
<u>engagements to myself</u> that I dare not promise''
(Stevenson 118).

Thoreau was schooled at Harvard, where he was an
average student but trained in many fields. Languages,
the social sciences, and mathematics were his
interests (Hall 406). He carried himself like a self-
tortured adolescent; unsure of his needs, unsure of
his future. But Thoreau <u>had</u> a plan for the future. His
ideas, not his appearance, were Thoreau. Charles
Nichols said, ''He transmitted these ideas into a
working philosophy, essentially transcendental,
optimistic, yet clear-cut and practical'' (Nichols
20). Thus, his thoughts lent themselves to the
naturalistic world as well as the political world of
his day. However, because of Thoreau's awkward social
presence, his thoughts were appreciated only by a few.

Those few who came to appreciate Thoreau's
thoughts did not include the nineteenth-century
government of the United States. Thoreau, like Marx,
despised government and took an active part in
opposing it. To Thoreau, ''man is the artificer of his
own happiness'' (Nichols 23). He felt that the
expediency of government usurped the power of
democracy that Thomas Jefferson had properly given to
the people. Thoreau once spent a night in jail for
refusing to pay a poll tax. He waited for a friend to

pay his bond because he resented paying a tax to a
government he would not support. Thoreau's night in
jail inspired the writing of Civil Disobedience, which
powerfully asserts his position. This work, said Tom
Fields, was similar to Gandi's philosophical
contribution in India. Thoreau, like Gandhi, based his
opposition to government on its loss of ''morality''
in governing. Said Thoreau, ''It is those men of
conscience who are willing to risk their necks for the
Right, who will, at last, fashion a state which can
afford to be just to all men'' (Nichols 24).

How was this justice lacking? Thoreau was
frustrated and angry that slavery had been for so long
protected by the government. When a Fugitive Slave Act
was finally put into effect, it served expediency
rather than morality. This situation prompted Thoreau
to assert that politics had been so ''superficial and
inhuman, that practically I have not fairly recognized
that it concerns me at all'' (Nichols 22).

Thoreau equally detested the Abolitionists,
saying they should withdraw from Massachusetts, for
their lobby was centrally an economic interest, not a
moral one. In short, Thoreau felt that if a government
''is of such a nature that it requires you to be the
agent of injustice to another, then, I say, break the
law'' (Fields 42). For a man has a right, says
Thoreau, as well as an obligation, to act his mind and
moral character.

It should then, of course, not be surprising to
us that Thoreau would cherish the moments he could
find away from politics, since the political forum had
become useless to him. He spent these times well. In
the quiet wild of Walden Pond, near Concord, Thoreau
built a hut, planted beans and potatoes, and stayed
for two years, developing his philosophy of the
individual. The result was Walden. He set one day of
the week aside for his gardening, all the rest for
meditation, reading, and writing (Fields 42). Walden
was an exercise in Thoreau's new life, a life which
denied government. Here, in the wild, man could learn
the beauty of the individual, the higher value of all
things which government seemed to overlook. Like
Emerson, Thoreau saw government attempting to educate
the wise man, although it was the government that
needed the education (Nichols 20). In ''Thinking Like
a Bream,'' Thoreau shows his awe at the universal
being of a thing. The bream exists not as a fish to be

studied by a scientist, but as a central force in the universe (Hall 407). Similarly, in his poems ''Smoke'' and ''Mist'' he illustrates the complexity in being of these two elements of nature (Gesner 226–27). Thus, the glory of nature and the bane of social convention, to Thoreau, was that we can understand those things ''sublime and noble only by the perpetual instilling and drenching of the reality around us'' (Nichols 22).

Thus, it is evident that Thoreau, as shown in his well-known works, from Walden to Civil Disobedience to A Week on the Concord and Merrimack Rivers, was preoccupied with the duplicity of the life around him. While acknowledging the beauty and spirit of nature, he bitterly criticized the imperfect society that man had built for himself. But his ideas went beyond those of the Enlightenment. As Stevenson said, ''He is not altogether one of us.'' Thoreau said that like a plant, man dies if he is forced to grow against his own nature. He saw the government as exercising this force in the 1840s and 1850s. And the people:

> ''The millions are awake enough for physical labor, but only one in a million is awake enough for effective intellectual assertion, only one in a hundred million to a poetic or divine life'' (Nichols 20).

It was this disappointment with man against a background universe of perfection that drove Thoreau to pursue a singular life devoted to self-improvement. He sought alone an entirely new basis for society that was not to be.

Works Cited

Fields, Tom. ''The Strange Genius Thoreau: Viewed as a Freak and a Bum in Early Concord Days.'' Newsweek, 9 Oct. 1939, p.42.

Gosner, George, ed. Anthology of American Poetry. New York: Avenel Books, 1983.

Thoreau, Henry David. ''Thinking Like a Bream.'' A Writer's Reader. Boston: Little, Brown and Company, 1985.

Nichols, Charles H., Jr. ''Thoreau on the Citizen and His Government.'' Phylon, March 1952, pp. 19–24.

Stevenson, Robert Louis. Familiar Studies of Men and Books. New York: Current Literature Publishing Company, 1916.

CHAPTER NINE

Writing from Formal Research

False facts are highly injurious to the progress of science,
for they often endure long . . .—Charles Darwin

What makes writing a "research paper" so different from other papers you write, so different that teachers talk about "*the* research paper," universities offer courses in "writing the research paper," and authors write whole books focusing exclusively on how to write this kind of paper?

Fortunately, this kind of paper differs less than you might think from the papers you've been writing throughout this semester. In a sense, all the writing we've discussed thus far has been writing from research. We've discussed making observations, collecting and organizing information, finding a thesis, writing, rewriting, and editing. For a research paper you still prewrite to discover what you already know and what you need to know. You still organize the material you gather and develop a working thesis. You still do a first draft, revise, and edit. The same processes you've been polishing all semester will serve you well as you undertake "the research paper."

Our focus, however, has largely been on informal research—the kind of investigation you do when you examine your immediate experience. Much of your college writing relies on this kind of research, but college writing also requires you to broaden your research base to include more formal investigation.

Clearly, however, there are differences between the two. First, even though all papers are based on research, the typical college research paper—long or short—relies more heavily on secondary research than firsthand experience. (In research done later in college and after you will often report the results of firsthand study and research. This text, however, covers only those types of research papers you are likely to encounter in your first two years of college.)

Usually the subject matter in these papers is less personal than papers you've written to date. Likewise, the format of research papers is more formal, with specific format requirements within each of the academic disciplines. These papers also tend to be longer—from five to twenty pages. Those closer to twenty pages are frequently called "term papers," and you're expected to work on them throughout much of a term, semester, or quarter.

Despite these differences, you will discover that many of the processes involved in writing research papers in any discipline are variations of those you've been practicing all semester. Formal research and the writing you do from it includes the same components as those used in all writing—except that now you will be using observations and information collected and organized by someone else. You will use their writing to enrich your own experience and to provide you with a broader base of support for your own ideas.

This chapter is not meant to be a complete guide to sophisticated types of research. Rather, it's an introduction for the beginning college student. We have tried to make this section utilitarian. Consequently, our first recommendation is that students buy a more detailed guide to the research process, preferably one designed specifically for scholars in their majors. If you haven't chosen a major yet, then the *MLA Handbook for Writers of Research Papers* (2nd ed., 1984) would be a good choice; it provides a discussion of the research process and contains a thorough treatment of documentation. Various disciplines require specific documentation formats; we'll be focusing on the MLA style, revised in 1984, used in language and literature. Confirm with your instructor the format you'll be expected to use. The *MLA Handbook for Writers of Research Papers* provides information about the MLA format.

Since formal research at the university almost always involves the library, we begin our research by first researching the library.

The Library

Although every university library is different, all students need to become familiar with certain general features. First you need to know where everything is. Find the card catalog, the circulation desk, the reserve desk, the reference room. (The card catalog is a file of the material held in the library. The circulation desk is the place where you check out books and obtain other information. The reserve desk has materials that instructors reserve for their students' use. The reference room houses reference books that generally cannot be taken out of the library.) Find out where the current newspapers and periodicals are kept. Then find the duplicating machines. Ask your librarian if the library has typewriters and computers for student use. Find the lounge. Then find out whether your university uses the Dewey Decimal System or the Library of Congress System to organize its holdings. After that look at the floor directory; it should tell you where the various collections are. Ask the librarian at any desk if there is any printed material about the library for first-time users.

If there is, collect it, read it, then file it in your favorite notebook. In other words, learn everything you can about your library. If you know where you are going and what to look for, you will save enough time each semester to go home early the day before spring break.

Your first destination after taking the overall library tour is the reference room or the central location of reference materials. Here you find general information, like that found in encyclopedias and dictionaries, but you also find sources like the card catalog and indexes which tell you where to look for more specific and current information than that found in encyclopedias and dictionaries. Reference librarians, who have been trained to understand the process whereby a scholar—that's you—finds information in a library, are willing to answer questions you may have about how to find things. They can save you time, help you avoid frustration, and ensure that your research is neither incomplete nor inappropriate. If you are looking for information and don't know how to proceed, ask your reference librarian.

EXERCISE 9–1

Take a tour of your library, then complete the following exercise:

1. What is the name of the reference librarian you spoke with?
2. During what hours is the library open?
3. Where's the library's phone?
4. What's the library's phone number?
5. What's the reference desk's phone number?
6. Does your library use the Dewey Decimal System or the Library of Congress System?
7. On what floor of the library would you find a book of criticism on American literature?
8. How many different libraries are there on campus? What are their specialties?
9. Are there typewriters for rent in your library?
10. Are computers available for students? If so, how do you arrange to use one?
11. Where can you make a photocopy of microfilm/fiche?
12. Where can you find out if a book has been checked out?
13. How can you request a return-call for a book that's already been checked out?
14. How long is the checkout period for books?
15. Where are current periodicals found?

College Research Papers

Now that we've looked at the nature of the research paper, we should tell you that there is no such thing as *the* research paper in college. Your literature professor expects one kind of research paper, your sociology professor yet another, your biology professor still another. The format each expects varies; the approach to the topic varies; even the expected style varies.

The first step in writing a research paper, therefore, is definition. You must ask your professor what he means by research paper when he assigns one. Ask for the proper approach, proper format, and proper documentation form. Ask your professor for a sample article or student paper so you can become familiar with the feel of a research paper in that discipline.

The Topic

Topics for research papers may be assigned or grow out of your own interests and experiences. In either case, you must begin by discovering the limits of your topic, by narrowing it, taking it down the ladder of abstraction. Before you can do this, however, you need to have some idea about what information is available to you; only then can you choose a direction.

Prewriting

The way to discover this information is to return to prewriting. Use whatever methods are appropriate: a journal, reading log, or electronic media log; brainstorming or freewriting; the journalist's questions, clustering, the grid. Find out what you know and, in this case even more important, what you don't. When you see gaps in your prewriting, you will know where to focus your research efforts. If you know far enough in advance that you have a research paper to write, you can begin assembling a notebook of material that *might* be appropriate to your topic. As you collect material, your ideas about the topic will begin to take shape.

Narrowing the Topic

After your initial prewriting, you've isolated several possible directions for your paper. Return to Chapter 2, pp. 36–39 and follow the steps presented there for narrowing your topic. Basically this involves grouping your ideas into categories, choosing one of the categories, and, if possible, developing a working thesis. Now the secondary-source level of research begins. After narrowing your topic, you now open it up again by collecting research material. Let's say, for example, you began with the general topic Environmental Threats. Through your initial prewriting, you came up with the following categories:

Lead Poisoning

Acid Rain

- The Ozone Layer
- Dioxin Poisoning
- Fouled Fishing Grounds
- Lead Pellets
- Unsafe Chemical Plants
- Deforestation

From these you choose Fouled Fishing Grounds. As you conduct your research, you discover problems with fishing all over the world. In particular, you discover information about mercury poisoning in the Great Lakes, cancerous tumors in fish off the coast of Massachusetts, the poisoning of wastewater from lumbermills in the West. While investigating the mercury poisoning, you become fascinated with the success story of the Coho's return to Lake Michigan.

Now you have progressed far down the ladder of abstraction and you are ready to write a paper on a more focused topic.

Finding and Evaluating Sources

Before you can reach this more specific topic, you must discover the information which can lead you from "Environmental Threats" to "The Return of the Coho to Lake Michigan." Of course, you will find a wide variety of information in the card catalog, indexes, and other bibliographies. One of your prime challenges is to decide which material might be appropriate for your topic. (One of the reasons you narrow your topic before going to the library is that in most cases you would never have enough time to do all the necessary reading if you began with a topic as broad as Environmental Threats.) Another challenge is to decide which of your prospective sources carries more authority.

Conducting Research

The assignment of a research or documented paper invariably requires that you develop some expertise in locating sources of information about your topic. In this section, we describe some of those sources and the process by which you locate them.

Libraries and the methods they use to catalog their materials differ, of course, so efficient use of the library depends in part on your familiarity with its methods and your willingness to seek assistance from librarians. In addition, you can approach the instructor who assigned the paper as a resource; he or she will probably be willing to assist you in your attempt to locate and evaluate source materials. Remember, also, that it takes time to obtain materials, especially if a book you need has been checked out or must be requested through the interlibrary loan system. Start researching *early* to avoid the panic that may set in if some needed materials can't be obtained quickly.

Limiting Your Reading

Learning to skim saves you valuable time. When you look up your subject in the card catalog, skim the descriptions of each item. Unless you are looking for a book with an up-to-date bibliography, you want to limit the number of works on your preliminary list. After you obtain the books on this list, skim their tables of contents, their introductions or prefaces. Check for a useful bibliography. When you check indexes, look for decriptions of the material; always work to limit the amount of material you need to read thoroughly. When you have periodicals in front of you, skim their introductions, then the first sentences of the paragraphs, or the headings dividing sections. This early effort saves time later.

Evaluating Your Sources

Often, the beginning researcher has a difficult time evaluating sources. After all, only an expert would be able to recognize the names of other experts in the field, know the best journals and publications, recognize which works by new writers contain substantive additions to the field. Since, most likely, you are not one of these experts, you have to rely on other assets. Fortunately, you have many at your disposal.

If you are writing a paper for one of your classes, your professor can generally provide you with the names of relevant authors, books, or journals. Reference librarians either know or can find out the names of the discipline's major publications. If you find more than one bibliography for your subject and you see names and titles mentioned frequently, these sources are probably important ones. (Make sure that you refer to at least one bibliography of recently published work; otherwise you might miss some important new work.)

The Interview

When students think about research, they rarely think about one of the most interesting, informative sources available: people in the community. In every community live experts on different subjects. Writing a paper on the possible effects of a value-added tax? Talk to a local merchant. Interested in reducing the national deficit by taxing foreign oil? Talk to a local filling station owner. Writing a paper on mandatory life sentences for repeat offenders? Talk to a local lawyer or police officer. Researching the state of education in your community? Talk to a teacher or a principal. Interested in the background of your family? Talk to aunts, uncles, grandparents.

In addition to the immediacy this firsthand research provides, the researcher discovers that information gained by interviewing experts is often more lively, more colorful, and more interesting when it appears in a paper than research from written sources. As William Zinsser states in *On Writing Well*, "Nothing so animates writing as someone telling what he thinks or what he does in his own words."

Chances are, unless you become a journalist or talk-show host, you will never get enough practice interviewing to refine your techniques. So here we offer you a brief guide to conducting and an effective interview.

Conducting an Interview

1. Do preliminary research first

Before the interview, do a background search on your topic. Find out what you already know about the topic and what you need to know. Unless you have some grasp of your topic, you won't know which questions to ask, which answers to pursue, and perhaps even whom to interview. Another aspect of your preliminary research is to gather some background information on the person you're interviewing. Once again, the depth of your information may depend on your ability to formulate successful questions. Knowing something about the person should also make you more comfortable during the interview.

2. Go prepared

Prepare a list of questions which you feel you *must* ask. The list may include others, but preparing an essential list—and perhaps memorizing it—guarantees you won't accidentally leave anything out.

Make sure you have two or three pens or pencils and sufficient paper. If you take a tape recorder, test it first; then take some notes during the interview—just in case.

3. Be personable

Remember that an interview basically consists of two people talking to each other. Don't start writing until you've established some contact. After you do start writing, don't keep your head buried in your notebook; eye contact shows your interest and keeps your subject talking.

4. Record your impressions

In addition to the subject's words, record your impression of the physical and emotional details of the interview. These impressions not only help you decide how to use the material you collect, they also provide vivid detail—color—with which to introduce the material in the paper.

5. Compile your notes while they're fresh

As soon after you complete the interview as possible, rewrite and sort your notes, adding to them as you see fit. Strive for accuracy. If you are going to use someone else's words in your paper, you owe it to that person to report accurately both the words and the sense of what that person had to say.

6. Integrate material into your essay

The material generated during the interview becomes part of your prewriting. Sort and categorize it together with your other research material.

The Card Catalog

The card catalog—those long rows of drawers placed conspicuously in a central location—is an alphabetical list of the materials in the library, by author, by title, and by subject. (Many libraries list by author and title in one file, by subject in another.) Some libraries now store their card catalog on microfilm or in a computer; the reference librarian will show you how to use this equipment.

The library uses one of two systems to organize its holdings: the Dewey Decimal System or the Library of Congress System. Your library may be using both or may be transferring holdings from the Dewey System to the Library of Congress System. Examining the call number (the number assigned to a work) on a book or in the card catalog quickly reveals the system under which a particular work has been classified. The Dewey Decimal System classifies books under one of the ten major categories, all of which begin with numbers:

000   General Works
100   Philosophy
200   Religion
300   Social Sciences
400   Language
500   Natural Sciences
600   Technology and Applied Sciences
700   Fine Arts
800   Literature
900   History and Geography

The Library of Congress System assigns works to one of twenty major groups, all of which begin with letters:

A   General works
B   Philosophy and Religion
C   General History
D   Foreign History
E-F   American History
G   Geography and Anthropology
H   Social Sciences
J   Political Science
K   Law
L   Education
M   Music
N   Fine Arts

P   Language and Literature
Q   Science
R   Medicine
S   Agriculture
T   Technology
U   Military Science
V   Naval Science
Z   Bibliography and Library Science

Each of these major groups is further divided into subgroups. In the Library of Congress System, some works on music are classified under ML—Literature of Music—or MT—Musical Instruction and Study. Language and Literature is all grouped under P, but numerous subgroups are used to classify works into smaller groups such as classical languages, romance languages, fiction and juvenile literature.

The entries in a card catalog give you specific and useful information about a work, information that helps you determine whether the work is one you need as you research your topic. Here are reproductions of author, title, and subject cards for a book on film, and an explanation of the information they contain:

Author Card

```
        2
  PN         McConnell, Frank D.      1942–
  1995.3         Storytelling and mythmaking :
| M26           images from film and literature /
              3 Frank McConnell.—New York :
                Oxford University Press, 1979.
              4 viii, 303 p. : ill. ; 22 cm.

              5 Bibliography: p. [291]–296.
                Includes index.
                ISBN 0-19-502572-5


              6   1. Moving-pictures and literature.
                  2. Moving-pictures—Plots, themes,
  7               etc. I. Title.
  PN1995.3.M26              791.43' 7
                                       78–27538
                                       MARC
  Library of Congress
  12018    876001   © THE BAKER & TAYLOR CO.    0140
```

1. The call number in the upper-left corner tells you where in the library the book is located. To find this one, you'd locate the P section, then PN, then 1995.3, then M26.

2. The name of the author and his date of birth (and death, if deceased) appear on the first line.

3. This section contains publication information. The name of the publisher

may reveal something about the book—its prestige or credibility. The date may also prove helpful. If you are seeking information about films of the 1960s, this book might help. But if you intend to concentrate on films produced in the mid-1980s, this book may only give you incidental background information.

4. This book has an introduction or preface and contains a total of 303 pages. It has illustrations. Its length suggests fairly thorough coverage, and the inclusion of illustrations might be helpful. The final notation in this section—22 cm.—lets the librarian know the book's height.

5. This section tells you that the book contains a fairly long bibliography (six pages) and an index. The index might help you locate specific information; a quick glance through the index might tell you whether the work addresses the topic in which you are interested. The bibliography might help you locate other sources. (The ISBN is an order number for the book.)

6. Here are the other headings in the card catalog under which the book appears. The Arabic numerals indicate subject headings; Roman numerals, title and author. The subject headings here suggest two categories you could check for other works on this topic and also indicate something about the book's content. The headings for this book suggest that the book deals with films and literature in a fairly scholarly manner, for it also deals with plots and themes.

7. Here the call number is repeated—Library of Congress on the left, Dewey Decimal on the right.

The remaining information is for the librarian's use.

The title card for this book differs from the author card in only one way: The title of the book is printed at the top of the card.

Title Card

```
                Storytelling and mythmaking.
    PN          McConnell, Frank D.       1942–
    1995.3          Storytelling and mythmaking :
    M26          images from film and literature /
                Frank McConnell.—New York :
                Oxford University Press, 1979.
                    viii, 303 p. : ill. ; 22 cm.

                    Bibliography: p. [291]–296.
                    Includes index.
                    ISBN 0-19-502572-5


                    1. Moving-pictures and literature.
                    2. Moving-pictures—Plots, themes,
                        etc. I. Title.
        PN1995.3.M26            791.43' 7
                                        78–27538
                                        MARC

        Library of Congress
        12018    876001    © THE BAKER & TAYLOR CO.    0140
```

The two subject cards differ from the others only in that the subject headings under which they are filed are printed at the top of the card.

Subject Cards

```
                    MOVING-PICTURES AND LITERATURE.
       PN           McConnell, Frank D.        1942-
       1995.3            Storytelling and mythmaking :
       M26           images from film and literature /
                     Frank McConnell.—New York :
                     Oxford University Press, 1979.
                          viii, 303 p. : ill. ; 22 cm.

                          Bibliography: p. [291]-296.
                          Includes index.
                          ISBN 0-19-502572-5


                          1. Moving-pictures and literature.
                          2. Moving-pictures—Plots, themes,
                          etc. I. Title.
       PN1995.3.M26               791.43' 7
                                             78-27538
                                               MARC
       Library of Congress
       12018    876001    © THE BAKER & TAYLOR CO.    0140
```

```
                    MOVING-PICTURES-PLOTS, THEMES, ETC.
       PN           McConnell, Frank D.        1942-
       1995.3            Storytelling and mythmaking :
       M26           images from film and literature /
                     Frank McConnell.—New York :
                     Oxford University Press, 1979.
                          viii, 303 p. : ill. ; 22 cm.

                          Bibliography: p. [291]-296.
                          Includes index.
                          ISBN 0-19-502572-5


                          1. Moving-pictures and literature.
                          2. Moving-pictures—Plots, themes,
                          etc. I. Title.
       PN1995.3.M26               791.43' 7
                                             78-27538
                                               MARC
       Library of Congress
       12018    876001    © THE BAKER & TAYLOR CO.    0140
```

So if you've found a title or author in a bibliography, you can track down the book's call number by checking the title or author card in the card catalog. If, however, you are searching for material on a topic but have no names or titles, you need to check the subject drawers of the card catalog.

Deciding what subject heading your topic is filed under can be tricky. If you looked under the subject heading "Films," for example, to find titles of books about films, you wouldn't find a thing. So to find out how topics are categorized under subject headings, check your library's copy of the *Library of Congress Subject Heading,* a reference work usually placed near the card catalog. There, under "Films," you'll find, "see moving pictures." The librarian can also help you identify the correct subject heading for your topic. Librarians work with a system that can be confusing even to experienced researchers, so don't hesitate to ask for assistance.

Reference Works

Besides using the card catalog, you may wish to consult general reference works. Many of these, especially encyclopedias, are best used for preliminary research; they don't provide the depth or detail that college-level research requires. They can help you strengthen your background on a topic, locate specific information on a topic, or verify the validity of some fact related to your topic. Because new or updated information may be important, check the date of each reference work and determine whether you need to consult a supplemental edition or a revised version of the original. These general reference works may also contain bibliographies and cross-references of value:

Encyclopedias

Collier's Encyclopedia
Columbia Encyclopedia
Encyclopedia Americana
Encyclopedia Britannica

Biographical Information (persons no longer living)

Dictionary of American Biography (U.S.A.)
Dictionary of National Biography (Britain)
Webster's Biographical Dictionary

Biographical Information (persons still living)

Contemporary Authors
Current Biography
International Who's Who
Webster's Biographical Dictionary
Who's Who in America

Gazetteers

Columbia-Lippincott Gazetteer of the World
Webster's new Geographical Dictionary

Atlases

National Atlas of the United States of America
National Geographic Atlas of the World
Times Atlas of the World

Yearbooks

Americana Annual
Britannica Book of the Year
Information Please Almanac
Statesman's Year-Book: Statistical and Historical Annual of the States of the World, 1864–
World Almanac and Book of Facts

In addition to the general reference works listed here, specialized encyclopedias and dictionaries exist for just about every area. Check the *Cumulative Book Index* or consult the reference librarian to find what is available.

EXERCISE 9–2

Examine a copy of one of the general reference works listed above. Then write a two- or three-sentence description of the work's focus and scope. (If you divide the list among classmates, you'll end up with an annotated bibliography of general reference works.)

EXERCISE 9–3

For each of the following fields of study, find the titles of at least two specialized encyclopedias or dictionaries that your library has among its holdings. You may want to divide this list as well.

Art	Literature
Biology	Mathematics
Chemistry	Medicine
Computer Science	Music
Dance	Philosophy
Economics	Psychology
Education	Religion
Film	Science and Technology
History	Social Sciences
Law	

EXERCISE 9–4

Describe in writing each of the specialized encyclopedias or dictionaries you identified in Exercise 9–3 so your classmates can determine the scope and usefulness of each.

EXERCISE 9–5

Turn back to page 7. Write a two- to three-page report in which you identify one of the writers listed and provide a summary of their contributions to the world's literature. Use at least two sources; one must be from a specialized encyclopedia or dictionary and one must be from a work you found in the card catalog. Be prepared to present your report orally to the class.

Bibliographies, Periodical Indexes, and Abstracts

Most of the books and articles you come across in your research have bibliographies of their own, a list of works the author cited or consulted. Use these bibliographies; scan them for titles of works that may provide you with information pertaining to your topic. You should also read each work keeping in mind that it can tell you about the sources it cites; it may be possible to discover from one article's content which other sources are most important to consider in your treatment of the topic.

The library has scores of books that list the titles, authors, publication information, and, sometimes, descriptions of articles on various subjects. These indexes, bibliographies, and abstracts help you find out what has been written on your topic. From them you can compile a list of works that may yield the information you need to explore a topic and support a thesis.

Quite often, periodicals offer the most recent information on a topic. A periodical is any publication that appears "periodically"—magazines, newspapers, scholarly or technical journals, house organs, or newsletters. A periodical index lists the articles that have appeared during a specified time on a particular subject.

The entries in a periodical index are listed alphabetically, according to a system that is explained in the first few pages. As you begin working with an unfamiliar index, read the explanation of its organization carefully so that finding the entires you need is easier.

Art

Art Index

Biology

Biological and Agricultural Index

Business

Business Index
Business Periodicals Index

Chemistry

Current Abstracts of Chemistry and Index Chemicus

Drama

Dramatic Index (1909–1949)

Education (1929–1964)

Current Index to Journals in Education
Education Index
Resources in Education (RIE), also known as ERIC

Engineering

Engineering Index Monthly and Author Index

Film

Film Literature Index
International Index of Film Periodicals

Humanities

British Humanities Index
Humanities Index

Language and Literature

MLA International Bibliography

Law

Index to Legal Periodicals

Medicine

Cumulative Index to Nursing and Allied Health Literature
Index Medicus

Music

Music Index

Philosophy

Philosopher's Index

Religion

Catholic Periodical Index: A Guide to Catholic Magazines
Religion Index One: Periodicals

Science and Technology

Applied Science and Technology Index
General Science Index
Science Citation Index

Social Sciences

Social Sciences and Humanities Index (1907–1974)
Social Sciences Index

General, Miscellaneous

Bibliographic Index: A Cumulative Bibliography of Bibliographies
*Biography Index: A Cumulative Index to Bibliography Material in Books
    and Magazines*
Book Review Digest
Magazine Index
Public Affairs Information Service
Reader's Guide to Periodical Literature
United States Government Publications Monthly Catalog

Special Indexes

Facts on File
The New York Times Index
Ulrich's International Periodical Directory
Vertical File Index: A Subject and Title Index to Selected Pamphlet Material

Federal Government Publications Indexes

You may also want to consult an index to publications printed by the federal government. These publications cover an enormous range of subjects and are a good source of historical as well as current information. Besides the four indexes listed below, you may also want to check in the library for a bibliography of government publications on a specific topic. Remember to work with the librarian; he or she will be skilled in locating the information you need.

Federal Government Publications

The American Statistics Index
Government Reports Announcements and Index
Monthly Catalog of the United States Government
Selected Government Publications

The library also has a collection of *abstracts*, works which summarize the content of articles published in certain journals. An abstract can be especially helpful if you want to know whether an article contains information useful to you. Here are a few:

Abstracts in Anthropology
Art Abstract
Biological Abstracts
Chemical Abstracts
Historical Abstracts
Key to Economic Science
Language and Language Behavior Abstracts
Physics Abstracts
Psychological Abstracts
Religious and Theological Abstracts
RILA (art)
RILM (music)
Science Abstracts
Sociological Abstracts

In addition to the abstracting services listed here, it's often possible to obtain abstracts as well as bibliographies through a computer search of centralized data banks. Although most of the information stored in these data banks is also available through printed sources, a computer search may speed up the process of locating sources.

Most of the sources listed in data banks, however, are relatively new, so you are likely to find only sources published within the last fifteen to twenty years.

Conducting a computer search also costs money and there is some waiting involved before you have the computer-generated bibliography in hand. Check with the reference librarian to see what computer services are available and ask whether requesting a computer search would be the most efficient way to compile the list of sources you need.

Guides to Reference Materials

You may also locate reference works in many areas through the following guides:

Barton, Mary N., comp. *Reference Books: A Brief Guide for Students and Other Users of the Library*
Gates, Jean Kay. *Guide to the Use of Books and Libraries*
Murphy, Robert W. *How and Where to Look It Up*
Sheres, Lairs. *Basic Reference Sources: An Introduction to Materials and Methods*
Walford, Arthur J., ed. *Guide to Reference Material*
Winchell, Constance M. *Guide to Reference Books*

EXERCISE 9–6

Divide the lists of indexes and abstracts among your classmates. Then go to the library to look up the titles assigned to you. Look through each work, recording your responses to the following:

1. What years does the work cover? Is it an ongoing publication?

2. What sorts of periodicals does it index? How many of them?

3. Describe the work, summarizing its purpose and usefulness.

4. How is the work organized?

5. Where in the library is the work located?

EXERCISE 9–7

Exchange your responses to the exercise with your classmates. If possible, have your descriptions of each work copied for each class member.

Compiling a Working Bibliography

A working bibliography is a list of all the material you've found that might be helpful to you as you research your topic and write your paper. From the indexes, abstracts, bibliographies, and card catalog you extract the titles, authors, and publication information of a number of books, articles, and other published materials. Compile a list of potentially helpful materials before you even look at the materials. This list is your working bibliography, and it is most useful if you keep it separate from the notes you take on the material itself.

You may compile a working bibliography in a number of ways. Your instructor may recommend a method not discussed here. Most important, however, is that you record all necessary information about the source, both to help you locate it in the library and to provide proper documentation in the paper itself. So an entry for a book in your working bibliography should include the author, title, place of publication, publisher, date of publication, and call number; for articles, be sure to include the volume and date of publication as well as the pages on which the article appears. Other sources require the same basic data—author, title, publication information. You may want to review the documentation section later in this chapter to ensure that you know what information is needed for documentation in your final list of works cited.

One method of recording information for a working bibliography is to use 3″ × 5″ cards, recording information about only one source on each card. One advantage of this method is that you can organize sources alphabetically or according to their location in the library. You can easily add a new source or discard one you won't need. Each card should contain everything needed to locate the source in the library and everything needed to prepare its entry in your final list of works cited.

In the upper-left corner of the card write the call number or library location of the source. Assign a code number to each entry, that is, 1–15 or A–O, and write that code in the upper-right corner. Then, as you take notes, you can save time by writing the code assigned to a source (rather than the full title and author) on the notes gathered from that source.

Instead of note cards, you may wish simply to keep your working bibliography on a sheet of notebook paper. As you find sources, write down all publication data. The advantage is that all your sources are available on a sheet or two of paper and you don't have to shuffle note cards. The disadvantage, though, is that the list can't be easily organized without a good deal of copying.

After compiling your working bibliography, you should have a good idea of the information available on your topic. If sources are plentiful, then you can proceed. But if, after working with the reference librarian and your instructor, you find that too little has been written on your topic, you are going to have to change your topic or your approach to it.

Once you've compiled a working bibliography, you can begin examining each source for the information you need to write your paper. As you examine sources, you will probably come across other materials that could be helpful. Add them to your working bibliography.

Begin with the sources that look most promising. A title, an author, a description of the source may indicate that it contains valuable information. You may wish to start with the encyclopedias or dictionaries for background information, then move on to books or articles. Or you may wish to pounce first on a particular book because it appears to have precisely the information you need. If you have a thesis firmly in mind, then your actual reading of sources can be directed by what each reveals about your thesis. If your thesis is not yet fully developed, you may have to take a more general approach, searching a wider area for information. The information gathered from your reading can then help you refine your unformed ideas into a workable topic.

If the sources don't pan out, if little information can be found to support your thesis, you may have to consider changing the thesis or changing your focus. Be alert to this possibility; if you continue with a topic that can't be adequately researched, you may find yourself facing a deadline with nothing substantial to submit.

Be alert also to information that changes your view of your subject. As you research, you may find that your opinion changes with your understanding. After a few days of reading and taking notes, you may wish to develop a thesis that's more compatible with your increasing knowledge. Check these changes with your instructor; he or she may be able to assist as you pursue the new direction.

Taking Notes

Now for the actual note-taking. Here again, several methods are available. You may take notes on larger, 4″ × 6″ note cards to distinguish notes from bibliographical entries. The advantages of note cards at this stage are several. Again, you can rearrange note cards easily as you draft and revise your paper. Information is easy to locate. Also, you can readily separate useful information from material that is not. If you use note cards, use only one side of the card and record only one piece of information from one source on each card. Make sure each card includes a code number to identify the source and the page number from which the information is taken. And add a heading at the top of the card (perhaps in different-colored ink) that classifies the material the card contains.

You may also take notes on regular paper, of course, following the same method. Here again, though, material may be difficult to arrange or impossible to locate quickly. Each sheet should include code numbers and headings, though.

Others prefer to avoid note-taking altogether by working from photocopies of articles or sections of books. The prime advantage of this method is that the bulk of the work can be done outside the library. Using this method, all the information is in front of you, so you can easily identify quoted material and don't have to wonder whether your notes are accurate. If you practice this method, be certain to record publication information on the first page of the copied material and keep all material from one source fastened together. You also need to highlight, bracket, or make marginal notes to isolate useful information.

Working from copied materials may make organizing more difficult, however. Headings don't work easily, although you can label sections of an article with a term that identifies what information appears there. Or, you can keep a list of headings on a separate sheet, noting under each heading the source and page number that contains the corresponding information.

So, some final reminders:

1. You must identify the source of each bit of information on note cards or paper; use the code number from the working bibliography or a brief title. If you duplicate an article or portions of a book, write all publication information on the first page of the material. Include page numbers from which information came.

2. You must be able to distinguish between quoted and paraphrased material. If you duplicate material, this is no problem. But if you take notes from a source, you must devise a system that clearly makes this distinction. Don't rely on your memory; after a few days you won't be able to remember whether you copied a direct quotation. In your notes, put quotation marks around all direct quotations—words, phrases, or sentences.

3. Check each section of your notes for accuracy. Make sure the notes come from the source you listed; make sure the notes come from the page or pages you indicated. Make sure you've recorded the content accurately. Taking some time to check for accuracy now will remove doubts you may have later as you write. If may also save you a last-minute trek to the library to check on some confusing detail.

Documenting Your Paper

In a research paper or report, you gather information about your topic from other sources. So in order to distinguish between your own ideas or observations and those of your sources, you must *document* the paper, indicating the sources from which your information was obtained. Then you must give credit to the source of an idea, a fact, a statement, a phrase. You must give credit both when you directly quote information and when you paraphrase it—that is, when you put the information into your own words.

Documenting properly is a matter of honesty and credibility. When you use information presented by another person, that person deserves to be acknowledged as the source of the information. Moreover, you are legally required to acknowledge the sources of your information. Published works are, in a sense, possessions, and to take from their owner without giving credit, to present borrowed information as your own, is plagiarism. Plagiarism, of course, is illegal and unethical, and, depending on your institution's policies, could have some very serious consequences, even if your failure to acknowledge a source is unintentional.

But documenting properly also contributes to your credibility. The claims and assertions you make have to be supported, and using the ideas, observations, and conclusions of others provides the needed support. By citing experts, you are demonstrating to your readers that you are knowledgeable about the current state of your topic. Your readers are also able to trace your information back to its source easily, a further indication of your credibility and the authority with which you are writing.

Styles of Documentation

Various disciplines use various styles of documentation. The one we are focusing on here is that used by the Modern Language Association (MLA). Widely used in the fields of language and literature, the MLA format is probably the format you will be instructed to use in your composition class.

A documentation format lends consistency to the way sources are referred to, quoted, and paraphrased. Any format, then, provides rules to be followed when a writer needs to cite the sources of his or her material. Some formats call for footnotes, others endnotes, and others parenthetical references within the text of the work itself. A documentation format sets a standard to be followed so that readers and writers both approach their work with the same set of expectations. A documentation format is a set of conventions that provide unity and continuity to the work done in a particular field or discipline.

Papers submitted to specific publications may have to follow the documentation procedures of a particular style manual. Different classes may call for different documentation styles. But most likely you'll have no reason to use the *Council of Biology Editors Style Manual* or the *American Medical Association Manual for Authors and Editors* right now.

However, you may have occasion to use the APA style—the style, that is, given in the *Publication Manual of the American Psychological Association*. It's one used often for college papers, especially in the social sciences. A brief overview of that style is contained in Appendix I (pp. 348–349). If you are doing a paper for a class which requires the APA style, however, you'll need to refer to a copy of its style manual. You should find a copy on reserve in the library or one may be purchased in the bookstore.

MLA Style of Documenting Sources

The good news here is that the new MLA style of documenting sources (see *MLA Handbook for Writers of Research Papers*, 2nd ed. 1984) allows writers to insert within the text of a paper a parenthetical reference to the source. That is, footnotes or endnotes are no longer necessary.

But before we get into a discussion about parenthetical references, let's consider what kinds of material must be documented. Basically, you must cite the source of *all* information you have taken from any source. Any material that is not your own, anything that you have borrowed—a fact, an observation, an idea—must be documented. And it must be documented whether you quote the material exactly as it appears in the original or you put the material in your words.

So what doesn't have to be documented? Material that is entirely your own, expressed entirely in your words, and material that is "common knowledge." An item is considered common knowledge if it is widely known, appears in several sources, and cannot be attributed to a single source. Information such as "Lansing is the capital of Michigan" is common knowledge and thus does not require documentation.

Parenthetical Documentation

The list of works cited at the end of your paper provides readers with complete publication information about each source. But in the paper itself you must indicate to your readers exactly which information was taken from a specific source. You must also indicate precisely where in a source a particular piece of information is found. So when you use words, ideas, facts, and observations that are not your own, a parenthetical reference lets your readers know from which source the information came. In most cases, the author's last name and the page on which the material appeared are sufficient for a parenthetical reference. Notice that if the author's name appears in the text, only page numbers are needed in the parenthetical reference. If a source has no author, use a shortened version of the title in the reference.

As you select information to include in the reference, use the procedures outlined in the section on preparing the list of works cited (p. 328) as a general guide. So if your source has four or five authors, your parenthetical reference need contain only the name of the first author, "et al.", and relevant page numbers. If a parenthetical reference cites two or more sources, use a semicolon between the sources. As you look over the following examples, notice how punctuation is used.

Sample Parenthetical References

Roberts, however, says that few writers and artists seemed concerned about the passing of the Obscene Publications Act in 1857 (618).

Few writers and artists seemed concerned about the passing of the Obscene Publications Act in 1857 (Roberts 618).

Weisner and Eiduson noted that about 17 percent of the families studied had recurring problems in managing their lives, difficulties that included drug and alcohol abuse as well as instability (62).

About 17 percent of the families studied had recurring problems in managing their lives, problems that included drug and alcohol abuse as well as instability (Weisner and Eiduson 62).

Redding and his colleagues conclude that additional study is needed to evaluate the effectiveness of the treatments currently available (821).

According to some researchers, additional study is needed to evaluate the effectiveness of the treatments currently available (Redding et al. 821).

The *Bowker/Bantam 1984 Complete Sourcebook of Personal Computing* advises that the hard copy produced by a printer can help a programmer locate program errors (27).

The hard copy produced by a printer can also help a programmer locate program errors (Bowker/Bantam 27).

Quoted Material

But, as the *Bowker/Bantam 1984 Complete Sourcebook of Personal Computing* asserts, "a printed program can be useful, especially if it is large, to debug or correct program statements" (27).

Weisner and Ediuson note that about 17 percent of the families studied "have continuing personal problems and a somewhat chaotic, changeable quality in their lives" (62).

Of the families studied in one project, about 17 percent had "continuing difficulties that include drinking, drugs, or personal problems and a somewhat chaotic, changeable quality in their lives" (Weisner and Eiduson 62).

If the quotation is longer than four typed lines, set the quotation off by beginning on a new line, indenting ten spaces. The quotation should be double spaced and it should not be set off by quotation marks.

```
Weisner and Eiduson were surprised at their results:
     When our project began, we had some concerns about
     the developmental well-being of the children reared
     in the alternate life-styles. Although many of the
     parents thought they were innovating in their
     children's best interests, we were less sure.
     However, judging by our developmental data through
     the first year of school, our concerns were not
     borne out. By school age, on average, the children
     in all four groups were doing well, and there were
     no major group differences in their physical or
     mental development, as indicated by overall health,
     school measure, cognitive and IQ scores, and social
     and emotional development scores on standardized
     tests. We do not expect the values and life choices
     of children raised conventionally to differ from
     those raised unconventionally as they grow older,
     however, we intend to track them into young
     adulthood to see whether such differences emerge.
     (60, 62)
```

Use long quotations sparingly. They are best used when they contain information that is extremely difficult to paraphrase or when the original has expressed something so well that you think your readers will benefit more from the original than from your paraphrase of it.

Quotations are also best used to support or illustrate a point. Don't use the quotation to make your point for you—making the point is your responsibility. In most cases, a quotation will not stand alone. You have to interpret the quotation for your readers; you have to show its importance and how it fits into what you are saying.

All quotations should be introduced in some manner. Phrases like the following are helpful:

According to Grayson, "_____" (   ).

As Miller points out, "_____" (   ).

Such an idea is illustrated by Aprile's contention that
"_____" (   ).

But Abrams claims that "_____" (   )

James, however, says that "_____" (   )

At least one researcher has suggested that "_____"
(   ).

A recent study reported that "_____" (   )

In *The Rhetoric of Fiction,* Booth asserts that "_____"
(   ).

This position is further supported by Lorenz's assertion that
"_____" (   ).

Tolstedt, moreover, insists that "_____" (   ).

Paraphrasing

When you paraphrase, you are putting into your own words someone else's idea or material. It is permissible, of course, to paraphrase a passage but to quote a key phrase or term—just remember to put quotation marks around the key phrase or term. And remember, always, to include the parenthetical reference at the end of the passage.

Parenthetical references are usually placed at the end of a sentence in which the material from that particular source appears. What do you do, then, if you've paraphrased a page or two of material from the original source? Because parenthetical references should be as concise and noninterfering as possible, you certainly don't want to insert a reference at the end of each sentence of your paraphrase.

Instead, construct the first sentence of your paraphrase in such a way that it provides a signal to your readers that a paraphrase is beginning. Then continue with the paraphrase. At its end, the parenthetical reference contains the page number(s) of the source from which you've drawn your material.

So when you embark on a long paraphrase, a sentence such as the following signals your readers that the material between it and the parenthetical reference all comes from the source cited in the reference.

Maus argues that a course in formal logic should be a part of the university curriculum.

That sentence can then be followed by a summary of the argument, and the parenthetical reference at the end signals the end of the information from that particular source. The reader assumes that all the words, all the phrases, all the sentences between the first one and the reference are your own, so be sure to use quotation marks if you find it necessary to quote a word or phrase directly.

Preparing a List of Works Cited

The readers of your research paper refer to the list of works cited to obtain complete publication information for the references which appear in the text of your research paper. The list of works cited is a bibliography; as such, it gives readers the information they need to locate a source should they wish to pursue any subjects or ideas contained in your research paper.

But it also contributes to the reader's sense of your credibility. By carefully documenting and preparing each entry in the list of works cited, you indicate to your readers that you have done a thorough and accurate job of giving credit to your sources of information or ideas.

The entries which follow are samples of the more common types of sources. As you prepare the list of works cited to accompany your research paper, follow the form given for each source you have used; simply substitute your own information. The completed list is alphabetized by the author's last name; works with no authors are alphabetized according to the first significant word in the title. If an entry runs more than one line, indent the second and subsequent lines five spaces. Should you have more than one work by the same author, the entry for that author's second and succeeding works should begin with three hyphens, followed by appropriate punctuation (comma or period, depending on type of entry), then one space. The remaining portion of such an entry follows the regular form.

Sample Entries

Books

An entry for a book should contain as much of the following information as is applicable: author, title, editor, translator, edition, and publication information (city, publisher, date).

A Book by a Single Author

Bell—Metereau, Rebecca. Hollywood Androgyny. New
    York: Columbia UP, 1985.
Chute, Carolyn. The Beans of Egypt, Maine. New York:
    Ticknor, 1985.
Kennedy, James G. ed. Stories East and West.
    Glenview: Scott, 1971.

A Book by Two or More Authors

When preparing an entry for a book by two or three authors, reverse only the
first name. When the book has more than three authors, list only the first and
et al. ("and others"). If the authors are editors or translators, use a comma
after the last name and add the appropriate designation.

Belcher, William F., and James W. Lee, eds. J. D.
    Salinger and the Critics. Belmont: Wadsworth,
    1962.
Howe, Jeanne, et al., eds. The Handbook of Nursing.
    New York: Wiley, 1984.
Kamm, Ernest R., Derald D. Hunt, and Jack A.
    Fleming. Juvenile Law and Procedure in
    California. Beverly Hills: Glencoe, 1971.

An Anonymous Book

Begin this entry with the title.

Bowker/Bantam 1984 Complete Sourcebook of Personal
    Computing. New York: Bowker/Bantam, 1983.

A Corporate or Government Publication

U.S. Dept. of Labor, Bureau of Labor Statistics.
    Employment, Hours, and Earnings, United States,
    1904—84, Vol. 1. Washington, D.C.: GPO, 1985.

A Translation

If you refer most often to the author, give the author's name first. But if you
refer most often to the translator, give the translator's name first.

Kundera, Milan. The Book of Laughter and Forgetting.
    Trans. Michael Henry Heim. New York: Penguin,
    1981.
Heim, Michael Henry, trans. The Book of Laughter and
    Forgetting. By Milan Kundera. New York:
    Penguin, 1981.

A Work in an Anthology

Hemingway, Ernest. ''A Clean, Well-Lighted Place.'' American Short Stories. Eds. Eugene Current-Garcia and Walton R. Patrick. 4th ed. Glenview: Scott, 1981. 471–475.

Periodicals

An entry for a periodical article should contain as much of the following information as applicable: author, article title, periodical title, volume, date, page number(s). The page number(s) appears last in the entry and should include all pages on which the article appears. If, however, an article begins on page 17, skips to page 20, and concludes on page 25, simply put 17+ to indicate that the article ranges over several nonconsecutive pages.

An Article from a Weekly or Biweekly Periodical

Parascenzo, Marino. ''Straight A's for Hershey Exile Larouche.'' Sporting News 20 Jan. 1986: 36.

Winkler, Karen J. ''Scholar Traces the Historical Connection Between Slavery and the Idea of Progress.'' Chronicle of Higher Education 27 Feb. 1985: 5–6.

Stengel, Richard. ''Good Field, Good Hit.'' Time 31 Oct. 1983: 117.

An Article from a Monthly or Bimonthly Periodical

Rothmeyer, Karen. ''Hot Properties: The Media-buying Spree Explained.'' Columbia Journalism Review Nov–Dec. 1985: 38–43.

Marzorati, Gerold. ''Leon Golub's Mean Streets.'' Art News Feb. 1985: 74–87.

Weisner, Thomas S., and Bernice T. Eiduson. ''The Children of the 60's as Parents.'' Psychology Today Jan. 1986: 60–66.

An Article in a Daily Newspaper

Petersen, Clarence. ''Men Still Find It Difficult to Open Up Their Emotions.'' Kansas City Star 26 Jan. 1986, D1+.

An Article in a Journal with Continuous Pagination

Roberts, M. J. D. ''Morals, Art, and the Law: The Passing of the Obscene Publications Act, 1857.'' Victorian Studies 28 (1985): 609–629.

Schlaefli, Andre, James R. Rest, and Stephen J. Thoma. ''Does Moral Education Improve Moral Judgment? A Meta-Analysis of Intervention

```
            Studies Using the Defining Issues Test.''
            Review of Educational Research 55 (1985): 319-
            352.
Redding, Gregory J., et al. ''Sleep Patterns in
            Nonambulatory Boys with Duchenne Muscular
            Dystrophy.'' Archives of Physical Medicine and
            Rehabilitation 66 (1985): 818-821.
```

An Article or Entry from an Encyclopedia, Dictionary, or other Alphabetic Reference Work

Begin with the author's name, if it is known. Many reference works give the author's initials at the end of an entry; a key is located elsewhere in the volume or in a separate volume. If the author's name is not known, begin with the entry's title as it appears in the work.

```
Dykuizen, George. ''Dewey, John.'' Encyclopedia
            Brittanica: Macropaedia. 1984 ed.
''Jung, Carl Gustav.'' Twentieth Century Culture:
            Biographical Companion. Eds. Alan Bullock, R.
            B. Woodings, and John Cumming. New York:
            Harper, 1983.
```

Miscellaneous Sources

Films

Generally, a film entry should contain the title, director, distributor, and year of the film. Other relevant information—writer, performer, composer, choreographer—appears after the director's name. If, however, you wish to refer to the contributions of one person, you may begin the entry with that person's name.

```
The Color Purple. Dir. Steven Spielberg. With Danny
            Glover and Whoopi Goldberg. Warner, 1985.
Meyjes, Menno, screenwriter. The Color Purple. Dir.
            Steven Spielberg with Danny Glover and Whoopi
            Goldberg. Warner, 1985.
Out of Africa. Dir. Sydney Pollack with Robert
            Redford and Meryl Streep. Universal, 1985.
```

Interviews

```
Wallace, Mike. Telephone Interview. 18 April 1981.
Safer, Morley. Personal Interview. 11 April 1981.
```

Lectures and Speeches

```
Martin, V. A. Class lecture. Southwest Texas State
            University, San Marcos, Texas, 6 May 1983.
```

Ong, Walter. Luncheon address. Questions of Morality
    and Literacy Conference, Rockhurst College,
    Kansas City. Mo. 29 July 1985.

EXERCISE 9–8

In early 1985 some of the major issues facing American society were (1) divesture of American business interests in South Africa, (2) social questions related to AIDS, (3) arms limitation agreements with the Soviet Union, (4) the increased professionalization and corruption of college athletics, (5) the Third World banking debt to Western countries.

Pick one of these issues to research.

- Write a report on the state of the issue in November 1985. Also focus on developments in the months immediately preceding (don't go back further than January 1, 1985.)

- Write a report on the developments between November 1985 and the time you are writing.

- Present an analysis of the current status of the issue.

- Write a paper in which, using the information in your research reports, you take a stand on one facet of the issue or you argue against the handling of the issue in the past.

The following pages present a sample research paper. As you read it, note the kinds of evidence the author uses to support her thesis.

Sample Research Paper

Today's Newspapers:
Are They Losing the Loyalty of Their Readers?

Author uses the inverted pyramid—moving from a general statement toward a specific thesis.

In the two–hundred–year history of the American newspaper, the newspaper business has become a competitive, massive, and complex industry, exerting an awesome power over its readers. Its primary responsibilities, however, have remained to inform, influence, and interpret for its readers and, as a business, to earn a profit. Through the years, however, the increasing complexity of subjects and interests has brought the newspaper to a content and to a style of writing and publishing that has left readers distrustful and irritated, no longer certain of their relationship with their newspapers.

During the two hundred years of its de–

velopment, the American newspaper has accumulated many different roles and seldom has abandoned any of them (Smith 13). In the eighteenth century the newspaper first expanded from local news into national politics. In the nineteenth century it extended its role to cover economic conditions as trade multiplied and a strong merchant class developed. At that time, it also took on a new set of roles from recreation, sports, and entertainment, becoming a mass medium by the force of its wide array of material. Lately newspapers have become nearly too expensive, too heavy to carry, too filled with information for any single reader to read thoroughly (Smith 320). There are now sections for sports, travel, finance, business, home, food, want ads, entertainment, fashion and magazine supplements. In 1973, Washington Post newspaper critic Ben H. Bagdikian reported that 83 percent of all newspaper pages added since 1950 are advertising and must of the remaining 17 percent are puffery for food, real estate, or clothing advertisements (Hynds 38). Despite—or perhaps because of—these changes, newspaper circulation peaked in the 1960s, as newspapers began falling out of step with readers because of their changing lifestyles and demographic shifting. Competition also had increased and the high costs of publishing and distribution threatened the newspaper industry's financial base (14).

This paragraph returns to the first sentence of the introduction and provides an expanded historical background.

Though the newspaper is in a period of transition as it moves to solve these problems with the computerization of production, the purposes of the newspaper remain unchanged. The newspaper continues to form readers' ideas and opinions, define their roles in society, and supply news of political, financial, and cultural affairs. It influences readers' lives as citizens, voters, consumers, and sports fans, as well as providing the basic information upon which they depend to perform the transactions of daily life (Smith 13–14). Traditionally, the news-

This paragraph returns to the second sentence of the introduction and begins the discussion of the current responsibilities of the newspaper.

paper's objective has been to inform, influence and entertain, and, of course, further
the economy through advertising (Hynds 13).
In addition, another function has recently
developed: that of self—improvement—helping
readers make their lives better and richer.
Historically, however, the newspaper's fore-
most purpose has been to inform readers and
to provide meaningful details so readers can
make their own judgments. Without question,
today's readers need knowledge of the world
around them to understand what is going on
and to survive in the world. It is evident
that the newspaper—the technician of the mass
mind—bears a great responsibility.

One of these responsibilities is to
serve as part of the political system of
checks and balances. In our country, a free
press serves a free people, helping them
maintain their freedoms (Hynds 27). Americans
traditionally have believed that journalists
must be allowed to work without unnecessary
government restrictions, that they be free to
criticize government activities at all levels. The public approves of the healthy fric-
tion constantly in evidence between the press
and government officials. The reader understands that the government feels it should
protect its secrets, and that the job of the
press is to dig them out for his information
(Cox 213). The same tension exists between
the press and the powerful, such as under-
world figures, who do not want their personal
interests made public. In covering a story
reporters are practicing their responsibility
to protect the public. The journalism trade's
most durable aphorism is: ''The business of
journalism is to comfort the afflicted and to
afflict the comfortable'' (Bruning 23).

In spite of the fact that newspapers
have long been perceived as the ''public
watchdog,'' readers—both the enthusiastic and
the skeptical—are beginning to accuse newspapers of not providing adequate information
and not presenting it clearly. Their charges
identify a new awareness readers have devel-

Here the author uses the plural to avoid sexist language.

Here the author inadvertently uses the traditional masculine form.

This paragraph begins the direct examination of the thesis presented in the first paragraph.

oped toward their newspapers. This new awareness surprised the press during the U.S. as-
sault on Grenada when reporters were banned
from the action, and the public approved
(Bruning 23). There also have been numerous
punitive libel judgments against newspapers,
something unheard of in the past. A report by
the National Opinion Research Center in Chicago found that only 13.7 percent of the
American people have a great deal of confidence in newspapers (Kilpatrick 4).

Following public exposure of stories
which embroidered reality, readers also began
to question the ethics of journalists. A
woman reporter on the Washington Post fabricated a story of an eight-year-old drug user.
She later admitted the story was not true.
Another well-known reporter who has written
for the New Yorker for many years was cen-
sured for presenting as real people composite
characters he had fabricated. To make his
stories more interesting, he put his characters in colorful situations, using vivid detail and attention-getting quotes as their
own (Henry 66). This alteration of facts to
develop a dramatic narrative has been dubbed
''The New Journalism,'' exemplified by the
books Roots and In Cold Blood. Though called
''true life'' novels, they are fictionalized
facts, in the New Journalism style, which the
readers accept as truth. This blurring of
fact and fiction helps destroy the public's
trust in the industry's integrity and credibility and breaches the ethics of journalism,
asserts David Shaw in Improving Newswriting
(66).

Other missteps annoy the reading public.
Readers soon lose confidence in what they are
reading in the newspaper when the news becomes too opinionated or analytical (Kilpatrick 14). They want the writer to state the
facts fairly and without bias so they can
reach their own conclusions. The absence of
the correction of errors of a news story may
confuse readers because they may have heard
or read the story differently, and they want

Since the author uses the source's name, she does not have to use it in the notation.

the straight truth. The reader, too, appreci-
ates good continuity in a story because he
wants to know the ending.

Readers further complain of rumor-mongering and sensationalism by newspapers,
charging that they are used to sell newspapers. Readers have also become particularly
sensitive to the invasion of a citizen's privacy. They believe that a determined reporter
may coerce or frighten an individual into
talking about things the individual prefers
be left unsaid (Cox 212). Readers often feel
empathy for the ''victims'' of such reporters.

Readers are also turning against their
newspapers because they are becoming more
difficult to read. One problem is the serious
obstruction to reading caused by the sprin-
kling of foreign words and expressions
throughout the newspaper. In a telephone conversation, Reader's Representative Donald
Jones of the Kansas City Star maintained that
''Latinate'' words used mostly in the business and financial sections better express a
thought than comparable English words. To
many readers they are an interruption. Furthermore, the creative skill of newswriting
has largely become hidden in a morass of ov-
erblown, specialized vocabulary, complex composition, and euphemisms. In fact, this so-
called ''Journalese,'' or ''jargon'' has almost become a second language used by news
writers, according to John Loder of Time
(78). It is responsible for such phrases as
''the right stuff,'' ''the gender gap,'' and
''life in the fast lane.'' Certain nouns seem
always to have a certain adjective: ''fact-
finding mission.'' Politics, the military,
and government are assigned special terms in
journalese: ''undererdog,'' ''uphill battle,'' ''coattail effect.'' Words have also
taken on different meanings in journalese.
''Outspoken'' means abusive; ''militant''
means fanatic. Then there are the offbeat
words—''ripoff,'' ''rap,'' ''dude''—which
also have no place in responsible news writ-

ing (Strunk and White 81). Sports writing
jargon is so pervasive that unless the reader
participates or referees the game, it is impossible to understand. Newspapers often rely
too heavily on difficult or uncommon words. A

section of a recent Kansas City Times used
such complex words as ''retrofit,'' ''synop-
tic,'' ''eschatology,'' ''miscreants,''
''commonweal.'' In order for news writing to
inform the reading public, it should be
plain, concise, orderly, and sincere. Journalese only serves to confuse the reader and
depreciate the English language.

  Readers want their information phrased
in simple words, not decorated with superfluous adjectives and adverbs. Below is an example of inflated language from an article in
the Chicago Tribune reprinted in the February
2, 1986 Kansas City Star. The subject is
''friendship'':

> Although friendship never went out
> of style, its visibility was
> obscured by two decades devoted to
> the sexual revolution and its
> fallout. The beneficiary of myriad
> sociological trends, from the
> dissolution of the nuclear family
> to the consequences of casual sex
> in a disease-panicked decade, good
> old platonic friendship is steadily
> making a comeback.

Although the subjects are dissimilar,
compare the above contemporary style with a
factual front-page report of an accident in
the September 18, 1880, edition of the Kansas
City Evening Star:

> As the first division of the
> procession reached Grand Avenue and
> Fifteenth streets this morning, a
> team of horses standing at the
> corner became frightened, and
> breaking away from the wagon dashed
> into a crowd of children, who were
> standing by a cistern box at the
> corner. The horses were fastened
> together by the neck-yoke and

consequently it was impossible for the children to avoid them, and they were knocked down by the neck-yoke and tramped under the hoofs of the thoroughly frightened horses.

The first is an example of today's journalese—muddy, overstated, and difficult, using $20 words when 10¢ words would do (Strunk and White 76). In the 1880s story, written when news was reported without embellishment, the writer takes the reader step by step through the action in a sympathetic and narrative style.

Author should have a page reference here.

Hynds maintains that, although it is many years from the 1800s to the present, the criteria for good news writing, from the reader's viewpoint, has remained the same. According to Paul Swenson in Improving News-writing (13), of primary interest to readers are people-oriented stories. Their second preference is stories of events triggered by man or nature. Next are the stories in which useful information is presented; then, problem situations, and finally, ideas which require effort to understand. Readers want complete and comprehensive news, an unbiased style and complete accuracy (285). They want simple, clean and direct writing without offbeat words, jargon and bloated vocabulary. A reader's plea to his newspaper is not ''Get it first,'' but ''First, get it right . . . and print it so I can understand it'' (Cox 214).

Another problem is the educational level, or grade level, of newswriting. What is the reading level of a newspaper? In seeking answers to these questions experts have devised a number of formulas to establish reading levels which take into consideration sentence length, number of syllables, and number and difficulty of words. No two formulas are alike. However, one—the Fry Graph—is most commonly used by classroom teachers who use newspapers in their teaching. The Fry formula, used to analyze recent front-page articles in several newspapers, produced results of comparably high reading levels in each. Applying the formula to a February 5, 1986, article in the <u>Wall Street Journal</u> about the dangers of being a member of a corporate board of directors, readability was found to be at the eleventh grade level. However, in describing how moose crowd the City of Anchorage in the wintertime, the readability dropped to a comfortable seventh–grade level. Two articles in the <u>Kansas City Times</u>, one on February 13, 1986, the other on March 7, fail to show this distinction. A story on El Salvador was written at a 14.5–grade level, while a story covering the Kansas City, Kansas, 100th anniversary celebration was written at the eleventh–grade level. Surprisingly, a simple article in the <u>Lee's Summit Journal</u> of March 7 which told of plans for a ''no drug–no alcohol'' senior high party also showed a readability level of 11.5. These few examples clearly demonstrate that newspapers are not writing for the ''man on the street,'' those people with less education. According to James L. Abbott, Newspaper in Education consultant, Brigham Young University conducted a comprehensive study of several major newspapers in 1982 and reported that the average reading level was then at the 11.19th grade—too high for the average reader. If newspapers want to reach a wide audience, they need to adjust their readability level to their readers' skills.

> Other examples of primary research done by author.

Fortunately, the newspaper is diversified into many sections; there is usually something in it for every interest and level of understanding. However, the audience of the newswriter—the reading public—cannot be informed by the newspaper if the newswriter does not write to be understood, whatever the subject. Newspaper editors should apply a readability formula to their newspapers and monitor their writers. If a writer becomes too sophisticated, he should be guided back to shorter sentences and more understandable words. One wonders if today's journalists are writing for their readers or for each other.

Newspaper readers know what they expect of their newspapers. They want accurate and understandable news, an unbiased, objective treatment of news, a good layout for easy reading, and, above all, a good writing style (Hynds 285). The newspaper helps set the boundaries of their personal, social, and business lives. Therefore, between the readers and their newspapers must be a relationship built upon respect, truth, trust, and faithfulness, just as in a good marriage (Cox 212).

This phrase takes the reader back to the introduction and signals the essay's conclusion.

Two hundred years have passed to bring the American newspaper to its present-day strength. However, in spite of its ''big business'' image, it must respond more directly to its readers' needs in order to fulfill its purpose of serving those readers. The newspaper must learn more about its readers, just as readers should understand the newspaper's goals and objectives. Newspapers must become more aware of readability and set standards for self-accountability. Readers must continue to question what they do not understand and insist that newspaper writing develop a clear and sincere style. They

The author suggests a course of action.

should complain of sensationalism, rumor-mongering, and bad judgment. As far back as 1801, Thomas Jefferson denounced newspapers for ''their lying faculties,'' and in 1803 he spoke of ''their abuses'' (Kilpatrick 4). Without criticism the newspaper will not attain fairness and objectivity as a responsibility to its readers, and readers will become its victims. As with other facets of life, if readers remain passive, their reactions may be interpreted as agreement and acceptance (Hughes 22).

Today's newspaper readers are confused. In the age of the 1980s newspaper, they find themselves trying to absorb the thoughts and opinons of others and adapting them to their own thinking. Readers accept that the purpose of the newspaper is to keep them informed about the world around them and help them adjust to changes in their lives. However, from

their standpoint, they feel the newspaper has
a responsibility to improve and simplify what
it offers them so they can apply it to their
lives. Perhaps today's newspaper readers have
come to expect too much and have neglected
their own mental abilities—as Socrates pre-
dicted in his warning against the printed
word—but the opportunity of the newspaper as
a teaching tool and a guide in the reader's
search for information and knowledge must not
be ignored. It is time for readers and newspapers to work toward better communication in
understanding each other. The newspaper must
think of itself as an ''information pro-
vider'' to the reader who is an ''information
consumer'' (Hynds 11), keeping in mind that
the reader must be able to understand and
trust what the newspaper prints. After all,
there will be no need for newspapers if there
are no readers.

Author took this allusion from previous knowledge; therefore there's no ciation.

The author concludes with a dramatic statement.

Works Cited

Abbott, James L. Telephone interview. 18 March 1986.

Bruning, Fred. ''Why People Distrust the Press.''
Macleans 16 Jan. 1984: 23.

Cox, David H. ''Readers—And Now Journalists—Find
Papers Unfaithful.'' Contemporary Education
Summer 1984: 212–215.

Henry, William A. III. ''Embroidering the Facts.''
Time 2 July 1984: 66.

Hughes, J. D. ''The Conscientious American Press:
Shaping the American Psyche.'' Contemporary
Education Fall 1982: 22–23.

Hynds, Ernest C. American Newspapers in the 1980s.
New York: Hastings House, 1980.

Jones, Donald. Telephone interview, 26 Feb. 1986.

Kilpatrick, James J. ''In Defense of the Media.''
Nation's Business Feb. 1984: 4+.

Loder, John. ''Journalese as a Second Tongue.'' Time
6 Feb. 1984: 78.

Shaw, David. ''The Blurring of Fact and Fiction.''
In Improving Newswriting. Ed. Loren Giglione.
Washington, D.C.: American Society of Newspaper
Editors Foundation, 1982.
62–67.

Smith, Anthony. Goodbye Gutenberg: The Newspaper
    Revolution of the 1980's. New York: Oxford
    University, 1980.
Strunk, William, Jr., and E. B. White. The Elements
    of Style. 3rd ed. New York: Macmillan, 1979.
Swenson, Paul. ''The Hard Work of Writing Better.''
    In Improving Newswriting. Ed. Loren Giglione.
    Washington, D.C.: American Society of Newspaper
    Editors Foundation, 1982.
    10–16.

EPILOGUE

The Writer's Circle

The Writing Process

For the past few months you've been working on making new methods part of your writing behavior. We would like to finish the class with a consideration of what happens during the processes of writing and reading. Understanding some of the variables involved in these activities should help you place the elements of the process in better perspective. This understanding should also help you comprehend the ideas and approaches we have presented in this text.

In Figure 9–1, "The Writer's Circle" (p. 344) we offer you a circular and rather tidy model of a series of intellectual activities which are rarely so simple and sequential. Nevertheless, the model should identify the complexities and variables present in the act of communication, complexities, and variables which form potential barriers to communication.

What we call the "subject" in "The Writer's Circle" could range anywhere from a house to be sold in a newspaper ad to an abstraction like "love" or your first trip to Niagara Falls. In any case, your goal as a writer is to convey your ideas about the subject to a reader. To this subject you apply the full extent of your perceptive ability. This ability, of course, is unique to each writer and is shaped by the writer's background, education, beliefs, environment, reading experience, ad infinitum. You focus your perception on a subject and translate or transform it into something uniquely your own. You might change the subject's "reality" because of who you are. For example, a friend of ours once told us that his family had a small place on the beach in California. The "small place" turned out to be a four-bedroom condominium in Laguna Beach. In his view it was small—in ours it was hardly that.

A next step in the communication process is to shape, through language, your internal perception into some form of (in this case) written communica-

FIGURE 9-1   The Writer's Circle

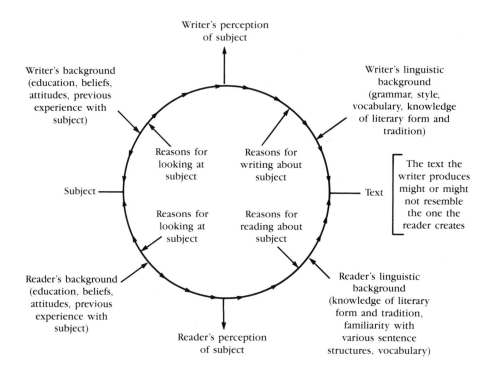

tion. Other forces are now at work. What is the nature of your linguistic repertoire? Your written piece is shaped by your vocabulary, your knowledge of grammar and sentence variety, your familiarity with literary form and tradition, and finally your ability to apply your repertoire to your perception of the subject, an ability which can vary depending on the subject matter. In other words, the more difficulty you have in shaping your perception of the subject, the more likely it is that you will have problems using the full extent of your repertoire successfully.

Ultimately, you produce a text, a piece of writing to be read. This text may correspond to the original subject with varying degrees of accuracy. Your trip to Niagara Falls, for example, could have been marred by a flat tire, a bad cold, and a favorite dress shrunken from the spray of the falls. But because of the passage of time and the mind's ability to use memory selectively, you have romanticized the trip in your mind. In this case, unless your reader was there with you, there is little chance that this change in "reality" will be noticed. Let's say you have decided (or that your memory has decided for you) to present the more romanticized version of your trip to the reader. There is still no guarantee that you will be able to shape your perception into a successful text. You have to narrate the events, select the right details, and choose the right words to convey the desired impression. Just as there is no certainty that your perception will correspond to the original subject, there is no guarantee that the text you produce will correspond to either the original subject or to the one you have created in your mind.

We complicate the situation significantly when we add a reader to our model. The reader, too, brings multiple biases to the act of communication. The reader's perceptive ability is shaped in much the same way as the writer's. Perhaps your reader feels that only sentimental fools ever visit Niagara Falls. In that case, successful communication might be impossible through no fault of your own. Perhaps your reader has never been to Niagara Falls and has no idea what it's like. In this case, you might fail to communicate because you focused on the events of your trip but didn't provide enough background about the place itself. In other words, the perceptions of the reader can significantly alter the response to your text.

Your reader's linguistic repertoire is also influential in shaping the response to your text. In short, how well can the audience read and understand the text's vocabulary, grammar, and literary form? Can the reader understand your allusions, your comparisons, your metaphors?

In addition, we add some new complications. How is your text presented? Neatly typed? Scribbled in pencil? In a slick magazine with pictures? Littered with factual errors and mistakes in grammar? In a magazine with a definite political, social, or moral slant? Different readers will respond differently to your text depending on the answers to questions like these. A friend, for example, probably wouldn't mind a text scribbled hastily in pencil; however, you know how your boss or your English teacher would respond to your writing if it were presented that way. Or, in a different kind of example, a reader with liberal politics might have difficulty accepting the perceptions offered in an article published in the *National Review,* a journal with a reputation for conservatism. The reader's response can even vary according to how he feels when he reads, where he's reading, how much time he spends on your writing, or why he's reading. Do you respond the same way to an assigned article as you do to one you've chosen in your favorite magazine?

Finally the reader produces a personal version of the original subject as first filtered through the writer's sensibility, the writer's linguistic and literary performance, the format of the text, and then through the reader's own sensibility and linguistic repertoire. How closely this end product resembles either the original subject or the writer's perception (sometimes called the writer's intention) depends on that immense variety of factors discussed here. Furthermore, to add one last qualification, the final perception varies somewhat from reader to reader. In fact, the final perception could even vary for the same reader depending on when the piece is read. *The Adventures of Huckleberry Finn* comes across much differently for a forty-year-old than it did for the same reader at twelve. The text hasn't changed, but the reader has. As John Steinbeck says, "A man who tells secrets or stories must think of who is hearing or reading, for a story has as many versions as it has readers" *(The Winter of Our Discontent).*

By now you are probably wondering how we ever communicate in light of all these potential barriers. The human species is most remarkable. We have established a social contract in which we generally agree to accept a set of limitations on our linguistic differences. The word "house" may carry different connotations for an urbanite from New York and a farmer on the Nebraska prairie; nevertheless, each can read the phrase "on the table in the house" and agree on its general meaning—despite the possible variations in personal interpretations.

In your writing too, you can count on this general agreement between humans to seek shared understanding. You must, nevertheless, be aware of the possibilities for misunderstanding and the different types of writing occasions which make more strenuous demands on both writer and reader.

Let's examine briefly what this means to you as a writer:

1. *You must examine your subject thoroughly so you have as great a capacity as possible to render it with essential detail and accuracy.*

Translation into Writing Skills: Thinking, prewriting, reading, and researching.

2. *You must carefully consider your relationship to the topic so you can understand and anticipate your own biases.*

Translation into Writing Skills: Prewriting which explores your own attitudes and past experiences.

3. *You must shape your internal ideas through language into a written text.*

Translation into Writing Skills: Skillful performance linguistically—vocabulary, diction, grammar, punctuation, sentence variety; use of appropriate literary forms—allusion, symbol, metaphor, paragraph, narration, description, comparison, and so on; ability to organize.

4. *You must match your intention and your performance to your vision of your audience.*

Translation into Writing Skills: Clearly stating your purpose and critically analyzing your audience; careful rereading and revising keeping your purpose and audience in mind.

5. *You must present your text to meet your reader's expectations.*

Translation into Writing Skills: Careful editing and manuscript preparation.

We have not attempted to provide a complete description of the complexity of the communication act; rather, we have presented a sequential view of a process that circles erratically more often than it moves smoothly ahead step by step. Even so, we feel that the work you have done throughout this text will help you become a more careful, more perceptive, more successful writer and reader.

THE LAST EXERCISE

You've finished a semester of college composition. In the course of the term, we've attempted to lead you to modify your writing behaviors to become more efficient, more effective writers. Write an informal essay in which you describe your progress in the class. Include your attitude about writing, the changes you've made in your approaches to writing, and the success of your efforts.

APPENDIX I

APA Documentation

Using the APA Style of Documentation

Like the MLA style, the APA uses parenthetical references within the text and provides complete publication information in the list of works cited. This section provides an overview of the APA style, focusing on how it differs from the MLA style as outlined in Chapter 9. But here again, you should consult the *Publication Manual of the American Psychological Association* for a paper using this style.

A parenthetical reference in the APA style includes the author, year, and page of the source, separated by commas and using the abbreviation "p." before the page number.

> Few writers and artists seemed concerned about the passing of the Obscene Publications Act in 1857 (Roberts, 1985, p. 618).

If the author's name appears in the sentence, the year appears after the author's name.

> Roberts (1985) says that few writers and artists seemed concerned about the passing of the Obscene Publications Act in 1857 (p. 618).

When a source has two or more authors, use all the authors' last names the first time you cite that source; in subsequent citations use only the first author's last name and "et al."

> The dime novel emerged in the 1840s as a result of "fast printing methods and cheap paper" (Hiebert, Ungurait, Bohn, 1974, p. 193).

> These popular books—usually romances, adventures, and westerns—often outsold more serious books and introduced the idea of "best sellers" (Hiebert et al., 1974, p. 193).

A list of works cited also appears at the end of a paper using the APA style; in this style, however, the list should be titled "references." Its entries are alphabetized by the author's last name. The year of publication follows the author's name; fewer words are capitalized and the name of the publisher is abbreviated less frequently.

Books

A book by a single author

Bell–Metereau, Rebecca. (1985). Hollywood androgyny. New York: Columbia University Press.

A book by two or more persons

Belcher, William F., and James, W. Lee. (Eds.). (1962). J. D. Salinger and the critics. Belmont, CA: Wadsworth.

Hiebert, Ray Eldon, Donald F. Urgurait, and Thomas W. Bohn. (1974). Mass media. New York: David McKay Company.

An anonymous book

Bowker/Bantam 1984 complete sourcebook of personal computing. (1983). New York: Bowker/Bantam.

A corporate or government publication

U.S. Department of Labor, Bureau of Labor Statistics. (1985). Employment, hours, and earnings, United States, 1904–84. (Vol. 1). (1985). Washington, D.C.: U.S. Government Printing office.

Articles

An article with continuous pagination

Schlaefli, Andre, James R. Rest, and Stephen J. Thoma. (1985). Does moral education improve moral judgment? A meta–analysis of intervention studies using the defining issues test. Review of Educational Research, 55, 319–352.

An article from a monthly or bimonthly periodical—separate pagination

Rothmeyer, Karen. (Nov.–Dec. 1985). Hot properties: The media–buying spree explained. Columbia Journalism Review, 38–43.

An article from a daily newspaper

Petersen, Clarence. (1986, January 26). Men still find it difficult to open up their emotions. Kansas City Star, p. Pl.

APPENDIX II

The Interest Inventory

Still at a loss for a topic or need a clearer direction for a vague topic? Try the interest inventory. List your favorite movie, sports, TV shows, books, magazines, hobbies, subjects at school. List your favorite kinds of people, clothes, music, art, family activities. If you need to do more, then you could take the same categories and list your least favorite. Now sit back and review your lists. Look for patterns, similarities and differences, things you feel strongly about. Somewhere in these lists there's a topic for you.

Here's a sample interest inventory. Notice that listing a reason for your choice gives you a head start in developing that interest into a topic.

Sample Interest Inventory

1. Favorite movie: `''Tender Mercies''`
because: `it's so Texas; I like the voices and the charac-`
`ters; I like what Duvall says near the end about happiness—`
`it expressed something I never could.`

2. Favorite sport: `rugby`
because: `It's a fast game—none of the waiting around like`
`baseball & football; more demanding—no pads, but does de-`
`pend on strength & skill.`

3. Favorite TV show: ''Hill Street Blues''
because: so many characters, each different--different personality & motivation; good, interesting stories that deal
both with society & personal lives & how society affects
personal lives.

4. Favorite book: ''The Blithedale Romance''
because: The main character is such a liar that it was fun
to figure out the truth and the lies. I didn't like it at
first, but I had to read it for class.

5. Favorite magazine: ''Time''
because: It has all the news. It talks about things that
happen that I can't always keep up with in the newspapers.

6. Favorite hobby: dancing
because: it's good exercise; it's challenging to learn new
steps and to do them well; I like the excitement of live music.

7. Favorite school subject: math
because: I'm good at it. Math makes sense--rules, principles. It's cumulative.

8. Favorite kinds of people: funny & nice
because: they're easy to talk to; make me laugh; are more
comfortable to be around than humorless ones; seem to approach life in an appealing manner.

9. Favorite kinds of clothes: casual pants, tops and jackets
because: they are fashionable but don't give me away; often
classics that can be worn for several years; nicely inter-
changeable & easy to add to.

10. Favorite kinds of music: country and western
because: It has a good sense of humor, clever lyrics, sometimes almost poetic lyrics. It's also fun to dance to.

11. Favorite kinds of art: Impressionism
because: the colors melt but stay separate, looking like the
world looks when I don't have my glasses on. They help me imagine.

12. Favorite kind of vacation: beach during winter at home
because: I like to get away from the cold weather, the snow,
ice, the coats and boots. Winter is so long that a few days
at a beach are good and refreshing.

This is just a sample; your answers are more detailed when you have more to say or when the question causes a flood of memories. Don't use your censor too much at this stage. Right now you are simply generating information you can use later. Conversely, don't write so much that you'll be bored with the inventory before you are finish.

Trying it for your least favorites can also generate ideas. The change in perspective should give you some new material.

1. Least favorite movie: _____
because: _____
_____
_____

2. A sport I don't like to watch: _____
because: _____
_____
_____

3. A TV show I'd never watch: _____
because: _____
_____
_____

4. Least favorite book: _____
because: _____
_____
_____

5. Least favorite magazine: _____
because: _____
_____
_____

6. A hobby I'd never take up: _____
because: _____
_____
_____

7. Least favorite school subject: _____
because: _____
_____
_____

8. Least favorite kinds of people: _____
because: _____
_____
_____

9. Least favorite kinds of clothes: _____
because: _____

_____
_____

10. Least favorite kinds of music: _____
because: _____
_____
_____

11. Least favorite kinds of art: _____
because: _____
_____
_____

12. Least favorite kinds of family vacations: _____
because: _____
_____
_____

Index